A CENTURY OF LUTHERANS IN OHIO

A CENTURY OF
LUTHERANS
IN OHIO

by

Willard D. Allbeck

THE ANTIOCH PRESS / 1966

The publication of this history has been made possible, in part, through the use of funds provided by the Ohio Synod of the Lutheran Church in America

Printed in the United States of America by The Antioch Press, Yellow Springs, Ohio

To my wife

Marie Neve Allbeck

a cheerful companion on field trips to old churches
and ancient cemeteries;

a patient partner in correcting galley proofs against
the vocal reading of the manuscript;

a warmhearted woman who devotedly encouraged
me in my pastoral ministry and in my seminary
teaching;

a mother and grandmother much beloved.

PREFACE

THE SOURCES for the history of Lutherans in Ohio constitute a fruitful area for investigation; they are not as complete as might be desired. It is hoped that in the course of time materials now apparently lost will come to light. For a dozen years or more this has been a field into which students in Hamma School of Theology have been directed for research. Their papers most often have treated the history of a local congregation, but they also have dealt with organizations, societies, biographies, and surveys of counties. In some instances the result of a study was published by the congregation or group concerned. A few are cited in this book.

There have been several by-products of this activity. One of these was an increase of interest in the Lutheran history of certain localities. Especially notable in this connection has been the work of Mr. Lewis Grote of Greenville, who for many years has been collecting data of Darke County. He was encouraged to compile his findings in manuscript sketches of congregations or of pastors. A second by-product of this general activity was the recovery of some documents and records whose existence had been forgotten. In the preparation of histories of congregations one of the chief benefits was the finding and assembling of scattered parish records. A third result was an increase in historical appreciation on the part of those who engaged in the research. It is hoped that the publication of this work will stimulate further results of this kind.

It became apparent that a comprehensive treatment of Ohio Lutheranism involving a more extensive investigation was desirable. Therefore, the preparation of this book was begun. Meanwhile, articles presenting portions of this research were published in several journals and are cited in the pages of this text.

Encouragement for this work has been heartily given by Presidents Clarence C. Stoughton and John N. Stauffer of Wittenberg University, and Deans Elmer E. Flack and Bernhard H. P. Hillila of Hamma School of Theology of Wittenberg University. Most generous assistance was received from members of the Wittenberg library staff, particularly Miss Ilo D. Fisher and Mrs. Luella Eutsler, as well as from Miss Dorothea Conrad, librarian at Capital University, and Miss Elizabeth L. Balz, librarian at the Evangelical Lutheran Theological Seminary in Columbus, Ohio.

Three faculty members of other theological seminaries gave the manuscript a critical reading. Professor Dorris A. Flesner of Northwestern Lutheran Theological Seminary, Minneapolis, Minnesota, reviewed the general structure and treatment. Professor Robert H. Fischer of the Lutheran School of Theology at Chicago (Maywood Campus), Illinois, provided a lengthy criticism both of the main thesis and of numerous details. Professor Fred W. Meuser of the Evangelical Lutheran Theological Seminary, Columbus, Ohio, not only suggested corrections, but also gave a helpful evaluation of the central theme in the light of the historical antecedents of the American Lutheran Church of which he is a member. While it has not been possible to employ all their suggestions, their opinions have aided me greatly in strengthening this narrative. I am profoundly grateful for their generous help. Errors which remain are to be attributed to me.

WILLARD D. ALLBECK

Hamma School of Theology
Wittenberg University

CONTENTS

A CENTURY OF LUTHERANS IN OHIO

INTRODUCTION

THE STORY OF LUTHERANISM IN OHIO is one of the areas in the history of Lutherans in America that has received insufficient attention. Both in general histories and in encyclopedias the statements concerning it are usually inadequate and occasionally inaccurate. There are many gaps in the published accounts, and many unanswered questions. Though there is an excellent treatment by Professor Meuser of the Joint Synod of Ohio as it became part of the American Lutheran Church, the works dealing with the previous century are not so competent nor of such high quality.

Previously published treatments have been chiefly synodical histories. They therefore were limited in outlook, and were propagandist in purpose. Those that included accounts of congregations had a parochial viewpoint which tended to obscure the larger issues of the church. The portrayal of the history of the synod rarely looked beyond its boundaries or glimpsed the total Lutheran scene. Thus these histories were partial and provincial.

Every history is to some degree an interpretation as well as a recital of facts. The narrative seeks to emphasize the major concerns of the group under discussion. In the case of synodical bodies the focus of their histories has been either on the theological stance or on the practical activities of the synod concerned, and events in its history have been related thereto. Connected with the confessional position was the related question of consistent Lutheran practice. When the practical program was the main theme, attention was largely on institutions. In either instance there was a neglect of other aspects of Christian life.

The present study seeks to supply some of what has been lacking. The research on which it is based has brought to light many details hitherto unpublished, information concerning persons and events which can enrich our knowledge and appreciation of our heritage. An extensive search has been made in primary sources in the interest of providing a reliable report. Without being exhaustive, it presents the Ohio story in considerable detail.

This account is intersynodical, with an effort at fairness toward all concerned. In a sense most Lutherans in Ohio are lineal descendants of the

Muhlenberg tradition brought to the state by the missionary pastors of the Ministerium of Pennsylvania. This is to say that Ohio Lutherans are all cousins, even if of forty-second connection rather than of the kissing kind. In spite of still unhealed estrangements within the family there has been a relationship, even when a hostile one, that should not be ignored. The conviction herein expressed is that the story of Lutherans in Ohio, including their dividedness, can be told to a considerable degree as a unit. The effort therefore is to see it in its larger relationships, whether there are intimations of future unity or not. In this way the history of Lutherans in Ohio is a reflection on a smaller scale of Lutheran history in America.

This account is written in the conviction that only a multiple approach is likely to be true to the complexities of the history. Theological concerns interact with sociological factors. Economic conditions are related to practical programs. The frontier had its effects, some of which remained as traces in the post-frontier period when isolation was other than geographical. The Lutheran Church, as is true of other churches, is a complex of doctrines, worship, missions, education, publication, organization, finances, etc. An effort has been made to recount something of these multiple features.

There is justification for limiting this survey roughly to the geographical boundaries of the State of Ohio, though this has not been adhered to rigidly. Ohio has occupied a unique position as in some respects the most typically American state. Its settlers came from Puritan New England, across the mountains from cosmopolitan Pennsylvania, up from the settled southern states, and from the foreign lands of Europe. Its inhabitants, forming such a cross-section of the nation, set the pattern for the population of states to the west. Moreover, its boundaries have been useful for administration both in the government and in the church. In past alignments and in present reorganizations designed for the future, Ohio constitutes an administrative church unit, whether called a district or a synod. This is the fact even when border areas in other states are involved.

Just as the geographic boundary for this account is approximate rather than precise, so the temporal limits are roughly a century rather than exactly so. The beginnings include hazily the first congregations, in somewhat clearer focus the first conferences, and in sharper detail the first synod. A century later the older patterns of life and organization were crumbling and about to be replaced by new ones. 1918 revealed some of this, 1930 showed more. The latter development has had exhaustive treatment by Dr. Meuser, making superfluous any further treatment of that area. Hence this study is justified in limiting itself to the previous century.

Finally, this work proceeded on the assumption that Lutheran history in America involves three overlapping phases: transplantation, adaptation, and expansion. At any given period one of these is likely to be dominant, but the other two are rarely absent. All three continue into the present in some degree. It should be clear that Lutheranism was brought to America by persons whose language was other than English. The Lutheran Church is a transplanted church. Yet it outgrew that condition and became fully and consciously American—a process of adaptation often painful. The church grew, both during immigration and during adjustment to the American scene, but with special vigor following those phases. This in the main is the present condition of Lutherans in America. And such precisely is the character of the Ohio story.

1 / STATEHOOD, SETTLEMENT, AND CHURCHES

WHEN OHIO BECAME a state in 1803 a strong flow of settlers into its area was already under way. With western Pennsylvania filling up and Kentucky already a state for a decade, the virgin lands north of the Ohio River were attracting the attention of many pioneers. Occupation of the land had been restrained partly by troubles with the Indians and partly by the delay of the Federal government in arranging for sale of the lands with legal title to the purchaser.

The United States government had been busy during the 1780's making treaties with the Indians, with the result that approximately two-thirds of the state was to be open for white settlement, the Indians to retain roughly the northwestern third. But the aggressiveness of the settlers caused apprehension among the Indian tribes. Intermittent clashes occurred until the Indian military power was broken by the Battle of Fallen Timbers in 1794, and the Greenville Treaty of peace was concluded. Thereafter, except for a flurry during the War of 1812, the settlers were relatively free of dangers from Indian raids.

The survey and sale of land was provided for in the Land Ordinance of 1785. Tracts of not less than 640 acres were to be sold at auction for not less than a dollar an acre. The survey of the land in the east along the Ohio River began that year in an area called the Seven Ranges. Large tracts of land sold to the Ohio Company and the Scioto Company were opened for settlement. The Virginia Military District lying west of the Scioto River offered parcels of land as bounties to Virginia veterans of the Revolutionary War. In the Western Reserve along Lake Erie, land was given as bounties or sold through the Connecticut Land Company. Other land agents were active, so that land was sold in all the areas outside the Indian reservation. Moreover, a Federal act of 1800 made it possible to buy plots as small as 320 acres with four years' credit.

Under such circumstances Ohio land was quickly occupied. In 1800 the population was over 45,000. Ten years later it had passed 230,000. After another decade it had gone beyond the half-million mark, and by 1830 was nearly a million.[1] The census of 1820 surprised the older states by showing that Ohio was fifth in the list according to size of population. By 1830 it had moved into fourth place, only New York, Pennsylvania, and Virginia being larger.

Such rapid movement of population created huge problems for organized religion. It was relatively rare that a group of people settled in Ohio as a congregation, bringing their pastor with them. For the most part the conditions were such that the inhabitants of a community had to form themselves into a new congregation and find someone to serve as pastor. In many instances the impulse to organization came not from the community but from the visit of an exploring missionary. Traveling preachers aroused the religious interest of some settlers, making them aware of their spiritual needs. Much of the time there had to be evangelistic work and conversions before church organizations could be formed.

There was never an "established church" in Ohio. When it became a state the separation of church and state was the accepted pattern of life in the United States. Therefore religious life in Ohio followed the free-church pattern. And because the migrants into the state came from many of the eastern states as well as from Europe, virtually all the older denominations were represented. Here were Congregationalists and Episcopalians of English ancestry, Scotch Presbyterians, Lutherans, and Reformed, and Dunkers in German-speaking areas, Methodists, Baptists, and later Disciples working indiscriminately among the settlers, and presently the fringe groups of Shakers and Mormons. A scattering of Roman Catholics of various national origins was to be found also.

The earliest organized religious work in the state was that of the Moravian missions. It was carried on among the Delaware Indians located in the area that became Tuscarawas County. The leading missionary was David Zeisberger. His sermon to an assembly of Indians, March 14, 1771, is reputed to be the first Protestant preaching in the Ohio area. The mission work was successful in winning many Indians to Christian faith and peaceful ways, but the disturbances of the Revolutionary War, a shameful massacre of Christian Indians in 1782, and a dispersion of the rest of the converts brought an end to the mission. Schoenbrunn and Gnadenhutten today are memorials of the notable Moravian activity. This area was later the scene of the settlement of many people of German ancestry and the organization of numerous Lutheran congregations.

---

[1] *United States Census,* 1850, p. ix.

Roman Catholics were not numerous in Ohio in the early years. The first priests in the area were French, either while this territory belonged to France and Jesuits were among the explorers or later at Gallipolis, a colony of French settlers. After 1800 Roman Catholics might be encountered among Germans in Perry County or among the Irish in Cincinnati. Bardstown, Kentucky, was the center of their activity.

Numerous members of the Society of Friends (Quakers) were found among one's neighbors in early nineteenth-century Ohio. They had come in many instances from slave-holding states—Virginia, the Carolinas, and Georgia—where they had suffered ostracism because of their anti-slavery views. Colonies of them located in Jefferson and Columbiana Counties in the east, around Chillicothe in the south, and in the Little Miami valley in the southwest. In each instance they were close to land where Lutherans made their homes.

The Scotch-Irish were numerous and influential in the settlements in Ohio. In 1792 the Transylvania Presbytery of Kentucky convened in the area that was to become Cincinnati, the purpose of the convention being to examine an applicant for ordination. This man as a layman had been serving a congregation of Presbyterians which had built a log church about two years earlier. He satisfied his examiners and was ordained. In eastern Ohio the Presbyterian congregations were supplied by ministers of the Pittsburgh Synod. In the Western Reserve the Presbyterians and Congregationalists combined in a Plan of Union whereby they avoided erecting rival congregations; but many of the ministers there were Presbyterians. When colleges and academies were founded in Ohio the officers and professors in many instances were Presbyterian clergymen. In the same areas were to be found from an early day members of the seceder groups from Scotland that later formed the United Presbyterian Chuch. One of their number, Jeremiah Morrow, was governor of Ohio from 1822 to 1826.

Members of the Congregational Church were to be found in areas settled by migrants from New England, namely, at Marietta and in the Western Reserve. Though the first settlers at Marietta arrived in April, 1788, it was not until 1796 that a church was organized there. Five years later the first congregation in the Western Reserve was formed. Numerous other organizations followed. Like the Presbyterians, the Congregationalists were active in promoting higher education.

On Christmas Day, 1750, a Virginian named Christopher Gist read from the Homilies of the Church of England to a group of Indians and white men at a spot where Coshocton now stands. But the Protestant Episcopal Church did not have an organized beginning in Ohio until after 1800. Congregations of settlers from Connecticut were formed, first at Worthington in 1804, and afterward in the Western Reserve. Bishop Philander Chase, who began his work in Ohio in 1819, greatly advanced the work of his church.

Baptists entered the state from Virginia and Kentucky. They claim that it was a Baptist congregation, and not a Presbyterian one, which was first on the scene at Cincinnati. They assert that Christopher Gist who held the Christmas service in 1750 was a Baptist rather than an Anglican. This much is certain: that Baptists were actively at work in the Ohio Valley and the Western Reserve about the turn of the century and soon were making substantial growth.

It was the Methodists, however, who made the most rapid progress, and were most likely to encounter Lutheran settlers. Circuit riders from Virginia and Kentucky make their appearance as soon as settlements were made. The first organization seems to have been formed on the Little Miami River in Clermont County. The first established "circuit" was formed in 1798 to cover the valleys of the Miami Rivers. In 1803, when Ohio became a state, the Methodists organized an Ohio District made up of five circuits. Expansion continued to be rapid. Edward Tiffin, the first Governor of the state, was a Methodist local preacher. Peter Cartwright, the famous Methodist circuit rider, was assigned the Scioto and Hocking Circuits in 1805–06. He wrote:

> I traveled in the State of Ohio in 1806, and at a largely attended camp-meeting near New Lancaster, there was a great work of God going on; many were pleading for mercy; many were getting religion; and the wicked looked solemn and awful. The pulpit in the woods was a large stand; it would hold a dozen people, and I would not let the lookers-on crowd into it, but kept it clear that at any time I might occupy it for the purpose of giving directions to the congregation.[2]

It was revival methods of this sort that greatly increased the number of Methodists, but which greatly offended the Lutherans.

The religious bodies which were German-speaking were those with which the Lutherans were most likely to have contact. The use of a common language was one factor. Besides that, they often settled in the same general area, seeking out rich land for farming. In many instances they came from German-language areas in Pennsylvania, Maryland, Vir-

---

[2] *Autobiography of Peter Cartwright* (Nashville, 1956), p. 62.

ginia, or North Carolina. Thus they brought with them to Ohio both a common German heritage and also a set of traditional antagonisms and divisions.

One group of churches had more or less of a strong Anabaptist heritage. Comprising this group were the Mennonites, the German Baptist Brethren, the River Brethren, and the United Brethren. Representatives of all these groups made their appearance quite early in the state. They were skillful and frugal farmers. In religion they were "plain people" as to dress and manner of life. Baptism by immersion was the usual practice. There was little interest in churchly, liturgical worship, or in doctrinal theology and catechetical instruction. They espoused a pattern of religion uncongenial to Lutherans.

Mennonites, the historical descendants of the Anabaptists, first came to the Hocking Valley in 1803. Soon afterwards others came to Columbiana and Mahoning Counties. A still later group located in Holmes and Tuscarawas Counties. Their descendants are still to be found in these and other localities. The German Baptist Brethren, also known as Dunkers, were occupying farms in Ohio during the first decade of its statehood; Montgomery and Miami Counties received most of the settlements. The River Brethren came to Ohio from Lancaster County, Pennsylvania, settling in Stark, Wayne, and Richland Counties in the same decade. This body today has the name Brethren in Christ. The United Brethren formed their first congregation in Ohio in Montgomery County about 1805. A little later other adherents of this denomination made their homes in the Hocking and the Tuscarawas valleys. This body has since merged in the Evangelical United Brethren Church.

Though these various Brethren churches in Lutheran eyes were always "sectaries," the Reformed could be accepted in a much more cordial way. In many instances in Ohio as in Pennsylvania the Lutherans and the Reformed joined in the construction of a church building. Though most of the German-speaking people who settled in Montgomery and adjoining counties had come from Pennsylvania, some came from North Carolina. From that state came also the first Reformed pastors to serve them: Jacob Christman in 1803, and John Jacob Larose in 1804. Central and northeastern Ohio were also localities where Reformed congregations were established.

Two other religious groups, though small numerically, are of romantic interest in the early history of Ohio. One is the Church of the New Jerusalem, adhering to the teachings of Emmanuel Swedenborg, the Swedish mystic. In the early decades of the nineteenth century John Chapman, famous as Johnny Appleseed, toured the central and western part of the state planting his apple seeds and distributing his Swedenborgian tracts. The other group was the Shakers (the United Society of Believers in Christ's Second Coming) whose settlements were near Lebanon in Warren County, and in Shaker Heights near Cleveland. The Shakers aroused much frontier curiosity by their celibate and communistic life, and by the peculiarity of their worship practices. Sometimes they aroused persecution also.

This summary of the religious bodies in Ohio at the beginning of the century will be definitely misleading if it leaves the impression that the great majority of the inhabitants were church members. The fact was quite the opposite, though there are no statistics available to support such a statement. But east of the mountains the churches could claim less than a quarter of the population; surely the situation was not better west of the mountains, and more likely was much worse from a church standpoint. The churches had to win their way patiently and persistently.

The accounts of life in general and of public morals in particular as given by observers of that day are far from flattering. Many of the inhabitants were rough and brutal. Drunkenness was common. Fights and brawls provided the exciting entertainment for the drab life of the day. William Burke, in touring the Methodist circuits in Ohio as presiding elder, often stayed overnight in the taverns which were filled with "the disorder and abuse of the unprincipled and half-civilized inmates." [3]

The religious scene was quite confused. If the observer was a clergyman the report is likely to be a dismal one. Even though the Presbyterians were the most prominent group in the state, the other denominations beginning to get a foothold might easily give an over-all impression of a confusion of tongues. Thus Jacob Scherer, a Lutheran pastor in North Carolina, made a missionary tour in Ohio in 1813. In his report he made the observation: "The spiritual condition of Ohio is dark; the people of all denominations are intermixed, and although they have many preachers among them, there appears to be a want of such who have sound doctrine and are of good repute." [4]

As might be expected under the circumstances, local congregations made efforts to win to their membership the people of other denominations who had no church of their faith in the community. On his way to Ohio,

[3] James B. Finley, *Sketches of Western Methodism*, pp. 85 f. Quoted in W. W. Sweet, *The Rise of Methodism in the West* (Nashville, 1920), p. 30.

[4] Quoted in G. D. Bernheim, *History of the German Settlements and of the Lutheran Church in North and South Carolina* (Philadelphia, 1872), p. 390.

Scherer got the impression that "Proselyting is carried on extensively here, and some of the Germans have united themselves with the Baptists and Methodists, but very few heathens have become Christians." [5] The Methodist itinerant James B. Finley reported that in Tuscarawas County he made Methodist converts of Moravian and Lutheran residents.[6]

The revival movement, to be discussed later, tended to scramble denominational loyalties, with especially disastrous results for the Presbyterians. Most Presbyterians in the Cincinnati area became members of the Christian Church, following the leadership of Barton W. Stone and others. Some of them in turn left the Christian Church to become Shakers. The peculiar practices and strange usages of Shakers in worship (including dancing) attracted the curious interest of many people, including the Lutheran missionary pastor Paul Henkel.

A very prominent feature of frontier religious life in Ohio was revivals. These varied in intensity from mild, orderly, evangelistic meetings on the one hand, to tremendously emotional, highly exciting camp meetings where there was little interest in decorum or solemn orderliness. It is the latter sort that was most often described by religious observers of the time.

The revival movement in the early days of Ohio statehood was part of the Second Great Awakening. The impulses felt in Ohio were derived from the phase of that Awakening centering in Kentucky. The famous camp meeting revival in Logan County, Kentucky, was held in 1800 and in subsequent years. As early as 1801 such camp meetings were attempted in Ohio at Eagle Creek in Adams County, and a little later the same year at Indian Creek in Harrison County. Thereafter they were repeated in other parts of the state, touching areas where there were Lutheran settlers.

Revivals were set up by most of the Protestant denominations for their own purpose, but the camp meeting were usually interdenominational, preachers of each church addressing the throngs at the same time in various parts of the camp. The Baptists, the Christians, the Methodists, and some of the Presbyterians were involved. Shakers used revival tactics, but usually on their own. It was the Methodists who made most use of revivals and profited most by them. The work of Peter Cartwright, for example, has already been noted.

Confronting the revival phenomena the Lutheran pastors were uncertain or antagonistic. C. A. G. Storch, a Lutheran pastor in North Carolina, in

[5] *Op. cit.,* p. 389.
[6] *Autobiography of Rev. James B. Finley* (Cincinnati, 1853), pp. 202 f.

1803 wrote a letter to a friend in Germany giving an impression of the American scene. Though reflecting conditions in North Carolina, the report was true for Kentucky and Ohio as well.

The present condition of this country is remarkable, both in a political and religious aspect. Party spirit is risen to a fearful height. Infidelity prevails to a great extent, both among the higher and the lower classes of society.

I still serve my old congregations, and I continue to preach the doctrines of Jesus Christ, the crucified, in simplicity, and have happily experienced the power of his grace upon myself and others. The prevalence of infidelity, the contempt of the best of all religions, its usages and servants, the increase of irreligion and crime, as remarked, have occasioned me many sad hours. . . .

By the side of this pestilence [infidelity] there prevails now for over a year a something, I know not what to name it, and I should not like to say *Fanaticism.* Christians of every denomination assemble themselves in the forest, numbering four, six, and sometimes ten thousand persons; they erect tents, sing, pray and preach day and night for five, six and eight days. I have been eyewitness to scenes in such large assembles, which I cannot explain. I beheld young and old, feeble and strong, white and black, in short, people of every age, position and circumstances as though they were struck by lightning, speechless and motionless; and when they had somewhat recovered they could be heard shrieking bitterly, and supplicating God for mercy and grace.

After they had thus spent three, and many even more, hours they rose up, praised God and commenced to pray in such a manner as they never were wont to do, exhorting sinners to come to Jesus, etc. Many of those who were thus exercised were highly ungodly persons before, and we can now discover a remarkable change in them. Even deists have been brought to confess Christ in this way. . . .

Opinions are various in regard to it; many, even ministers, denominate it the work of the devil; others again would explain it in a natural way or in accordance with some physical law; while others look upon it as the work of God. . . . This thing has occasioned me no little uneasiness. In our German congregations nothing of this kind has yet been manifested.[7]

If Storch was uncertain in his judgment in the presence of the revival movement, there were other Lutherans who had made up their minds against it. The Ministerium of Pennsylvania in deciding to send Paul Henkel in 1811 as traveling preacher in the states of Ohio, Kentucky, Virginia, and Tennessee, advised him "to have no dealings with campmeetings, if he should find such departures from our evangelical ways."[8] Those who came

[7] Quoted in Bernheim, *op. cit.,* pp. 348, 351 f.
[8] *Documentary History of the Evangelical Lutheran Ministerium of Pennsylvania and Adjacent States* (Philadelphia, 1898), p. 428.

west of the mountains were not all convinced of the wisdom of the Ministerium's judgment. The question of revivals was to be a troublesome one in
subsequent years.

Meanwhile there were many persons who looked at the evidences of
religion with indifference or amusement, perhaps even with a touch of
cynicism. For example, Judge John Cleves Symmes writing to his daughter
September 18, 1809, from Cleves said:

> My hired people have all gone abroad as we have no steady meeting in
> this place, although there be as many modes of worshipping the Supreme
> God as people fancy to themselves. One sect, Quakers, worship him in silence,
> sitting with hats on from beginning to end of their meeting. Another sect,
> the Methodists, worship him by grunts and groans, stamping, raving and
> roaring like so many bulls and wolves, and crying amen at every ten to
> twenty words of the preacher. Another sect, Newlights, worship him by
> screaming, clapping hands, crying hell fire and damnation as loud as they can
> yell, tumbling down lying on their backs.[9]

At a time when the most pressing concern was to clear the land and produce a living from it, or in the villages to get a store going and government
established, it is not surprising that such secular affairs received major attention. Among public buildings there was more likely to be a tavern, a store,
a government office, and perhaps even a jail before there would be a church.
Intense interest in religion therefore would generally appear somewhat
ridiculous.

In this chaotic religious condition the churches faced the task of bringing
piety, order, and authority. Little of this could be achieved without proper
leadership. Untrained laymen could make some progress but were likely
soon to reach their limits. The Baptists had the most success with local
leaders who were farmer-preachers. The Methodist system took men who
seemed to have the needed talents and put them to work under supervision,
gradually increasing the range of their work and responsibilities. Among
Presbyterians it was generally expected that a minister have a reasonably
good academic education, and the same would be true of the Congregational churches. For the most part the German Baptist groups, like their
English-speaking brethren, had little interest in an educated ministry. In
general, therefore, the Lutherans and the Reformed with whom they frequently were united, both favored a trained and duly authorized ministry.
But they found themselves in a population where lay preachers or ministers

[9] Alta Harvey Heiser, *West to Ohio* (Yellow Springs, Ohio, 1955), p. 77.

with no theological education were not only commonly found but who also made a strong appeal to settlers suspicious of academic attainments and scholarship.

Under these circumstances it was easy for clerical impostors to prosper, for a time. They evidently were men with a smattering of religious information and with better-than-average fluency of speech. They appeared in a community where nothing was known of their background; there they preached, taught school, perhaps practiced medicine, performed marriages and other services, and soon moved on to some other locality. They had no license or ordination by any established church body. Sometimes the reason for their short period of residence was the revelation of immorality or dishonesty in their lives. In other instances there is no information, and one can suspect merely a restless, roving spirit uncongenial to long residence in one place. At best they were religious opportunists, concerned more for their own survival than for community service. At worst they were impostors who severely damaged religious life when their misdeeds were exposed. Time and again in the history of the earliest Lutheran congregations in Ohio there is fleeting mention of a man who performed pastoral functions; but his name appears in the clerical roll of no synod, and there is no evidence that he had ever received either licensure or ordination. In this respect the Ohio churches repeated the experience of the earliest congregations on the Atlantic seaboard before the arrival of regularly ordained pastors. To cite an example, Lutherans in the vicinity of New Reading and Thornville in Perry County were ministered to in 1803 by a man named Eierman, but nothing further is known of him.[10]

Amid the rush and turmoil of settling the land, clearing the forest, platting towns, establishing government, and setting up communications, the churches of Ohio began to emerge. All shared the same financial problems, the same primitive conditions, the same struggle to supply their needs and to become established. They were to have the common experience of solving one problem only to find others awaiting their attention. The story of Lutherans in Ohio includes both the facts of beginnings and expansion as well as the interpretation of the way in which problems were met and adjustments made.

The problem for Lutherans was further complicated by the fact that Lutheranism was varied rather than uniform in character. Both in Germany

---

[10] C. L. Martzolff, "Lutheranism in Perry County, Ohio" *Ohio Archaeological and Historical Publications,* XXVIII. p. 379.

and in the German settlements along the Atlantic seaboard impulses of several theological sorts were being felt. The clergy rather than the laymen on the farms were those most informed on these matters. It is impossible to tell which theological trend had most adherents.

In simplest terms particularly as appearing on the Ohio scene, the varieties may be grouped under four headings. Pietism gave major attention to matters of life and conduct, to faith rather than to doctrine. A second trend placed the emphasis on theological matters, on pure doctrine, classical Lutheran teachings, and the points which distinguished Lutherans from all others. A third grouping included those more or less affected by rationalism; based in part on philosophical grounds and in part on common sense, this tendency disparaged traditional Christian teaching, thereby reducing Christian faith simply to moral conduct. A fourth variety was interested in uniting Lutherans and Reformed either in organization or in fellowship. Such "union" emphasis discouraged distinctive Lutheran doctrine.

These trends, and variations of them, were imported into Ohio from Germany as well as from Pennsylvania and neighboring states. They were the basis of tensions among Lutherans in Ohio, as the following pages will show. They must be recognized if the history of Ohio Lutherans is to avoid being oversimplified and thereby falsified.

2 / PEOPLE AND PASTORS
1800–1812

THE BEGINNINGS OF LUTHERANISM in Ohio are to be found in the settlements of German-speaking people. In many instances these people had been born in Germany but had lived for a time in states along the Atlantic coast, especially Pennsylvania, Maryland, Virginia, and North Carolina. Some settlers had been born in these states. A few of them came directly from Germany. But in every case German was the language they used ordinarily and by preference, both in business and in church. Because they tended to settle in colonies, their communities were called "German"—Germantown in one instance, German Township in several instances, or "little Germany" as a local nickname. Because most of them were farmers, their rural life and their language tended to isolate them from other residents, so that there is some basis for the statement that Lutherans, though "of much local importance, did not affect the great body of Ohio's population." [1]

The principal areas of Ohio in which Lutherans were to be found in the first quarter of the nineteenth century were three. One was in the northeast part of the state in the tier of counties immediately south of the Western Reserve. Because this was hilly country, forming the watershed between Lake Erie and the Ohio River, it was called the "Backbone Region." Faust says that this "is distinctly the Pennsylvania German part of Ohio, and its principal business was farming." [2] But the distinction must be shared with the other areas. It was in the counties of Columbiana, Stark, Jefferson, Harrison, and Tuscarawas that Lutherans settled in sufficient numbers to form congregations.

The second area was just south of the center of the state, viz., Perry, Fairfield, and Pickaway Counties. Muskingum County formed something of a bridge between the two areas. Settlers in this central district arrived by way of the valleys formed by the Muskingum, Hocking, and Scioto

[1] Carl Wittke, ed., *History of the State of Ohio* (Columbus, 1942), II, 38.
[2] A. B. Faust, *The German Element in the United States* (Boston, 1909), I, 422.

Rivers. Here on the rounded hills on the edge of the glaciated area the pioneers found rich land.

The third area was Montgomery County and environs to which settlers had come by way of the Great Miami River valley. There were a few Germans among the first settlers in the Dayton area in 1795–96. At the turn of the century there were Lutherans in and about Miamisburg, among whom prominently were the Gebharts. Funeral records of First Lutheran Church, Miamisburg, show that most early members came from Berks, Lebanon, York, and Schuylkill Counties in Pennsylvania. When Paul Henkel on a missionary tour through southern Ohio in 1806 visited Montgomery County he conducted services and made a list of twenty-two heads of families in Washington Township, which at that time included the Miamisburg area. He noted that "most of my hearers are from Pastor Schulze's congregation in Pennsylvania." [3]

The western boundary of Washington Township at that date was the Miami River. West of it was German Township including Germantown. In 1804 "Philip Gunkel headed a colony of twenty-four families" from Berks County. He was a miller and looked for a mill site, choosing the place where Little Twin Creek enters Big Twin. That came to be Germantown. Most later settlers were from Pennsylvania. [4] In this township Paul Henkel listed the names of 102 heads of families. [5] The name of Philip Gunckel heads the list. This prosperous settlement with its strong flavor of German influence and language attracted yet other migrants to whom these factors were important. A considerable proportion of the inhabitants were Lutheran.

The men whose names are given in Henkel's lists were by no means all Lutheran. His lists rather are of German-speaking settlers. Many of them were Reformed. Indeed in his tour of Montgomery County, Henkel was accompanied in most cordial relationship by Jacob Christman and John Jacob Larose, Reformed pastors in the area whom Henkel had known when they were pastors in North Carolina. Larose had moved to Ohio as late as 1804. [6] Henkel rejoiced in seeing his friends again. It is certain that in

---

3 Clement L. Martzolff, ed., "Rev. Paul Henkel's Journal," *Ohio Archaeological and Historical Publications,* XXIII, 191. Christopher Emanuel Schulze was pastor in the Tulpehocken area of Berks County, Pennsylvania, 1770–1809.

4 A. W. Drury, *History of the City of Dayton and Montgomery County, Ohio* (Chicago-Dayton, 1909), I, 873.

5 Martzolff, *op. cit.,* pp. 204 f.

6 *Ibid.,* pp. 190, 214. Henry Harbaugh, *The Fathers of the German Reformed Church* (Lancaster, Pennsylvania, 1858-1859), III, 28 ff.

Montgomery County the Reformed and the Lutheran settlers, united in their use of the German language, worked together in church matters. It was quite different with Germans of other denominations. The Lutherans had nothing to do with them. There were many Germans in Montgomery County in townships other than the two mentioned. In some instances the settlers were Tunkers, sometimes called German Baptists, who congregated in certain areas. In other instances it was the Methodists whose influence was dominant. Methodist itinerants were in the area quite early. The first German sermon in Dayton was preached October 15, 1809, by Heinrich Boehm, a Methodist who the next year made that town his headquarters.[7] While it is true that the German Methodist movement did not get into full swing until the beginning of the work of Wilhelm Nast in 1835,[8] the Methodists, who soon became by far the largest denomination in the state, sought to win Germans as well as others.[9] Besides the Methodists, the Lutherans had as neighbors the United Brethren who combined in themselves the revivalism of the Methodists and certain traits of the Mennonites. In the course of time Montgomery County became one of the leading United Brethren strongholds, with a theological seminary and a publishing house in Dayton. It was in Perry Township that a congregation of the United Brethren settled in 1819.[10] Soon the United Brethren were found in other townships as well.

Lutherans were to be found not only in the southernmost townships of Montgomery County but also in the townships just north of them, particularly in Jefferson and Jackson Township. At the same time they occupied land in Preble County and neighboring areas. In Lewisburg and vicinity Lutherans were forming congregations at an early date.

If Germans from Pennsylvania predominated in Montgomery County, it was otherwise with the counties to the east through which Paul Henkel traveled. To the area that comprised the Virginia Military District in Ohio had come settlers from the south Atlantic states. At New Market in Highland County Henkel found Germans from Maryland and from Virginia, and at Brush Creek of the same county there were Virginians also. Settlers from North Carolina were encountered in Warren County at Springboro

---

[7] Helmut Trepte, *Deutschtum in Ohio bis zum Jahre 1820* (Dresden, 1931), p. 152 n.

[8] Paul F. Douglas, *The Story of German Methodism* (Cincinnati, 1939), pp. 21 ff.

[9] *Ibid.*, pp. 99 f. Douglas gives no adequate account of German Methodist preachers before Nast.

[10] Trepte, *op. cit.*, p. 155. Trepte is mistaken in identifying the United Brethren as "Herrnhuter" however.

and Clear Creek. Even in Montgomery County there had apparently been some Southerners, for Henkel met some whom "I knew elsewhere." [11] Some indication of the size of these settlements may be seen in the fact that at Clear Creek Henkel recorded thirty-three names of men, at New Market thirty-two, and at Brush Creek twenty-nine.

There were German-speaking settlers in Chillicothe and Ross County from an early date. Detailed surveys of the records of deeds to land reveal numerous German names. Some of these people were brought to Ross County as redemptioners, working out their terms of service there and remaining as inhabitants. Others came from Pennsylvania and perhaps elsewhere. Chillicothe, the first capital of the state, was dominantly English-speaking. The German-speaking settlers, instead of forming a foreign language colony, became rapidly Americanized. When Paul Henkel visited the area in 1806 he had difficulty in finding anyone who was willing to admit his German heritage.[12] Since English-speaking Lutheran churches were almost unknown at that date, there was no interest in organizing a Lutheran congregation in Chillicothe which would of course be German-speaking. Henkel got the impression that "the German inhabitants of the place are prejudiced against German pastors. They were probably possessed with what many others are possessed, stupid pride and lightmindedness." [13]

It was quite otherwise in Perry, Fairfield, and Pickaway Counties. Here the concentrations of German-speaking people were sufficient to maintain their identity. Language and Americanization were not obstacles to the formation of Lutheran congregations. Here again there was a pattern of fraternization with the Reformed but a coolness toward Methodists, Baptists, and United Brethren.

It was the eastern part of Pickaway County in particular that became Lutheran territory because there were located the German-speaking people who gathered in Lutheran, Reformed, and other churches. The majority of them had come from Pennsylvania. In Salt Creek Township, in which Tarlton is located, the settlers bore such names as Shoemaker, Lutz, Stumpf, Dunkel, Braucher, Holderman, and Reichelderfer.[14]

The first Lutheran settler in Perry County was Christian Binckley. He came from Maryland in 1801 with three sons and three daughters, most of

---

11 Martzolff, *op. cit.*, pp. 185 ff.

12 *Ibid.*, p. 184.

13 *Ibid.*, p. 194.

14 *History of Franklin and Pickaway Counties* (Cleveland, 1880), pp. 250 f.

them married. A year later another Lutheran family, that of John Peter Overmeyer, arrived from Pennsylvania.[15] Within another two years others had arrived until there were about twenty families with such names as Anspach, Humberger, Emrich, Cooperrider, and Mechling.[16]

The families of John Cooperrider and Peter Walser from Fayette County, Pennsylvania, were early Lutheran settlers, also in Perry County. They were among the charter members of Good Hope Church in Hopewell Township. J. Wagenhals, a young schoolteacher who later became a pastor, preached to them in the Cooperrider house. It was not until 1817, however, that a formal organization of a congregation occurred and a log church was erected.[17]

It was much the same story in Fairfield County. In Clearcreek Township settlers had arrived in 1806 and 1807 from Pennsylvania. In the cemetery of Israel's Church the gravestones of Jacob Huffer and of John Hartman state that they had been born in Berks County, Pennsylvania. Some of the settlers were Reformed, some were Lutheran.[18] "Lancaster, named after the Pennsylvania city . . . was settled originally by Pennsylvania Dutch, joined by Wurtembergers and some Swiss." [19]

In Jefferson County on the eastern edge of Ohio the first Lutheran settlers came for the most part from Pennsylvania. In 1800 the families of George and Martin Ostertag and George Bauer came from Fayette County, Pennsylvania.[20] John Reinhard, the first resident of Ohio to be ordained to the Lutheran ministry, wrote: "In the year of our Lord, 1804, I and my family, in connection with three other families, moved to Jefferson County in the State of Ohio. Upon our arrival here we found five other families which had preceded us, and in the next year another family followed us." [21] The parish record book of the Germano congregation includes the statement: "According to the wonderful leading and providence of God, in the years of our Lord 1802–1805 large numbers of Germans began to settle in

[15] C. L. Marzolff, "Lutheranism in Perry County, Ohio," *Ohio Archaeological and Historical Society Publications*, XXVIII, 375 ff.

[16] *Ibid.*, p. 380.

[17] P. A. Peter and William Schmidt, *Geschichte der Allgemeinen Evang.-Lutherischen Synode von Ohio und anderen Staaten* (Columbus, 1900), p. 374.

[18] *Lutheran Standard*, V, 12, August 4, 1847, p. 2.

[19] Eugene H. Roseboom and Francis P. Weisenburger, *A History of Ohio* (Columbus, 1953), p. 113.

[20] E. B. Burgess. *Memorial History of the Pittsburgh Synod* (Greenville, Pennsylvania, 1925), p. 725.

[21] *Lutheran Standard*, January 29, 1851. Quoted in Burgess, *op. cit.*, p. 62.

this region." [22] Most of these settlers came from Pennsylvania, though others in the county around Annapolis came from Maryland and Virginia. For example, there was Baltzer Culp, born near Frankfort-am-Main, Germany, who settled in Virginia in 1783, but moved to Knox Township, Jefferson County, Ohio, in 1805.[23] Some had been soldiers in the Continental Army and others were Hessians who had served with the British. "Martin Zwuedert, whose children spelled their names Swickard, was one of the Hessians captured at Trenton." [24]

The story of the organizing of congregations in these areas must be traced by the activity of pastors. For except for Good Hope Church in Jefferson County, these early congregations either did not keep records or lost them. The records of Good Hope Church, now disbanded as a Lutheran congregation, are in the archives of the Pittsburgh Synod.

Ohio first appears in the records of the Ministerium of Pennsylvania in 1804 when a petition was received from Columbiana County asking that Mr. George Simon be received into the Ministerium.[25] The Ministerium adopted the resolution: "That Mr. George Simon be given a license as candidate in the congregations which ask for him, with the admonition that the Ministerium desires that he receive further instruction." [26] He was therefore the first resident of Ohio to receive a Lutheran license to perform ministerial acts. A year later the convention received the news that Mr. Simon had died.[27]

The petition likely was inspired by John Stough (Johannes Stauch) who had been visiting that community. Stough with his bride had moved some 160 miles west of Hagerstown, Maryland, in 1787. Since he was a devout man, other settlers induced him to perform marriages and other clerical acts even though he had no ministerial license. Settlers in (West) Virginia near Morgantown and in southwestern Pennsylvania were requesting his services.[28]

---

[22] Burgess, op. cit., p. 63.

[23] Lutheran Standard, V, 10, July 7, 1847, p. 3.

[24] Burgess, op. cit., p. 728.

[25] Documentary History of the Evangelical Lutheran Ministerium of Pennsylvania and Adjacent States, p. 343.

[26] Ibid., p. 347.

[27] Ibid., p. 351.

[28] Stough's autobiography, translated by his son, is in the collection of the Lutheran Historical Society at Gettysburg Theological Seminary. It was published serially in The Lutheran Observer beginning June 12, 1857. Later it appeared in The Lutheran Visitor and was copied serially in The Lutheran Evangelist beginning February 25, 1881. It was

After his wife died he took his children back to Hagerstown in the spring of 1793 and went on to Philadelphia to the convention of the Ministerium. The minutes report that "A certain Johannes Stauch handed in a petition from Virginia asking for admission. Several congregations are in that region without a preacher the nearest being one hundred and fifty miles from an ordained preacher." [29] The Ministerium *"Resolved:* That Mr. Stauch receive a license as catechist in Redstone, Morgantown and Salem, under the supervision of the ordained preacher in Martinsburg." [30] With this, the lowest rank in the order of ministers, he made his headquarters in Fayette County, Pennsylvania—the Redstone area.

The next year he came again to the convention of the Ministerium, asking that he be advanced in rank to that of candidate. The Ministerium *"Resolved,* That on account of the great distance from an ordained preacher, Catechist Stauch be granted a full license, but that it extend only over Redstone and other congregations near it on the frontier." [31] But this gave him plenty of latitude. He recalled: "I had ten preaching places in German Lutheran settlements, from one hundred miles to one hundred and sixty miles distant, to which I travelled every four weeks." [32] He was absent from six of the next ten annual conventions of the Ministerium, probably because of the great distance, but finally was advanced to the rank of ordained pastor at the convention at Easton in 1804. This was the same convention at which George Simon was licensed. If he were to receive the "further instruction" ordered by the Ministerium, it likely would be at the hands of Stough, the only ordained pastor in the area beyond the mountains.

Since Stough in reality had the whole frontier as his parish, he traveled "in thinly settled parts of Ohio, Kentucky, Western Virginia and Pennsylvania." [33] On such a preaching tour in 1802 he held preaching services in the cabin of Adam Rupert, a Revolutionary War veteran, who lived in Unity Township, Columbiana County, Ohio. As a result "Salem" or "Union"

---

printed in *The Lutheran Standard,* 1907, numbers 42, 43, 45. It is given in C. V. Sheatsley,*History of the Evangelical Lutheran Joint Synod of Ohio* (Columbus, 1919), pp. 12 ff., and in E. B. Burgess, *op. cit.,* pp. 29 ff. It is reprinted in two family histories, that of the Bowman, and of the Hester families. W. D. Allbeck, "John Stough, Founder of Ohio Lutheranism," *Lutheran Quarterly,* XII (1960), 25 ff.

[29] *Documentary History,* p. 265.

[30] *Ibid.,* p. 266.

[31] *Ibid.,* p. 273.

[32] Sheatsley, *op. cit.,* p. 21.

[33] *Ibid.,* p. 24.

congregation was formed and a log church was built in 1803 or 1804.[34] He was in Springfield Township (now Mahoning County) in 1803 where a congregation of Lutherans and Reformed was gathered. "On June 4, 1804, the members of the Lutheran and Reformed congregation voted to build a church or meeting house on the land of Peter Meserle." [35] This was known as the "Old Springfield Church." [36]

Stough gathered congregations in Jefferson County also, and conducted services there at stated intervals beginning in 1805. As John Reinhard remembered it, it was soon after his family had settled that "Rev. J. Stauch appeared in our midst, but living eighty miles from here, he could come only once in eight weeks." [37] Stough continued to explore the needs of other settlements as well, and for the expense of his travels received payment from the synod. For the Ministerium of Pennsylvania in June, 1806, "*Resolved, That Mr. John Stauch shall be paid for his labors outside the congregations he has accepted in the State of Ohio, just as other traveling preachers.*" [38]

In October, 1806, after he resigned his parish in Pennsylvania because of dissension among the members, he moved to Columbiana County, Ohio, settling in Center Township where he bought 160 acres of land from Bezaleel Wells and wife for $480.[39] During the next two years he made a trip back to his former parish in Pennsylvania to conduct services every fourth week the first year and every eighth week the second year.[40] Meanwhile he cultivated the missionary opportunities in the territory around his home in Columbiana County. The first license to perform marriage ceremonies in the county was the one issued to him November 18, 1806.[41] His first recorded wedding was of Christian Crist and Susannah Slosser on on December 23, 1806.[42] The extent of his parish cannot now be precisely determined, but it included Germano in Harrison County[43] and a location

[34] H. M. Smiley, *History of the Bowman Family* (Lisbon, Ohio, 1909), p. 45. Horace Mack, *History of Columbiana County*, p. 251, places it on the southwest corner of the Forney section, number ten. On Adam Rupert, cf. *Official Roster of the Soldiers of the American Revolution Buried in the State of Ohio*, p. 318.

[35] *Parish Record Book, Zion Lutheran Church, New Middletown, Ohio*, p. 1.

[36] Smiley, *op. cit.*, p. 45; Mack, *op. cit.*, p. 319, states that the church was on the southwest corner of section fourteen.

[37] Burgess, *op. cit.*, pp. 62 f.

[38] *Documentary History*, p. 371.

[39] Smiley, *op. cit.*, p. 46. Bezaleel Wells, surveyor and judge, owned large tracts of land in eastern Ohio. He founded Steubenville and Canton.

[40] Burgess, *op. cit.*, p. 38. Sheatsley, *op. cit.*, p. 29.

[41] Smiley, *op. cit.*, p. 46.

[42] *Columbiana County Marriage Record Book*, I, 19.

[43] Burgess, *op. cit.*, p. 730.

in Stark County.[44] In both instances the congregation was formed in 1805 and was Lutheran and Reformed.

The extent and spirit of Stough's work is best indicated by this quotation from his Journal.

> The first year after my move into Ohio I organized twelve congregations in the counties of Columbiana, Jefferson, Warren, Stark, Beaver and Mercer (the last two named in Pennsylvania), and continued to preach in Washington County every four weeks the first year, and after every eight weeks, as it was seventy miles distant and over bad roads. My heart sickens within me when I behold the wide waste in our beloved Zion. Children baptized within the pale of the church crying for spiritual food or instruction, and all for want of laborers in the harvest field. And many that are truly pious were spiritually starving and wandering in the wilderness of sin and lost to the church and to heaven. Men came as far as thirty miles and told me their deplorable condition, bade me come and preach the gospel in their houses.[45]

Stough reported to the convention of the Ministerium in June, 1808, that during the previous year he had baptized 323 persons, confirmed forty-three, administered communion to 356, and buried eleven.[46] That report is fairly typical of his reports for subsequent years through 1812. The number of of people to whom he ministered is impressive, considering that they were not concentrated in one town but were scattered over the farms of a considerable area. The numerous baptisms, presuming that most of them were of children, are indicative of large families. To accumulate such totals Stough was in effect riding a circuit. To the Ministerium in 1809 "Pastor Stauch reported 14 congregations without names in Columbia [sic], Jefferson and Trumbull counties and 5 vacant congregations. Baptized, 351; confirmed, 49; communicants, 505; deceased, 9; schools, 3." [47]

Besides his regular parish, extended as it was, he was concerned about the settlers on the ever-advancing frontier. A journal of his travels was submitted regularly to the Ministerium. For example, the journal presented to the 1807 convention indicated that during the previous twelve months he had spent 122 days on tour and had covered 1300 miles.[48]

---

[44] Article by Johann Raeber in *Der deutsche Pionier*, 1871, p. 53.

[45] Burgess, *op. cit.*, p. 37. Sheatsley, *op. cit.*, p. 29.

[46] *Documentary History*, p. 393. Theodore G. Tappert, "The Diaries of John Stough, 1806–1807," *Lutheran Quarterly*, XII (1960), 44 ff.

[47] *Ibid.*, p. 403.

[48] *Ibid.*, p. 380. Microfilm Collection of the Concordia Historical Institute, no. 173, "Stauch Papers."

Because the number of new settlements and congregations was increasing rapidly, and there were not sufficient pastors to occupy them all, the Ministerium of Pennsylvania in 1805 decided "to appoint traveling preachers, who shall make a tour each year." It was *"Resolved,* That forty dollars a month be allowed each traveling preacher, and that one month's salary shall be paid in advance." These men were to be provided with the necessary credentials. Besides six other tour areas it was *"Moved,* that a traveling preacher be named for the district called New Pennsylvania (in the State of Ohio), from the Capital New Madrid, to Lake Erie. This motion was approved and Mr. Forster was appointed." [49]

The area indicated in the resolution is rather vague, but some information is available concerning the preacher. William Forster had been given a license as candidate by the Ministerium of Pennsylvania in 1798 at the request of some congregations in Shenandoah County, Virginia, and was ordained in 1802. We may suppose that he made his preaching trip into Ohio during the summer when the weather was fit for traveling. At the next convention in June, 1806, he and another traveling preacher made their reports. The convention ordered 4,000 copies of extracts of these reports to be printed. He had covered a wide area, going as far south as Point Pleasant, (West) Virginia.[50] The formation of a congregation at New Reading, Perry County, may be attributed to this preaching tour. Stough, too, visited the area of Fairfield and Perry Counties, preaching and baptizing. He collected names of settlers and sent them to Forster to interest him in coming to Ohio. Zion congregation in Thorn Township, Perry County, organized in 1805 or 1806, was a fruit of Forster's work.[51]

The convention of the Ministerium of Pennsylvania in June, 1806, which heard Forster's report and which voted to remunerate Stough for his travels, voted also to appoint Paul Henkel as traveling preacher with the usual pay of forty dollars a month for the actual time he was on tour.[52] This was the man whose journal lists the settlers already noted in this chapter. Henkel at this time was fifty-five years old and was pastor in New Market, Vir-

---

[49] *Documentary History,* pp. 356 f.

[50] Martzolff, "Rev. Paul Henkel's Journal," *op. cit.,* p. 179. Microfilm Collection of the Concordia Historical Institute: William Foster and J. G. Butler, *Brief Account of Their Journey to Ohio, 1805.*

[51] *Ibid.,* pp. 211 f. The date 1805 is given in A. A. Graham, *History of Fairfield and Perry Counties,* pp. 406 f.

[52] *Documentary History,* p. 370.

ginia.[53] On July seventh he set out with his wife, crossed the mountains, and followed the valley of the Kanawha River to its junction with the Ohio River at Point Pleasant. There he crossed the river into Ohio, went to Chillicothe, and traveled across the southern counties as far as Germantown, Montgomery County. His return journey followed the same route and he reached home September fifteenth. The journal, edited by Martzolff, is a very interesting document. It displays his missionary zeal, his earnest piety, and his devotion to the German language. At the 1807 convention of the Ministerium of Pennsylvania Henkel "read a part of his journal, from which it appears that he traveled 128 days in the service of the Synod, baptized 158 children, and received $106.05 on this journey." [54]

The Minutes of the 1807 convention show that Forster was absent without excuse. Stough was absent also, but sent his excuse and the journal of his travels. Though there was a desire to continue to support Stough on his tours, the small amount of money in the treasury permitted appointing only one traveling preacher, and he was to work in Virginia. The needs of Ohio, however, had been expressed in several letters requesting visits by traveling preachers.[55]

In 1808 another man joined the small force of pastors working in Ohio. He was Andrew Simon, though the Minutes of the Ministerium of Pennsylvania nowhere give his first name nor any indication of the area in Ohio served by him, except at the beginning. The convention of the Ministerium that year received "reports of Mr. Stauch's labors in his congregations, in which he at the same time requests that Mr. Simon, if he was examined and found capable, might go to the district of Jefferson and Trumbull" Counties in Ohio.[56] The Ministerium not only voted to give him a license as a candidate, finding his qualifications adequate,[57] but also voted him a grant of thirty dollars to help him continue his theological studies.[58] He had been voted $100 the previous year. It was decided that he should be a traveling preacher "whose district shall be restricted to the small towns and

[53] *Dictionary of American Biography*, VIII, 538. William B. Sprague, *Annals of the American Lutheran Pulpit* (New York, 1869), pp. 92 ff. W. J. Finck, "Paul Henkel, the Lutheran Pioneer," *Lutheran Quarterly*, LVI, 307 ff. B. H. Pershing, "Paul Henkel, Frontier Missionary, Organizer and Author," *Lutheran Church Quarterly*, VII, 125 ff.

[54] *Documentary History*, p. 380.
[55] *Ibid.*, pp. 375 f.
[56] *Ibid.*, p. 391.
[57] *Ibid.*, p. 395.
[58] *Ibid.*, p. 388.

northern parts of Pennsylvania and the State of Ohio. It was, however, distinctly understood that neither of the traveling preachers shall encroach upon any congregations where preachers are already stationed." [59] As evidence of the fact that Andrew Simon began his ministry in northeastern Ohio and across the line in Pennsylvania there is a record of a baptism by him, August 14, 1808, in Good Hope Church, Mercer County, Pennsylvania. [60]

Soon, however, he located in southwestern Ohio. The convention of the Ministerium in 1808 received a letter containing "hearty thanks from the congregations in the State of Ohio, who thank the Synod, that the traveling preacher, Mr. Paul Henkel, visited them; also the request that the said pastor settle and make his home with them. Whereupon it was resolved, that the traveling preacher, Mr. Simon, shall visit them." [61] At this same convention "a letter from Miami was read, in which request is made that one of the traveling preachers visit them." [62] This points to Montgomery County, and there it was that Simon settled. A wedding at which he officiated, October 19, 1809, is on record at the Court House. He purchased land on December 23, 1812, paying $200 for fifty-two acres.

But he was to be a disappointment to his Lutheran brethren. The first year of his ministry was satisfactory. He attended the synodical convention, reporting that he had been on tour for five and a half months and had received $74.62. The Synod voted him an additional fifty dollars. [63] Moreover, the convention received "letters of thanksgiving from Ohio, thanking that the traveling preacher, Mr. Simon, preached the Gospel unto them, and asking that he be appointed their permanent preacher. Moved and seconded that the request be granted, and his license be prepared for this congregation." [64] He never again attended a convention of the Ministerium of Pennsylvania, nor sent an excuse, nor submitted a statistical report. He attended the second Special Conference in Ohio in 1813 but was absent from all the others as well as from the conventions of the Ohio Synod in 1818 and 1819. Thereafter his name disappears from the minutes. His last recorded wedding in Montgomery County was dated August 19, 1819. It has been stated that he moved to Indiana and began the practice of medicine. [65]

[59] *Ibid.*, p. 389.
[60] Burgess, *op. cit.*, p. 580.
[61] *Documentary History*, p. 390.
[62] *Ibid.*, p. 391.
[63] *Ibid.*, p. 408.
[64] *Ibid.*, p. 401.
[65] Trepte, *op. cit.*, p. 160.

The Ministerium of Pennsylvania in 1812 had to take some action "concerning the Christian and conscientious question of Mr. Simon: Whether he be permitted to give communion to Reformed people also, it was *Resolved,* That in *case of necessity* it might be given to any Protestant in good standing, if he cannot have the services of his own pastor." [66] Likely this liberal ruling suited Simon, but in his parish were members with stricter views. As a result the next year the Ministerium of Pennsylvania had before it "a letter from three congregations in the State of Ohio in which several complaints are made against their pastor, Mr. Simon, in which he is accused of not abiding by the old Lutheran form of doctrine." [67] The ministerial session resolved "That Pastor Lochman [the secretary], in the name of the Ministerium, should hold up before him, in the spirit of love, the complaints brought against him, and fraternally admonish him, not only to conduct himself more circumspectly, but also to abide by the pure old form of doctrine, and to make no innovations, or there would be hesitation about renewing his license in the future." [68]

Defending himself against the charges of introducing innovations, Simon's reply to the secretary came before the convention the next year and was considered satisfactory.[69] Because no notice of this action reached him, the convention of 1815 had before it a "letter from Mr. Simon in which he complains that his letter to the last year's Synod had not been answered. He also defends himself against several complaints, and expresses the desire to continue as a member of our body. Inclosed was a favorable testimonial from his congregations." The secretary affirmed that he had sent a letter even if Simon had not received it. Whereupon it was *"Resolved,* That Pastor Lochman write to him again, and assure him that we still recognize him as a worthy member of our body." [70]

In Ohio, however, he was not in such good favor with his fellow-pastors. In 1819 Pastor Leist asked the Ohio Synod "whether a minister of our connection who behaves contrary to the Ministerial Order and criticizes the rules of the church, disrupting parishes, should be recognized, or should be advised to give up his office." The Synod resolved that every preacher should observe the Ministerial Order, and it was *"Resolved,* That Mr. Simon, who already has been admonished many times to behave according

[66] *Documentary History,* p. 437.
[67] *Ibid.,* p. 454.
[68] *Ibid.,* p. 460.
[69] *Ibid.,* p. 468.
[70] *Ibid.,* p. 478.

to the Order, once more should be requested by the officers of Synod, and if no improvement follows he in the future can not further be a member of our connection." [71] That was the end of the synodical connection for Mr. Simon. He had never been ordained, but had been functioning during these years simply on the basis of a license.

John Samuel Mau was another pastor who was a problem.[72] The first notice of him is in a parish record in Westmoreland County, Pennsylvania, where his daughter was baptized.[73] The next notice is in the Minutes of the Ministerium of Pennsylvania in 1790:

> Dr. [H. E.] Muhlenberg [the president] reported to the Synod that in the summer of the past year, a man named Mace, who for some years had been a schoolmaster in Pennsylvania, had through diligent study acquired a fair knowledge of theology, and at present lives in Kentucky, had asked him for a license, which he, after a closer examination of his abilities, had also granted him. The Dr. hoped that partly the inconvenience of calling a Synod without loss of time, might sufficiently justify his action. The Synod found these reasons satisfactory, and declared the license granted Mr. Mace valid.[74]

Thus his first license was dated 1789, three years after he had moved to Kentucky. In 1795 it was reported that a District Meeting in Virginia had renewed his license, and at his request was asking for permission to ordain him.[75] The most the Ministerium would grant was a renewal of his license for "Lexington, the Falls, Danville, and Limestone in Kentucky." [76]

After moving to Ohio about 1804, he settled in Montgomery County, where he bought a quarter section of land on June 11, 1808. The first wedding recorded by him in the county was performed August 31, 1809.[77] And about this time he was also teaching school in German Township. In

---

[71] Minutes, Evangelical Lutheran Synod of Ohio and Neighboring States, 1819, p. 7.

[72] This was his name as he wrote it, but it appears also as Maw, Mow, Mann, Marr, or Mace as various printers interpreted the handwriting.

[73] William A. Zundel, History of Old Zion Church, p. 35.

[74] Documentary History, p. 231.

[75] Perhaps this was part of the purpose of his trip made in the winter of 1794–95. His brief journal, now in the possession of Mrs. Mabel Bobbitt, Waldron, Indiana, tells of a journey made from Martinsburg, Virginia, to Bethlehem, Pennsylvania, to see his mother. He wrote that he was born March 3, 1752, in Bethlehem, Pennsylvania. Cf. W. D. Allbeck, "A Journal of John Samuel Mau, 1794–1795," Lutheran Quarterly, XIII (1961), 155 ff.

[76] Documentary History, pp. 276, 280. The Falls is now Louisville, and Limestone is Maysville.

[77] Montgomery County Marriage Record Book, I, 23.

1813 he attended the Second Special Conference of Lutheran pastors in Ohio. The Minutes read:

> Mr. Mau, who a few years ago at the General Conference was duly furnished with credentials to serve as a licensed candidate in the State of Kentucky, announced his presence at the Special Conference. He admitted with regret that in his weakness and precipitancy he had dealings with the so-called New Reformed or Independent Brethren[78] and had been misled to believe and accept certain fanatical teachings, as a result of which he had given offense to his church, but not willingly and intentionally, and that in all this he had meant well both toward God and his fellowmen; he said he desired to be restored to the membership of the church and to serve again as a regular preacher.
>
> It was resolved that the officers of the Special Conference should report the matter to the General Conference and request a new certificate for Mr. Mau inasmuch as we have trustworthy evidence that his life and conduct are such as to commend him as a preacher of the Gospel.[79]

The Ministerium of Pennsylvania (the "General Conference" mentioned above) at its convention a month later received

> a report from a Special Conference which had been held in Fairfield County (Ohio), October, 1812 [actually May, 1813], signed by Pastors Henkel and Stauch, in which they, together with others, petition for a license for Mr. Samuel Mau. They certify that he has heartily repented of the wrong he committed in leaving the Evangelical Lutheran Church, and express the firm hope that in the future he will be useful and profitable to the church of God.[80]

The following action was taken at the ministerial session:

> With reference to Mr. Mau, who had been recommended for readmission into the Ministerium by Pastors Henkel and Stauch, it was resolved, that the Ministerium allow him a license for such congregations in Kentucky as the ordained members of the State of Ohio shall assign him.[81]

There is no evidence that Mau ever attended a convention of the Ministerium of Pennsylvania, or ever was ordained. He was absent from the Special Conference in Ohio which approved his reinstatement, though he did attend the Special Conferences in 1815 and 1816. His address in 1815

---

[78] Followers of P. W. Otterbein.

[79] *Minutes, Second Special Conference*, p. 8.

[80] *Documentary History*, p. 425.

[81] *Ibid.*, p. 460.

was Twin Creek, Ohio, and in 1816 it was Preble County. He is listed as absent from the early conventions of the Ohio Synod, and beginning with 1822 his name drops from the record. The Synod was not eager to exclude him. The convention of 1819 had before it

> A letter of Mr. Mau in which he complains indirectly about the whole Special Conference held last spring in Germantown and appears to be afraid he might not henceforth be considered as a member of our connection.
>
> *Resolved*, That the officers of Synod shall advise him in writing to try to control his passion somewhat more and also at the same time to comfort him that if he calms himself and truly manages his office, he has entirely nothing to fear that he would be excluded from our connection.[82]

Back of Mau's complaint was the fact that in the Germantown congregation there was dissension which involved him. For his guidance there had been read the section of the Synod Order referring to the conduct of ministers, but he had been offended by the reproof.[83]

The 1821 convention of the Ohio Synod considered

> A letter from Mr. Mau in which he leaves himself to the judgment of Synod concerning charges that he is sympathetic to sectarianism (*schwaermerisch gesinnet*).
>
> Received two letters from two congregations of Mr. Mau wherein they show their satisfaction with their preacher; they ask also about a certain report whether or not it is established that last year's Synod had excluded their pastor [the old Mr. Mau] as a member of their Synod, as last year's secretary, Mr. Dill, reported to them through a copy of the original.[84]

The Ministerium was not fully agreed on the matter but resolved that it did not desire to exclude Mr. Mau if he held sufficiently to the Ministerial Order.[85] Evidently Mau did not conform sufficiently to the Synod's ideals. His last recorded wedding in Montgomery County occurred January 14, 1819. He supported himself by teaching, being the first school-teacher in the Twin Valley. He is described as being "somewhat eccentric." He made his will October 30, 1828, naming his wife, Eve Catherine, three sons, and four daughters as heirs, his wife being appointed administratrix of his estate September 20, 1830. He died in the summer of 1830.

The careers of Simon and Mau indicate pointedly some of the problems of the church and the ministry in pioneer days. These two men made a

---

[82] *Minutes, Joint Synod of Ohio and Other States*, 1819, p. 6.
[83] *Ibid.*, p. 15.
[84] *Ibid.*, 1821, p. 4.
[85] *Ibid.*, p. 8.

certain contribution to the religious life of the settlers who otherwise would have been neglected. But they lacked the attitudes needed for the construction of organized church work.

The synod, whether the one already functioning in Pennsylvania or the one soon to arise in Ohio, was an organization whose main interests were cooperation and good order in church work. Pastors and congregations were united in a synod in order that they might work together, and by their union have strength for tasks too large for single parishes. Their cooperation meant that they could have funds for sending traveling preachers into new settlements. It meant that they might encourage each other in their frontier loneliness. Their union gave weight to appeals for aid. Federated together, they could look forward to such growth that they could educate their own pastors more nearly sufficient in number for their needs. If each pastor or congregation were independent, there could be none of these things.

The synod also stood for good order. It was organized so that pastors and congregations working together would avoid conflicts. In the brotherly atmosphere of synod they could arrive at mutual agreements as to boundaries and areas of work. The synod was a forum where complaints could be heard and adjusted as far as was possible. Good order required also that only suitable men be certified as pastors. This was not a narrowly denominational matter, for strict Lutheranism was unknown in frontier Ohio. It meant not only that disreputable and unqualified men should not be certified as preachers but also that each pastor and congregation should be willing to submit to the principles and practices commonly agreed to in the synod.

Neither Simon nor Mau was a synod man at heart. Essentially they were independent preachers whose connection with other Lutheran pastors was casual and minimal. They went their individual ways unwilling to submit themselves to the discipline of fellowship. Parochial-minded, they had no interest in the wide work of the church throughout the state. If there was a frontier mentality, the spirit of wanting to go it alone, they apparently had it.

Simon and Mau bring to view also the desperate needs of the settlers for spiritual services. To be without church services and sacraments for years was disturbing to at least some of the pioneers. Whenever opportunity for such pastoral services was offered, there were those who welcomed them heartily. Even though the man who presented himself was not ordained and had only a license issued years ago, he was the best that could be had, and he was accepted. He might turn out to be a disappointment, as these two men did, but until better pastors were available, these had to be accepted and endured.

The standards of the ministry are exhibited also in the persons of Simon and Mau. It was not so much that they lacked formal training; none of the other Lutheran preachers in Ohio had a really adequate education in theology. All of them had served an apprenticeship with a license before being ordained. The requirements of the period of licensure were small enough, but neither Simon nor Mau was willing to meet them, as presumably they might have done. Nor was the problem that of working part time at something else. All Lutheran preachers in Ohio had to do some farming to maintain their families. Some of them dabbled in medicine as Simon did. Having read a simple book on medicine they gave advice to those seeking medical help when no physicians were available. Some of them added to their incomes as Mau did by teaching school. This was good community service.

What marks off Simon and Mau was the fact that the ministry was not for them a primary task to which their other activities were secondary. Rather they were independent characters, each seeking to make his way and maintain himself by whatever wits and abilities he possessed. Preaching was just one of the several things he could do and he used it along with the others for a livelihood. When the synod was not satisfied with that, he and the synod went their separate ways.

The cases of Simon and Mau remind us also that Lutheran pastors in frontier Ohio had to deal with the sectarian movements around them. The excited revivals in Kentucky attracted many visitors from Ohio, as Paul Henkel discovered on his tour. Revivalism spread into Ohio. The new settlements heard plenty of laymen's religion marked by vigorous physical displays. The old forms of religion with their theological bases tended to be ignored, and the new excited voices and ideas were to be heard. Both Simon and Mau were affected by them. Other pastors, such as Stough, were disturbed also, but not to the degree that they suffered estrangement. Forster was accused of preaching much on the Apocalypse without understanding it.[86] But their fellowship helped them to preserve their balance—a benefit lost to the independents.

If Simon and Mau were disappointments as pioneer pastors, it was quite different with John Michael Steck and G. Henry Weygandt in western Pennsylvania. Both of these men were important for the organizing of Lutherans in Ohio, even though they do not exhaust the list of

[86] *Documentary History*, p. 431.

Lutheran preachers on the frontier. At least six others had crossed the mountains westward into western Pennsylvania before 1812.[87]

John Michael Steck, who was born at Germantown, Pennsylvania, October 5, 1756, had studied theology under Dr. J. H. C. Helmuth in Philadelphia. Apparently without license or ordination by any synod, he began his ministerial career in 1784 at Chambersburg. Five years later he was called farther west to congregations in Bedford and Somerset Counties, but soon moved westward again into Westmoreland County where he spent the rest of his life. He died at Greensburg July 14, 1830.[88]

The first notice of Steck in the minutes of the Ministerium of Pennsylvania was in 1796 when he attended the convention to apply for a license. Having successfully passed the examination, he was granted a license for the congregations of "Greensburg, Herolds's, Bruschkrik, Ridge, at Jacobskrik, and at Allegheny in Westmoreland County." [89] But he had been working in that parish for almost five years by that time. The first record of a Communion conducted by him is dated October 11, 1791.[90]

Synodical minutes give some indication of Steck's interest in the organized work of the Church beyond his parish. Though he crossed the mountains only three times to attend conventions of the Ministerium of Pennsylvania—in 1796 when he was licensed, again in 1798 when his license was renewed, and in 1806 when he was ordained—he was fairly faithful in sending his statistical reports. He was present at three of the seven Special Conferences of the Western District; at two of them held in Pennsylvania he was elected president—1814 when he was host to the Conference at Greensburg, and 1815 at Somerset; the third was in 1817 at New Philadelphia, Ohio. He was host to the convention of the Ohio Synod at Greensburg in 1822, and attended two other conventions. Though he had the frontiersman's spirit of independence, he valued the fellowship of his brethren in the ministry, and he was willing to submit to such orderly regulations as that fellowship in synod entailed. Thus he conformed to the modest requirements for ordination, and continued in synodical membership to the end of his life. [91]

[87] Burgess, *op. cit.*, p. 51, lists these names: Anton Ulrich Luetge, Abraham Gottlieb Deschler, Johann Friedrich Wilhelm Lange, Philip Muckenhaupt, John Carl Rebenach, and Wilhelm Heinrich Scriba.

[88] Sprague, *op. cit.*, p. 148.

[89] *Documentary History*, p. 287.

[90] Burgess, *op. cit.*, pp. 633 ff. See picture of church record, p. 640.

[91] For an account of his life see the article on his son, M. J. Steck, in *Evangelical Review*, VIII, 105 f.; J. C. Jensson, *American Lutheran Biographies* (Milwaukee, 1890), p. 753; Sprague, *op. cit.*, p. 148.

The ministry of G. Henry Weygandt covered about thirty-eight years, the first half of it in Washington County, Pennsylvania, and the rest in Wayne County, Ohio. Born May 2, 1779, in Northumberland County, Pennsylvania, he was brought by his parents to the new settlements in Washington County. There he was confirmed by Pastor Stough. It will be remembered that for several years after he moved to Ohio Stough continued to be regular supply preacher in the Washington County parish. Since this was burdensome he was looking for a successor in that field. Thus when he attended the convention of the Ministerium of Pennsylvania at Hanover, May 28–30, 1809, he had with him Henry Weygandt as an applicant for a license. A letter from Washington County requested Weygandt's services. Examination revealed that he had a fair amount of knowledge but needed to continue his studies. Accordingly he was given a license as catechist and directed to study under the supervision of Pastor Stough.[92]

A year later, when the examining committee reported that he had "improved much," his license advanced him in rank from catechist to candidate.[93] He attended the conventions faithfully during the next five years with one exception, and on Stough's recommendation was ordained as deacon in 1815.[94] Though absent thereafter, he sent his reports regularly.

His record of faithfulness to the Special Conference was just as good. He was host to the first convention of the Conference. He was absent from the second convention only because the Conference had sent him to the synod convention with a petition for authority to ordain in the West. He carried with him also the sermons and diaries of his fellow candidates. The third convention elected him secretary-treasurer, and the fifth and seventh conventions chose him to be treasurer. In his letter of excuse for absence from the sixth convention he included a plea "for keeping up the dear German language" by the Conference.[95]

When the Ohio Synod met for its first convention in 1818 Weygandt participated and was elected treasurer. The next year he was chosen secretary. In the years that followed he shared loyally and regularly in the Synod's conventions and work. In 1828 or 1829 he moved to Wayne County, Ohio, where he served eight congregations, namely, Immanuel's, Salem's, Wooster, Bachman's, Milton, Franklin, Kiefer, and Newman's Creek. He died October 7, 1847, and was buried at Doylestown, Ohio.[96]

---

[92] *Documentary History,* pp. 397, 400 f., 406 f.
[93] *Ibid.,* p. 420.
[94] *Ibid.,* pp. 478, 483 f.
[95] *Minutes,* p. 32.
[96] *Lutheran Standard,* V, 18, October 27, 1847.

These were the men who performed ministerial functions as Lutherans in Ohio before 1812 when the first conference was held. They saw the virgin forest breaking open with clearings for farms and villages. The population reported by the Census of 1800 was 45,365 people scattered around the state. By 1810 that figure had leaped to 230,760. The days when a few pastors in isolation could serve the needs of the swelling population by a few preaching tours was about over. It was high time that they organize themselves for the work, for the population in the next decade would jump to 581,434. The First Conference, held in 1812, came none too soon. The story of that organization must be told in the next chapter.[97]

[97] The form of church organization developed by Lutherans in the free-church situation of the United States differed from that in Europe where state-church patterns existed. For a careful study see Robert Fortenbaugh, *The Development of the Synodical Polity of the Lutheran Church in America to 1829* (Philadelphia, 1926).

3 / UNITING FOR STRENGTH
1812–1817

THE FIRST LUTHERAN CONVENTION west of the Allegheny Mountains was held in 1812. Who sent out the summons, setting the place and the date, is not recorded. In the crisp weather of October 17, 18, and 19 the meeting was held in the hills of Washington County, Pennsylvania, in Stecher's Church, of which Henry Weygandt was pastor. That was the beginning of organized cooperation among Lutheran pastors and congregations in the new Wast. It was designated a "Special Conference" of pastors of the Ministerium of Pennsylvania.

The plan of Special Conferences had been suggested in the Ministerium of Pennsylvania as early as 1781. The difficulties of travel in those days made trips of any distance quite tedious. Between conventions of that Ministerium (or Synod, as it was sometimes called) it was thought desirable that "the ministers dwelling close together in one county or district confer" on mutual problems.[1] Two years later the Conferences were officially organized.[2] In the Constitution of the Ministerium of 1792 the organization and the functions of the Special Conferences are specified. A Conference was to consist of neighboring pastors and a lay delegate from each congregation. Meetings were to be held as needed. A chairman and a secretary were to attest the minutes; their office ceased with the close of the meeting. The Conference should "promote the welfare of the respective congregations and of the German schools within the District" and should deal with such business and matters of the congregations as may be presented, without, however, intruding upon the special functions of the Ministerium.[3]

A redistricting of the Conferences was made in 1801, with the instruction that they should meet at least once a year. At this time a Western District

[1] *Documentary History of the Evangelical Lutheran Ministerium of Pennsylvania and Adjacent States*, p. 175.

[2] *Ibid.*, pp. 190 f.

[3] *Ibid.*, pp. 258 f.

was named, but with no place or date of meeting indicated.[4] The fact was that there were too few men to form a Western District at that time. Buttler was at Cumberland, Maryland (listed as Fort Cumberland); Steck was in Greensburg, Pennsylvania; and Stough was cultivating western Pennsylvania and eastern Ohio.

John George Buttler had gone to Cumberland shortly after his ordination in 1805.[5] Every year without exception he traveled from his mid-mountain parish to the convention of the Synod. John Stough, who had much farther to travel, did not have as good a record of attendance as did Buttler, but it was much better than Steck's. About every third year Stough made the long trip to Synod, and when he was absent he usually sent an excuse and his reports.

It is apparent, therefore, that these men who kept their affiliation with the Ministerium of Pennsylvania knew of the plan of Special Conferences. When they attended the conventions they heard the reports of the Conference meetings in other districts. The desire for such a meeting in their western area would be most natural. Moreover they had opportunity to know each other and to become acquainted at the synodical conventions. Buttler and Stough were present in 1806 at Hagerstown, Maryland, when Steck was ordained. At that same convention they heard the report of William Forster who sometime during the previous twelve months had made a missionary tour of Ohio. This was the Forster who was to join them very soon in Ohio. And at that convention they could talk with Paul Henkel who was appointed to be a traveling preacher in western Virginia and Ohio that year, and who in a few years was to settle in Point Pleasant, (West) Virginia.

These few pastors were soon joined by others. Andrew Simon was licensed and sent as traveling preacher in Ohio in 1808, and the following year Henry Weygandt was given a license for Washington County, Pennsylvania, where he was to spend the next twenty years of his life. A year later E. H. Tiedemann came over the mountains to Somerset, Pennsylvania, with a catechist's license. But 1812 was a big year: four men received ministerial licenses to serve as pastors in the west. They were Anthony Weyer, John Rinehart, Henry Huet, and Jacob Leist. At long last there were enough pastors west of the mountains to form a Special Conference. And there was the prospect of more to come.

[4] *Ibid.*, pp. 319 f.
[5] For his life see Jensson, *op. cit.*, pp. 127 f., and Sprague, *op. cit.*, p. 72.

The first notice of Anthony Weyer is in 1810 when he was fifty years old, and it is vague in its details. It reads:

> In reference to the letter of Rev. Mr. Stauch, in which he recommends one Mr. Anton Weier to the Ministerium as a pastor, it was moved and approved that the letter be answered in the name of the Ministerium in a fraternal [liebevolle] manner, approving his conduct in reference to Mr. Weier, and that Rev. Mr. Lochman write the answer.[6]

It seems that Weyer and his wife, Catherine, were among the first settlers in Stark County. Perhaps Stough had been teaching him and wanted him brought to the attention of the Synod, though neither man attended the convention.

Two years later the Ministerium of Pennsylvania received a petition "from the congregation in Belmont, Jefferson, Guery [sic] and Muskingum Counties, that we admit Mr. Anthony Weyer." [7] The request was granted. Weyer was examined along with the other applicants and was given a license.[8] But there is a postscript to his case. The ministerial session "Resolved, That Rev. Mr. Lochman earnestly reprimand Mr. Forster in the name of the Ministerium for assuming the right to grant Mr. Weyer a license." [9] Evidently Weyer had been functioning as a preacher before 1812 in the counties indicated.

Weyer did not again attend a convention of the Ministerium of Pennsylvania, and no reports of his ministry appear in the minutes of that body. But he was faithful to the Special Conferences in Ohio, attending all but the fifth, and even then sent his report. He was elected secretary at the third convention. In 1813 his address was given as "near Washington, Guernsey County." That year the Third Special Conference directed him to serve congregations around Canton, and there he continued for the rest of his life. His congregations in Stark County in 1826 were Jerusalem's, Henrich's, Paulus, Israel's, Salem's, Bethlehem's, and Union.[10] He was absent from the first convention of the Ohio Synod, but was ordained by it in 1819. From 1821 to 1823 he held the office of treasurer. He died March 30, 1829, in his sixty-ninth year.[11] He is buried in the cemetery of Warstler Church, Plain Township, Stark County. His firmness as a Lutheran was indicated

[6] Documentary History, p. 418.

[7] Ibid., p. 441.

[8] Ibid., p. 444.

[9] Ibid., p. 445.

[10] Minutes of the Synod of Ohio, 1826, p. 15.

[11] Ibid., 1829, p. 22.

by a letter written by him in 1821 to the Tennessee Synod approving the doctrinal position of that Synod.[12]

John Rinehart (Reinhard) was a pioneer farmer who reluctantly accepted ministerial status and actively served congregations only about thirteen years. His name in the court records and on his tombstone is in the Anglicized form "Rinehart." The most that is known about him comes from an autobiographical article published in *The Lutheran Standard*, January 29, 1851.[13]

According to the tombstone he was born March 14, 1776, so that he was twenty-eight years old when he and his family moved from Washington County, Pennsylvania, into the wilds of Jefferson County, Ohio. Several families in Island Creek Township began meeting for religious purposes and were visited by John Stough at intervals. Rinehart was one of the officers of this small congregation. Stough urged that in the periods between his visits Rinehart should be a lay catechist, and ultimately become a pastor. After "much anxiety and uneasiness of mind, I consented to devote myself to the ministry until the Church could be supplied with better qualified laborers," he wrote.

Thus in 1812 the Ministerium of Pennsylvania had before it a petition "from the congregation in Jefferson County, State of Ohio," to admit him to the ministry. Rinehart was present at the convention, was approved, and was given a ministerial license.[14] This was the last time he attended a convention of that Ministerium, and only in 1815 did he send a report.

When the Ohio Synod was formed in 1818 he was present and was ordained. He was not prominent in the organization and held no office. For some years he was faithful in his obligations to the Synod, but after 1825 he attended only three conventions. After 1833 his name disappears from the roll without explanation. Yet the articles in *The Lutheran Standard* speak of him with respect, indicating no trouble. He made missionary trips for the Synod, one in 1819 to Fort Wayne, Indiana, another in 1823 to Sandusky, Ohio. For the latter trip he was remunerated at the rate of fifteen dollars a month.[15]

The congregations he served were all small rural ones in Jefferson County, all of which are now disbanded. Good Hope Church, in the locality

---

[12] Socrates Henkel, *History of the Evangelical Lutheran Tennessee Synod* (New Market, Virginia, 1890), p. 44.

[13] Reprinted in Burgess, *op. cit.*, pp. 62 f.

[14] *Documentary History*, pp. 441, 444.

[15] *Minutes*, 1823, p. 5.

now called Osage and earlier named Bowling Green, was the base of his operations. There is the possibility that he preached in neighboring counties, as his successor did. Trinity Church, Carrolton, lays claim to his ministry. His first recorded wedding was of Michel Stull and Betsy Misser, December 10, 1812.[16]

In 1825 he relinquished his active ministry to James Manning who took charge of the Jefferson County congregations after being licensed that year. Evidently Rinehart felt that Manning was a "better qualified laborer." It may be presumed that he devoted his full time to farming. He had bought land from Martin Swickart on June 6, 1807, paying $620 for 125½ acres.[17] It is not clear what land he had been occupying before that time. His first wife, Susanna, had died February 8, 1806. Perhaps it was in connection with his marriage to his second wife, Barbara, that on June 16, 1808, he bought from John Kay for the sum of fifty-five dollars,

> one set of blacksmith tools, three feather beds and bedding, two chests, one trunk, one corner cupboard, two copper tea kettles, one large copper kettle, three bed steads, one moily [sic] cow, two dutch ovens, one pot, one side saddle, one copper coffee pot, three sets of china ware, one half dozen pewter plates, one dozen spoons, forty yards of cotton, one half dozen windsor chairs, one looking glass.[18]

He subsequently bought other pieces of land, indicating success in his farming.

His continued interest in the work of his Synod is indicated by a contribution to the treasury accompanied by a letter which was published in the November 28, 1856, issue of *The Lutheran Standard*.[19] He wrote to exhort others to support the Synod liberally. His death occurred June 7, 1861. He was buried between his wives in the cemetery of Good Hope Church, Osage.

John Henry Huet had likewise been a member of Stough's parish in Washington County, Pennsylvania. Born February 14, 1772, near Hagerstown, Maryland, he had been brought to western Pennsylvania where Stough confirmed him October 29, 1791. While still in Pennsylvania he married Esther Simon, April 30, 1793. They had fourteen children, so that there is a large number of descendants who now spell the name "Hewitt." His name appears in the records usually as Heinrich Huet.

16 *Jefferson County Marriage Record Book*, number 2, p. 4.
17 *Deed Record Book B*, p. 192.
18 *Deed Record Book B*, p. 392.
19 Reprinted in Sheatsley, *op. cit.*, pp. 46 f.

At the convention of the Ministerium of Pennsylvania in 1812 Huet applied for admission, and a congregation in Washington County endorsed his application. After he received his license he evidently went to the congregation concerned, for at the Special Conference in May, 1813, his address was given as Canton Township, Washington County, Pennsylvania. Yet in June of that year the Ministerium of Pennsylvania recorded "an expression of thanks from several congregations in the State of Ohio for sending Mr. Huet to serve as pastor in their congregations." [20] Perhaps he had made some missionary tours. He attended no further conventions of the Ministerium of Pennsylvania. But he was present at the first Special Conference west of the mountains in 1812 and was loyal to that organization. He was present also at Somerset, Ohio, in 1818 when the Ohio Synod was organized, and there he was ordained.

He moved to Trumbull County, Ohio, before 1815. From that center he served congregations in that area and in Mercer County, Pennsylvania. In that area he spent the rest of his life. He died on February 16, 1855, and is buried in Lake Park Cemetery in Youngstown.

The most important of the four men licensed in 1812 was Jacob Leist. He was born on January 8, 1788, likely in Snyder County, Pennsylvania. It is not known when he moved to Ohio, but on April 25, 1812, he bought land from his parents.[21] Before this time he had been thinking of becoming a pastor. In June, 1811, he attended a convention of the Ministerium of Pennsylvania to apply for a license. The minutes report that "Mr. Leist was put off with a hopeful prospect." [22] Whether he was expecting to preach in Pennsylvania or Ohio is not clear.

The next year he applied again, his application being buttressed by a request from congregations in Fairfield and Pickaway Counties. Both petitions were granted.[23] He shared actively in the Special Conferences, being host to the first Conference to convene within Ohio, the meeting at Israel's Church (near Amanda) in 1813. He was ordained at the organization meeting of the Ohio Synod in 1818. His entire ministry was spent in the area between Lancaster and Circleville, Ohio. By 1854 he had retired from the active ministery. He died, November 7, 1870, at his home in Pickaway County, and was buried in the town cemetery at Tarlton.

[20] *Documentary History*, p. 454.

[21] *Pickaway County Deed Record Book*, Vol. A, p. 351.

[22] *Documentary History*, p. 433.

[23] *Ibid.*, pp. 439, 444.

His importance is shown by the fact that he was elected secretary of Synod in 1821, and was president for three years, 1825–27. He was president of the English District formed in 1857, presiding at the organizing convention. He continued a member of that District even after it was separated from the Joint Synod. He instructed some candidates in theology. He was in charge of the Synod's first effort to establish an institution of learning, the school at Tarlton with three students lasting only through the winter of 1818–19. He was active in the support of the Seminary at Columbus. He survived all the others who were pastors at the beginning of organized Lutheranism in Ohio.[24]

The only evidence that these pastors had any communication with each other is their attendance at synodical conventions. Of the seven men who came to the Conference in October, six had attended Synod at Carlisle, Pennsylvania, in May. It must be assumed that an announcement of the Conference was sent to all concerned. The place selected was about in the middle of the large area served by all the these pastors. Buttler would have about as far to travel from Cumberland to Washington County, Pennsylvania, as would Simon from Montgomery County, Ohio, though neither of them attended. The time selected was a period when there was a lull in farm work and before bad weather arrived. It was at the time of a full moon, making travel and evening meetings easier.[25] The following May it was resolved that thereafter the Conference convene "the last Saturday before the full moon in the month of October." [26] In 1814 this was changed to September.

The first Special Conference, which met October 17 to 19, 1812, was concerned exclusively with church problems, so far as the minutes show. There was plenty of preaching. A sermon was delivered by every minister, including a visiting itinerant preacher named Heim and by a Reformed pastor named Mannenschmidt; only the pastor loci was exempt from preaching. One sermon was in English; it was by Weyer. At the Communion service "the pastors appeared first and then the congregation." [27]

24 W. D. Allbeck, "Jacob Leist, Pioneer Pastor and Synod President," *Wittenberg Bulletin*, LV, 4 (May 1958). Leist outlived by six months Andrew Henkel, pastor at Germantown. According to the obituary account in the *Minutes* of the District Synod of Ohio of 1870, page 29, Henkel had also been one of the pioneers, serving in Perry and Muskingum Counties in 1812, but efforts to verify this have failed.

25 Data furnished by Dr. Lloyd R. Wylie, Professor of Astronomy at Wittenberg University.

26 *Minutes of the Special Conferences*, typed translation by Sheatsley et al., p. 8.

27 *Ibid.*, p. 2.

Matters of business were few. There were two requests from congregations for pastors; certain of the pastors were assigned to visit the petitioners. It was voted to hold the annual meetings of the Conference four weeks before Synod—a decision which meant a meeting in May, and which was reversed the next spring by returning to the time of the full moon in October. It was decided to send Pastor Weygandt as the Conference's representative to the next Synod "with a petition to grant the right of ordination, so that better order may be achieved in our Special Conference." [28] The place of the next meeting was decided upon as Clear Creek, Fairfield County, Ohio. That is all the business recorded in the minutes. No officers are listed.

There are reasons for thinking that Stough was the leader of the Conference. He and Forster were the only ordained pastors present; the other members of the Conference in attendance had only licenses. Buttler, Steck, and Henkel, all of whom were ordained, were absent. Stough's name appears first on the roll. He preached the first sermon, and it was he who gave the closing address. Perhaps he also presided at the business sessions. At any event it is quite clear that at the next convention, in May of 1813, he was the chairman.

Stough's leadership is shown also in the fact that most of the licensed pastors were urged or helped into the ministry by him. He had requested the Synod to send George Simon to Jefferson County, Ohio.[29] Weygandt came out of a congregation Stough served in Washington County, Pennsylvania, and when he was given a ministerial license he was directed to do his theological studying under the supervision of Stough,[30] who later recommended him for ordination. Weyer was first brought to the attention of the Ministerium by a letter from Stough recommending him. An answering letter was ordered to be sent to Stough "approving his conduct in reference to Mr. Weier." [31] The nature of the "conduct" is not stated, but the implication seems to be that Stough was training Weyer for ministerial service. Both Huet and Rinehart were encouraged to enter the ministry and were instructed by Stough. Of Leist's early years we have no record. Later, in 1815, Abraham Schneider, recommended by Stough, was directed by Synod to study under his supervision.[32] Thus it appears that there was a

[28] *Loc. cit.*
[29] *Documentary History*, p. 391.
[30] *Ibid.*, pp. 407, 478.
[31] *Ibid.*, p. 418.
[32] *Ibid.*, pp. 478, 483 .

sort of "Stough circle" which formed the nucleus of the new Conference. This group could easily be the majority in any voting. And the loyalty of these men to Stough not only strengthened his leadership, but also, because their parishes were in or near Ohio, made Ohio the center of the Conference's interest.

This first Special Conference of 1812 was important also in that it revealed a state of mind which desired a degree of independent authority, and which also was confident of the permanence of Lutheran organization in this new area. Evidence of the desire for authority is seen in the petition for the right to ordain. Confidence in the future is to be observed in the provision for future meetings and in the arrangements for visiting vacant congregations. There could scarcely be any doubt, in spite of the declaration of war, that population would increase and that the number of congregations and of pastors would grow. A foundation therefore could be laid.

The next two Special Conferences were held in Ohio, then two were held in Pennsylvania, and then two more in Ohio. Thereafter, in 1818, the Conference became a Synod; the story of it will begin in the next chapter. At this point it will be of interest to see what developments appeared in the Special Conferences.

In accordance with the action of 1812, the second Special Conference met at Clear Creek, Fairfield County, Ohio, May 15 to 18, 1813. Except for Pastor Weygandt, all the pastors were present who had attended the first Conference, and in addition Henkel and Andrew Simon were there. This was the only Special Conference that Simon ever attended—whether for lack of interest or because of poor health cannot be determined. With the Pennsylvania men absent, the Stough circle was easily the majority. The fact that the services were held "in the church" indicates that there was a building. The one English sermon was preached by Henkel. Here, for the first time, officers are recorded: Stough as president, and Henkel as secretary. Stough was chosen to preside at all subsequent Conferences except the fourth when Steck was in the chair, but the duties of secretary were performed by a series of pastors.

At this second Conference a discordant note for the first time arose. Forster had a complaint to make: he had been serving a considerable number of congregations over a wide area, and now some of these congregations wanted Jacob Leist as pastor; he objected to the petition of two congregations to this effect. The Conference overruled him, declaring the congregations vacant, and referred the appointment of a pastor to Synod. Also at

Ziegler's Church in Pleasant Township, Fairfield County, there was trouble; a majority of the members desired Leist, and only six wanted to retain Forster. Conference advised Forster to yield, a thing he was reluctant to do.

It is possible to interpret Forster's attitude as being the result of missionary zeal. Surely there were enough uncultivated areas in Ohio to make it unnecessary for Leist to intrude into the Fairfield County area. Concerning Forster, Sheatsley wrote, "We are told that when asked as to the extent of his field he arose and with outstretched arms dramatically exclaimed: 'The entire North West Territory is my field.' " [33] How well he accepted the Conference's decision against him cannot be told, but it is certain that he left the convention before it closed.[34] He was absent from the next two Conference conventions, and before the following one could meet he was dead.[35] Even the Ministerium of Pennsylvania voted against him, for it concurred in the decision of the Ohio Special Conference.[36]

At the meeting at Clear Creek in May, 1813, it was decided to return to full moon time in October as the time of conventions. Accordingly the third Special Conference convened October 2 to 4, 1813, in St. Jacob's Church in Stough's parish in Columbiana County, Ohio. Possibly this was too many conventions for one year, for only Rinehart, Huet, and Weyer met with Stough. A year later it was Steck's parish in Greensburg, Pennsylvania, which was the scene of the convention, and some sessions were held in the courthouse. At this fourth Conference only Stough and Weyer came from Ohio—all the others were Pennsylvania pastors.

The fifth Special Conference was held in 1815 at the eastern extreme of the district—Somerset, Pennsylvania, where Pastor Tiedemann's congregation had erected a new church building. Since Somerset was not too far from Cumberland, Maryland, Pastor Buttler attended and preached one of the sermons, though his name does not appear among those listed as present.[37] This was the only Conference he attended. He died December 12, 1816. Apparently Cumberland was too far east to be included actively in this western district. Once more it was the case that Pennsylvanians predominated, the Ohio area being represented only by Stough, Mau, and Huet

[33] Sheatsley, *op. cit.*, p. 40.

[34] *Minutes*, p. 7.

[35] His grave is on a farm in Perry County. The county records do not list any marriages performed by him. Others (one being Leist) officiated at the weddings of his children during his lifetime.

[36] *Documentary History*, p. 452.

[37] *Minutes*, p. 23.

—and even part of Huet's parish was in Pennsylvania. Never thereafter were Pennsylvania pastors a majority at any convention; from that time on the Ohio pastors predominated.

For its sixth meeting the Special Conference went to (New) Lancaster, Fairfield County, Ohio. At this convention, held August 31 to September 4, 1816, all the Pennsylvania pastors were absent, but eight others were present. Some of the sessions were held in the courthouse, as was true the following year when the convention met in New Philadelphia, September 20 to 24, 1817. At this seventh and last Special Conference attendance of pastors reached the peak, twelve being present. Steck, senior, and Weygandt had come from Pennsylvania, and Paul Henkel from (West) Virginia; the other nine were Ohio pastors. Thus it could not be otherwise, when the Conference became a synod, than that it should be an Ohio synod.

Of the transactions of these seven Special Conferences, a great deal, of course, was typical convention business. It followed the pattern customary in the Ministerium of Pennsylvania. It had to do with the time and place of conventions, with the printing of minutes, with the purchase of a minute-book, with a treasury and the payment of bills. The minutes of the second Conference give the first record of money received from congregations: Stough had brought $2.00, Weyer $2.00, Rinehart $7.34, and Huet $6.74— a total of $17.08. The fourth Conference got a jolt when it received the bill of the delegates to Synod: for the clerical delegate $25, for the lay delegate $52.50 (of which the Conference voted to pay $34.05). Perhaps there were some plain words spoken, for the following year the delegate's expense was only $12.00.

Part of the routine business was giving answers to congregations which were requesting pastors. If any parish could find an ordained man who was willing to serve it, he could be called; the approval of Synod or Conference was not required. But since ordained men were very few, congregations usually had to look for a young man who was preparing himself for ordination by studying under some pastor, and who meanwhile as a candidate for ordination was given a license to perform ministerial acts. Such candidates were not free to accept calls, but could serve only those congregations to which they were assigned, either by the Synod or the Conference. This is the reason why petitions from congregations were part of the routine business. Even at the first Special Conference there were two such petitions. Sometimes, because of the shortage of clergymen, the best that could be done was to direct the nearest pastors to visit the petitioning congregations a few times during the year and conduct services.

Routine business usually included some miscellaneous items. Some of these had to do with worship in the congregations. There was the recognized need of a hymnbook. The fourth Conference voted to publish one to cost not more than fifty cents. When it was printed Pastor Schnee urged the other pastors to accept the new book, but the Conference merely left it to the discretion of these men.[38] Apparently the Conference had not heeded the resolution of the Ministerium of Pennsylvania "that no member or several members in our connection have a right to have a new hymn-book prepared or printed without the consent of the Synod."[39]

Another matter was the observance of certain days in the year. The third Conference voted to recommend to the congregations that they observe July fourth as a day of solemn prayer and January first as a day of thanksgiving "since God has granted our Church such great progress in this part of the world."[40] The seventh Conference recommended that during the first three days of October the Reformation be celebrated, and that the regular Gospels and Epistles of the church year be read when possible.

The intellectual side of life also received some attention. The sixth Special Conference voted to encourage the congregations to establish German schools. A year later the need of books was recognized so that the Conference voted to sponsor a German A-B-C book and first reader. For the benefit of adults it was decided to have the Augsburg Confession, with a preface by Pastor Steck, printed with the Conference minutes. At other times the minutes were supplemented by a sermon (Weygandt's, p. 27) or "something useful" (by Schnee, p. 19) or "edifying articles" (by Leist and Henkel, p. 35).

The statistical reports indicate a good deal of the pastoral activity of those days. They also leave much to be desired, chiefly because in those days the statistical items were not sharply defined. For example, in reporting communicants it is not clear whether the number reported is that of all persons who had received Communion at least once during the year, no person being counted more than once, or whether it means the total number of times the pastors gave communions to individuals with the possibility that some persons might have communed more than once. Be that as it may,

---

[38] *Minutes,* p. 33. The title page reads: *Das Neue Gesangbuch, zum öffentlichen Gottesdienste und zur häuslichen Andacht. Zum Druck verordnet durch eine Special Conferenz der Evangelisch Lutherischen Prediger im westlichen Theil von Pennsylvanien und dem Staat Ohio.* (no date) Pittsburgh. *Gedruckt von Jacob Schnee.* The preface is signed by John Michael Steck, President, and Jacob Schnee, Secretary.

[39] *Documentary History,* p. 476.

[40] *Minutes,* pp. 11 f.

Pastor Leist in 1813 reported 157 communicants, 52 confirmations, and 171 baptisms. Stough that same year had 143 communicants, 29 confirmations, and 165 baptisms. If we may think of the communicants as adults and the baptisms as of children, the figures say something both of pastoral activity and of the birth rate. Only very large congregations today can report so many baptisms. Steck, senior, had the largest parish, with 707 communicants; Huet was next with 557. Considering the fact that the usual parish consisted of a half a dozen small scattered congregations connected by bad roads, these are astonishing figures.

In view of the fact that this Western District, in which the seven Special Conferences were held, became a synod in 1818, it is of interest to observe the relation of these Conferences to the Synod—the Ministerium of Pennsylvania. First of all was the matter of attending the conventions of the Synod. From the very beginning it was felt that it was sufficient if one man made the trip, serving as a delegate of the Western District representing his fellow pastors west of the mountains. Weygandt was chosen as delegate at the first Special Conference and duly appeared at the Synod convention the following spring.

In order that this arrangement might be recognized and regular, it was voted in 1813 to ask, "Is the Synod satisfied if our Special Conference send only one preacher annually to the Synod?" [41] The Synod answered, "Yes," [42] and this answer was so reported to the next Special Conference.[43] Accordingly until 1818 there was always at least one pastor from the Western District in attendance at Synod.

Next in importance in the proceedings of the Special Conferences was the question of the control of candidates for the ministry, licensing them, assigning parishes to them, and ordaining them. The first Special Conference promptly expressed itself on this matter. Its delegate to the next Synod was sent "with a petition to grant the right of ordination, so that better order may be achieved in our Special Conference." [44] No notice of this petition appears in the minutes of the Synod. Probably this was asking too much, for the Synod consistently kept control of ordinations in its own hands.

A year later the Western District made more modest requests. It asked the Synod, "Has our Special Conference the right to pass on the sermons

---

[41] *Minutes*, p. 11.
[42] *Documentary History*, p. 467.
[43] *Minutes*, p. 14.
[44] *Minutes*, p. 2.

and diaries submitted by the candidates? Has the Special Conference the right to change the parishes of the candidates and note such changes in the respective candidates' licenses?" [45] The Synod discussed these questions carefully. It decided to answer the first question in the negative, directing instead "that the representatives for each time, from the western district, shall bring with them to the Ministerium the sermons and diaries of their candidates for the purpose of examination." [46] The second question was answered in the affirmative. When these answers were reported to the fourth Special Conference, the impression was given that the answer to the first question, instead of being a "no," was a qualified "yes." The Conference understood that it did have the right to examine the papers of candidates, even though it must also submit them to the Synod. Hence it adopted a resolution requiring the candidates to submit their sermons and diaries to the Conference for evaluation, specifying that diaries were to run from Conference to Conference time, and that all sermons and diaries were to be placed in the hands of the delegate to Synod. Synod seems to have raised no objection.

The Special Conference of 1816 decided to go further. It resolved "that we send a unanimous request to the Ministerium asking that we be allowed to establish our own ministerium." [47] President Stough was elected delegate to take this petition.[48] The Synod, however, was unfavorably disposed toward this request, resolving "that permission could not be granted to the Conference of Ohio to form a Ministerium of their own, but that the Ministerium might be commissioned to draw up a plan through which particular difficulties might be removed." [49] A plan was devised and sent to Ohio. It appears at the end of the minutes of the Special Conference of 1817 as a "Memorandum for our Brethren in the State of Ohio" signed by the president and the secretary of the Ministerium of Pennsylvania. It reads:

> *Resolved*, That the ordained preachers of the Special Conference in the State of Ohio, or a majority of them, be allowed to license applicants as candidates or catechists, and to renew their licenses from year to year.
> *Resolved*, further, that after this each candidate and catechist in Ohio shall send his diary and one sermon to the Ministerium Meeting each year.[50]

[45] *Minutes*, p. 11.
[46] *Documentary History*, p. 467.
[47] *Minutes*, p. 54.
[48] *Minutes*, p. 35.
[49] *Documentary History*, p. 500.
[50] *Ibid.*, p. 506. *Minutes*, p. 43.

The reaction of the Special Conference to this compromise arrangement is not stated officially in the minutes, and therefore must be inferred. Sheatsley suggested that "perhaps the document did not reach the Conference during the session and was later added to the minutes by the secretary," [51] but this inference is not necessary. We have no way of knowing how careful a secretary Andrew Henkel may have been; some of his colleagues had not been meticulous secretaries. It seems unlikely that he would have failed to record action on a matter as important as this. There was ample time for the Synod's decision on June fifth to have reached the Conference September twentieth. Even if there had been delay in the correspondence, the Synod's action was known, for Stough and a lay delegate from New Lisbon as well as Schneider from New Philadelphia had attended the Synod convention at York. In view of this, it seems most likely that the Conference somehow made up its mind, even if it did not do so by formal resolution.

The fact was that it began to function as a synod. It had asked the Synod for permission to form a ministerium with the right and authority to do two things: to grant and renew licenses; and to ordain. The Synod had granted the first, but withheld the second. The Conference proceeded to assume what had been denied. It decided to proclaim Weygandt, previously ordained with the rank of deacon, to be a pastor, signifying the action with a handclasp. Moreover, it referred to itself as a "synod" when the time and place of the next convention were determined. Some of the pastors of that day in writing their memoirs speak of the Ohio Synod as beginning in 1817. And it must be noted that no pastor of this Western District either attended the 1818 convention of the Ministerium of Pennsylvania or sent a report—something which was a marked break with the past.

Why the Ohio men exceeded the limits permitted them by the Ministerium of Pennsylvania is not clear. Perhaps they interpreted the action of the Synod liberally instead of literally. Feeling very keenly the need for pastors in Ohio, and noting that some discretion was granted, the Conference may have felt that the emergencies of the new West justified stretching the authority granted. This would imply a continuing friendly spirit toward the Ministerium of Pennsylvania. This friendliness is substantiated by the fact that both Stough and Paul Henkel wrote friendly letters to the Synod in 1819, that a report of the second Ohio Synod convention was sent to the Synod in Pennsylvania, and that there was friendly correspondence also in 1820.

[51] *Op. cit.,* p. 57.

Perhaps, however, this was an act of independence, the fresh frontier spirit rising up against the conservative East, the evidence of resentment over the Synod's reluctance to grant autonomy. It is noteworthy that except for Stough, Steck senior, and Paul Henkel, the men in the Western District did not have close ties with the East. They were either born in the West, or grew up there. Of the younger men only Weygandt seems to have been faithful in attending Synod or in sending his excuses. A few of the others sent reports once or twice. But generally it was true that they went over the mountains to secure a license, but never again attended a convention of the Ministerium of Pennsylvania.

Graebner intimated that resentment was involved. He represented these pastors as saying, "Does not ony one yet see that although we are considered by them to be poor, suffering, uneducated simpletons, yet we labor amid great blessings, and daily bring poor souls under Jesus' blood-marked banner of peace?" [52] This would account for the spirited determination to do their own work, to have their own treasury, and to depart in some particulars from practices in the East, e.g., omitting the rank of ordained deacon.

At this distance it is hard to decide what were the factors. It seems likely that Stough, Henkel, and others who had lived in the East and had the conservatism typical of older men, desired to preserve the connections with the Ministerium of Pennsylvania. It may have been their influence which preserved the cordial relations between the two synods. They likely were responsible for the fact that the Ohio Synod adopted in toto the constitution of the Pennsylvania body.

It would seem that the younger preachers, who had grown up on the frontier, who went to Synod only to get a license and never went again, whose ties with the East were very few, had an independent spirit. Under the influence of the older men the desire of the younger men for a synod was channeled into a petition to the older synod. When that petition was only partially granted, the younger men could no longer be restrained. This view is given by Andrew Henkel in an article concerning his father, Paul Henkel. Speaking of 1817 he said,

> the brethren having met in conference at New Philadelphia, passed Resolutions relative to forming themselves into an independent Body. This measure was strongly urged by several of the younger brethren, but equally opposed by the elder. There being but three ordained ministers present (one of whom

[52] A. L. Graebner, *Geschichte der Lutherischen Kirche in America* (St. Louis, 1892), p. 675.

was my father), and their consent being indispensable to carry out the design, strong efforts were made to overcome their objections; and they finally did yield, and the desired object was accomplished.[53]

Whatever the reasons for their independence, these pastors served congregations over a wide area. In eastern Ohio, where the Ohio River leaves Pennsylvania, is Columbiana County, in which were a number of congregations served during all this period by Pastor Stough whose post office address was Lisbon. There came to work just north of him in 1815 Pastor Huet who made his headquarters at North Lima, now Mahoning County (a county later formed of parts of Trumbull and Columbiana Counties) serving congregations there and across the line in Pennsylvania.

Stough knew of Lutherans west of him in Stark County. They wrote to the Pennsylvania Ministerium in 1812 asking for a preacher.[54] Four years later Weyer came as pastor to the area, having his mail addressed to Canton. South of Stough, in Jefferson County, Rinehart was pastor during all this period. Rinehart's nearest neighboring pastor to the west was Schneider in Tuscarawas County who in 1816 began serving the New Philadelphia and Sugar Creek congregations. South of them in Belmont, Guernsey, and Muskingum Counties Weyer had been assigned to work in 1813, staying three years.

To the southwest lie Perry and Fairfield Counties where Pastor Forster worked until his death in 1815. Andrew Henkel came as pastor at Somerset, Perry County, in 1816. The next county to the west is Pickaway where Leist was pastor all this period. Since Fairfield County lies between Perry and Pickaway, it was the area over which there was a contest in 1813 between Forster and Leist as to who should serve the congregations. It will be remembered that the Conference and the Synod decided in favor of Leist. In 1814 three congregations in Fairfield County petitioned the North Carolina Synod for a pastor.[55] Three years later Pastor Michael John Steck had settled at Lancaster in Fairfield County.

Leist's nearest clerical neighbor to the west was some sixty-five miles away in Montgomery County. Pastor Andrew Simon was there at least between 1813 and 1816, if not longer. In 1814 the Synod in Pennsylvania received "A request from three congregations on the Miami in the State of Ohio, which ask for a pastor, and at the same time give the information that many more congregations could be gathered in the neighborhood.

[53] Sprague, *op. cit.*, p. 93.
[54] *Documentary History*, p. 438.
[55] G. D. Bernheim, *op. cit.*, p. 401.

Upon motion, it was resolved that the Synod provide for them by sending a traveling preacher there." [56] Evidently it was in keeping with that resolution that it was decided "That Mr. Rudisill be traveling preacher in the State of Ohio, in Twien church, Stettler's and Gebhardt's congregations, and in their neighborhood, and that thirty dollars be paid him in advance." [57] The following year it was reported that "Mr. Rudisill was unable to undertake his journey because of illness." [58] The "Twien church" referred to was doubtless the church on Twin Creek in Montgomery County. In the latter year Pastor Dill was called to Germantown, though his name does not appear on the roll in Ohio until 1818.

West of Montgomery County is Preble County against the Indiana state line. Here Mau was pastor from 1816 on. At the southwest corner of the state is Hamilton County where Lutherans were to be found in and around Cincinnati. There Pastor Zaeslein carried on his uncertain work beginning in 1814. Up the Ohio River some seventy miles from Cincinnati is Scioto County where there were Lutherans in Green Township. They petitioned the Ministerium of Pennsylvania for a pastor in 1817, but their request was referred to the Special Conference in Ohio for action.[59]

It is thus apparent that Lutheran congregations were to be found chiefly in eastern, central, and southwestern Ohio. In the summer of 1813 Pastor Jacob Scherer of North Carolina made a missionary tour through central and southwestern Ohio. He reported:

From Clarksburg we went to Marietta, where we crossed the Ohio River, and passing New Lancaster we came to Dayton on the 17th of June. On this route I baptized seven children and one adult.

On the following Sunday I preached twice among the Germans who are mostly from North Carolina, and intend building a church desiring to have a preacher from that state. From here I visited my uncle, Christian Scherer, in which neighborhood I preached four days, from the 24th to the 27th to large congregations; baptized five children. The spiritual condition of Ohio is dark; people of all denominations are intermixed, and although they have many preachers among them, there appears to be a want of such who have sound doctrine and are of good repute.

On the 29th of June we left the state of Ohio and proceeded on our homeward journey. . . .[60]

[56] *Documentary History*, p. 467.
[57] *Ibid.*, p. 469.
[58] *Ibid.*, p. 476.
[59] *Ibid.*, p. 502.
[60] Bernheim, *op. cit.*, p. 389.

Scherer's two weeks in Ohio are of interest in demonstrating that settlers had come from North Carolina, and that they had the interest and good will of the synod in that state. But the time was too short for his observation of conditions to have been more than superficial.

Besides those in Ohio, the Western District included congregations in Pennsylvania. In Washington County on the western edge of the state Pastor Weygandt was working through these years, and Huet was there in Canton Township from 1813 to 1815. Pittsburgh was the center of activity for Pastor Schnee in 1814 and 1815. In the Greensburg area John Michael Steck was pastor throughout this period. Farther east, with Somerset as the center, Tiedemann was the pastor beginning in 1814. In the northwest corner of the state, with Meadville as the post office, Colson was sent as traveling preacher in 1816, and Heyer two years later.

The only other congregations included in the Western District were those of Cumberland, Maryland, and Point Pleasant, (West) Virginia. The connection of the former ceased after 1815. The latter's relation began with Paul Henkel's pastorate in 1813.

The activity of Lutheran pastors in forming a Conference was parallel to that of other Protestants in the same decade in two respects. First, the organization included a wide area surpassing the geographical boundaries of the State of Ohio. Second, the association of pastors and congregations provided for local active propagation of denominational work independent of control by church bodies in the East.

Presbyterians from their centers in Kentucky formed an Ohio Presbytery in 1783. Their Ohio Synod was established in 1814 and a Western Reserve Synod in 1825. The United Brethren constituted a Conference in Ohio in 1810. Methodists whose circuit riders traveled in Ohio as well as in neighboring states formed an Ohio Conference consisting of five districts in 1812. The Society of Friends, usually less interested in centralization, nonetheless had developed a Yearly Meeting in Ohio in 1813. The Protestant Episcopal Diocese of Ohio dates from 1818, with Philander Chase soon the first bishop. The German Reformed were united in an Ohio Classis in 1820, which became a Synod four years later.

The second decade of the century thus was important for the organization of Protestant churches in Ohio.

4 / THE OHIO SYNOD
1818–1833

THE YEARS 1812 TO 1817 had been a period of developing self-reliance for Lutheranism in Ohio. It had been a sort of apprenticeship in which lessons of expansion and self-government were learned. Not only was organized Lutheranism in the state gaining in strength but it was also acquiring a spirit of independence. It had arrived at the stage where it had the determination and the ability to go it alone. 1818 marks its beginning as a separate synod.

Fifteen years later the Ohio Synod had grown until it seemed to be too large to continue as a single body. The increased number of Lutheran congregations in western Pennsylvania and Ohio created a situation in which local areas desired to become independent synods just as the Ohio Synod had done. More roads had been opened, but travel was still by horse—a tedious process at best, and quite irksome in a synod whose east-to-west extent was almost three hundred miles. The pressure for independence was relieved by the decision to form districts. 1833 was the year of the first convention of the *Joint* Synod of Ohio—"Joint" because consisting of districts. Thus the years 1818 to 1833 mark a distinct period of Ohio Lutheranism.

THE FIRST CONVENTION

When the delegates assembled on Saturday, September 14, 1818, for their first regular synodical convention, they were beginning a new venture for Lutherans in the state. They had come over the rolling country of Perry County to the hilltop village of Somerset to meet in a little church surrounded by its graveyard. The cemetery is still there with its accumulation of graves and tombstones, but the old church is gone. A large boulder bearing a bronze tablet marks the site of the convention.

The roll of those present included four ordained pastors—Stough, Paul Henkel, Dill, and Weygandt—and six men with licenses—Leist, Rinehart, Huet, Andrew Henkel, Michael John Steck, and Schneider. Seven others were listed as absent. Lay delegates present numbered eight. Among the visitors was the Reformed pastor, John Jacob Larose, who preached to the convention at one of it services. This small convention was actually much larger than most other early Lutheran synods in America had been at the time of their organization.

There is no record that a constitution was adopted. Instead it was presumed that the usages of the Ministerium of Pennsylvania would be followed. This seems the intention when it was *"Resolved:* That pastors conduct themselves according to the rules of the Mother Synod." [1] Moreover it appears that the delegates (or perhaps only the secretary) did not have clearly in mind what the body was to be called. Three times in the minutes the word "Conference" is used, and as many times the word "Synod." The title page calls it the "General Conference of the Evangelical Lutheran Preachers in Ohio and Neighboring States." Even though the name apparently was not officially decided, the convention knew that it needed officers. It elected Stough president, Paul Henkel secretary, and Weygandt treasurer for the year.

The business of synodical conventions in those days, after the election of officers, was concerned with letters and documents placed in the hands of the president. Some of the letters were petitions from congregations requesting a pastor, perhaps naming the man they desired and asking a license for him if he were a layman. There would also be petitions from men desiring licenses. Other letters came from congregations served by men with licenses reporting whether or not the people were satisfied with the pastoral service they were receiving. Besides these letters the men with licenses placed on the president's desk their journals for the past year and copies of one or two of their sermons. The president appointed the members of the convention as committees among whom all these papers were divided for study and report. Most of this was routine: "The congregations of Mr.—— say that they are satisfied with him and request that he be sent to them for another year." And Synod would approve in most instances.

The continual difficulty was there were not enough preachers to fill the needs. The most that could be done in many instances was to send some

[1] *Minutes,* p. 6.

of the pastors on preaching tours, just as the Ministerium of Pennsylvania had done. This was to be the program of the Ohio Synod for some years to come. To cover the expense entailed it was resolved that each pastor take up an offering in his congregations, the funds to be assembled in the Synod's treasury.

To increase the number of preachers, this first convention of the Ohio Synod took two actions which, though not immediately successful, were ultimately to be fruitful. The first was its resolution "that the Synod from now on should make all possible provision to train young preachers and to instruct them in the Latin and Greek languages as well as in all other sciences and learning which are necessary for this important pastoral office." [2] What was in mind was an educational institution. The second action was a resolution to gather funds from the parishes for the purpose of assisting needy young men in their education.

Both of these actions were ventures of faith. Student aid would be sufficiently difficult to secure, considering the weakness of the many small congregations struggling to establish themselves. But at first it involved no fixed charges, since the funds to be expended would only be those received. To start a school, however, would involve regular annual expenses and commitments of a contractual nature. It was a brave resolution for a new synod, especially when it is remembered that the seventy-year-old Ministerium of Pennsylvania had not yet accomplished it.

The result was that a school of academy grade was begun near Tarlton on October 1, 1818. Pastor Leist, thirty years old and ordained at this convention, was in charge, although most of the teaching was done by David Schuh, a young man whom he was instructing in theology. Three boys formed the student body. At the end of the winter Schuh went to Somerset and instruction soon ceased. The only record of this frail effort is a letter of Pastor Samuel Kaemmerer who had been one of the three students.[3]

Besides these long-range plans there were some immediate actions which were taken at this convention to increase the number of pastors. This body had constituted itself an independent synod instead of continuing as a conference or district of another body in order that it might have in its own hands the power of ordination and licensure. So it advanced to ordination

[2] *Loc. cit.*

[3] *Lutheran Standard,* March 12, 1851.

three men who previously held licenses. These first ordinands were Jacob Leist, John Rinehart, and Henry Huet. In addition it accepted on its roll of licensed catechists two men, Michael Wachter and Charles Henkel.

The new synod took notice of the need of parish education. It "*Resolved, that it is the duty of pastors to establish Sunday schools and to admonish parents to send their children.*" [4] It was concerned to propagate its doctrinal convictions, and therefore resolved to have Paul Henkel prepare briefly and inoffensively a statement as an appendix to the minutes indicating the differences between Lutherans and others on such doctrines as that of baptism, the Lord's Supper, etc. What Henkel wrote fills twenty-two pages of the printed minutes. Finally the Synod made provision for future conventions to be held on alternate years east and west of the Muskingum River. With this it adjourned.

The members of the Synod doubtless would consider this convention memorable if only for the reason that it was first. But more than this was the fact that it showed vigor and courage. The opportunities for the growth of Lutheranism in the state were obvious to any who observed the steady arrival of new settlers. The increase in the number of congregations during the previous six years was a token of hope for the future. Under the providence of God the hopes expressed in the plans resolved upon in convention would be realized. Of this the members of the Synod were sure.

EXPANSION

Meanwhile during the first fifteen years of the Synod's existence its internal affairs were being dealt with so that considerable success could be recorded. Statistics at their best are open to question; they are near their worst at the period under discussion and therefore can serve only as rough indicators. Of the seventeen pastors, thirteen submitted reports in 1818. The total number of communicants then was 3,551. The statistics for 1833 are quite incomplete also, but the tabulation shows thirty-four pastors, 159 congregations and 13,252 communicants. Thus in fifteen years the number of pastors had doubled, and the communicant membership had quadrupled. In terms of communicants the Ohio Synod in 1833 was the second largest Lutheran synod in the nation; the Ministerium of Pennsylvania was first with some 23,000 members. The rest of the synods were much smaller than Ohio.[5]

---

[4] *Minutes,* p. 7.

[5] The statistics are given in the *Minutes* of the Ohio Synod of 1833, p. 37.

Finances are of interest, too. In 1823 the congregations contributed to the synodical treasury $57.99¾, which was about two cents per communicant. Ten years later the contributions amounted to $304.44¼, or about three cents per communicant. This indicates an increase in the willingness to support the synodical program—even in fractional currency—and in the financial ability to do so.

OHIO AND THE GENERAL SYNOD

For some years Lutherans in Ohio had to face the problem of Lutheran unity on a national scale. It arose the year after the Ohio Synod was formed, and consisted of a proposed plan for a nation-wide organization of Lutheran synods in a General Synod. Lutherans in Ohio had to decide whether to join this larger movement or to remain independent.

It is interesting to observe that the problem arose at the time when local interests were competing with national interests for supremacy. In the United States those who favored a strong national government were vigorously opposed by those who advocated states' rights. The sentiment of the majority of the people in Ohio was of the latter kind; Federalists were a minority. Edward Tiffin the first governor, and the other state officials were anti-Federalists. Perhaps the most striking instance of Ohio's effort to assert the state's rights against the nation was the attempt to give a preferred status to state banks by placing a heavy tax on national banks in Ohio. It was even claimed that Ohio, as a sovereign state, was supreme over affairs within its borders.

There were pastors in the East who were troubled by the fact that Lutheran congregations in the various states were separated by hundreds of miles. They saw that the number of synods was increasing and that more might be expected. They felt that there was a widespread desire for a national organization of Lutherans to preserve the bond of love and unity, and to avoid unnecessary and injurious divisions.

The Proposed Plan (*Plan-Entwurf*), first prepared at a convention of the Ministerium of Pennsylvania in 1819, suggested that the national organization have the name, "General Synod." This was to be a federation, for the synods were to retain control of their internal affairs. The synods were to delegate to the General Synod the power to prepare books of worship, determine grades of the ministry, authorize new synods, and hear appeals. The number of delegates from a synod to a convention of the General Synod was to be in proportion to the size of the synod. But lest the delegates of one or two large synods outvote all the small synods together, it was proposed that major issues must have the approval of the majority of the synods.

Mild as this plan may appear today, it looked too "federalist" for some of the Lutherans of that day. The constitution that was finally adopted made the General Synod a federation without power, merely a "joint committee" of synods which could do no more than give "advice, counsel or opinion" on books of worship and other matters. Quite prominent was a disavowal of central power limiting a synod's independence in any way. Unity among Lutherans was to be by conference and agreement, and also by cooperative work in education of ministers, in missions, and in works of mercy.

In the mid-twentieth century it would seem that the idea of a General Synod represented broad vision, a sense of future possibilities, conscious adaptation to the American scene, and a preservation of Lutheran unity and identity. Objections to the General Synod appear to be near-sighted, sectional, contentious, and even preposterous. But such objections did appear, compelling the big Ministerium of Pennsylvania—as large as all the other synods combined—to withdraw, as did also the Ministerium of New York. The General Synod was reduced to an insignificant membership of three small synods. There was doubt whether in its feeble condition it could survive at all.

In view of the prevailing spirit of independence in Ohio, and of the fact that the Ohio Synod had so recently asserted its independence of the Ministerium of Pennsylvania, it is not surprising that the Ohio Synod did not join the General Synod. What is surprising is that in 1819, when the Ohio Synod received an invitation to share in forming a General Synod, it considered the Proposed Plan and accepted it.

A year later this was reversed, and an action was taken that was to be decisive for many decades to come in settling a policy that the Joint Synod of Ohio was to be an independent synod in America. The action therefore was highly important.

The optimistic spirit expressed in "the hope that the united body of Lutheran preachers can work with more influence in the kingdom of Jesus" [6] went into eclipse in 1820 when Pastor John Michael Steck, who had been absent the previous year and again could not be present, sent his excuse in which he voiced his opinions against the Proposed Plan. "He

[6] *Minutes*, 1819, p. 10.

recommended to the Synod the fourth, sixth, and seventh sections of the Proposed Plan for mature consideration, and expressed therewith his dissatisfaction with the same." [7] A committee appointed to study the matter presented the following statement which was approved by the Synod:

> According to the report which we have received from the Synod of New York and also from the Synod of Carolina, we conclude that the end design of the Proposed Plan for establishing a General Synod cannot yet be attained. Therefore we move that the resolution of the previous Synod held at Canton concerning the reception of the Proposed Plan be again taken up; that we desire to let the matter rest until we see the constitution of the General Synod. If it pleases us then we will accept it. If not we will not be inclined to join ourselves to the same.[8]

The fact was that Stough was aware of what was brewing even before the Synod convened August thirtieth; for he sent word to the convention of the Ministerium of Pennsylvania in May that some members of his synod were unwilling to accept the Proposed Plan.[9]

The reasons for the opposition to the Proposed Plan are not clearly recorded. Perhaps it was the fear that "through the adoption of the Proposed Plan we would convey a large part of our rights into the hands of some few persons, namely the delegates to the General Synod." [10] This was the sentiment expressed in a printed document stating the views of some members of the Ohio Synod.[11] They further stated, "we are completely convinced from church history that the papacy had quickly established itself in a similar way." [12]

Pastor Steck pointed his questioning finger at Section Four of the Proposed Plan which would give to the General Synod exclusive right to publish liturgies if a majority of the synods approved. There is no way of knowing whether or not Steck had a part in preparing the printed document just referred to, since it was anonymous. But it objected to liturgical uniformity as being contrary to Article VII of the Augsburg Confession. It wanted freedom in worship.

[7] *Minutes,* 1820, p. 3.

[8] *Minutes,* 1820, pp. 6 f.

[9] *Documentary History,* p. 552.

[10] C. O. Kraushaar, *Verfassungsformen der Lutherischen Kirche Americas* (Gütersloh, 1911), p. 443.

[11] *Bedenklichen Ursachen, Angegeben von einigen Evangelisch-Lutherischen Predigern im Staat Ohio und verschiedene Andere, warum sie den Plan-Entwurf der so-genannten Central-Synode nicht annehmen wollen,* printed in the 1820 *Minutes* of the Tennessee Synod.

[12] Graebner, *op. cit.,* p. 701.

Steck had placed a question mark after Section Six also. This section declared that each synod was sovereign in its own affairs. But to this was added a proviso that the rules of a synod should not be in conflict with the principles of the general body, though the General Synod might take action only in cases of appeal. The objectors believed that the General Synod would become an incorporated body able to enforce its regulations by the power of the state. Thus it seemed that though the front door was firmly closed to federalism the back door was wide open to it, and synodical freedom was in danger.

David Henkel of the Tennessee Synod, who was in correspondence with John Lewis Markert and other pastors in Ohio, vigorously opposed the General Synod on this point as on others. After noting that the management of a General Synod seminary would be in the hands of a board of directors, he said, "This looks like Federalists' work, yea, like monarchy itself. A few to govern a whole free, independent community is too much to swallow. But it is evident that Federalists are at the head of the matter." [13]

Section Seven to which Steck referred proposed giving to the General Synod the authority to arrange a uniform system of classification of ministers. In the Ministerium of Pennsylvania a young man was first a catechist, then advanced to the rank of candidate, and finally to that of an ordained pastor. The North Carolina Synod objected to that system. It was hoped that the General Synod would settle the difference in a way acceptable to all the synods. The Ohio objectors feared that they would be bound by a system satisfactory to the eastern synods but unacceptable in Ohio.

The anonymous printed document raised objection also to Section Five which gave the General Synod control of the formation of new synods. Pastors desiring to organize a synod would be required first to get the consent of the General Synod. This proposal was called "more popish than apostolic." And the question was asked "If for example, a general conference according to the Proposed Plan had existed in the United States before our Synod in Ohio was established, who can believe that it would have been established?" [14]

All these objections breathed a spirit of independence. They gave evidence of fears that the Ohio Synod might find itself in the minority on certain issues, and be compelled to yield to the majority. This dread of

[13] Letter of 1823 printed in *The Lutheran Observer*, April 15, 1864.

[14] Graebner, *op. cit.*, p. 702. Cf. H. E. Jacobs, *A History of the Evangelical Lutheran Church in the United States* (New York, 1893), pp. 358 f ,.for the anonymous document in *Americanische Ansichten von dem Gottesdienst und andern Eigenheiten der Deutschen.*

compulsion was real enough, even though the compulsion was entirely illusory. Such, however, was the spirit of the time.

On another matter which was not illusory there was a fear also. In this case it was a matter of language. The Ohio Synod was predominantly a German-speaking body, and some pastors wanted it to remain so. But in the eastern synods, and therefore in the General Synod, English was making large advances. It must have been known in Ohio that the members of the committee that composed the Proposed Plan were pastors most active on introducing English into the public worship of their congregations. In this objection to the General Synod the spirit of independence is joined by a conservatism in language.

The objectors did not necessarily speak the sentiment of all pastors of the Ohio Synod. Some of them could and did preach in English. It is not clear when this was first done in a congregation, but at the very first Special Conference, 1812, there was a sermon in English by Weyer. This precedent may have been followed annually, but at least there is a clear record in 1815 of an English sermon by Stough, and in 1816 and 1817 ones by A. Henkel. At the first convention of the Synod, 1818, "Mr. Stauch delivered a stirring address on 2 Tim. 2:15. After this Mr. Henkel, Sr., preached in the English language on 2 Cor. 5:20." [15] So Paul Henkel preached in English, even though he ardently preferred German! This increasing use of English will be discussed later, but at this point it is interesting to note that in 1825 when the General Synod authorized 500 copies of its minutes in German and 1,000 in English, the Ohio Synod ordered 1,200 copies of its minutes to be printed in German and 500 in English.[16]

At the convention in 1821 the Ohio Synod had the text of the constitution of the General Synod before it. Stough seems to have been a friend of the General Synod, for he brought up the constitution as an item of business. That document, shaved clean of all federalist powers, should have laid to rest the fears in Ohio. But the prejudice remained, and the best Stough could get was a decision to postpone action for a year for further investigation. Ohio would wait and see.[17]

The hopes of the friends of the General Synod seemed to be realized in 1822 at the convention held at Greensburg, Pennsylvania. To be sure, this was in the parish of Steck, senior. Geisenheiner of Pittsburgh and three other pastors of the Ministerium of Pennsylvania were present—members

---

[15] *Minutes,* 1818, p. 3.
[16] *Minutes,* 1825, p. 9.
[17] *Minutes,* 1821, pp. 5 f.

of a body that a year previous had approved the Constitution of the General Synod by a vote of sixty-seven to six. Once more the Ohio Synod discussed the constitution of the General Synod article by article, reaching a decision to send two men, John Peter Schmucker and Michael John Steck, to the next convention of the General Synod to confer on the matter of membership. Both were young men; Steck was twenty-nine years old, and Schmucker apparently was a few years older. Steck, in part trained by his father at Greensburg, had been pastor at Lancaster, Ohio, since 1816. Schmucker had just come to Newark, Ohio. He had been a delegate of the North Carolina Synod at the organization meeting of the General Synod in 1820 and had signed the constitution. A few years later he left the Lutheran Church and joined the German Methodists.

This Greensburg convention was held in September, 1822. The next convention of the General Synod was not held until October, 1823, thirteen months later. In the interval matters in the East took a decided turn. Among the congregations the fears of central authority and tyranny boiled up to such alarming heights that the Ministerium of Pennsylvania felt it the part of wisdom to withdraw from the General Synod. To the Ohio Synod convention in 1823 came a letter from Pastor Steck, senior, bearing this news and suggesting that the resolution to send Schmucker and Steck, junior, be rescinded. It was so voted.

Thus after some uncertainty the earlier decision to remain independent continued as a settled policy. It appeared that the General Synod was doomed to failure, or at least to insignificance. Many years were to elapse before the General Synod would include a majority of the Lutherans in America, and then only briefly. Before that time arrived other factors arose which prevented the union of the Joint Synod of Ohio with the general body.

Meanwhile the General Synod did not give up hope of winning the Ohio Synod. The 1825 Minutes of the General Synod included a "Pastoral Address" which contained a paragraph concerning each of the Lutheran synods in America. The paragraph on the Ohio Synod came formally to its attention through the report of a committee which advised "the Synod to pass it over in silence until Providence shall in the course of time make it appear clear to us." [18] Yet the General Synod believed it had friends in Ohio for in the decision to establish a theological seminary (soon begun at Gettysburg) Pastors Stough and J. Steck (likely meaning the younger Steck) were appointed to solicit funds in Ohio and Indiana.

[18] *Minutes,* 1826, p. 5.

Nor was that the end of it. In 1833 mention is made of "a letter from Pastor D. F. Schaeffer, President of the (so-called) General Synod in which he expresses the desire that the Ohio Synod might send a delegate to the next session of that body." The letter was read to the convention which "Resolved that the secretary of this Synod communicate to Pastor Schaeffer the assurance of our unfeigned love and regard." But a footnote remarks: "Of the ten Lutheran synods in the United States four belong to or constitute this General Synod. These four synods number seventy-seven, and the six not belonging to it 152 ministers." [19] The spirit and intent of the footnote are obvious.

Associated with J. M. Steck in opposition to the General Synod was Paul Henkel. Indeed, he may have been the one who first raised objections. There can be no doubt that he was the point of contact with the Tennessee Synod, which objected strenuously to the General Synod. Henkel became a member of the Tennessee Synod at its organization in 1820. In its minutes of that year it appended the Ohio objections to the Proposed Plan of a General Synod. A few months before he died in 1825, Paul Henkel sent a letter to the Ohio Synod expressing his opinions against the General Synod and hoping that this synod might always remain with the old evangelical order.[20] The Tennessee objections were much like those of Ohio, with some additions in the area of doctrine. Thus Paul Henkel, whose name continued on the roll of the Ohio Synod as long as he lived, introduced into the discussions on the General Synod an element of Lutheran doctrinal conservatism. His son, Charles, pastor at Columbus and later at Somerset, was "most pronounced and bitter in his opposition" to the General Synod.[21] This element would in the future greatly strengthen the Ohio Synod's decision to remain independent.

CHANGE IN LEADERSHIP

Leadership in the Synod was changing also. Before 1830 it was mostly the men of the Stough group who were elected officers of the Synod. Stough himself was president six times. Weygandt, Rinehart, and Weyer held some office at one time or another. All of them had been frontiersmen. But now younger pastors who reached maturity or who arrived after the frontier

[19] *Minutes,* 1833, p. 8.

[20] *Minutes,* 1825, p. 4.

[21] M. L. Wagner, *The Chicago Synod and Its Antecedents* (Waverly, Iowa, 1909), p. 32.

had moved farther west were stepping into the leadership. By 1830 death had removed from the Synod Paul Henkel and John Michael Steck, John Casper Dill and Anthony Weyer. Late in 1828 Stough concluded his active ministry in Columbiana County. Early in the spring he sold his farm to his son-in-law, then moved to Crawford County, buying land adjoining the farm of one of his sons, where he lived in retirement. Rinehart turned his parish over to James Manning in 1825, apparently returning to farming. To replace these men there came to the fore Paul Henkel's sons, Andrew and Charles, and John Michael Steck's son, Michael John.

The change in leadership indicates the decline, if not the end, of the Stough influence with his preference for a mild form of Lutheranism. Since he was a pioneer missionary whose early training was pietistic, his main concern was to bring the Gospel to the new settlements, gathering Christian believers into congregations. Most of the time he did this in cooperation with the German Reformed. There are indications that he had a friendly attitude toward other denominations. Speaking in his memoirs of prayer meetings he said: "I have always found these meetings to be true nurseries of a religious life among all Christians of every denomination and language." [22] In another connection he wrote, "We are also strengthened and encouraged by brethren in sister churches." [23] In his memoirs references to Lutheran doctrines or to the Lutheran Confessions are altogether lacking. His theological outlook is indicated by his reading: "My principal books for fifty years have been Starke's Commentary, Spener's Explanation of Luther's Five Principles, my catechism, hymnbook and the Holy Bible." [24] Doubtless this was the pietistic kind of Lutheranism he taught the men he instructed for the ministry in Ohio, though nothing from their pens has survived as evidence of their own views.

It was in keeping with Stough's friendly attitude toward members of other churches that he attended an interdenominational meeting in Lisbon which was held to encourage the establishing of Sunday schools in as many places as feasible. [25] It was in the same spirit that when the Synod met at New Philadelphia in 1826 a Methodist minister named Plimpton was made an honorary member of the convention and allowed to preach to the Synod in English.[26] Typical of the Stough spirit also is an anonymous letter of 1828 by a "respectable Minister in Ohio":

[22] Burgess, op. cit., p. 37. Sheatsley, op. cit., p. 30.
[23] Burgess, op. cit., p. 38. Sheatsley, op. cit., p. 31.
[24] Burgess, op. cit., p. 39. Sheatsley, op. cit., p. 36.
[25] Ohio Patriot, Lisbon, Ohio, July 17, 1819.
[26] Minutes, pp. 6, 12.

Here in Ohio the harvest truly is plenteous, but the laborers are few. We have many churches but cannot so watch over them as to resist effectually the enemy, who seeks to destroy our members. This fact causes indeed in our official operations many difficulties. But we have the consolation to know that the pure Evangelical doctrine will be sustained and that the church of Christ will finally triumph over all its enemies. If God spares me until the next meeting of the General Synod I am determined to pay it a friendly visit. We are not so prejudiced against the General Synod as some to the East represent. I trust that the Great Shepherd, Jesus Christ, will soon control and direct all matters to the promotion of his church's welfare.[27]

It may have been the same pastor who wrote another letter.

Before I left home I resolved to make it my business at the Synod to rouse the sleeping energies of our Church, to encourage them to the recommendation of Sunday schools, to larger contributions to our missionary fund, to the spread of our Intelligencer, the introduction of the Catechism and Liturgy of the General Synod, etc. After the business of the individual churches had been transacted, I spoke upon the important subjects which lay so near my heart for many years, and the approbation and deep attention which was visible to every eye . . . you ought to have seen.[28]

The indications of interest in a more doctrinal Lutheranism come from men outside the Stough group. Thus when in 1817 it was voted to publish the Augsburg Confession with the minutes of the convention, a preface for it was to be prepared by "Pastor Steck" [29]—evidently John Michael, the father, rather than Michael John, the son, who was then only a licenced candidate not yet ordained as pastor. Such theological training as Father Steck had was received from J. C. F. Helmuth, a Philadelphia pastor whose Lutheranism was colored by a hearty pietism. Ten years later when the Synod authorized the appointment of a committee to prepare an English translation of Luther's Catechism, the members of the committee were Andrew Henkel and Michael John Steck, young men not of the Stough group.[30] The same thing happened the next year when a committee was appointed to prepare a "Liturgy arranged according to the spirit and doctrines of our Church," though other men constituted the committee. Moreover, as was noted earlier, when the Synod in 1818 wanted a statement on Lutheran doctrine it committed the task to Paul Henkel. It is quite evident that it was the Henkels who had much to do with developing a more doctrinal Lutheranism in Ohio as opposed to the doctrinal indifference of revivalism.

[27] *Evangelical Lutheran Intelligencer,* III, 1 (April 1828), pp. 41 f.
[28] *Ibid.,* III, 6 (August 1828), p. 129.
[29] *Minutes,* p. 41.
[30] *Minutes,* p. 6.

Further evidence is to be found in the standards for the admission of pastors to the Synod. During the first decade candidates were examined concerning their piety and education. Men transferring from other synods were accepted readily. But after the Ohio Synod was ten years old it began to be more particular. A man had gotten himself accepted as pastor by some congregations in Trumbull County and then applied for admission to Synod. But the Synod rejected his application since it was "credibly informed that he always acted inordinately when he was a member of the Maryland and Virginia, and the West Pennsylvania Synods, and because it appears by all information that he acts thus yet." [31] After this experience the Synod decided to establish a regulation: "*Resolved,* That in future every one who having been a member of another Ministerium applies to Synod for admission, shall be strictly examined without regard to any previous examination or the place he came from." [32] How this worked in practice is shown by this report of the examining committee the next year: "That the conversation they had held with the Pastors Ruth and Greenwald had convinced them in a satisfactory manner that these brethren were neither infected by the poison of Rationalism nor inflamed by the wildfire of Fanaticism, and that therefore this Ministerium need not hesitate to receive them into their midst." [33] It is interesting that the committee consisted of Charles Henkel and C. G. Schweizerbarth. It was this same Schweizerbarth, pastor at Zelienople, Pennsylvania, who as secretary of Synod probably wrote the sharp footnote to a report in the printed minutes asserting that "The American Sunday School Union has sectarian views, [and] is hostile to the Lutheran Church." [34]

THEOLOGICAL SEMINARY BEGUN

The second effort of the Ohio Synod to begin an educational institution was successful. The first effort had been premature because there had not yet been the right combination of competent teacher and synod support. The second effort came at a more favorable time. Its success was highly important for the Synod both in providing training for prospective pastors and also in furnishing a visible focus for synodical loyalty. The institution was a tangible evidence of the Synod's life.

[31] *Minutes,* 1829, p. 8.
[32] *Minutes,* 1831, p. 13.
[33] *Minutes,* 1832, p. 28.
[34] *Minutes,* 1833, p. 4.

In the area west of the mountains Presbyterians of one strain or another had been the first to get theological institutions founded. There had been Service Seminary in Beaver County, Pennsylvania, begun in 1794, Pittsburgh Seminary in 1825, and Western Seminary in Pittsburgh in 1827. The Protestant Episcopal Seminary at Gambier, Ohio, dates back to 1824. Roman Catholics had begun a school at Bardstown, Kentucky, in 1811, and another at Cincinnati in 1829. The Lutheran Seminary thus came quite early in theological training in this area.

Late in 1827 five young pastors and some laymen assembled in Zanesville for an "English Special Conference." Among their resolutions was a very respectful request that the Synod consider establishing a training school for pastors. When this request came before the Synod the following spring the result was the appointment of a committee consisting of three middle-aged pastors: Andrew Henkel, Leist, and Heincke. The committee was charged with the duty of devising a plan for establishing a theological seminary. Since Leist had been involved in the previous attempt which ended in failure, it is not surprising that the committee a year later reported unfavorably. A seminary would of course "be of great benefit." But "for the present we are not in the possession of the means to effect or commence such an institution." This the Synod approved.[35] This does not seem unreasonable in view of the fact that the total amount received by the treasury of the Synod during the year was $169.67.

It was only a year after this discouraging decision that the situation completely changed and the Synod voted to begin a school.[36] A letter had come from Reverend E. T. Hazelius, D. D., President of the Evangelical Lutheran Synod of New York, suggesting that Ohio candidates for the ministry study at Hartwick Seminary in that state. The committee to consider this correspondence consisted of two young pastors, C. G. Schweizerbarth and John Wagenhals, and a lay delegate, C. O. Wolpers. The committee felt that it was too far and too expensive for students to go to New York. Even if those obstacles could be overcome,

> It is the special desire of the Church in the West to have an institution for the education of our ministry within her own borders where her interests might generally concentrate and from whence as from a fountain head the doctrines of the Augsburg Confession of Faith might be promulgated literally, purely, and unadulteratedly, and the mild and tolerant spirit of our

---

[35] *Minutes,* 1829, p. 11.
[36] See the centennial volume, *History of the First Lutheran Seminary of the West: 1830–1930,* by C. V. Sheatsley (Columbus, 1930), and *These Hundred Years, The Centennial History of Capital University* (Columbus, 1850).

discipline shed abroad its benign influence; and where the characteristics of Lutheranism which neither malice nor art can destroy nor time efface might be preserved.

The committee report expressed the opinion that a beginning need not be expensive; remember that Francke began the Halle Orphan Asylum with only eleven gulden—$4.40. Since God will help,

The Committee therefore propose—
1. That, whereas, the first and principal obstacle in the way of erecting a Seminary consists in affording a salary to the teacher, inquiry be made whether a man of requisite abilities might not be found among us who would, at least for a short space of time, engage to teach the elementary principles in this institution gratuitously. And,
2. Whether the second obstacle, which is the obtaining of suitable school books, might not be removed by accepting the offer made by several Ministers and friends of such an institution who proposed through the medium of their friends in Germany to furnish books sufficient to lay the foundation of a suitable library.

Before the afternoon session closed, the Synod

Resolved, That this Report be accepted, and that it be the duty of the officers of the Synod to inquire whether there be a man of the necessary qualifications in our connection who would take charge of such an institution according to the plan proposed by the committee.

The next morning the consideration of the report was continued.

The President [Andrew Henkel] stated to the Synod that he, having consulted with [Candidate] Schmidt, was informed by him that he would consent to take charge of such an institution provided no one else among the brethren should be so disposed.

With this assurance the convention took action:

Resolved, That an institution for the education of young men for the Ministry be erected; That Candidate Schmidt, whose kind offer to take charge of the institution we gratefully receive, be hereby appointed teacher of the same, and that all Ministers belonging to this body be advised to recommend to him those young men who wish to enter upon the Ministry. *Resolved,* That this institution be entitled *The Theological Seminary of the Evangelical Lutheran Synod of Ohio.*

Before the convention adjourned the professor-elect submitted for inspection the outline of a three-year course of study which the Synod approved.[37]

37 *Minutes,* 1830, pp. 9–14.

For most of the next nine years Wilhelm Schmidt was the only professor in the Seminary. He began the instruction of two students October 1, 1830, in his home in Canton where he was pastor. Born December 11, 1803, the son of a pastor of a village in Wurtemberg, Germany, he had received a theological training at the University of Halle-Wittenberg before coming to America.[38] With three brothers he settled in Holmes County, Ohio, and founded the town of Winesburg. When some congregations near Canton asked him to be their pastor he applied to the Synod for a license. He brought with him testimonials from the University of Halle-Wittenberg signed by the chancellor and others. He had letters of recommendation from two professors there and from the president of the Ministerium of Pennsylvania. When read to the Ohio Synod in 1828 they created sufficient attention to be quoted in the minutes.[39] Given a license as candidate that year, he was advanced to ordination at the same convention which approved him as professor. This twenty-six year old pastor, the only member of the Synod with a formal academic training in classical and theological studies, modestly accepted the responsibility for starting a seminary. To this task he devoted himself with competence and with such complete devotion that in nine years he had burned out his life.

The first winter of teaching by Schmidt was proof to the Synod that a seminary could exist. The 1831 convention acted to give support to the school by electing a Board of Directors, consisting of four pastors and four laymen, to serve for one year. The membership of the Board is interesting. The pastors were Andrew Henkel and Jacob Leist—members of the committee that had said "no" to starting a seminary in 1829—C. G. Schweizerbarth and John Wagenhals—members of the committee that gave a vigorous "yes" to the idea in 1830. They represented a geographic distribution, though the Synod may not have given that any consideration. Schweizerbarth of Zelienople, Pennsylvania, represented the east; Leist of Tarlton and Wagenhals of Lancaster represented the center; and Henkel of Germantown the west. No one of the lay members of the Board was a delegate to the 1831 convention. They were the "Hon. Gustavus Swan (of Columbus), a lawyer and real estate man, and his friend and business associate Judge Christian Heyl"[40] who was a member of the Columbus parish where

[38] See the article by Paul H. Buehring, "Wilhelm Schmidt, Founder of the Columbus Seminary," *Lutheran Quarterly*, VII ,4 (November 1955), pp. 348 ff. An account of his life as given in the *Proceedings of the Western District of the Evangelical Lutheran Synod of Ohio*, 1840, in German appeared in English translation in *Lutheran Observer*, VIII, 25 (February 19, 1841).

[39] *Minutes*, pp. 9 f.

[40] *These Hundred Years*, p. 12.

Schmidt was soon to be pastor; John Leist who was a member of the Tarlton parish and likely a brother of Pastor Jacob Leist; and F. A. Schneider.

To define the work of the Board of Directors the Synod adopted four resolutions:

> *Resolved,* That these Directors are hereby authorized by the Synod to make the necessary arrangements for the Theological School, and to receive donations.
>
> *Resolved,* That the Board of Directors meet on the first day of September A.D. 1831 at New Lancaster, Ohio, and hereby be empowered by Synod then and there to decide finally upon the location of the Theological School, if it should consider such a measure necessary for the prosperity of the Institution.
>
> *Resolved,* That the Directorium shall compose a constitution for the Theological School and lay it before the next Synod.
>
> *Resolved,* That the Synod recommend to every one of its members in the most affectionate and urgent manner to collect as many contributions for this Theological School as his opportunities will permit.[41]

In the summer of 1831 Schmidt accepted the call to the four-congregation Columbus parish, moving there with his family and students. It was Columbus that offered the largest subscription of funds for the school. The two Columbus members of the Board certainly were influential. Thus the decision to locate the Seminary in Columbus scarcely could have been otherwise. The Board purchased fourteen acres of land on which a building was erected during 1832-33, though with an indebtedness of over $1,100. The size of the student body grew slowly. A library was accumulated. Dr. Hazelius sent fifty theological books from the Gettysburg Seminary and twenty of his own. The Synod adopted a resolution of thanks to Dr. Hazelius and his colleagues for this evidence of "their sincere interest in the establishment of a Seminary in the West." [42]

The 1832 convention of the Synod was held in Columbus. In the presence of the delegates Professor Schmidt examined his students in German, Latin, and Greek. Eight students gave orations on the Reformation. Their speeches, according to Schweizerbarth the secretary, "met with general applause." As Secretary Schweizerbarth summed it up in the Minutes,

> The visible blessing wherewith the All-Merciful crowned the feeble attempts which this Synod made in dependence upon Him to found a Theological School in the West filled all hearts with joy, with gratitude, with hope, and

[41] *Minutes,* 1831, pp. 16 f.
[42] *Minutes,* 1832, p. 12.

strengthened in all the resolution to unite all their efforts in word and deed to promote its further advancement.[43]

The Synod voiced its appreciation of the work of Professor Schmidt, setting his salary at $150 and voting $300 out of the balance in the treasury for the Seminary building. It was hoped that the enthusiasm aroused would result in larger giving in the congregations, for the total receipts to the synodical treasury during the year had been only $289.06¼.

Thus in 1833 the Ohio Synod had a Theological Seminary in Columbus consisting of a professor assisted by an advanced student, a small student body, the beginning of a library, and a two-story building whose second story was unfinished. Finances were so limited that correspondents were warned to send all their letters to the professor post-paid. The Synod authorized the active solicitation of funds for the Seminary; Professor Schmidt in Philadelphia, New York, and Baltimore; Pastor Schweizerbarth in Pittsburgh and western Pennsylvania; Pastor Charles Henkel in Virginia; and Pastor Heincke in Cincinnati and western Ohio. The results of these renewed efforts would determine whether or not this educational venture could survive.

RELATION TO THE REFORMED

From the beginning of church organizations in Ohio it had been common for German Lutherans and German Reformed to combine in the erection of a place of worship. Lutheran pastors cooperated with their Reformed colleagues in religious activities, in conducting funerals, and on other public occasions. One of the speakers at the ceremony of laying the cornerstone of the seminary building was a Reformed minister. This was typical practice. If such cooperation was possible on the parish level, the question was bound to be raised as to whether or not it could exist also on the synodical level. The decisions of the Ohio Synod by 1833 were to become the precedent in this matter for years to come.

The record indicates that the Lutheran attitude toward the Reformed was friendly but formal, courteous but cautious. There was willingness to meet and talk, but no willingness to surrender loyalty to what was considered distinctively Lutheran as contrasted with what was Reformed. The Ohio Synod refused to violate the ecclesiastical proprieties. A Western Special Conference in 1819 asked if it might hold a conference with the

[43] *Minutes,* 1832, p. 11.

Reformed ministers of the area. The Synod replied that it could not conscientiously receive this request until after a report from the Reformed Synod.[44] That was the end of the matter at that time.

From time to time there was an exchange of printed minutes between the Lutheran Ohio Synod and the Reformed Synod of Ohio, and even with the West-Penn Classis of the Reformed Synod of Pennsylvania. For example, in 1827 the Ohio Synod voted "to return our thanks to these [Reformed] brethren for their love and friendship and to send them twenty-five copies of the Minutes." [45]

Two years later the Lutherans were confronted with a proposal for union. The Synod appointed a committee to confer with the German Reformed committee concerning a time for a joint meeting.[46] Three years more elapse before there is another record of what was taking place. Then there was a report that a majority of the German Reformed Synod of Ohio were favorable to union with the Lutherans provided the terms were satisfactory. Since only fifteen of the thirty pastors were present, the Lutheran Synod "*Resolved,* That with regret we feel ourselves constrained to postpone the expression of our sentiments upon this subject till the next Synod on account of the absent Fathers and Brethren." [47] A year later when the matter came up for consideration the Lutheran Synod declared its willingness to enter into a union,

> *Provided* terms of union can be found which are based on truth and righteousness, and secure the principles of the Evangelical Church. . . . But that we wish that our Calvinistic brethren might communicate unto our Synod their views on such "terms." [48]

At the same time German Reformed students for the ministry were invited to attend the Lutheran Theological Seminary in Columbus. What the Lutheran "terms" for such a union would be was indicated by the provision in the model constitution for congregations, authorized by the Synod in 1833, which required Lutheran pastors "to preach and teach according to the doctrines of the Symbolical Books of the Lutheran Church." [49] Since that was the doctrinal attitude of the Lutheran Ohio Synod, it must have

[44] *Minutes,* 1819, p. 6.
[45] *Minutes,* 1827, p. 3.
[46] *Minutes,* 1829, p. 14.
[47] *Minutes,* 1832, p. 19.
[48] *Minutes,* 1833, p. 15.
[49] *Ibid.,* p. 27.

been clear to any unbiased observer that there would not be a union of Lutheran and Reformed synods in Ohio.

THE PROBLEM OF BOUNDARIES

How much area the Ohio Synod should cover was bound to be a problem as population and the number of congregations increased. When the first Special Conference met in 1812, the Western District was not defined. Nor do any of the Minutes of the Ministerium of Pennsylvania set any boundaries. The District certainly included western Pennsylvania. For a brief period Pastor Buttler and Cumberland, Maryland, were included. When Paul Henkel became a member, Point Pleasant on the Virginia side of the Ohio River was added. By specific action in 1813 the Ministerium directed the Western District to supervise Samuel Mau's work in Kentucky. Beginning with 1827 the Ohio Synod was sending pastors on tours into Indiana.

Until the day when transportation facilities were improved and railroads were built, the Synod had to wrestle with the difficulties of travel to conventions. It could have been warned by the experience of the Pennsylvania Synod which had tried to preserve its unity by a system of districts, but saw the out-lying districts become independent synods. Facing the same problem the Ohio Synod had no better solution. It wanted to preserve its unity over an ever-increasing area, and it did not want to lose sections of that area by the rise of new synods. The story is one of some failures but of ultimate success; for the Ohio Synod, after trains began to run, became a nation-wide body.

On the positive side was the effort to cultivate "Special Conferences." The earliest one on record was held in Germantown, June 6, 1819. Its minutes are included in the minutes of the Synod for that year. The exact area involved is not specified, but it evidently was the western half of Ohio. In 1823 the Synod adopted a resolution to establish three districts: first, the western part of Pennsylvania; second, Ohio east of the Muskingum River; and third, Ohio west of that river; each district to have an annual "Special Conference." [50]

There is no record that the first two districts held a meeting, but the Third District held a convention on September 6, 1824, the place of meeting not being recorded.[51] The Synod took action on the resolutions submitted by the District. No subsequent conventions of the District are reported in

[50] *Minutes*, 1823, pp. 6 f.
[51] *Minutes*, 1825, pp. 9 f.

the Synod's minutes, and it appears that the plan adopted in 1823 was allowed to lapse. All three of the districts were German. Yet curiously enough an English Special Conference was held in Zanesville on October 15, 1827.[52] Whence came the authorization for it is not clear. This seems to have been its only meeting.

The restoration of the district organizations came about because of the threatened organization of an independent synod in western Pennsylvania. During the 1831 convention of the Synod, Pastor Schweizerbarth, the secretary, arose to deliver a message committed to him. He told of a meeting held in Greensburg, Pennsylvania, the previous April tenth. It had been attended by ten pastors, three of them of the Ohio Synod and the other seven of the West Pennsylvania Synod. He had been the secretary of the meeting. From it came a request to the Ohio Synod to approve the formation of a new synod between the mountains and the Ohio state line.

All this tended to sharpen the question of synodical boundaries. Originally the Pennsylvania Synod claimed everything westward until its western edge was fixed at the mountains by the organization of the Ohio Synod. The congregations west of the Susquehanna River separated from the Pennsylvania Synod and in 1825 held their first convention as the West Pennsylvania Synod. This new synod was soon sending missionary pastors westward over the mountains. It therefore found itself unwilling to accept the mountains as its western border, and thus came in conflict with the Ohio Synod.

The matter came before the Ohio Synod in 1831. At the convention that year attention was called to the "opinion" of the West Pennsylvania Synod in its minutes "that the boundaries of the several States [Ohio and Pennsylvania] should justly be regarded as the boundaries of the two synods." [53] The members of the committee reporting this item declared that

> they cannot at all consider it an act of justice that the above mentioned boundaries should be dictated to the Synod of Ohio, especially as beyond the line of the State of Ohio five of our esteemed Brethren reside, whose separation from this body would not be calculated to promote "the best interests of our evangelical Zion" in the West, and whose continued union with us, we for this reason heartily wish. Your Committee is therefore of the opinion: that Synod should not give its consent to said line of demarcation.

And Synod heartily concurred.[54]

[52] Minutes, 1828, p. 7.
[53] Minutes, 1831, p. 9.
[54] Ibid., p. 10.

That was good lusty loyalty, but it did not remove the difficulty. The fact was that by no means all the Lutheran pastors in western Pennsylvania —or Ohio, for that matter—were members of the Ohio Synod. In Burgess' list of twenty-six pastors who had been in western Pennsylvania from 1818 to 1831, four belonged to the Pennsylvania Synod and nine to the West Pennsylvania Synod.[55] Pastors of the West Pennsylvania Synod continued to come over the mountains into western Pennsylvania congregations until they outnumbered the Ohio Synod men. Their contacts were with the East and they showed little disposition to become members of the Ohio Synod. The distance to an Ohio Synod convention was often actually greater than to one of their own synod. Moreover, most of them had participated in the separation of the West Pennsylvania Synod from its parent, and they were reluctant to separate again.

It doubtless was apparent to the Ohio Synod that it could not hold western Pennsylvania exclusively, no matter what its claims might be. It simply did not have sufficient pastors for all the German settlements and congregations which were arising. When a congregation organized itself, it got a pastor wherever it could and usually was willing to belong to the synod where he had his membership. For example, a congregation in Warren, Pennsylvania, had as pastor in 1852 a man named Conrad Kuehn, and because he was a member of the Buffalo Synod the congregation's affiliation was there. Later when it called as pastor a member of the Pittsburgh Synod it became part of that body. The most that the Ohio Synod could do was to hold to itself as many of the Western Pennsylvania pastors and congregations as possible, and let the rest go.

This was exactly the Ohio Synod policy. For this reason it was opposed to the formation of a new synod in western Pennsylvania. The same attitude prevailed in the West Pennsylvania Synod and continued a decade later when a proposal was made for forming a new synod in the mountain counties. But in spite of opposition the Allegheny Synod came into existence in 1842. And the story was repeated in 1845 with the formation of the Pittsburgh Synod. Thus synodical boundaries overlapped.

Merely to oppose the formation of a new synod was a negative approach. The committee reporting the matter felt that the Synod "should do everything in order to satisfy the just wishes of these Brethren. . . ."[56] It noted that

[55] *Op. cit.,* pp. 51 f.
[56] *Minutes,* 1831, p. 11.

the principal reason why our Brethren in Pennsylvania are desirous to form themselves into a new Synod seems to be those two, 1. That they see their efforts to promote the welfare of the Church paralyzed by the want of a Treasury under their own control; and 2. That the long journey to the Synod is connected with heavy expenses to themselves and with serious injury to their Congregations on account of their long absence.[57]

The Pennsylvania pastors expressed their entire loyalty to the Ohio Synod, but also showed their concern "for the northwesterly part of Pennsylvania to which heretofore a somewhat step-motherly care had been extended." [58] They believed that a synod there, concentrating its energies on that area, could get more rapid results.

The committee's suggestions resulted in the following actions:

> *Resolved,* That the Synod of Ohio shall be and hereby is divided into two District Synods, which shall meet for two successive years yearly within their respective Districts.
> *Resolved,* That every third year a General Synod shall be held whereat the Members of both Districts shall convene and alone Ordination take place.
> *Resolved,* That the District Synods shall have their separate Treasuries but be obliged to pay over one half of the collected moneys to the General Synod.
> *Resolved,* That the District Synods shall have power to license Candidates and Catechets.
> *Resolved,* That the Pastors Weigandt, Wagenhals, and Schweizerbarth shall be a Committee who shall lay before the next Synod, which is a general one, a plan in which the boundaries of both districts, as well as their relation to the General Synod, shall be accurately defined.[59]

In these resolutions the words "General Synod" are to be understood as "Joint Synod"—the later appellation of the Ohio Synod.

The following year the committee suggested that

> . . . the most proper line of demarkation would be to commence at Cleveland, run along the canal to New Philadelphia, and from thence in a straight direction to Marietta.
> *Resolved,* That this line of division be adopted for the present time.
> *Resolved,* That as heretofore this Synod retain the name of Ohio Synod, and the eastern part of it be called the Eastern District of the Ohio Synod, and the western part be called the Western District of the Ohio Synod.[60]

It is not clear from the wording to which District the towns named in the line of demarkation should belong. The Synod had no congregations at that

57 *Ibid.*, p. 12.
58 *Loc. cit.*
59 *Op. cit.*, pp. 12 f.
60 *Minutes*, 1832, p. 17.

time in either Cleveland or Marietta, and New Philadelphia found itself in
the Eastern District. One could wish that the wording of the last resolution
had been followed, but soon there arose among the districts the custom of
calling them "district synods." Thereby comes some confusion.

The plan thus devised proved wise in practice. The line of demarcation
between the districts was far east enough in Ohio to make western Pennsylvania a large part of the Eastern District. A new synod in Pennsylvania
was prevented for the moment. The desires of the pastors in that area
were satisfied. And when finally the Pittsburgh Synod was organized, the
Ohio Synod lost little of its strength in that area, either of pastors or congregations.

The Ohio Synod took yet another step. Northwestern Pennsylvania
needed attention, and the thing to do was to work there. Hence the Synod
adopted the following:

> *Resolved*, That Candidate Kuchler visit as a Missionary the Counties of
> Crawford and Erie, Pennsylvania, for one month, and that he receive 15
> dollars in advance.
> *Resolved*, That Pastor Schweizerbarth visit the same Counties as a Mis
> sionary for one month and that he likewise receive 15 dollars.[61]

Kuchler duly made his missionary tour in October, 1831, reporting to the
next convention of Synod that he preached thirteen times within twenty-two
days, baptized three, confirmed thirteen, administered the Lord's Supper to
twenty-four, and collected five dollars and fifteen cents.[62] There is no evidence, either in the minutes or the treasurer's report, that Schweizerbarth
made a tour; and he was the secretary of Synod in 1832. But note is taken
that year of a letter from Elihu Rathbun reporting

> That the condition of the German Lutherans in Crawford county, Penn
> sylvania, was . . . extremely destitute [Candidate Rathbun preached in the
> English language only] and the wish expressed that Synod might send a
> supply to them during the year.

Whereupon it was "*Resolved*, That Pastor C. G. Schweizerbarth visit the
Congregations of Candidate Rathbun once in the course of this year in
order to preach to them in the German language." [63] The expectation was
that he should spend a month on tour.[64] In this instance it is certain that
Schweizerbarth did not make the tour, for in the Minutes of 1833 there is

[61] *Minutes*, 1831, p. 13.
[62] *Minutes*, 1832, pp. 8 f.
[63] *Ibid.*, p. 16.
[64] *Ibid.*, p. 18.

a report of a Missionary tour which J. H. Hohnholz made in the north-western part of Pennsylvania in the stead and at the request of Pastor Schweizerbarth (who was appointed thereto last session) according to which he had during 23 days preached 11 times, traveled 221 miles, and collected $5.72 cents for the fund of Missions.

After the President had inquired of Pastor Schweizerbarth why he had not himself undertaken the mission, the latter stated that accumulated ministerial business made it utterly impossible for him to leave the sphere assigned to him by his Master—the Head of the Church.

Resolved, That John H. Hohnholz receive $12 for his missionary services performed in the stead and at the request of Pastor Schweizerbarth.[65]

Thus some territory in Pennsylvania continued to be cultivated.

The next time that talk of a new synod arose the place was Ohio. A conference, summoned by Pastors Stough, Weygandt, and Fast, assembled in New Philadelphia in April, 1832. The minutes of the meeting read strangely. After spending Saturday in preparatory services, and Sunday in Communion and preaching, the convention was ready for business on Monday. But no one of the twelve pastors or three lay delegates wanted to propose anything. Yet the notice of the meeting had called the men to assemble "in order to transact important business relative to the north-western part of the State." Finally a letter of excuse was read from an absent pastor in which he expressed his fears about the formation of a new synod. The letter was referred to a committee to discuss over the noon hour. In the committee the desire for a new synod came out in the open, though the majority was opposed. When the committee's report came before the afternoon session, there was prolonged discussion. Then there was a motion to continue in union with the Ohio Synod. Six pastors and one layman voted for it, two laymen—Dr. Jehu Stough and Dr. Samuel Stough—against it, the others not voting.[66] The Synod took note of this conference and rejoiced over its decision.[67] It was not until 1840 that the unity of the Ohio Synod was broken by the formation of a new synod; but that is a story for a later chapter.

SUMMARY

The Ohio Synod, which began its independent existence in 1818, held fifteen annual conventions. After it had grown to such a size as necessitated subdivision into districts, it held its first convention as a Joint Synod in 1833,

[65] *Minutes,* 1833, p. 14.
[66] *Minutes,* 1832, pp. 26 f.
[67] *Ibid.,* p. 12.

thus beginning a new chapter in its history. During these fifteen years it had made its decision to remain an independent synod without inclusion in any general body of Lutherans—a decision that was to continue for a century. Its outlook was becoming more decidedly Lutheran in theology so that union with the Reformed was not possible. Moreover, it had begun a theological seminary which would be a center for its activities and its loyalties.

5 / A HERITAGE IN TENSION

LUTHERANS IN OHIO had to face the question of what adjustments to make to the American way of life. Should they resist all influences that would Anglicize them, thereby remaining a German island in an English-speaking area? Should they take prompt steps to make themselves like their American neighbors in language and outlook? Or was there some position in between wherein they might retain some of their treasured heritage while conforming to the ways of the new land when prudence directed? These questions were insistent. No Lutheran settler in Ohio could ignore them for long. If he had previously resided in an eastern state, he likely had given some answer to them already. If he had emigrated from Germany they were new to him. In any case the answers given were to affect his church deeply.

His perplexities, in so far as they affected his church, centered about several foci, which, however, were interrelated. There was, of course, the problem of language. But this was so tied up with the religious practices and thought patterns of Germany that it seemed to many that to yield at any point was to surrender everything. The advocates of change were not content simply to translate their church services into English; they wished to make other changes as well. American influences did not stop simply with language. The issues therefore tended to be confused and confusing.

The first and most obvious problem was language. German might be spoken in the home. Communities usually permitted its use in schools or churches if the constituency desired it. In some communities it might be spoken in places of business. And there were German-language newspapers. Yet there was no evading the fact that all about were English-speaking people who were greatly in the majority and who would not accommodate themselves to the language of a minority. There was no help for it: the Germans must learn to speak English. The only alternative was to avoid business and social contacts with non-Germans.

The decision to retain German in the family, the school, and the church was in some instances an expression of a desire to be loyal to a heritage.

There was much in German literature of which to be proud. German hymns constituted a great treasure. The devotional and liturgical products of German church life were to be highly esteemed. Some of those who valued such things had received a thorough education in Germany. Cultured people of this sort could look only with sorrow upon their unlettered brethren who were willing quickly to become Americanized. Such, for example, was the view of Edward Hengstenberg who spent about a year studying the conditions of Germans in the United States. In his report, published under the title *Germans in North America,* he stressed the importance of preserving the true German culture, language, and spirit.[1]

Under such a point of view the change to English was looked upon as being something of a betrayal. To give up German in church and school was an evidence of disloyalty. The immigrant who adapted himself quickly to American ways could not escape the suspicion of being something of a turncoat. As a German he should remain German, in the view of many persons. Paul Henkel scolded those who weakened at this point. "I reproved him that he held his and his wife's mother tongue in such little esteem, and did not teach it to their children," he wrote of a man at Brush Creek.[2]

Willingness to change language was attributed in some cases to worldly ambition and pride. The German settlers wanted to get on in the world: to do so necessitated becoming Americanized. To German pastors such as Paul Henkel such conduct was to be deplored. Of one man and his family Henkel wrote, "although both his parents are German, and so brought up, the foolishness of others led them to bring up their children in the English language."[3] In another instance, "we started early to visit another German family who would like to be English if only they had the necessary gifts and ability. . . . The wife was ever filled with the love of pride; the same drew her to the English."[4] The Germans at Chillicothe tried to conceal their nationality; they "do not willingly acknowledge it," wrote Henkel.[5] "The German inhabitants of the place are prejudiced against the German pastors. They are probably possessed with what many others are possessed, stupid pride and lightmindedness."[6]

---

[1] This report was published serially beginning March 20, 1847, in the *Evangelische Kirchenzeitung* edited by his brother, Ernest W. It was translated with critical notes by W. M. Reynolds and published serially in *The Lutheran Observer* beginning December 10, 1847 (XV, 15).

[2] Martzolff, "Rev. Paul Henkel's Journal," *op. cit.,* p. 188.

[3] *Ibid.,* p. 167.

[4] *Ibid.,* p. 176.

[5] *Ibid.,* p. 184.

[6] *Ibid.,* p. 194.

These may have been somewhat exceptional cases, for it would seem that most Lutherans who grew to maturity using German preferred it for their worship. The hymns and prayers had a more familiar sound in their mother tongue. The use of English always required the difficult mental process of translation. It was so much easier in German. In that language the dear God was so much nearer. It was difficult enough to worship God in a strange land without adding the further burden of a strange tongue. Let the use of German in church continue, yes, even require it!

The result was a certain isolation from the rest of the community and a certain misunderstanding by it. The Lutheran church, being German, was therefore foreign. It could not appeal to the unchurched in the area unless they were German-speaking. Because of language ties, the Reformed and the Lutherans often united in the erection of a building. The confessional distinction was obscured in the mind of the English-speaking community which saw the use of German as the most prominant characteristic. Customs, such as those connected with Christmas or with confirmation, were therefore regarded not so much as being Lutheran but as being German. As the years progressed the pressure of such community misunderstandings was certain to be felt within Lutheran congregations.

Young people especially were sensitive to community attitudes. Born in America, they had no nostalgia for the Fatherland. The label of "foreign" was particularly offensive to them. Unless they were distinctly isolated by living in scattered rural areas or in predominantly German settlements, their contacts made it possible for them to learn English easily and naturally. No amount of German conversation in the home or training in the German text of Luther's Catechism could prevent the gradual development of the use of English as their primary language. No matter how slowly this process occurred, there was continually through the decades a constantly increasing number of young people who rebelled at the requirement of German in church.

As a consequence many young folks left the Lutheran Church, either to be without any church connection or to find membership in some other denomination. Lutheran comments bewailing this condition were common in the literature of that day. The President of the English Synod of Ohio, in his report to the convention in 1837, made this statement:

> What is most painful to contemplate in the picture is the fact that the accessions to the communion of other churches are in many instances derived from the youth of Lutheran families who, not understanding the German language and not possessing the advantage of English ministrations in the

church of their fathers, are necessitated to attach themselves to other churches. [7]

Perhaps those who ceased to be Lutherans had other reasons in addition to language for their change of membership, but the use of German was the focus of complaint.

Yet there were many persons who for a variety of reasons could not bring themselves to the decision to make the break. Family and church loyalty, the absence of any other church to which to go, distaste for the denominations represented in the community, and the cultivated ability to understand German, if not to speak it, were sufficient factors to keep many of the younger generation in the Lutheran Church.

Gradually their desire for services in English became vocal. At first there might be a request for an occasional English sermon in addition to the German one. If that were successful, they asked for services entirely in English. Presently there arose demands that English be on an equal basis with the German. To accomplish this, there would be motions to amend the constitution so that the word "German" would be dropped from the name of the congregation, and that the appropriate article would read: "Services shall be conducted in the German and English languages." When the demands were refused and the motions defeated, as was many times the case, the minority party withdrew and formed a separate English Lutheran congregation.

The formation of English Lutheran parishes must not always be interpreted as hostility to things German. These people were not all Germanophobes. They permitted occasional German services in their churches. Pastors of "English" Lutheran congregations could and sometimes did preach in German. Bilingual pastors were much in demand and were seen as the solution to the language problem. D. P. Rosenmiller, pastor in Dayton, wrote:

> It is almost indispensably necessary that every minister of our church locating in the West should be able to officiate in these two languages. By this arrangement our European brethren will become attached to our institutions and they and their children secured from the proselyting arts of several German sects who are becoming numerous in the West.[8]

There is ample evidence that "English" Lutheran pastors preached willingly and acceptably in the German language. This, however, was intended only

[7] *Minutes of the Synod and Ministerium of the English Evangelical Lutheran Churches in Ohio and Adjacent States,* 1837, p. 6.

[8] *Lutheran Observer,* XIII, 1 (August 29, 1845), p. 2.

as a temporary measure to be used until such time as all their members could satisfactorily worship in English.

Bilingual pastors, however, had their own problems. Rosenmiller describes them in an article entitled "Peculiar Difficulties to Lutheran Clergymen Arising from the Use of Two Languages." [9] According to this account, the bilingual pastor finds that it is quite hard to be polished in both English and German. If he makes mistakes in either language he arouses ridicule among the champions of the language concerned. Yet he cannot limit himself to the language of his training because both languages are demanded. He is constantly in danger of getting words from the other language in his sentences so that his speech becomes a ludicrous mixture. It is one of the burdens of his office that every sermon must be repeated in the other language, thereby doubling the strain upon his physical resources. And finally, even when he has done his best, the English part of his parish resents his German, and the Germans have a prejudice against his English.

German congregations which resisted the encroachment of English were by no means without their problems. Sometimes it seemed that they were fighting for a lost cause. If they did not think of it in those terms, at least their opponents so interpreted it. A resident of Wooster described it in this way:

> Some congregations have been preached to death and others in a measure ruined by this unreasonable opposition to English preaching. In a few instances preachers in the plentitude of their wisdom have preached against English preaching. But after all a minister confined entirely to the German is for the most part slenderly supported. There are some exceptions; but in general it is true that a German minister is very hard run here in point of support.[10]

Very likely all Lutheran pastors in Ohio in the 1830's had meagre salaries, whatever their language. Despite losses, Lutheran congregations in Ohio using the German language were increasing in number and size in these decades. Loyalty and hard work continued to bring results.

The field for work in German was continually being replenished by migration from Germany. The losses to the English could be ignored in view of the thousands of newcomers from abroad. They increased the strength of German churches already in existence. Settling in areas where Germans had been few, they opened possibilities for founding new congregations. They overtaxed the capacity of the Synod to supply them with

[9] *Lutheran Observer*, XVII, 26 (June 29, 1849), p. 2.
[10] Letter signed "Tully," in *Lutheran Observer*, IV, 35 (April 21, 1837), p. 137.

pastors. Thus by creating an increasing field for service exclusively in German they strengthened the determination to persevere in that language. The decision to resist the inroads of English was reinforced.

The larger, long-range view was certain to be that the preservation of German alone was a forlorn hope. However, those who were struggling to maintain church services in German were unable to see it that way. The perpetuation of the Lutheran congregations as German in every way seemed to be not only possible but even vitally necessary. But those who were familiar with the developments in the Lutheran congregations along the Atlantic coast as well as those who saw the whole national situation, were sure that the German would in time give way to the English. So Hengstenberg, back in Germany after his survey, reported:

> The tendency of the German population is always towards the English language; no resistance on the part of the ministers can be of any avail; let them persist stiffly in preaching German, and the people would fall off by crowds to the Presbyterians, Methodists, Baptists and Episcopalians, a dead loss thus not only to the German nationality but also to the Lutheran Church.[11]

This, it will be remembered, was the conclusion of a man ardently interested in preserving the identity of national German culture and language.

On the other hand, those who were agitating for the prompt adoption of English in Lutheran congregations found their cause reinforced by the spirit of American nationalism. The United States had become a nation whose increasing strength and wealth was a source of pride to her citizens. The American way of life, though exaggerated by the Know-Nothing Party consisting of native-born, Protestant men, was certain to affect the thinking of Lutherans as well as of others. Those who favored the dominant use of English in church united in the "adoption of strictly Lutheran and American principles." A spokesman of this viewpoint said, "Our church is American, our people are all American in the second and often the first generation; the American character and spirit must therefore pervade our institutions if we desire them to flourish. . . . Whatever it [American character] is, we must follow it if we wish to give our institutions a popular, that is, a truly American name." [12]

Thus it was that those who wanted purely German Lutheran congregations stood their ground against those who worked to have English services.

[11] *Lutheran Observer*, XVI, 6 (February 11, 1848), p. 2.
[12] Ernst L. Hazelius, *History of the American Lutheran Church* (Zanesville, Ohio, 1846), p. 288.

Each party, its attitudes being hardened by strong emotions, found it increasingly difficult to have any patience with the other. Epithets appeared, labelling the Germans as "Europeans" to indicate their foreignness, and, in one instance at least, calling the English speaking party "Irish" as a term of contempt. Amid suspicion and misunderstanding, Lutheranism in Ohio was facing stormy days.

A second point of difficulty was the problem of the methods to be used in the work of the congregations. Those who had grown up in Germany were accustomed to the practices of long established precedent. Parishes there were well defined, and the clergy were supported by taxation. Baptism, confirmations, and stated services of worship were all that were required to maintain the Church. But in Ohio and the growing West there was the necessity of organizing congregations anew. Provision had to be made for the support of pastors from the free contributions of the people. The clergy had not only the duty of preaching, confirming, and administering the sacraments; they had also the task of gathering into the Church's membership those not already enrolled. In the free-church condition in America mere confirmation and residence was not sufficient to constitute membership; there had to be voluntary admission. This placed upon the pastors a task of evangelism unfamiliar in Germany.

For many years there had been Lutherans who thought of membership in a congregation not simply as an enrollment but also as an evidence of personal faith and piety. The Church was not only an agency to provide baptisms, funerals, and so forth, but was an assembly of the devout. The members were expected to show the evidences of pious living. Such pietism had been brought over from Germany and was common in the Lutheran congregations of the American colonies. It was carried over the mountains into the settlements of the Ohio valley. If piety was the mark of church membership, it was only logical to make it a condition for admission to a congregation. It follows, therefore, that there should be used methods appropriate to detecting and arousing this piety.

Some aspects of this German pietism were soon found to be in accord with phases of American religious life colored by Puritanism. Christianity in New England had laid considerable stress on inner religious experience, devotional practices, and strict morals. These same things were emphasized by the Methodists, the Presbyterians, and others with whom the Lutherans came in contact in Ohio. When the barrier of language was overcome, the Lutherans sometimes found congenial spirits in these others as together they were battling the irreligion of the new West. And if these others found certain methods successful in winning the godless to Christian faith, it was to be expected that some Lutherans would imitate their methods.

During the second quarter of the century some American churches experienced a steady surge of revivalism. The Second Great Awakening continued until about 1835. Camp meetings were replaced by periodic revival meetings in local areas and churches. Meanwhile Charles Grandison Finney had become one of the dominant leaders in the movement. Though most of his activity centered in western New York and northeastern Ohio, his influence extended over a much wider area. His revivalist theories and methods were extensively copied. His earlier activities, which had been attended by hysterical manifestations such as fainting or shrieking, had been replaced by meetings conducted with decorum. Nevertheless his concern for methods that produced conversions impelled him to adopt practices sharply in contrast with those in traditional use. Disagreements over the theological and practical aspects of such revivals produced discord among Congregationalists and Presbyterians. Though revivals were much in the public eye, it was by no means certain that revivalism would completely dominate the ecclesiastical scene.

In any event, the stress on "experimental religion" appeared among Lutherans quite vividly. When that was the case, other matters were quite secondary. What was of primary importance was that each individual should have a conscious experience of repentance and faith in which after a period of marked anxiety he had found blessed relief. He would be a praying Christian. Church membership was quite a secondary matter. Baptism and confirmation would have their appropriate places. What was to be expected first of all was that the individual had a glorious sense of the grace of God in his heart. Without that, the services of worship and the Church's liturgy were mere formalism.

To meet this need the proper measures must be employed, keeping always in mind, however, the conservative character of the Lutheran Church. Extremes must be avoided. If the deadness of inactivity were to be discarded, it was necessary to shun the disorderly excesses displayed among the sects. This attitude, when officially expressed, appeared in these words: "On revivals of religion your committee beg leave to recommend opposition to all disorder and *ultraism* on the one hand, whilst on the other we earnestly encourage our churches to promote genuine revivals by faithful preaching of the word, by prayer, and such other means as accord with the holy religion of the blessed Redeemer." [13] To advocate this was to

---

[13] *Minutes* of the English Synod of Ohio, 1841, p. 13.

encourage the use of "new measures." By this phrase was designated the practices of American church life adopted by Lutherans which included Sunday Schools, "protracted meetings," prayer meetings, missionary societies, etc.

Sunday Schools had to win their way into the practices of Lutheran congregations in Ohio. They appeared most prominently among congregations where English was used. When the Ohio Synod in 1836 authorized the formation of an English District (or Synod), the latter body at its first convention reported nine Sunday Schools among it forty-six congregations. Within four years, during which time the number of congregations increased about fifty per cent, the number of Sunday Schools had trebled. These schools were looked upon by those who formed them as important means of making contact with the unchurched.

A "protracted meeting" was really a series of preaching services continued day after day until a satisfactory number of conversions had occurred. The days of the "protracted meeting" might be few or many. Such a meeting in Ashland in 1842 lasted twenty-three days.[14] Meetings of ten to fourteen days were more usual. There would be fervent preaching in the afternoons and evenings, with the mornings being devoted to earnest conversation with those concerned about their salvation. Two or three pastors would cooperate in conducting the preaching services—an ordeal that taxed a man's physical strength. Church members who had never had an experience of conversion, as well as the unchurched, were the objects of the sermonic efforts. A pastor, writing from Wooster, described such a meeting in these words:

> We had one of the most interesting revivals I ever witnessed, and not less than sixty were hopefully converted to God. . . . With a few exceptions the most perfect order and harmony prevailed. . . . We had no "mourner's bench" but we had anxious seats. We invited all who were convinced of sin and wished to have the prayers of the church to occupy the front seats in the church where they were conversed with and instructed in the use of means in order to their salvation.[15]

The pastors in charge of the meeting were expected to keep control of the situation and prevent excessive displays of emotion. One of the accusations made against protracted meetings was that they degenerated into wild commotion. There may have been times when even among Lutherans the usual decorum was lost. A report from Ashland stated:

[14] Letter by Walter Sloan, *Lutheran Observer*, X, 20 (January 20, 1843), p. 3.
[15] Letter by J. H. Hoffman, *Lutheran Observer*, VII, 28 (March 13, 1840), p. 3.

We had no confusion, but considerable noise—and dear br. how could it be otherwise? Fifty and sixty souls crying to God for mercy—some finding peace and praising God, christians conversing with and praying for mourners, etc. The people came eight and ten miles, and the house was always filled to overflowing, particularly at night. About two hundred souls were converted at that meeting, and 79 added to the Lutheran church by confirmation and baptism, and some more will unite with the church hereafter.[16]

To persons accustomed to the formal dignity of German worship, such meetings were spectacles that were highly offensive. Protracted meetings were thought of in terms of their worst examples, and were associated in their minds with the camp meetings where people rolled in the aisles, barked like dogs, or developed spasms of convulsive bodily jerks. It was assumed that Lutheran revivals were no different from these others. Hence there were published attacks on protracted meetings, describing them as marked by the most disorderly displays. Answering such an account in *The Lutheran Standard,* Benjamin Kurtz said in an editorial, "The description there given of new measures is a monstrous chaos of exaggeration; it is a perfect caricature; there is not a friend of new measures in all the church who would subscribe to it." [17]

The viewpoint of the Germans is well represented by Frederick Wynecken who in 1843 published his impressions under the title, *Die Noth der deutschen Lutheraner in Nord America.* Concerning the English-speaking Lutherans, he declared that "they are violent defenders of the 'New Measures,' and in their mode of conversion entirely Methodistic." A translation of his description of revivals reads:

> To New Measures belongs especially the holding of what are called *protracted meetings,* that is, large assemblages which are often extended one or two weeks, whereby it is intended to promote a so-called *revival,* and several preachers are always present. Here nearly the whole day is occupied in preaching, the intervals being filled with *prayer-meetings.* The sermons are systematically adapted to work in still increasing degrees upon the feelings, a more vehement sermon and a more powerful preacher always succeeding the previous one. Prayers, songs set to worldly and enrapturing tunes, groaning and sobbing and ejaculations do their utmost to excite the feelings and the nerves. Toward night, when the excitement has reached its highest pitch, a call is made to sinners who wish to be converted. Whilst some start the liveliest tunes and others pray, a bench is set before the pulpit (the mourners' bench) and another call is made to sinners by a preacher. The others dash among the audience endeavoring in a high voice to speak to

---

[16] Letter by W. J. Sloan, *Lutheran Observer,* X, 32 (April 14, 1843), p. 2.
[17] *Lutheran Observer,* X, 50 (August 18, 1843), p. 2.

individuals, urging them to lay aside false shame, to come now at length and escape the wrath to come. Finally the bench is filled with kneeling and penitent sinners, and now the confusion reaches its highest pitch. The kneeling sinners sob and groan and shriek frequently as though they stood bodily before the judgment seat of Christ, whilst some preachers are speaking to them. The congregation prays aloud partly for them and partly with them, the other preachers still go about among the benches with loud and shrieking appeals to them to come forward. Other squads sing the most different tunes through each other, whilst others again upon their own account, some of them sobbing, with exclamations, with sighs and prayers, and the clapping of hands raise the nervous excitement and play upon the feelings to the very highest point. No wonder that with such preparatory excitement by the preaching, and with such powerful aid afterwards the penitent are perfectly confounded and fall into complete ecstacy connected with convulsions and visions never before imagined. As their whole attention is now turned towards the obtainment of grace of what other form can these convulsions and visions be, or in what other sphere can they move than in that in which at the moment all the feelings, yea the whole soul revolves, and what explanation can they get of their experience but that Christ has heard them and received them into his grace? The "Spirit" has ended his work, but not in general before the most revolting exhibitions are made. Frequently the penitent fall down as though they were dead, then suddenly awake, and shout and leap several feet high in the air, which however is done in a distracted state and as tho' compelled by an invisible power. Frequently also the "Spirit" breaks out in the most terrible contortions and convulsions, and frequently into laughter which is contagious and carries the whole congregation along with it. There are instances when even the greatest scoffers who were slinking away in dismay from the hubbub of such a meeting have fallen down as dead at the door. Around such a one the faithful assemble, pray and sing over him, and when he awakes he feels himself as beneath the bands of the Almighty, who has seized him in the midst of his course and cast him to the earth.

The translation of this passage was made by W. M. Reynolds who adds this comment:

> There are not six out of three hundred ministers stigmatized as "New Measure Men" who pursue anything like the course which you indicate, or would tolerate the fanaticism which you describe. Your description is not even a caricature of protracted meetings among Lutherans. There are indeed a few inexperienced or injudicious brethren who have admitted into their religious exercises disorders which we deplore, as some of them also already do, but their number is small.[18]

18 "Position of the American Lutheran Church," *Lutheran Observer*, XI, 49 (August 9, 1844), p. 1.

Another writer, using the name "Scrutator," charged that Wynecken's ideas about revivals were not derived from his own observation. Indeed, Wynecken's viewpoint was "too fanatical" and "too bigoted" to enable him to understand American practices correctly.[19] The most that could be claimed by the apologists for revivals was that the protracted meetings were conducted in as orderly a fashion as was possible. The charge that in essence they were Methodistic could not be successfully denied. But the charge was made that "many of our Lutheran and Reformed preachers together with a majority of their parishoners hated Methodism much more bitterly than they did sin and the devil." [20]

An editorial in *The Lutheran Standard* listed the criticisms of protracted meetings:

1. They lead Christians to undervalue the ordinary means of grace. . . .
2. They produce an unhealthy tone of feeling.
3. They produce so many spurious conversions.
4. They have in so many instances unsettled the pastoral relation.
5. They lead rash and inexperienced young ministers . . . to denounce the motives and piety of old and long-tried servants of God. . . .
6. They cause the old and pious fathers of our congregations to be set aside as being dead formalists. . . .
7. They lead to the introduction of extravagent measures. . . .[21]

Another feature of the "new measures" was the use of prayer meetings. It was expected that members of the church would meet together for some Bible study and prayer, and that laymen as well as clergymen would offer public prayer. In fact, the willingness and ability to pray in public was looked upon as being one of the marks of a converted Christian. Of a congregation in West Carlisle, Coshocton County, it was said, "Two years ago we had but two praying members here, now we have some fifty or sixty." [22] The practice of what was sometimes called "social prayer" was to be found not only in the parishes but also at synod conventions. The proceedings, after describing the formal occasions of worship, record the following: "Besides the above named exercises, prayer meetings were held in the morning at half past eight o'clock. The meetings were generally large and characterized by good order and deep solemnity, and it is believed that much good was affected." [23]

[19] *Lutheran Observer*, X, 49 (August 11, 1843), p. 1.
[20] Typed *Autobiography of Rev. Joshua Crouse*, p. 76.
[21] *Lutheran Standard*, I, 8 (December 7, 1842), p. 2.
[22] Letter by Jacob Seidle, *Lutheran Observer*, VIII, 46 (July 16, 1841), p. 3.
[23] *Proceedings* of the English Synod of Ohio, 1839, p. 4.

The German pastors and their congregations in Ohio generally were opposed to the "new measures," preferring to conduct the work of the parish with the "old measures" of catechetical instruction and confirmation. With these traditional methods they hoped to cultivate a true sense of piety and devotion. Avoiding the excitement and emotionalism of revivals, they sought a true faith aroused and sustained by the means of grace. This they understood to be the genuinely Lutheran expression of church life.

"Old measures" were described by Editor Greenwald in the very first issue of *The Lutheran Standard* in these words:

> Among the time-honored customs of the Lutheran Church which have been eminently blessed of God in the conversion of sinners and the edification of Christians, besides the faithful preaching of the Gospel and the administration of the Sacraments, we may particularly name the instruction of youth preparatory to confirmation; the catechizing of the children of the Church by the Pastor or the Sunday School; the weekly lecture for exercises of devotion; family instruction and worship; pastoral visitation to the sick; and the maintenance of a mild, but Christian discipline. These measures, although old, are not antiquated, and wherever they have been faithfully pursued, the church has been built up.[24]

So the lines were drawn, and opposing parties faced each other across the line of "measures." The criticism of their opponents might make them careful to occupy defensible positions, but from these they were not easily moved. The "new measure men" declared themselves:

> *Resolved,* That inasmuch as many of the members of the Lutheran Church in Ohio are prejudiced against what they call "new measures," therefore, resolved that this Synod recommend to all its members the importance of conforming as much as possible where practicable to the customs, manners, forms and usages of our fathers, without injuring the cause of vital Godliness—and that they attend faithfully to the long established and excellent system of catechetical lectures where it is expedient—and that they recommend uniformity in worship—and that in conducting revivals of religion we be careful to obey the injunction of the apostle:— "Let all things be done decently and in order"—and that our licentiates and young men pay particular attention to these suggestions. But that we highly approve of extraordinary efforts to awaken sinners, and bring them to the knowledge of truth as it is in Christ.[25]

Opposition to "new measures" was looked upon as antagonism to genuine piety and spirituality. W. G. Keil, preaching the presidential sermon at the meeting of the English Synod at Zanesville in 1840, affirmed:

---

[24] *Lutheran Standard,* I, 1 (September 21, 1842), p. 2.
[25] *Minutes,* English Synod of Ohio, 1842, p. 14.

Neither should we dread, as some men do, the use of extraordinary means and the wonderful effects that may follow. Some men seem to abhor what are called "new measures and revivals" more than the old monster sin, with all his noise and woe. To them a "revival preacher," so-called, with his protracted meetings, his anxious seat, and his crying falling sinners, appears to be a more disgusting, dangerous scene than the ungodly "hireling" with all his bitter opposition to vital religion.[26]

Since "experimental religion" was desirable above everything else, the "new measure men" were prepared to defend it at all costs. As they saw congregations increased and enlarged by protracted meetings, they regarded opposition to them as sheer perversity.

The answer to this problem was certain to affect parish practice in many ways. One of these was the method of transferring members from one congregation to another. If the person applying for admission came from a congregation with similar views concerning "measures," there would be no problem. But if the two congregations differed on this matter, then what should be done? The Ministerium of Pennsylvania considered the question, "Can a Lutheran minister with a good conscience admit pretended members of our church who have been confirmed by a so-called 'New Lutheran preacher' without being catechised to the celebration of the Lord's Supper without a previous examination?" The Ministerium answered, "No." That decision was reviewed in Ohio:

> If the preacher has reason to believe such privileged persons to be unsufficiently acquainted with the christian religion, your committee coincide in this opinion. But we would also ask, shall a member who has been catechised and confirmed by a so-called "OLD Lutheran preacher," who lives in open vice and is also unacquainted with experimental religion, be admitted to the Lord's Supper? We answer, NO." [27]

Among the "old measure men" the charge of unspirituality rankled. They looked upon the protracted meetings as mere occasions of "animal excitement." The emotionalism of the revivals was viewed with deep suspicion. To call the "new measures" by the adjective "Methodistic" was more than merely applying an epithet. The word represented a keen resentment against the all too successful efforts of the Methodists to win members from Lutheran adherence. Hengstenberg had noticed this, and wrote:

> Their concern to proselyte, not so much to the gospel as to their own particular sect, may be seen especially in the zeal with which they endeavor, often by unworthy artifices, to alienate members of regular German churches

[26] *Minutes* of the English Synod of Ohio, 1840, p. 29.
[27] *Minutes* of the English Synod of Ohio, 1841, pp. 15 f.

from their pastors whom they style reproachfully "hireling ministers" and to draw them into their own body as the only one that can truly provide for the salvation of their souls.[28]

If Methodist practices were thus offensive, it was rather shocking to find Lutherans adopting measures quite similar to those in use among the Methodists.

"New measure" ministers were accused of contributing to discord, faction, and schism. Editor Greenwald protested that

> the worst feature in the conduct of new measure ministers is the disposition so constantly exhibited to intrude into old and long established congregations that are served by pious and good pastors, and by low and dishonorable machinations to create disturbance and set brethren at variance. . . . Is there not room enough in this great western valley for all to operate and do good, without cutting up and dividing our little congregations that even with all their united exertions are scarcely able to support the ministrations of the Gospel among them? [29]

A third problem concerned the attitude to be taken toward the confessional writings of the Lutheran Church. During the first decade of Lutheranism in Ohio the energies of the pastors were absorbed in establishing a beachhead and enlarging it. There was little time or strength for questions of doctrine. But with the passing of the years and the developing strength of organization there came to be an increasing sense of church identity. And this was bound to raise the question of what sort of adherence to the Augsburg Confession and associated documents was to characterize Ohio Lutheran pastors and congregations.

Since the first pastors came from eastern states, the attitudes prevalent there were carried westward. Though the details have been in dispute, it is possible to interpret the evidence as showing that rationalism had seriously affected loyalty to the Confessions there. The Book of Concord had become an unknown volume. Even the Augsburg Confession and Luther's Small Catechism had largely fallen into disuse. And if they were used, their distinctive doctrines were interpreted rationally. It did not seem reasonable to accept the doctrine of the "real Presence" in the Lord's Supper. In a similar way other doctrines were rationalized. The net result was to create an indifference to doctrinal positions and creeds. It was looked upon as being typically American to have liberty in these matters.

[28] *Lutheran Observer*, XVI, 10 (March 10, 1848), p. 2.
[29] *Lutheran Standard*, II, 32 (May 31, 1844), p. 2.

For the English-speaking Lutherans in America, Gettysburg Lutheran Theological Seminary largely set the tune. The Seminary was established and supported by the General Synod and therefore had the interest of an increasing number of synods. Though small, it was the chief source of ministerial supply for congregations desiring English preaching. The theological pattern at Gettysburg was one which accepted evangelical doctrines common to Protestant denominations and those doctrines contained in the Augsburg Confession. Gettysburg graduates, trained in that viewpoint, were rather few in Ohio before 1840, but thereafter their number increased steadily.

Samuel Simon Schmucker, President of Gettysburg Seminary, was the champion of these views. Reacting against rationalism and deism, he espoused a thoroughly orthodox and biblical theology. However, he described his position as one of modified loyalty to the Augsburg Confession. The statement which he advocated for the General Synod and for Gettysburg Seminary was that the Augsburg Confession is a substantially correct interpretation of the fundamental doctrines of the Bible. In his view certain statements of the Augsburg Confession, though "substantially correct," were capable of fuller treatment which gave them a somewhat different meaning. In this way pastors could make avowals of acceptance of the Augsburg Confession while actually adopting only parts of it, as Schmucker had done in his *Elements of Popular Theology* of 1834.

During the 1840's a different attitude became prominent. It accepted the Augsburg Confession completely, and was willing to include the other documents of the Book of Concord in that approval. Persons with that viewpoint were called "Old Lutherans." They had been found for some time in the Tennessee Synod. Some German "Old Lutheran" immigrants settled in Ohio, Indiana, and Michigan. Others were the Saxons who settled in Missouri and who furnished much of the leadership of the Missouri Synod. To such persons the statements of the confessional writings were unquestionably true testimonies of the teachings of God's Word. Their voices were to be heard in the synods they joined or which they formed. They propagated their position in print. They promptly made other Lutherans in America aware of their presence.

Meanwhile a number of Schmucker's former students became dissatisfied with the position of their professor. A group of young pastors, stimulated in part by the writings of the "Old Lutherans," concluded that Schmucker's position was untenable. To their minds it was unethical to claim the name "Lutheran" while denying the doctrines distinctive of Lutheranism. A mutilated Augsburg Confession could not be a true mark of Lutherans. These views were published especially in the *Evangelical Review,* begun in 1849. The editor was William M. Reynolds, who, in another journal, made this statement:

> I seem to be called upon to define my position, am charged with having changed my views, and accepted what is denounced as "old Lutheranism," and am asked whether I am willing to stand upon the "doctrinal basis of the General Synod." I am free to confess, and rejoice to say that *I have changed my views in relation to several very important points* within the last two years. . . The result of my investigations has been to lead me to a hearty reception of the doctrines of the church as expressed in the Augsburg Confession and the Shorter Catechism which I believe to be faithful expositions of the meaning of the word of God.[30]

When Reynolds attacked the accuracy of Schmucker's account of Lutheran attitudes toward the Confessions in America, there ensued a debate in the columns of *The Lutheran Observer* running through twenty-eight issues over a period of eight months. [31] In Schmucker's opinion, all that was necessary for Lutherans in America was "absolute assent to the Bible as the only infallible rule of faith and practice, and qualified assent to the Augsburg Confession." [32] Reynolds' judgment was that this "American Lutheran system" of Schmucker was a "confessionless faith," the result of rationalism in theology.[33] Schmucker stated that his views had not changed through the years, saying of himself, "we are as near the doctrinal basis of the Augsburg Confession at present as ever we were. The doctrine of the bodily presence of the Savior in the Eucharist as taught by Luther we always regarded as unscriptural." [34] Reynolds recognized this as a denial of a doctrine of the Lutheran Church and asked, "How then can anyone who rejects the Augsburg Confession be a Lutheran?" [35] Schmucker in defense talked a great deal about liberty, about freedom from the bondage of creeds, about the right to make changes; he mentions Old Lutherans, Puseyites, Formalists, etc. And concerning the "real presence" he quoted

---

[30] *Lutheran Observer,* XVIII, 14 (April 5, 1850), p. 1.

[31] The debate was opened by Reynolds with a series of articles entitled, "Memoranda upon the Historical and Doctrinal Basis of the American Lutheran Church," beginning with the issue of September 21, 1849 (XVII, 38). It closed in the issue of May 10, 1850 (XVIII, 19).

[32] XVII, 35 (August 31, 1849), p. 2.

[33] XVII, 39 (September 28, 1849), p. 1.

[34] XVII, 45 (November 9, 1849), p. 2.

[35] XVII, 48 (November 30, 1849), p. 1.

other authors who, as he observed, "refine it away until little of its peculiarity is left." [36] Reynolds would have none of that, saying, "For such a system that usurps a name to which it has no claim, that opens the door to every form of opinion, but turns away with contempt from those which have the strongest claims upon its regard and sympathy, I confess that I cherish no very high respect." [37] Schmucker had noticed that "For about ten years past a new and very serious movement has been on foot. It was commenced by some ultra-Lutherans from Germany, gradually aided by accessions from Europe, and even by some few of our countrymen. Its aim is to elevate the whole mass of the former Symbolical books of our church in Germany to binding authority amongst us." [38] To which Reynolds boldly asserted, "If, therefore, the American church wish to remain Lutheran it must retain these Confessions." [39] The nativism which colored Schmucker's attitudes shows itself in his reply:

> We close these articles with the earnest hope that our ministers and laity will vindicate their rights as American Lutherans and will not suffer themselves to be deprived of their Protestant liberties by the influence of old Lutherans who have not yet been amongst us long enough to appreciate either our civil or religious institutions.[40]

Reynolds considered such a play to the galleries as contemptible: "Such demagogueism is unworthy of a theologian. S. S. S. very well knows that we ask no man to receive the Augsburg Confession or any article of faith in the Lutheran system unless he believes it." [41]

This controversy between two men in Gettysburg is of interest in Ohio, not only because Reynolds was soon to move to this state, but also because many readers of *The Lutheran Observer* were following the debate with great interest. This is shown by a report to *The Lutheran Observer* of an action of the English Synod:

> Whereas the parent Church of the Reformation, of which we claim to be a part, has been agitated during the last year on Symbolical and Progressive Lutheranism in this country. Having carefully examined the subject at issue which has appeared in the columns of the Observer from the pens of Prof. S. S. Schmucker, D.D., and Prof. W. M. Reynolds, we deem it our

[36] XVII, 45 (November 9, 1849), p. 2.
[37] XVII, 52 (December 28, 1849), p. 1.
[38] XVII, 46 (November 16, 1849), p. 2.
[39] XVII, 52 (December 28, 1849), p. 1.
[40] XVIII, 11 (March 15, 1850), p. 1.
[41] XVIII, 15 (April 12, 1850), p. 1.

duty to give some expression of our views as an ecclesiastical body on this exciting subject.

Resolved, That we believe the Sacred Scriptures to be a sufficient rule or guide in all matters pertaining to faith and practice.

Resolved, That we believe progressive Lutheranism to be strictly in accord with God's holy word which teaches us to grow in grace and in a knowledge of the truth.

Resolved, That we heartily approve of the spirit and course pursued by the Rev. Prof. S. S. Schmucker, D.D., in his Historical Sketches of the progress of American Lutheranism, and that we deem the view taken of the subject by him to be in accordance with the doctrinal basis of the General Synod of the Evangelical [Lutheran] Church in the United States.[42]

It proved to be exceedingly difficult to maintain peace and unity among Lutherans in Ohio. The "Old Lutherans" were thoroughly convinced of the soundness of the theology of the confessional writings. They were bound in conscience to preach and teach in accordance with them. They regarded departure from them as denials of Lutheranism. There was no way of yielding on this point. Yet the "American" party was just as strongly convinced of its position. It accepted the point of view that the keynote of the Reformation was liberty—a liberty it was determined to maintain. Between the opposing parties there seemed to be no possibility of reconciliation unless one yielded its position.

Besides these three problems there were other related perplexities. One of these had to do with catechetical instruction. Some congregations insisted upon it with all the vigor possible. Others neglected it and had to be reminded of its values. In such instances it was usually related to protracted meetings. Either the catechetical instruction was given those converted in a revival, or a protracted meeting was begun at the end of the instruction. Such instruction was less likely to be strongly doctrinal than in congregations where the catechism was unrelated to a revival.

There was also the problem of open communion. Union congregations, combining Lutheran and Reformed, had to face this issue, the outcome tending to be that the Lutheran celebration of the Lord's Supper was exclusively for the Lutherans. On the other hand, where revivals and doctrinal indifference prevailed there was a disposition to admit any Protestant to the communion. The English Synod expressed itself on this matter:

Brother Surface having stated that some of his members were opposed to his giving an invitation to members of Sister churches at communion seasons and having appealed to this synod for decision, therefore,

[42] XVIII, 25 (June 21, 1850), p. 1.

> *Resolved,* That we as a synod consider this practice not only Scriptural, but also consistent with the liberal principles of the Lutheran Church.[43]

Differences of opinion appeared also with reference to the use of Sunday. "Sabbath observance" was the phrase used among persons of the Puritan tradition. Immigrants from Germany were unlikely to have any traditional restrictions concerning what might be done on Sunday. Strict prohibitions concerning pleasurable activities on that day would seem strange to them. But the Anglicized Lutherans in Ohio were very likely to feel the pull of the religious life of their communities where Christian people observed the day very solemnly, in marked contrast to the behavior of unbelievers. Thus the English Synod declared itself:

> *Resolved,* That inasmuch as the Lord's day is desecrated to an alarming extent in our country in various ways, therefore we would earnestly recommend to the people within our synodical bounds a stricter observance of this Holy day.[44]

A similar problem was that of temperance. Here again the Anglicized Lutherans were likely to follow the pattern of the English-speaking churches in America in opposing the use of alcoholic beverages. It was expected of a truly converted Christian that he would totally abstain from such drinking. The Presbyterians and Congregationalists had adopted resolutions against intemperance and the use of intoxicating liquors. Various temperance societies had been formed to propagate the ideal of total abstinence from the use of alcoholic beverages. Books and pamphlets advocating this position were issued in large numbers. During the 1840's the movement attracted a large following. Its program found ready acceptance in congregations and Sunday Schools. The use of hard liquors, or even of beers and wines, was considered incompatible with a devout Christian life.

English-speaking Lutherans tended to accept the temperance point of view and to participate in the various societies. The very fact that the Lutheran immigrants from Germany were accustomed to the use of beer made them suspect in the eyes of the others. Thus one pastor wrote, "The German Lutherans have a congregation here, but their members are nearly all dissipated." [45] An indefensible statement of that kind reveals the intensity of the sentiment against drinking.[46] When the English Synod met in

---

[43] *Minutes,* 1840, p. 6.

[44] *Minutes,* 1839, p. 12.

[45] Letter of J. Livengood to Synod President, *Minutes* of the English Synod, 1843, p. 29.

[46] The German pastor reacted vigorously, as did also the church council, in the columns of *The Lutheran Standard* of May 31, 1844.

1837 it discussed the question, "Shall this Synod take an active part in the Temperance Reformation of the present day?" A lay delegate offered the motion "That it be considered the duty of every minister of the Gospel to aid in promoting the cause of Temperance, and that it be recommended to each member of this synod to use his influence in driving out the monster vice, Intemperance, from among the people of his charge." The Synod members indicated that they were unanimously opposed to intemperance, but they declined to commit every one to the temperance movement at that time.[47] Yet two years later the synod was willing to declare, "*Resolved,* That this Synod rejoice in the onward march of the Temperance Reformation, and that we as a body make greater efforts in our respective Pastoral Districts in the promotion of this good cause." [48]

Related to all these problems was the attitude toward *The Lutheran Observer,* which was published in Baltimore, Maryland, and edited for the most part by Benjamin Kurtz. Beginning in 1831, it was for some years the only Lutheran church paper in English in America. It attempted to serve the interest of its readers not only in church matters but also in secular and home concerns. It had articles on "Balloon Ascension" (April 4, 1834), "Locusts" (May 9, 1834), "Women at 21" (May 30, 1834), "Soap Making" (July 4, 1834), "Use of the Tomato" (August 8, 1834), "On Bathing" (August 29, 1834), and "Ladies' Pockets" (October 3, 1834).

The *Observer* was interested in the cultivation of English in Lutheran congregations. It was devoted to revivals, defending them editorially and printing a stream of reports of protracted meetings. It was in accord with Schmucker's position on accepting the Augsburg Confession; in this matter its doctrinal indifference made it favor church union. An editorial, "Union of the Evang. Lutheran and German Reformed Churches," declared: "This has ever been a favorite topic with us; as well publicly as privately have we pleaded for it, since we have had the control of the Lutheran Observer we have not hesitated to employ our editorial privilege in advocating it." [49]

From the beginning the *Observer* supported the temperance movement. During the first year it carried articles entitled, "The Difference that Whiskey Makes" (September 1, 1831), "Ardent Spirits Do Not Increase Strength" (September 15), "American Independence Secured Without Rum" (October 1), and "Rum Drinking Minister, Read This!" (November 1). Presently it was printing a "Temperance Department" in its columns.

[47] Letter by W. G. Keil, *Lutheran Observer,* V, 14 (November 24, 1837), p. 55.
[48] *Minutes of the English Synod,* 1839, p. 12.
[49] IV, 12 (November 11, 1836), p. 46.

The *Observer* had considerable circulation in Ohio. In an editorial, "The Lutherans in Ohio," it was stated that "a large proportion of the recent accessions to our list have come from Ohio." [50] Pastors acted as agents for the paper, those in Ohio listed in 1840 were: E. Greenwald of New Philadelphia, Wm. G. Keil of Senecaville, G. Leiter of Mansfield, John B. Reck of Shanesville, F. J. Ruth of Bucyrus, and J. B. Hoffman of Massilon.[51] The difficulties they had in making remittances because of unstable currency and a financial depression of the 1830's are indicated in this notice:

> The Rev. J. H. Hoffman of Wooster, Wayne County, Ohio is authorized to act as general and travelling agent for the Lutheran Observer in the State of Ohio. Brother H's receipt for money paid for the Observer will be valid; but we would request him and others if possible to make remittances in Eastern funds, as we are subjected to heavy losses by the reception of foreign notes. Yesterday we were obliged to pay a Broker 12½ per cent. to change a genuine but uncurrent Ohio bank-bill.[52]

Yet inspite of financial difficulties, and though criticized, the *Observer* had many subscribers and warm friends in Ohio. One enthusiastic correspondent wrote: "I am happy to add however that even here your paper has many and very warm advocates, and these its advocates certainly are among the most intelligent and enlightened." [53] The tone of that comment indicates something of the party spirit taking sides for the *Observer*.

On the opposite side were those who were highly critical of the paper. Because of its position both on revivals and on doctrine it was distasteful to many readers. Occasionally an article would arouse specially unfavorable reactions. Thus in 1836 there had appeared an article discussing baptism and the Campbellites. A letter to the editor said:

> It was brought up before the Synod and handled very roughly. The Rev. ——— pronounced it *ketzerisch* [heretical] and anti-Lutheran, and had not a friend of yours interfered and explained, it would have been formally condemned by an open resolution. Thus they labor here to prejudice the people against your paper.[54]

In printing the letter the editor commented, "We receive considerable support from the church in Ohio, and this support is constantly increasing. We

[50] IV, 41 (June 2, 1837), p. 163.

[51] VIII, 17 (December 25, 1840), p. 4.

[52] V. 20 (January 5, 1838), p. 3.

[53] Letter of "A Looker On" after the Synod of Ohio convention at New Lancaster, 1836. *Lutheran Observer*, III, 47 (July 15, 1836), p. 186.

[54] III, 51 (August 12, 1836), p. 203.

look forward to the period when we shall have thousands of readers in Ohio."

The *Observer* had its severe critics in Ohio. One of them wrote:

> New measures are nursed, advocated, and zealously propagated by that paper. The editor is carried away farther and farther by these extravagant measures. Some years ago he evinced much modesty, reserve and forbearance. He is assuming a bolder and more decided position. In proportion as he progresses on new measure ground, he recedes from the ancient landmarks of genuine Lutheranism.[55]

The dissatisfaction at times was expressed directly to the editor of the *Observer*, as witness this letter:

> Instead of less of that disgusting stuff about got-up Revivals, Screaming, Clapping of Hands at the Hypocrite's Bench, you have more of it every week. You and the other Revival-Boys are advocating this Rail-Road christianity according to which they become sinlessly perfect in an hour, for the same reason for which the Presbyterians have adopted it, that our people might not desert to the Methodists. . . . Alter, for the Lutheran Church's sake, the name of your paper; call it *New Measure, Fanatical, Methodistical, Anti-Lutheran Engine, or Advocate of Screaming, Falling, Clapping of Hands, of Hypocrisy and Lies.*[56]

Likely there were many others whose dislike of the *Observer* had not reached such a stage of ferment that it boiled over in such terms of exasperation. Yet the letter gave voice to a widespread dissatisfaction with the *Observer*. To meet the needs of English-speaking Lutherans in Ohio of more conservative tastes there was begun in 1842 *The Lutheran Standard.* Of its founding and progress we will speak later.

These were the perplexities of Lutherans in Ohio in the 1830's and 1840's. By that date the lines were rather well drawn. Though there were some pastors who occupied an intermediate position, for the most part they were to be found in one of two parties. On the one side were those who were devoted to the German language, to "old measures," to the Lutheran confessional writings, and to the usages concerning Sunday and beverages customary in Germany. To them the *Observer* was offensive. On the other side were those who earnestly advocated the use of English and of "new measures." They accepted but part of the Augsburg Confession. They propagated temperance, Sabbath observance, and reading the *Observer*. Each of

---

[55] Article, "Measures," signed "BETA," *Lutheran Standard,* II, 19 (March 1, 1844), p. 3.

[56] Letter with signature deleted, V, 23 (March 30, 1838).

these parties was so earnestly committed to its point of view that there was no apparent way of reconciling them.

This situation, of course, was not peculiar to Ohio, as Wyneken observed in his *Die Noth der deutschen Lutheraner in Nord America:*

> A deep split has for several years divided the whole Lutheran church and is breaking her to pieces. A large portion of the English Lutherans, although very active and zealous as is common in America, have *totally* fallen away from the faith of their fathers. . . . They attack the doctrines of our church. . . . They are the zealous defenders of "new measures" and altogether Methodistic in their mode of conversion.[57]

In most states one or the other of the two parties was largely in the majority and dominated the scene. Ohio was one of the few states in which the two sides stood facing each other with sufficient strength to contest the area. For this reason the Ohio story is particularly important.

Though the English party was the weaker of the two, it was vigorously convinced that its opponent was deficient in spirituality. Hence there was the pressing need of cultivating "vital religion." For this reason it pressed on with home missionary activity, defining it in these terms:

> When the general corruption of the church, or the wickedness of influential members, countenanced or connived at by the minister—a deplorable destitution of spiritual food for hungering souls—a bitter and obstinate persecution of English services, revivals, prayer meetings, temperance measures, etc., is the cause of the dissatisfaction, there can be no doubt of the propriety of interposing a counter influence to save these wanderers from being finally lost to the church of their fathers or their affections. . . . A sufficient number have already been lost to the church,—the world has swallowed up multitudes, and other denominations have fattened long enough upon the spoils of Lutheran families and Lutheran churches—it is time that something efficient were done to prevent these disastrous consequences.[58]

Having justified their position in such terms, the "new measure" men were satisfied in their own minds that it was proper for them to attempt to organize congregations in localities where German Lutheran congregations already existed. It was inevitable that there should be resentment and bitterness which became vocal at synodical meetings. Thus there appeared in the proceedings of the Western District of the Joint Synod this action:

> *Resolved,* That we deeply regret to hear from members of our Synod that enemies of the church are endeavoring to intrude upon their congre-

---

[57] Translation in *Lutheran Observer,* X, 49 (August 11, 1843), p. 1.
[58] *Minutes* of the English Synod, 1842, p. 20.

gations and to impede the progress of the Lutheran faith; and that we warn our church members against all such and admonish them firmly to adhere to *pure Lutheranism*.[59]

In order that this sentiment might express itself as a protest, it was further

> *Resolved,* That the officers of this synod be requested to write to the "General Synod," the "Synod of the West" and the "Independent English Lutheran Synod of Ohio" to inquire whether or not they approve of the frequent, unwarranted intrusion of some of their members into the congregation of others, there to perform ministerial functions.[60]

These irritations from the English synods were particularly aggravating to the German synods which were having difficulty on another front. The German-language newspapers published or circulating in Ohio had secular, if not actively anti-religious, attitudes. Especially was this so after the arrival of the Forty-eighters—the political refugees of the Revolution of 1848. Many papers of radical sentiment made their appearance. Religious Germans, whether Lutheran or Roman Catholic, felt themselves under severe attack. Cincinnati became a center of culture, but also of rationalist and anti-clerical propaganda. Many of the Forty-eighters were committed to ideals which included abolishing slavery, ending social injustice, and dispelling superstitions—by which they meant religion. German Lutherans, facing this vigorous anti-religious attack, felt that they were being stabbed in the back by English Lutherans who weakened the old doctrinal loyalties, and in addition were abolitionists.[61]

CONCLUSION

Though the task of becoming established and of finding a livelihood was the major concern of first- or second-generation migrants to Ohio, the relation of Lutherans to the world about them was a problem that could not be ignored. Language was the most obvious difficulty. To some degree the question of German or English was superficial. Yet it often became the core around which other problems assembled.

As long as language was not a controversial issue, the questions of "measures" or of social issues could be faced on their own merits. However,

---

59 *Lutheran Standard,* II, 40 (July 26, 1844), p. 2.

60 *Lutheran Standard,* II, 40 (July 26, 1844), p. 3.

61 Carl Wittke, *The German-Language Press in America* (Lexington, Kentucky, 1957), chapter 6.

when language became a battle line the use of German became a center around which clustered matters of doctrine and practice. This was so during the 1830's and 1840's before the influence of the Missouri Synod was strongly felt in Ohio. As we noted in the preceding chapter, Lutherans in Ohio were growing in their appreciation of Lutheran doctrine. A gradual increase in the use of English occurred at the same time, though symptoms of strife began to appear.

An example may be found in the career of Matthias Loy. As a student at the Seminary in Columbus in 1847 his impression of the house-father, Christian Spielman, and of Professor W. F. Lehmann was that "both were then more pronounced in their Lutheranism than was usual in the Ohio Synod, but by no means in antagonism to the prevailing sentiment." [62] Lehmann, besides his teaching, ministered to a German and to an English congregation. Loy gives the impression that there was doctrinal and linguistic peace at that time. Some troubles were past; others were to follow.

[62] M. Loy, *Story of My Life* (Columbus, 1905), p. 85.

6 / COMPLEXITY AND COMPETITION
1833–1855

THE 1833 CONVENTION of the Ohio Synod, which marked the beginning of its existence as a Joint Synod consisting of two districts, was an indicator of the developing complexity connected with its growth. The larger the Synod became, the more difficult it would be to maintain the unity that marked its founding. Increase in size meant also that the diverse tendencies would gain followings large enough to make separate existence possible, thus leading to division and schism. When division occurred the result was a certain rivalry and competition within the territory of the Synod of Ohio and Neighboring States which at times was unhappy and unseemly. The twenty-two years following the 1833 convention form a period which, so far as the organizational life of Lutheranism in Ohio was concerned, was marked by these two aspects of complexity and competition.

Before describing these aspects in detail, it will be well to indicate the general trend. Within the Joint Synod the growth it experienced led to the formation of other districts in addition to the first two—the Eastern and the Western. The third district to be established was an English one without geographical boundaries, formed solely on the basis of language, thus leaving all the German-speaking congregations in the Eastern or Western Districts. Later in this period a fourth district was erected with geographic boundaries and was called the Northern District. During these years it was expected that the conventions of the Joint Synod would be attended by all the pastors and delegates from all the districts. But the growing size of the Synod made this a problem. The resulting decision was that the conventions of the Joint Synod would consist only of delegated pastors and laymen. By the end of this period the conventions were designated as "Delegate Synod" meetings.

The other aspect of the period was the appearance on the territory of the Joint Synod of other synods independent of it and rivaling it. In the eastern area the persistent demands for a synod in western Pennsylvania ultimately resulted in the formation of a Pittsburgh Synod which experienced a vigorous growth. Within the State of Ohio on two occasions the majority of the English District separated from the Joint Synod. In the first instance it called itself the English Synod of Ohio, later changing its name to the East Ohio Synod because it had peaceably subdivided, the western part taking the name of Wittenberg Synod. Meanwhile another group of pastors and congregations in southwestern Ohio organized the Miami Synod. Still another group interested in union with the German Reformed organized the short-lived Tuscarawas Synod. A small number of staunchly German pastors, dissatisfied with Joint Synod policies, withdrew about the middle of this period and shared in the formation of the Evangelical Lutheran Synod of Missouri, Ohio and Other States. Within the area of the Western District of the Joint Synod, which included parts of Indiana, there was a problem due to the organization of other synods. The appearance of all these rival synods was bound to affect the policies and positions of the Joint Synod as it faced the issues before it.

THE ENGLISH SYNOD

As was noticed earlier, the Joint Synod was not actively hostile to the English language, the evidence being that an English sermon was included in convention programs, and an English translation of the minutes was published. By 1830 at least three pastors, William G. Keil, Elihu Rathbun, and James Manning, were doing their work entirely in English. During the 1833 convention at Zelienople, besides the German service and communion, there was an English service at which Charles Henkel preached and Manning and Emanuel Greenwald "administered the sacrament of the Lord's Supper to a few members in the same language."[1] Somewhat earlier the Synod had appointed a committee to prepare a liturgy in English which was adopted and ordered printed in not more than 300 copies.[2] A thousand copies of an English translation of Luther's Small Catechism were to be published at a price of twelve and one half cents each, and another thousand with the Augsburg Confession at eighteen and three quarters cents each.[3] All this points to the willingness of the Synod to meet the needs of English congregations.

The next step was the formation of an English District, or District Synod as it was sometimes called. At the 1836 convention the Joint Synod authorized the appointment of a committee to prepare a constitution for

[1] *Minutes*, p. 3.
[2] *Minutes*, 1830, p. 8.
[3] *Minutes*, 1831, pp. 14 f.

such an English body. The committee recommended the use of the Joint Synod's constitution with such slight verbal changes as would be necessary, together with five supplementary articles providing for continued connection with the Joint Synod, an exchange of delegates and of minutes, the annual payment of half the receipts into the treasury of the seminary, and adherence to the Augsburg Confession. The convention adopted the report with a further provision forbidding the English District from uniting with any other body without the approval of the Joint Synod.[4]

Before leaving the convention the pastors interested in the project got together, chose officers, and selected a time and place for the first convention of their own. By this arrangement the members convened at Somerset on Saturday, November 5, 1836, for a preparatory service, a Communion Service on Sunday, and business sessions beginning on Monday. Pastor James Manning was president.[5] Besides Manning of Annapolis there were three other ordained pastors: E. Greenwald of New Philadelphia, Charles Henkel of Somerset, and John B. Reck of Tuscarawas County. Five licensed candidates were present and a sixth was absent. These men served forty-six congregations with 1,173 communicants.

Some of the adopted rules sound a bit quaint.

> If members of the Convention shall have anything to say to the President alone, he shall not therefore go out of the convention, but such things must be done when the Convention does not sit.
> When the members give their votes they shall be simply given as *Yea* or *Nay* and no further observations shall then be admissible.[6]

The intention was that the clergy should be in control. No layman could be president or secretary. A lay delegate could vote only if his pastor was present, and even then could never vote on ministerial matters. Thus the number of lay votes could not be greater than that of the pastors.[7] The doctrinal article of the constitution read:

> The Augsburg Confession of Faith shall be the unalterable symbol of the doctrines of this Synod, and all the members of this Synod shall ex animo profess adherence to all its doctrinal articles, complete and entire, without any reservations.[8]

[4] *Minutes,* 1836, pp. 13 f.
[5] *Minutes of the Synod and Ministerium of the English Evangelical Lutheran Churches in Ohio and Adjacent States,* 1836, p. 3.
[6] *Op. cit.,* p. 20.
[7] *Op. cit.,* p. 18.
[8] *Op. cit.,* p. 24.

This beginning was peaceful and auspicious enough. But the editor of *The Lutheran Observer* was eager to aggravate any irritations or tensions between the English District and the Joint Synod. He interpreted the position of the English pastors in the German-speaking conventions of the Joint Synod as being "in effect gagged and deprived of an inestimable right of uttering their ideas on the floor of the Synod, and no wonder that they will no longer submit to such odious restrictions."[9] The article in the constitution requiring the District to remain a member of the Joint Synod he called "fetters around themselves and their successors," or in effect a failure to "maintain their liberty." He declared that the Joint Synod would have authority over the English group, whereas the General Synod was entirely an advisory body in relation to its constituent synods.[10]

There was at least one man in Ohio who shared these views. A letter signed with the initials "P.A." declared:

> As the great object was the formation of an English Synod, and that too with the full consent and unanimous permission of the German Synod, the English members then present yielded to the restrictions placed upon the powers of the new Synod; for it is was absolutely certain that on no other terms would the permission be granted. . . . We shall eventually (Providence permitting) make all things straight.[11]

This was certainly not the view of all his colleagues, but it indicated a cloud rising on the horizon. The growing trend in the English body became clearly evident in 1839. A committee reported that the General Synod "has also taken favorable notice of the English Synod of Ohio, and your committee hope that this Synod will ever cherish the most friendly feelings toward said General Synod."[12] That was a view quite at variance with that prevailing in the Joint Synod.

A further point of irritation came as a result of a resolution adopted that same year by the Joint Synod. It declared "that the members of the English Synod shall be entitled to a seat and to vote in the meetings of the Eastern and Western Districts if they choose to be present, as well as the members of those Districts at the English Synod." Since those districts easily outnumbered the English body, some members of the latter group regarded this resolution with some suspicion. A committee called it "an unusual and

[9] *Lutheran Observer,* IV, 5 (September 23, 1836), p. 19.
[10] *Op. cit.,* IV, 22 (January 20, 1837), p. 87.
[11] *Op. cit.,* IV, 27 (February 24, 1837), p. 107.
[12] *Minutes,* 1839, p. 13.

unsafe precedent." [13] It was declared that this resolution "confers privileges which this Synod will not claim and which the District Synods ought not to exercise." [14] This was adopted, Pastor Roof registering his dissent.

The next step was the adoption by the Synod of the following:

> *Resolved,* That a committee be appointed, consisting of three ordained ministers, whose duty it shall be to suggest such amendments to the constitution of our Synod at its next session as will make the document more consistent with our views and feelings as Lutherans and friends of liberty.[15]

The tone of the resolution is obviously ominous. A year later when the committee reported it recommended that the sections of the constitution binding the English Synod to the Joint Synod "should forthwith be expunged, and that our Synod and Ministerium should be *free* and independent of all others." [16] This was adopted by the necessary majority, the secretary recording that there was only one loud negative vote. With this the English Synod became independent.

But there were five pastors with their lay delegates who desired to continue their relation to the Joint Synod. They were Charles Henkel, James Manning, E. Greenwald, J. A. Roof, and Amos Bartholomew. They declared the majority action unconstitutional, and met at another location to continue as the English District of the Joint Synod. The officers elected were identical with those chosen in 1836: Manning president, Greenwald secretary, Henkel treasurer. For a short time there were accusations and counter-accusations between the two bodies, but it was obvious that the separation was permanent, and perhaps inevitable. For the continuing English District held much the same attitudes toward doctrines and practices as did the Joint Synod.

The independent English Synod, however, had a different disposition which promptly displayed itself. A report of its convention appeared in *The Lutheran Observer* signed "R"—likely J. B. Reck, the president. In his defense of the legality of the Synod's action and his statement of the reasons for independence he said,

> We as Lutherans, who have been freed from the yoke of Popery, do not feel disposed to bend our necks to any modern yoke by whomsoever invented. Again, we wish to be what we professed. This body called itself *The English Evangelical Lutheran Synod of Ohio,* while she was recognized, and in real-

13 *Op. cit.,* p. 7.
14 *Op. cit.,* p. 13.
15 *Op. cit.,* p. 14.
16 *Minutes,* 1840, p. 8.

ity was, only a *branch* pinned to the sleeve of the Germans. This the minority confessed. Moreover, too many of the German Synod are opposed to prayer meetings, temperance societies, etc.; and therefore we could not concur nor cooperate with them. Besides we wished to unite with the General Synod of the Lutheran Church, as we used her hymn book and wished to adopt her discipline, for we know of no other.[17]

As might be expected, this produced further revision of the constitution. There was dissatisfaction with the article professing adherence to the Augsburg Confession, and therefore also with the section prohibiting any alteration of that article. Thus it was said,

> The article binding us *ex animo* to profess adherence to every minutia and shade of doctrine of the Augsburg Confession of Faith is a palpable violation of the distinguishing principle of Lutheranism—"that liberty of conscience and the free exercise of private judgment in matters of religion are natural and unalienable rights of man, of which no government, civil or ecclesiastical, can deprive us." [18]

Accordingly, the constitution adopted in 1842 had no doctrinal article. In matters of practice it was affirmed that "giving an invitation to members of sister churches at communion seasons" is "not only Scriptural, but also consistent with the liberal principles of the Lutheran Church." [19] In some congregations there had been "flourishing prayer meetings, extensive awakenings and revivals of religion" during the year.[20] The constitution which was recommended to synods by the General Synod was adopted. The English Synod applied for membership in the General Synod and was accepted in 1843.

The only remaining question was that of sharing in the support, control, and patronage of the Theological Seminary in Columbus. Quite obviously the Joint Synod would not permit the seceding English Synod to share in the control of the institution. Plainly also the English Synod under such circumstances refused to share in the support and patronage. This led to a resolution in 1842 to establish a literary and theological institution of its own. Ezra Keller, a pastor in Hagerstown, Maryland, was invited to be the first professor. In the summer of 1844 he began the instruction of four students of theology at Wooster. The next spring the institution received a charter under the name Wittenberg College with a theological and a

---

[17] *Lutheran Observer*, VIII, 35 (April 30, 1841).
[18] *Minutes* of the English Synod, 1841, p. 8.
[19] *Op. cit.*, 1840, p. 6.
[20] *Ibid.*, p. 8.

collegiate department, and was located at Springfield.[21] With the founding of this institution the separation of the English Synod from the Joint Synod was complete.

The reasons why there arose within the Joint Synod a group of pastors with a different outlook are various. In 1840 there were seventeen pastors in the English Synod and five in the English District. Biographical data is lacking on most of these men but where it is available the indication is that these pastors were of a third or fourth generation in America. Marcus L. Hanson has advanced the thesis that the second generation in America struggles to discard every taint of foreignness by becoming completely Americanized, but the third generation seeks to recover valuable elements of its European heritage.[22] This is true if the struggle for Americanization has ended successfully in the second generation. The pastors of the English Synod, though thoroughly Anglicized in their own persons, found themselves in a continuing struggle over this matter in the Joint Synod. Their continual reference to it was as the "German" Synod. They could not think of the other pastors simply as fellow-Lutherans whose use of another language was quite incidental and unimportant. Language was a battle line. In this they were influenced by the "nativism" of the time which colored the columns of *The Lutheran Observer*.[23] In contrast, the viewpoints of "native Americanism" were specifically rejected by the Eastern District of the Joint Synod.[24]

It would seem unjustified to think of the attitudes of the English Synod simply as importations from the East. Eleven of the seventeen pastors in 1840 had received their ministerial training and licensure or ordination in Ohio. One of these was Abraham Weills who was the first graduate of the Theological Seminary in Columbus, and another was Andrew Kuhn who had studied there also. The others had studied theology privately under the direction of pastors of the Joint Synod. Six of the seventeen had studied in the East before coming to Ohio. F. J. Ruth (as was the case also with E. Greenwald) was born in Frederick, Maryland, and studied theology there under David F. Schaeffer, a conservative for his day. Four others, Solomon Ritz, George Leiter, John H. Hoffman, and Henry Bishop, had

---

[21] See H. H. Lentz, *A History of Wittenberg College 1845–1945* (Springfield, 1946) and W. D. Allbeck, *Theology at Wittenberg* (Springfield, 1945).

[22] Cf. Sydney E. Ahlstrom, "The Lutheran Church and American Culture: A Tercentenary Retrospect," *Lutheran Quarterly*, IX, 4 (November 1957), pp. 336 f.

[23] See for example, the issue of November 15, 1844; and George M. Stephenson, *The Founding of the Augustana Synod 1850–1860*, p. 26.

[24] *Lutheran Standard*, III, 10 (February 12, 1845), p. 3.

been students at Gettysburg Theological Seminary under S. S. Schmucker. And John B. Reck had studied under Schmucker before he was a professor. The predominance of Ohio-trained men certainly indicates that responsibility for the views of the English Synod cannot be laid at the door of the Gettysburg Seminary. Instead, it may be affirmed that these were the views of Anglicized Lutherans in both East and West at that time.

The position of the English Synod can be understood in the light of several circumstances of that day. First is the fact that during the first part of the century indifference to doctrine was combined with a popular rationalism to produce a spirit which had no taste for theological strictness. Especially in areas recently emerged from frontier status there was a distinct preference for a common-sense religion. The chief concern was conversion and morals. A second fact is this, that all the Lutheran magazines published in English before 1842 fostered the broad, tolerant, independent spirit which the English Synod shared. One hunts in vain in the publications of that time printed in English for any other point of view. A third fact is the accommodation of Anglicized Lutherans to certain of the denominations around them, even to the extent of joining them. For example, Pastor John Stough's daughter, Mary, married Martin Hester whose family became Methodists and among whose descendants are a number of Methodist ministers.[25] A friendly attitude toward people of other denominations therefore needs no special explanation when it is found among members of the English Synod.

MIAMI SYNOD

The number of English-speaking Lutheran congregations in southwestern Ohio continued to increase. The pastors of some of them were members of the English Synod. Therefore it was suggested that a committee be appointed "to devise a plan to divide this Synod and propose a boundary." [26] A year later the proposed plan was approved, a notice was issued, and an organizing convention was held at Xenia, October 16 and 17, 1844. The officers were C. F. Schaeffer, president, D. P. Rosenmiller, secretary, and John Surface, treasurer. The Synod was organized with eight pastors, two licensed candidates, and two lay delegates. The two candidates and three of the pastors had been members of the English Synod. Two others

---

[25] See Martin M. Hester, *History and Genealogy of the Descendants of John Lawrence Hester and Godfrey Stough* (Norwalk, Ohio, 1905).

[26] *Minutes* of the English Synod, 1843, p. 24.

came from the Joint Synod, and three from the Synod of the West.[27] An absent candidate from the Maryland Synod petitioned for inclusion.

The Miami Synod attempted to occupy a position between the attitudes of the Joint Synod and of the English Synod, though it was actually much closer to the latter. Typical of this attempt is this passage from the report of President Rosenmiller in 1848:

> The Miami Synod was formed upon the basis of *mutual concession for the sake of mutual good-will in reference to measures.* Let this always be kept in view, and let the Miami Synod remain as it has been heretofore, the Olive Branch held up between the two ultra parties which have so frequently threatened to rend in pieces our ancient and beloved Zion.[28]

This middle position was to be one of inclusiveness and toleration, the "adoption of strictly Lutheran and American principles." [29] It was the intention to conserve a distinctive Lutheranism and at the same time to escape the reputation of foreignness. The Synod "shall not be fettered by foreign languages, usages or opinions, but shall sanction those which, while they conform to the Word of God and the spirit of our church, are likewise adapted to the circumstances of our native country." [30]

A doctrinally conservative pressure was applied by C. F. Schaeffer of Lancaster and his cousin, D. P. Rosenmiller of Dayton, during the few years they were members of the Synod. Schaeffer, who for three years had been a professor in the Theological Seminary at Columbus, was sympathetic to doctrinal Lutheranism, and by the same token was dissatisfied with the theology of S. S. Schmucker at Gettysburg. It was in Schaeffer's report as president that there occurs this passage:

> We promptly and gladly declare our firm adherence to the Augsburg Confession of faith as a successful exhibition of divine truth. We acknowledge the unrivalled excellence of Luther's Small Catechism and the blessed results arising from a judicious and faithful course of catechetical lectures. . . . We agreed to pronounce our unqualified disapprobation, on the one hand. of all that tends to substitute mere formality for enlightened Christian zeal, . . .

---

[27] A. J. Imhoff, *History of the Evangelical Lutheran Synod of Miami* (Philadelphia, cir. 1894), p. 10. is inaccurate on this point. From the Synod of the West came A. Reck, J. Crigler, and J. Krack; from the Joint Synod D. P. Rosenmiller and C. F. Schaeffer; from the English Synod Ezra Keller, J. Surface, George Sill and candidates J. Lehman and H. Baker. A. J. Weddle of the Maryland Synod was absent. Keller had transferred from the Maryland Synod to the English Synod of Ohio, but John Surface had not transferred to the Synod of the West as Imhoff states.

[28] *Proceedings*, 1848, p. 5.

[29] *Proceedings*, 1845, p. 9.

[30] *Ibid.*

and, on the other hand, of all that promotes mere animal excitement or fanaticism.[31]

In comparison with some extremists in the General Synod, the Miami Synod through the years considered itself quite restrained and moderate. But the sympathy with "new measures" which marked the men who had come from the English Synod was reinforced by the young pastors who were graduating from Wittenberg and Gettysburg. There can be no doubt that the Miami Synod shared in the attitudes of the other Anglicized synods in the United States. Yet from the beginning it cultivated this tradition of moderation which was useful in restraining its more liberal members.

In adopting for itself the constitution recommended by the General Synod it approved a preliminary paragraph stating: "We believe that the Scriptures of the Old and New Testaments are our only and infallible rule of faith and practice; we receive the Augsburg Confession of faith and Luther's Smaller Catechism as writings in which the doctrines of the word of God are set forth in a manner substantially correct." [32] This form of statement was typical of the General Synod usage, particularly in the questions asked of candidates for ordination. The phrase "substantially correct" was to be a source of future difficulty. Some members of the Synod believed that the Augsburg Confession was "correct" without any qualification. The Synod's debate on this matter will be described in a later chapter.

WITTENBERG SYNOD

Another subdivision of the English Synod occurred in 1847 when permission was given the pastors in northwestern Ohio to form a new synod. The dividing line was to run from Cleveland through Ashland and Mount Vernon to Springfield, that is, to the National Highway which was the northern boundary of the Miami Synod. On or northwest of that line were nine ordained pastors and six licensed candidates of the English Synod. Eight of these fifteen men were present at the English Synod convention at Washingtonville when permission to subdivide was given. They at once got together—the date was June 8—and organized as a synod. The officers chosen were F. J. Ruth, president, J. Livengood, secretary, and J. Seidle, treasurer. It was voted to adopt the same form of constitution as that of the Miami Synod but without its preamble containing a statement of adherence

31 *Op. cit.*, p. 10.
32 *Proceedings*, 1845, p. 29.

to the Augsburg Confession. It was voted also to join the General Synod.[33]

The reasons for the formation of a new synod were stated for the readers of *The Lutheran Observer* by the secretary, Pastor Livengood. He was quite eager to affirm that the division involved no unpleasant animosities. It was not a schism. Instead, there were two practical reasons. The first was that the distance to conventions of the English Synod was great enough to involve too much expense and time for the pastors and delegates of northwestern Ohio. The second reason was that the English Synod had become too large to be entertained by many of the small congregations which desired to be host to synodical conventions. The newly organized small Wittenberg Synod would remove these difficulties.[34] These reasons, however, soon lost their validity as the Synod began to make rapid growth.

In temper and outlook the Wittenberg Synod was no different from the English Synod. It took the same position on revivals and other practices. It shared the same view of Lutheran doctrine. It supported the same policies at Wittenberg College. It was merely a territorial division of English Lutheranism in Ohio, and had no other distinguishing characteristic.

These three synods, The English Ohio, the Miami, and the Wittenberg, represent a permanent separation from the Lutheranism of the districts of the Joint Synod. The two kinds of Lutheranism occupied the same geographic area, often even the same localities. Occasionally there were tensions and a lack of good will. Rival congregations were erected in some places. The separation was of the sort that left no hope of reunion, no points of cooperation, to say nothing of fellowship, no bridges to conversation and mutual understanding. Some pastors in the Joint Synod hid their hostility to the English language under a profession of doctrinal convictions, accusing the English synods of being un-Lutheran. Many of the pastors of these English synods considered the Joint Synod un-American; they concealed their indifference to Lutheran doctrine under a zeal for evangelizing the multitudes of people outside the church. Many years were to pass before there was a change in the temper of these synods.

TUSCARAWAS SYNOD

The disposition to subdivide and to form small independent synods was not limited to the English-speaking segment but was found among the

---

[33] There were no published minutes of the Wittenberg Synod before 1850. An account of the organizing convention appeared in *Lutheran Observer*, XIV, 45 (July 9, 1847). The action of the English Synod was reported in the same journal a week earlier.

[34] *Ibid.*

German-speaking party as well. An evidence of this was the short-lived Tuscarawas Synod. It was formed by members of the Synod of Michigan living in northern Ohio, with the consent of the parent body. The organizing convention was held in Massillon, July 2, 1848. Pastor J. M. Steiner of Massillon was chosen president, and Pastor W. B. Rally of Mt. Eaton, Wayne County, was secretary.[35] From the notice of the second convention a year later it appears that the Synod consisted of five pastors serving congregations in Holmes, Coshocton, Wayne, Stark, and Medina Counties.[36]

A reorganization took place at the third convention held on Trinity Sunday in May, 1850, at Hayesville whereby the Synod took the name *Deutscher Evangelischer Kirchenverein in Ohio,* a title sometimes translated "German Evangelical Church Association" or simply "Evangelical Church Union." [37] The constitution was signed by the following pastors, though it is not clear that all of them attended the meeting: Augustus G. Georgii, W. B. Rally, John M. Steiner, John F. C. Haase, Sebastian Doeppenschmidt, Frederic W. Weiskotten, John P. Conradi, Holm G. Holm, Mathias Gallster, and John G. Abele—such were the spellings.

Its object was a union of the Lutheran and the Reformed Churches. As was the case in the Union Church in Germany, Scripture was to be doctrinally explained by the Augsburg Confession and Luther's Catechism or the Heidelberg Catechism. Where there was disagreement in doctrine simply the words of Scripture were to be used, each party having the freedom to interpret texts according to his confessional preference.

Soon afterwards this body became part of *Der Deutsche Evangelische Kirchenverein des Westens,* an organization begun in 1840. It ultimately was called the Evangelical Synod of North America.

In the eyes of the Joint Synod of Ohio and its English District this reorganization of the Tuscarawas Synod into the *Kirchenverein* was an abandonment of the Lutheran name and faith. The Lutheran bodies disapproved "a mere external Union where there is a want of internal union." This attempt at union did not reduce the number of church bodies in Ohio, but simply increased the number by one. Moreover, the Joint Synod accused the *Kirchenverein* of proselyting.[38]

[35] *Lutheran Standard,* VI, 62 (August 2, 1848), p. 3.

[36] *Op. cit.,* VII, 10 (July 4, 1849).

[37] *Op. cit.,* VIII, 20 (November 6, 1850). Carl E. Schneider, *The German Church on the American Frontier* (St. Louis, 1939), pp. 391 f. *The Minutes of the English Evangelical Lutheran* (District) *Synod and Ministerium of Ohio and Adjacent States,* 1850, pp. 11 f., give the fullest summary of the minutes of the Hayesville convention.

[38] *Minutes* of the English District, 1850, p. 12. *Minutes* of the Joint Synod, 1851, pp. 21 f.

The brief existence of the Tuscarawas Synod (named likely for the river valley near the center of its area) pointed up a problem confronting the Joint Synod. A considerable, though undetermined, number of its congregations were joined to those of the German Reformed Church in the owning and maintaining of church buildings and cemeteries. The Tuscarawas Synod represented the threat that such dual congregations might actually combine to form a unity which was neither Lutheran nor Reformed, but simply Union. The basic tie in such instances was the German language, therefore the English synods were less troubled by this problem. To meet the issue the Joint Synod sought to strengthen the confessional loyalty of its parishes. In 1850 its Western District declared itself against the continuance or the further organization of joint Lutheran and Reformed congregations. A union congregation with no Lutheran identity at all was intolerable.

Yet union was considered the ideal church condition by many emigrants from Germany who had been members of union churches there. Some of the pastors in Ohio and neighboring states had been sent there by union missionary societies in Europe. As early as 1834 two missionaries from the Basel Society, John Gerber and George W. Metzger, were in Ohio ministering to Swiss settlers.[39] These two men did not join the Lutheran Synod. Later from Basel came John M. Steiner to the Canal Dover and Massillon area, and Charles F. Besel to the Benton area in Holmes County, both of whom were in the Tuscarawas Synod.[40] Frederick W. Weiskotten at Miltonsburg had come from the Mission House of the Rhenish Missionary Society in Barmen, Germany. He was ordained by the Tuscarawas Synod in 1849. He participated in the organization of the *Kirchenverein* though later he became a member of the Lutheran Ministerium of New York.[41]

Four missionaries of the Hanau Society (Hessian Society for German Protestants in North America) came to Ohio and became members of the Joint Synod. They were J. G. Abele, Charles Sebastian Doeppenschmidt, John Philip Conradi, and Adolph Conradi.[42] Abele, licensed by the Western District of the Joint Synod in 1847, was pastor at Canal Dover. He asked to be dismissed because he favored union congregations, as did the society which sent him to America. His request was granted. He joined in organiz-

[39] Schneider, *op. cit.*, p. 50.

[40] *Lutheran Standard*, V, 22 (December 22, 1847); VII, 10 (July 4, 1849). Schneider, *op. cit.*, p. 487; footnote p. 161.

[41] *Lutheran Standard*, VII, 20 (November 21, 1849). Schneider, *op. cit.*, pp. 391, 395.

[42] Concerning the Hanau Society see Schneider, *op cit.*, footnote p. 365.

ing the *Kirchenverein,* was ordained by it, and was elected its secretary.[43] Doeppenschmidt, pastor at Trenton and later at Stone Creek, was licensed by the Joint Synod in 1848. He was ordained at Massillon, July 15, 1849, by a committee of the Tuscarawas Synod and joined the *Kirchenverein.*[44] J. P. Conradi, who moved from Wooster to Loudenville in 1847, had been licensed by the Joint Synod in 1845 and was ordained by it three years later. He, too, was a charter member of the *Kirchenverein.*[45] Adolph Conradi, whose relation to John Philip is not clear, was both licensed and ordained with him by the Joint Synod the same years. He was pastor at Hamilton until 1847 when he went to New Bremen, where he died of cholera August 10, 1849.[46]

Five other pastors in the Tuscarawas Synod or the *Kirchenverein* had Lutheran connections. Augustus B. Gockelen was president of the Tuscarawas Synod in 1849 while pastor at Malaga, but later he joined the Western District of the Joint Synod while pastor at St. Mary's. Later he was pastor at Wapakoneta where he died April 30, 1853.[47] A second man was Matthias Galster who, strangely enough, was licensed in 1845 and ordained in 1848 by the English Synod. He was pastor in Stark County and later at Canal Dover. He, too, was in the *Kirchenverein.*[48] John F. C. Haase, who had been a professor in Eisenach, Germany, was ordained in 1848 by Steiner and Rally, a committee of the Michigan Synod, to be pastor of a Lutheran and Reformed congregation at Canal Fulton. He went with the *Kirchenverein.*[49] H. G. Holm, who had come from Schleswig, Germany, was ordained by Gockelen and Rally, president and secretary of the Tuscarawas Synod, in 1849. Though he signed the *Kirchenverein* constitution he promptly turned to the Western District of the Joint Synod where he was a member until his death in 1881. His address was Buena Vista, Tuscarawas County.[50] W. B. Rally had been a member of the Ministerium of Pennsylvania.

[43] *Lutheran Standard,* VII, 18 (October 23, 1850). *Minutes* of the Western District, 1847, p. 14; 1850, pp. 13, 27. Schneider, *op. cit..* pp. 391. 486.

[44] *Minutes* of the Joint Synod, 1848, p. 37. *Lutheran Standard,* VII, 14 (August 29, 1849). Schneider, *op. cit.,* p. 392.

[45] *Lutheran Standard,* V, 4 (April 14, 1847). *Minutes* of the Joint Synod, 1848, p. 26. Schneider, *op. cit.,* p. 391. He was Lutheran again in 1867.

[46] *Minutes* of the Joint Synod, 1848, p. 26. *Lutheran Standard,* VII, 14 (August 29, 1849).

[47] *Lutheran Standard,* VII, 10 (July 4, 1849); VIII, 9 (June 19, 1850). *Minutes* of the Western District, 1853, pp. 22 f.

[48] *Minutes* of the English Synod, 1845, p. 18. *Lutheran Observer,* XVI, 21 (May 26, 1848). Schneider, *op. cit.,* pp. 391 f., 486.

[49] *Lutheran Standard,* VI, 9 (June 21, 1848). *Minutes* of the English District, 1850, pp. 11 f.

[50] *Minutes* of the Joint Synod, 1851, p. 41.

There were other pastors whom the Joint Synod was able to keep within the Lutheran fellowship in spite of influence from union missionary societies in Germany. Two such men with training in the *Rauhes Haus* near Hamburg were J. G. Theiss and J. M. Schladermundt. Theiss, in applying for admission to the Western District, presented a letter of recommendation from Wichern. Licensed in 1849 and ordained three years later, he continued in that District until his death in 1886.[51] The same can be said for Schladermundt who was licensed in 1843 and ordained four years later. While pastor in Springfield he combined Lutheran and Reformed adherents in St. Johns Church.[52] He died in 1874.

The list of pastors in the Joint Synod who had been sent to America by societies not strictly Lutheran, and who were in the Lutheran body rather than the union *Kirchenverein,* could be further extended. Other societies with emissaries in Ohio were the Bremen, the St. Chrischona, and the Gossner (Berlin). In some instances a society combined its interest in America with its foreign mission work. In other instances it was a distinct society for work among emigrants, the German Protestants in North America. The relation of these societies to Lutheran synods in America has not been adequately studied.

It is important to observe the problem which the Tuscarawas Synod and the *Kirchenverein* presented, for it was to be prominent and persistent in decisions on confessional loyalty to be made by the Joint Synod. In most of the historical accounts the confessional Lutheranism of the Joint Synod has been compared only to the weak confessionalism of the English synods. Part of the picture also was the influence and rivalry of union congregations; for the *Kirchenverein* increased in strength in Ohio. Back of this was the practical problem of maintenance and survival. Population was chiefly rural and the congregations were small; therefore a union congregation seemed to have a better chance of being large enough to provide needed funds.

W. B. Rally favored the *Kirchenverein* because the Lutheran synod "increasingly pressed toward sworn adherence to the Formula of Concord in all it declarations, so that the little congregations are divided and a preacher must serve eight to twelve congregations in order to secure sufficient livelihood." [53] Some pastors and congregations therefore would find the pressure for union too strong to resist. Lutheran congregations, in self

[51] *Lutheran Standard,* VII, 22 (December 19, 1849).
[52] *Lutheran Standard,* V, 9 (June 23, 1847). Schneider, *op. cit.,* p. 146.
[53] Schneider, *op. cit.,* p. 391, footnote.

defense if for no other reason, were impelled to examine and affirm their Lutheran convictions, even if at considerable cost to themselves.

SYNOD OF THE WEST

In the course of time it became apparent that the "West" was becoming much larger than the Joint Synod of Ohio, even with its title of "and Neighboring States," could claim or serve. Pastors settled in southern Indiana, Kentucky, and Tennessee where they were too far from the center of Joint Synod activity. A summons was sent out for a meeting at Jeffersontown, Kentucky, to be held October 11, 1834, for the purpose of organizing a synod. But only three clerical and three lay delegates appeared and action was postponed for a year.[54] "We could not organize a synod in consequence of not having ministers enough present. We have made arrangements to form a synod next October." Jacob Crigler was chairman and W. Jenkins secretary of this unsuccessful meeting.[55]

A year later there was success. Convening in Louisville, Kentucky, the delegates met for worship on Sunday, October fourth, in the Methodist Protestant Church. The business session began on Monday. Five pastors were present: Jacob Crigler of Boone County, Kentucky, W. Jenkins of Bedford County, Tennessee, George Yeager of Jefferson County, Kentucky, P. Rizer of Floyd County, Indiana, and John J. Lehmanowsky of Rush County, Indiana. With them were four lay delegates. Another pastor, D. Scherer, wrote explaining his absence and asking to be included. Crigler was the president, Jenkins the secretary, and Yeager the treasurer.[56] The name "Synod of the West" was that which was used.

The Joint Synod received word of the formation of this new Lutheran synod on its southwest border and took notice of it in a friendly way. It appointed Charles Henkel to be its representative at the next convention of the Synod of the West to be held on Boone County, Kentucky.[57] There may have been a desire to establish a friendly relationship in view of the possibility that the Western District would have boundary problems with the Synod of the West in Indiana, or even in Cincinnati.

---

[54] *Minutes* of the General Synod, 1835, p. 7. Microfilm of manuscript Minutes.

[55] *Lutheran Observer,* November 14, 1834, p. 47. The *Lutheran Cyclopedia* (St. Louis, 1954), p. 1126, is mistaken at this point.

[56] *Lutheran Observer,* III, 12 (November 13, 1835), p. 47. Microfilm of manuscript Minutes.

[57] *Minutes* of the Joint Synod, 1836, p. 8.

Because of illness Charles Henkel was unable to attend the 1836 convention of the Synod of the West.[58] Since he was a member of the English
District formed that year, and since the bilingual Synod of the West had
a preference for English, it was between these two bodies that friendly relations were cultivated. At the first there was a bit of a strain because an Ohio
pastor named N. B. Little, on being welcomed by the Synod of the West,
was reported to have accused the Ohio men of believing that "baptism is
regeneration." The English District repudiated the charge, saying it believed
baptism was simply a means of regeneration.[59] The Synod of the West
disavowed the accusation and declared its desire to have a friendly relation
with the Lutherans in Ohio.[60]

When the majority of the English District became the English Synod in
1840 it was with the latter body that the Synod of the West continued
friendly dealings. This was in keeping with its spirit and character. Its
proceedings were published in English, even though an equal number of
were printed in a German translation.[61] The constitution it adopted followed closely the form recommended by the General Synod. Its constitution had no doctrinal article. It did not even have a doctrinal question for
candidates for ordination such as the General Synod form had.[62] Doctrinally
these synods were much alike. The English Synod declared that "We entertain for our beloved brethren of that Synod sentiments of profound respect
and fraternal affection." [63]

Beyond this there was the suggestion that the two synods work together
in some common enterprises. In 1841 the English Synod had before it four
proposals for joint action with the Synod of the West. First was cooperation
in supporting a mission in Cincinnati for a year. Pastor A. Reck was willing
to be the missionary for a salary of at least $400. Second was a proposal to
start publishing a paper to be called the *Western Lutheran Observer*. On
both these items the English Synod voted to recommend both projects to its
congregations, but it took no action committing it to definite financial obligations. A third item was an invitation to join in establishing a Theological
Seminary of the West, and fourth concerned an exchange of delegates as
a mark of Christian Friendship.[64]

[58] *Minutes,* Synod of the West, 1836, p. 3.
[59] *Minutes* of the English Synod, 1836, p. 8.
[60] *Op. cit.,* 1838, p. 9.
[61] *Minutes,* Synod of the West, 1836, p. 5.
[62] *Op. cit.,* pp. 14 f.
[63] *Minutes* of the English Synod, 1842, p. 9.
[64] *Op. cit.,* 1841, p. 14.

The fourth item was adopted as a practice already in vogue, since J. J. Lehmanowsky was present representing the Synod of the West. But on the third item it was

> *Resolved,* That it gives us unfeigned pleasure to hear that the Synod of the West is about erecting a Theological Seminary on the manual labor system within their bounds, but that we cannot see our way clear to co-operate with them because they exclude us from participating in the government of said institution and because its constitution shall not be subject to alteration after its final adoption.[65]

A year later word came from the Synod of the West that it was willing to accept the conditions indicated. But for the second time the English Synod declined on the ground that an institution was needed in Ohio. Occupying as it did chiefly northeastern Ohio, the English Synod had Wooster in mind as the place of its institution, and as a result could not consider feasible a place in southern Indiana or Kentucky. Out of this came the resolution which led to the founding of Wittenberg College in which the Synod of the West was invited to share on the identical terms it had last proposed.[66]

In reality the Synod of the West was not in a position to accept the invitation. Because it covered a large territory involving five states, it had to face the fact of subdivision as soon as its growth made such a thing possible. Morever, there were tensions between the German- and the English-speaking pastors. Distance was the main problem. In 1843, in response to a petition from three pastors, a committee presented a resolution favoring subdivision into three synods: the Synod of the West occupying the State of Indiana; the Synod of Illinois which would include congregations in Missouri also; and a Synod of Cincinnati for churches in Kentucky, Tennessee, and southwestern Ohio. However, action was postponed until the next convention.[67] The next year action was deferred again, but by that time the members in southwestern Ohio were sharing in the organization of the Miami Synod. Thus when action finally was taken in June, 1846, the division occurred as proposed, except that instead of a Synod of Cincinnati there was a Synod of the South West. At this same convention it was resolved that the "Literary and Theological Institute" of the three synods should be in Illinois.[68]

After 1846 there is no record of contacts between the Synod of the West and those in Ohio. A few years later it had ceased to exist, its members

[65] *Op. cit.,* p. 15.
[66] *Op. cit.,* 1842, p. 9.
[67] *Minutes,* Synod of the West, 1843, pp. 17, 22.
[68] *Lutheran Observer,* XIII, 45 (July 3, 1846).

joining other synods in the areas in which they were located. It failed because it had attempted to be an inclusive synod both territorially and linguistically. Such an effort was possible when the Ohio Synod began, having the entire field to itself. By 1850 this possibility had disappeared. The Synod of the West, when reduced in territory to the State of Indiana, found itself more constantly in competition with other Lutheran synods in the state. It suffered the schismatic loss of its most conservative Lutheran German-speaking pastors. It had a continual conflict with the unionism of the *Kirchenverein des Westens* and of the followers of Alexander Campbell. In addition to all this was the indifference to religion, the worldliness, and sometimes the rationalism of the populace.

OTHER SYNODS IN INDIANA

Along the pathways of the Ohio River settlers came to Indiana from the eastern and southern states. Missionary tours were made in the state by men sent by the Ministerium of Pennsylvania and the North Carolina Synod, and later by the Ohio and the Tennessee Synods. Likely the first Lutheran pastors to make preaching trips into Indiana were from southwestern Ohio—Samuel Mau, Andrew Simon, and John Caspar Dill. But the first settled pastor was John Lewis Markert who was a member first of the North Carolina and later of the Tennessee Synod. In the course of the years other Tennessee Synod pastors arrived, bringing with them a staunch loyalty to the Lutheran Confessions and a fierce antagonism to the General Synod. They retained their connections with the Tennessee Synod just as the Ohio pastors in Indiana did with their synod.

The next step was to form a new synod. On August 15, 1835, six pastors and seven laymen met at St. John's Church in Johnson County and organized the Evangelical Lutheran Synod of Indiana. The ordained pastors were John L. Markert, Christian Moretz, and Eusebius S. Henkel; the ordained deacons were Abraham Miller, Conrad F. Picker, and Ephraim R. Conrad. Picker and Conrad served congregations in Missouri. The three deacons were ordained as pastors at this convention. No officers are indicated, but the constitution of the Tennessee Synod was the form adopted.[69]

The Indiana Synod, like its Tennessee parent, continued the feud with the General Synod. It was convinced that the General Synod was a pernicious development in the Lutheranism of America. There could be no affiliation or compromise with such a general body, but only continued

[69] Martin L. Wagner, *op. cit.*, p. 71. Socrates Henkel, *op. cit.*, p. 88.

antagonism and separation. These views were expressed formally in convention:

> *Resolved,* That said General Synod is a human invention, that many of the doctrines and practices thereof are contrary to the Bible and the ancient usages and practices of the Lutheran Church; we therefore warn every Lutheran in the United States to be aware of them and not to be entangled with any of their unholy doctrines and practices; and we earnestly entreat such as have been deceived to shake off the shackles.[70]

This resolution was followed by an extended "Expose of the General Synod" filling pages nine to thirty. This was not a fair, objective evaluation but a polemic which portrayed the General Synod's weaknesses both genuine and imaginary.

The Synod of the West raised the question of the possible union of the two synods.[71] Correspondence produced the appointment of committees to confer on the matter. The Synod of Indiana showed interest in the project and formulated conditions for union. A report to this effect was made to the Synod of the West which recorded its reaction as follows:

> *Resolved,* That we cordially reciprocate the good feeling of the Indiana Synod towards this as evidenced by their earnest desire for union; but that however desirable such union may be, it is utterly impracticable, if such sentiments as the following, contained in a letter from Rev. A. Miller, dated June 18th, 1840, addressed to the corresponding committee of the Synod of the West, have general prevalence among the members of the Indiana Synod, viz.: 1. "That the Synod of the West rescind the resolution which attaches it to the General Synod. 2. That we oppose the falsely called benevolent societies of the present day—such as Tract, Temperance, Missionary, Bible, and a host of such like *fantastical* societies"—and be regarded by them as an unconditional proviso.[72]

With this action the efforts at union were dropped.

With the changing membership of the Indiana Synod there came to leadership a pastor named Ephraim Rudisill who began propagating the doctrine of the destruction of the wicked rather than their resurrection and judgment. When he and some associates in 1848 attempted to get Synod approval of "Destructionism" the result was confusion and a minority seceded. Two years later he was able to convince the continuing majority that

---

[70] *Proceedings of the Seventh Session of the Evangelical Lutheran Synod of Indiana,* 1842, p. 8.

[71] *Minutes,* Synod of the West, 1836, p. 4.

[72] *Journal of the Sixth Annual Session of the Evangelical Lutheran Synod of the West,* 1840, p. 14.

he did not hold the heretical doctrines with which he was charged by the minority. Meanwhile Eusebius Henkel had espoused Universalist views and had demitted the ministry for two years. These doctrinal disturbances were a severe injury to the Synod, though it continued until 1859 when it disbanded and reorganized under the name "Union Synod of the Evangelical Lutheran Church." [73]

The minority seceding party consisted of two pastors, Abraham and David Miller, and a licensed candidate, John F. Lautenschlager, whom they ordained. This "Miller Faction," claiming the name and rights of the original Indiana Synod, found itself involved in law suits which uniformly were decided in its favor. But the cost of the litigation exhausted its resources, so that by 1851 it had ceased to exist.[74]

Another body, the Indianapolis Synod, made its appearance about the same time. When the Synod of the West made its three-way division in 1846, the body in Indiana suffered the loss of four conservative German pastors who disapproved of the General Synod. These men, John F. Isensee, John George Kunz, F. W. Wier, and J. J. Meissner, held their first meeting at Indianapolis, September 3, 1846. Isensee and Kunz were Gossner missionaries sent to America in 1840. The Synod affirmed its loyalty to the Lutheran Confessions.[75] At the second and third conventions the formal organization of the Synod was completed. Soon, however, some of the pastors joined the Missouri Synod and the others united with the Southern District of the Joint Synod of Ohio. In 1852 the Synod ceased to exist.[76]

Within the Miami Synod the pastors and congregations in Indiana constituted the Wabash Conference. With the Synod's consent[77] this group organized itself as the Olive Branch Synod at a convention held in Indianapolis, October 28 to 30, 1848. Four ordained pastors, Hugh Wells, A. H. Myers, Samuel McReynolds, and Samuel Sayford, and two licensed candidates, Franklin Templin and Obadiah Brown, together with one layman, formed the original membership.[78] The Synod, in keeping with its antecedents, joined the General Synod in 1850. Its official contacts and exchange of visitors were with synods of that national body rather than with synods in Indiana hostile to it.

[73] M. L. Wagner, op. cit., pp. 148-160, 177.
[74] Wagner, op. cit., pp. 144-147.
[75] Report in Der Lutheraner, III, 11, cited by H. M. Zorn, "Beginnings in Indianapolis," Concordia Theological Monthly, V, 25 f. (January, 1934). Schneider, op. cit., p. 185.
[76] Wagner, op. cit., p. 104.
[77] Proceedings of the Miami Synod, 1848, p. 11.
[78] Proceedings of the Olive Branch Synod, 1848, p. 4.

Later there was another synod formed when some pastors of the Olive Branch Synod together with those of the Wittenberg Synod located in Indiana with the consent of their respective synods combined to form the Synod of Northern Indiana. The organizing convention was held in Columbia City, October 25 to 27, 1855, attended by eight pastors and three lay delegates. H. Wells was elected president, G. Miller secretary, and D. Smith treasurer.[79] This body joined the General Synod also.

Through the years the Ohio Synod (the Joint Synod) continued to work in the state. As early as 1827 Pastors A. Henkel and Henry Heincke were each directed to spend a month visiting pastorless groups in Indiana.[80] Two years later Jacob Gruber of Preble County, Ohio, was designated as missionary. He soon made congregations across the line in Indiana part of his parish. Similar provision for visiting preachers was made in subsequent years, for there were reported in the minutes continued requests for pastors. The first Ohio Synod pastor to have an Indiana address was G. F. L. Gerhard at Corydon in 1833. Through the years the number of pastors of the Western District of the Joint Synod resident in Indiana continued to increase. During the 1840's pastors of English synods appeared, and missionaries of the General Synod Home Missionary Society were at work in the state.[81] Late in the decade pastors of the Missouri Synod were there also. In Fort Wayne members of that body established a school conducted by Dr. William Sihler, instruction beginning in November, 1846, with construction of a building expected to begin the next spring.

Efforts to achieve Lutheran unity in the state were unsuccessful. An invitation was issued to all Lutheran pastors in the state to attend the convention of the Olive Branch Synod in Indianapolis, September 1, 1853, for the purpose of uniting in one synod.[82] Nothing came of it. There was one matter, however, on which all Lutheran synods in Indiana were agreed, namely, the union program of the *Kirchenverein des Westens*. Editor Benjamin Kurtz expressed in *The Lutheran Observer* the objections later to be repeated in the resolutions of the English synods. In his opinion the members of the *Kirchenverein* should have joined either the Lutheran or the Reformed synods. He considered these synods to be broad enough in their doctrines and practices to satisfy all concerned. Moreover, the organiza-

---

[79] *Evangelical Lutheran*, December 14, 1855. *Proceedings of a Convention and the Minutes of the First Session of the Evangelical Lutheran Synod of Northern Indiana*, 1855.

[80] *Minutes of the Ohio Synod*, 1827, p. 7.

[81] Report in *Lutheran Observer*, September 3, 1846.

[82] *Evangelical Lutheran*, August 12, 1853.

tion of the *Kirchenverein* merely created a new sect in America.[83] The Synod of the West voiced much the same objections later the same year,[84] as did also the English Ohio Synod.[85] The German synods would of course be expected to raise objections on confessional rather than practical grounds.

An example on the parish level of the contest between Lutherans and members of the *Kirchenverein* occurred at Evansville. A congregation there wrote to the Ohio Synod seminary at Columbus for a pastor. In response two men were commissioned to serve congregations in southern Indiana. But before they had arrived on the scene in June, 1845, a pastor of the *Kirchenverein* preached to the Evansville congregation. With the arrival of the Ohio pastors the congregation was divided, one part being Lutheran, the other part Evangelical.[86]

PITTSBURGH SYNOD

From the beginning Western Pennsylvania had been part of the territory of the Joint Synod of Ohio. Yet there were recurrent demands for a separate synod in that area, as was noted in Chapter V. In a period when there was a rapid increase in population, but the means of travel were poor, there quite naturally were two reasons for organizing new, though small, synods: great optimism for future growth and convenience in holding conventions. When these two reasons were compounded with Americanizing trends, the impulse to form a new synod was almost irresistible.

It was William Alfred Passavant, the twenty-three year old pastor of First English Lutheran Church in Pittsburgh, whose energy brought the new synod into being. He and four other pastors had discussed the project at an informal meeting at Butler, Pennsylvania, in late August, 1844. His invitation brought together eight pastors and eight lay delegates in his church the middle of January, 1845. The assembly proceeded to organize itself January fifteenth as The Pittsburgh Synod of the Evangelical Lutheran Church.[87] It was specifically declared that members of the Synod were free to support such literary, theological, or benevolent institutions as suited their prefer-

83 *Lutheran Observer*, VIII, 52 (August 27, 1841).

84 *Minutes*, Synod of the West, 1841, p. 10. Quoted in full in Schneider, *op. cit.*, pp. 130 f.

85 *Minutes* of the English Synod of Ohio, 1841, p. 20. Schneider, *op. cit.*, p. 131, footnote, fails to note that this is the English Synod, not the Joint Synod.

86 Schneider, *op. cit.*, p. 186.

87 *Proceedings of a Convention and of the First and Second Sessions of the Pittsburgh Synod of the Evangelical Lutheran Church*, 1845. Burgess, *op. cit.*, pp. 69 ff.

ences. There also was to be no distinction between "old and new measures." Michael J. Steck was elected president and Passavant secretary.

The pastors who were the charter members of the Synod were but eight of the twenty-nine working in Western Pennsylvania, according to the tabulation made by Burgess. Steck had belonged to the Eastern District and Abraham Weills to the English District of the Joint Synod of Ohio—the only members of that body to join the new Synod. Passavant's membership was in the Maryland Synod; Gottlieb Bassler was a member of the West Pennsylvania Synod; G. F. Ehrenfeld and Samuel D. Witt were on the roll of the Allegheny Synod. The remaining two men had had connections with the English Synod of Ohio: Elihu Rathbun who had been a member of that body from the beginning, and David Earhart who received a license in 1844.

A second convention, held in Shippenville, Pennsylvania, June 5 to 10, 1845, completed the formal organization and incorporation of the Synod. A year later a "Missionary Constitution" was adopted whereby the Synod set itself aggressively to the development of its territory. The organizers claimed that Western Pennsylvania heretofore had been merely the marginal area of other synods, and therefore was neglected. The new Synod set itself to correct this condition. The result was a rapid growth in the number of pastors, congregations, and communicants in the Synod. This did not come about by the transfer of congregations from other synods, least of all from Ohio synods. Instead it was the fruit of active missionary work producing many new congregations. The Pittsburgh Synod quickly surpassed the strength in Western Pennsylvania of other synods. In 1853 it could report thirty pastors, eighty-nine congregations, and 5629 communicants.

The Pittsburgh Synod attempted to follow a pattern of moderation and inclusiveness while maintaining a strong Lutheran character. In contrast to bodies that limited themselves to one language, whether German or English, this Synod was bilingual, with a steadily increasing predominance of English. In 1846, 400 copies of the Minutes were printed in English, 300 in German.[88] In 1852 the proportion was 500 English to 200 German.[89] At this latter convention most of the preaching was in English, though some was in German. In this Synod where language was not a battle-line the transition to English could be made with less pain. In the English-speaking congregations the work of evangelism was not limited to people of German

[88] *Minutes,* 1846, p. 32.
[89] *Minutes,* 1852, p. 41.

ancestry but was directed to the general population. Increasingly the pastors and people were American-born.

On the question of revivals the Synod attempted to be moderate, though the majority of the pastors were opposed to such practices. Steck was of the majority opinion. Passavant in the first years of his ministry was a revivalist but soon came to the opposite position. Though the pastors that were added to the synodical roll from year to year had received theological instruction at Gettysburg or Wittenberg, rather than at Columbus, it continued to be true that men of conservative spirit were in the majority.

Evidence of conservatism may be seen in the attitude toward the General Synod. A proposal to join that body came before the 1851 convention and was defeated. The argument of the majority was that affiliation with the General Synod would cause distractions and divisions in some congregations. Moreover, the General Synod tolerated slavery and admitted slave-owning delegates to its conventions.[90] A year later the proposal was renewed with the declaration that joining the General Synod did not commit the Pittsburgh Synod to a pro-slavery position. This time the vote for the proposal was ten clergy and seven lay delegates, the vote against was nine clergy and three laymen.[91]

In spite of the fact that the Pittsburgh Synod occupied part of the territory included in the Eastern District of the Joint Synod of Ohio, efforts were made to cultivate friendly relations between the two bodies. Passavant had been designated as the representative of the Pittsburgh Synod to attend the convention of the Joint Synod in Columbus in 1848, but being unable to be there he wrote a letter in which he noted that his Synod had received a representative of the Eastern District of the Joint Synod. He thought this "a sign that the day would not be distant when all who confess the Augsburg Confession would no more be separated through mistrust and jealousy, but through trust and sympathy would stretch forth the hand of brotherly love." In response the Joint Synod "*Resolved*, That the Synod has received with joy the fraternal sentiments of the Pittsburgh Synod toward our body, and expresses herewith the assurance of the same feelings." It chose President Mechling to be its delegate to the next convention of the Pittsburgh Synod.[92]

However, there were irritations. The eagerness of the Pittsburgh Synod to form English congregations sometimes meant invading a community where a German congregation of the Joint Synod existed. Moreover, some

[90] *Minutes,* 1851, p. 18.
[91] *Minutes,* 1852, p. 20.
[92] *Minutes* of the Joint Synod, 1848, p. 17.

Pittsburgh Synod men were revivalists. The Eastern District of the Joint Synod declared "That we very much desire to stand on good terms with the Pittsburgh Synod, and therefore regret that its members repeatedly preach in the congregations of our members without their knowledge and consent." [93]

At this convention of the Eastern District, Gottlieb Bassler was present as the representative of his synod, expressing the desire for amicable relations. The Eastern District thereupon adopted some resolutions in the interest of peace (*Friedensvorschlaege*). These specified that both bodies renounce acts of intrusion, that both agree to recognize only congregations and pastors teaching pure doctrine, that both bodies discipline offenders, that all members of both bodies avoid causes of strife, and that the two bodies accept delegates from the other.[94]

All this was duly reported to the Pittsburgh Synod. The accusation of interference was irritating. The terms of peace, even though concurred in by Bassler, gave the impression of an ultimatum. There were counter-charges of being intruded upon. Therefore a statement was adopted as follows:

> In regard to the alleged interference of our members with the churches of the English District Synod of Ohio, we would offer the following preamble and resolution:
> Whereas, the above Synod has from time to time charged our members with irregularity and intrusion and interference with their churches without sustaining them;
> *Resolved,* That we hereafter disregard all such charges unless accompanied with proper proof and regularly preferred before this body.
> *Resolved,* That whereas the delegate of Eastern District Synod of Ohio has not appeared, therefore their proposed regulations "Friedens Vorschlaege" be laid on the table.[95]

With this irritated response, which the influence of Bassler and Passavant could not prevent, negotiations for friendly relations ceased. Each body went its own way, largely ignoring the other. Before long each body was involved in other controversies which engrossed its attention. The Eastern District of the Joint Synod of Ohio faced the necessity of cultivating its growth in Western Pennsylvania without regard for the policies of the Pittsburgh Synod, and thereby being forced into the position of being the German Lutheran body in the area.

[93] *Minutes* of the Eastern District, 1850, p. 22.
[94] *Ibid.,* pp. 25 f.
[95] *Minutes* of the Pittsburgh Synod, 1851, pp. 14 f.

THE MISSOURI SYNOD

The Lutheran Church - Missouri Synod, whose original name was "The German Evangelical Lutheran Synod of Missouri, Ohio, and Other States," had considerable strength in Ohio from its beginning in 1847. This came about because there were Ohio pastors with their congregations who either never belonged to the Joint Synod or withdrew from it because of their dissatisfaction with it.

The focus of dissatisfaction was language, but around it clustered the other doctrinal and practical matters which were disturbing Lutherans in the mid-century decades. The issue became acute in connection with the Theological Seminary at Columbus. At first there had been no tension, for it is reported that Professor Schmidt sometimes conducted classes in English. Moreover, it was a desire for expansion and adaptation to the needs of the field that led the English District in 1837 to express a desire for an English professor.[96] Two years later, when a vigorous appeal was made by the Board of Directors for larger financial support of the Seminary and for some assistance for Professor Schmidt "who must do the work of two teachers," the question of preparing pastors for English congregations was raised. The answer given was:

> That the Synod not only considers it constitutional that instruction in the Seminary be given also in the English language as has heretofore been the case, but also deems it necessary and useful to appoint this requirement, with the condition, however, that thereby the instruction by means of the German language would not be repressed.[97]

The death of Professor Schmidt on November 3, 1839, a month before his thirty-sixth birthday, was a severe blow to the Seminary. The next professor was Charles F. Schaeffer, a pastor at Hagerstown, Maryland, who was bilingual but with a preference for English. He arrived in May, 1840. In November, 1842, he was joined by Friedrich Winkler, pastor at Newark, New Jersey, a man with preference for German. Tension between the two professors developed to such a degree as to jeopardize the whole institution. The Board of Directors called for the resignation of both professors. Schaeffer complied, but Winkler refused and continued to conduct classes.

It was argued that the German language was necessary in theological instruction because there was no Lutheran theological literature in English,

96 *Minutes* of the English Synod, 1837, pp. 15 ff.
97 *Minutes* of the Joint Synod, 1839, p. 18.

because those trained in English have a weak Lutheranism, and because German is necessary to preserve the true character of the Lutheran Church.[98]

To remove the turmoil the Joint Synod was called into extra session at Zanesville in June, 1844. A committee to which the Board's report had been referred expressed the judgment that Winkler was less at fault than his colleague in the dispute, but regretted that he had not been removed also. The Synod's action was:

> *Resolved,* That according to the constitution of the Seminary the German language is the only medium through which theological instruction must be given; but the same constitution authorizes the teaching of the English language theoretically and practically, so that students may thereby be enabled to preach in both languages where the wants of the church require it.[99]

The vote on this resolution was thirty-eight to ten, members of the English District casting votes in the negative.

This victory of the German party aroused prompt indignation. Emanuel Greenwald, editor of *The Lutheran Standard,* criticized the action in the issue of July 12, 1844, arguing that the constitution of the Seminary permitted lectures in English. The Synod soon became aware that the Zanesville decision was having an adverse effect upon the finances and enrollment of the Seminary. Within a year Winkler was dismissed and the Synod meeting at Lancaster reversed its decision, this time by a vote of forty-two to twenty-four. The statement reads:

> As the Seminary is and shall remain German, and the principal lectures are to be given in the German language, all theological students shall be required to learn the German language in the College. But inasmuch as the wants and welfare of the church require that ministers be educated so as also to be able to preach readily in the English language, all theological lectures shall be delivered also in the English language. In order, however, to secure the doctrines of our church, German textbooks shall be used in theological lectures until they shall appear in such English translations as shall be sanctioned by the Synod; but in all German lectures the German textbooks shall for all time to come be retained.[100]

Here was the answer to Editor Greenwald's question, "Is the Seminary at Columbus exclusively a German Institution?" In his editorial he said,

---

[98] Letter by "Guiliemus," *Lutheran Standard,* II, 41 (August 2, 1844), p. 2.

[99] *Ibid.,* II, 45 (August 30, 1844). *Minutes* of the Joint Synod, 1844, pp. 21 f.

[100] *Lutheran Standard,* III, 34 (July 30, 1845), p. 4. *Minutes* of the Joint Synod, 1845, pp. 10, 14.

"We could name nearly a half dozen ministers who pursued their studies there who either cannot preach in the German language at all, or who do so with much difficulty." [101] Here also was the answer to those who were irreconcilably committed to the exclusive use of the German language. The Synod closed the door on any possible reversal of its action. Since the Board of Directors of the Seminary favored this Lancaster decision, Jacob Leist, the president of the Board, introduced and secured the adoption of a resolution amending the constitution of the Seminary so that nominations to Board membership could be made only by directors.[102] For those who wanted the Seminary to be exclusively German this was utter and final defeat.[103] The twenty-four who voted in the negative entered a formal protest in the minutes, but to no avail. Among the signers of the protest was Professor Winkler, but more important was Dr. Wilhelm Sihler, a well educated man who had come with credentials from the Lutheran Missionary Society of Dresden, Germany, and had settled in Pomeroy, Meigs County, Ohio, early in 1844.[104] In June of that year he was ordained by the Western District of the Joint Synod. His leadership was at once apparent.

Joined to the language question was a doctrinal matter which focused upon two words in the liturgy. In Germany the union of the Lutheran and Reformed Churches bridged their difference on the doctrine of the Lord's Supper by adding the words, "Jesus said," to the formula of administration in the liturgy: "Take and eat; This is my body." The liturgy in use in the Joint Synod at that time included the same two words.

At the Zanesville convention Dr. Sihler and three others presented a petition asking that the two words be removed from the Synod's liturgy. Action on the petition was deferred until the next regular convention, but with the request that the church papers give full publicity to the matter. The next year at the convention at Lancaster the overwhelming decision was to retain the liturgy in its current form, including the disputed two words, and to declare it to be the duty of pastors to use this liturgy.[105]

101 *Lutheran Standard,* I, 3 (November 2, 1842), p. 2.

102 *Minutes* of the Joint Synod, 1845, p. 19.

103 Edward Hengstenberg's report, translated and published in *The Lutheran Observer,* has been noted in Chapter V, footnote 1. The narration of the troubles in the Seminary at Columbus appeared in the issue of February 11, 1848. Hengstenberg wrote that at the beginning "an active controversy grew up between the two men . . . the passionate recklessly violent temper of the German, the obstinacy of the irritable American with his offended and proud reserve. Prof. Winkler had right on his side, but he fought for a good cause in a very fleshy, acrimonious and offensive way."

104 *Lutheran Standard,* II, 17 (February 16, 1844), p. 2.

105 *Minutes* of the Joint Synod, 1844, p. 19; 1845, p. 22. *Lutheran Standard,* II, 45 (August 30, 1844), p. 2.

Four months after the Lancaster convention a meeting was held in Cleveland for the purpose of considering what action to take, perhaps to form a new synod. Most of the pastors and teachers present there had been sent to America through the influence of Wilhelm Loehe. They were men committed to a strict confessional Lutheranism. Some of the pastors had no connection with any synod in America, a few others belonged to the Michigan Synod, and six of those present were members of the Joint Synod of Ohio.

A document renouncing all connection with the Joint Synod was signed by the following members of that body: Dr. Sihler, F. Winkler, A. Schmidt of Cleveland, George Burger of Van Wert County, J. Adam Ernst of Marysville, C. August T. Selle of Columbiana County, William Richmann of Fairfield County, and A. Saupert of Evansville, Indiana (though Richmann and Saupert seem to have been absent at Cleveland). The reasons for the secession were listed under two categories. The first was ecclesiastical and confessional. Under this heading it was asserted that the Joint Synod had laid on the table the question, "What synods are Lutheran?"—a question intended to condemn the General Synod; that it had rejected the petition to abolish from the liturgy the words in the formula for administration, "Jesus said"; that it did not acknowledge all the Symbolical Books nor pledge their ordinands to them. The second category was labeled "moral" and asserted that the basic German nature of the Seminary was being compromised with English for the sake of finances. "This is the main cause of our secession." [106]

The Cleveland meeting did not organize itself as a new synod because more time was needed to bring that about. Sihler and his associates desired to include in a strictly confessional synod many pastors and congregations much farther west. The leader of the western group was Pastor C. F. W. Walther who wrote to Pastor Adam Ernst at Marysville heartily endorsing the project, and indicating that the opposition of some congregations to the formation of a synod was being overcome.[107] A year later a meeting consisting of the Loehe men and those farther west was held at Fort Wayne where a constitution was drawn up and signed. This made it possible for a convention to be held in Chicago beginning April 26, 1847, where officially began "The German Evangelical Lutheran Synod of Missouri, Ohio and Other States."

---

[106] The document in English translation appeared in *The Lutheran Standard*, III, 52 (February 18, 1846), p. 3. The account of the meeting in Walter A. Baepler, *A Century of Grace* (St. Louis, 1947), p. 87, tells only of confessional objections.

[107] Baepler, *op. cit.*, pp. 85 f.

The loss to the Joint Synod of Ohio in 1847 in the number of pastors was not large. Only a small minority of those who signed the protest at Lancaster seceded. Sihler was in Fort Wayne preaching and teaching. Pastor A. Saupert was located in Evansville, Indiana. C. A. T. Selle had become pastor of the congregation in Chicago in which the organizing convention was held. Within Ohio, Ernst of Marysville and F. W. Richmann of Lancaster were members of the new Synod by secession from the old. Other Ohio pastors in the new Synod who had not been members of the Joint Synod of Ohio were J. G. Streckfus of Willshire, Jacob Trautman of Port Clinton, J. E. Schneider of Marion, and Adam Detzer of Bryan. Nor was the number of congregations they served large. Most of these congregations were but recently organized and small. Of the six pastors working in Ohio only Ernst and Streckfus were pastors of congregations joining the new Synod, and therefore had the status of "voting members" since the congregations of the other pastors had not yet elected to join the Synod.

In another sense the secession was a serious matter for the Joint Synod. Amid the shortage of pastors every loss was deplorable, and men as capable as Dr. Sihler were rare. The hope of winning into Synod membership the independent pastors who held strict doctrinal views and who formed the link with the Loehe missionary impulse in Germany was now at an end. Moreover, there would now be competition for the German element in Ohio just as the English synods were rivals for the English-speaking population. The Joint Synod which attempted to solve its problems with firmness and moderation had lost its extreme English wing because of its firmness, and now was losing its extreme German wing because of its moderation which was condemned as error, if not heresy. As conflict leaves behind it a legacy of suspicion and misunderstanding, so the estrangement in Ohio left unhappy results.

THE JOINT SYNOD

The loss of the extreme English wing in 1840 and of the extreme German faction in 1845 was not a mortal blow to the Joint Synod of Ohio. It still continued to be the largest Lutheran body in the state. In losing irreconcilable elements it was freed from some of its irritating problems and therefore able to concentrate on others. Both of the seceding factions had been blind to history; the English wing in its zeal for Americanizing was blind to the history of Lutheran confessionalism; the German wing in its zest for pure doctrine and practice, and consisting of men newly come to

America, failed to understand what had made this nation what it was. The pastors who had been born in America, who preached in both languages, and who had spent all their ministerial lives in the Joint Synod, recognized that a practical policy would be something short of the extremes.

Two-thirds of the pastors who favored the German side and who signed the protest at Lancaster remained in the Joint Synod. With their colleagues they actively cultivated their territory. The result was that the Synod continued to grow. Even though in mid-century roads, canals, and even railroads were making travel easier, the increase in membership made advisable the erection of another district in addition to the Eastern, the Western, and the English.

Therefore in 1851 the Joint Synod adopted a committee's report recommending the formation of a northern district with these boundaries: from Cleveland south along the Ohio Canal to the southwest corner of Wayne County, thence west along the southern borders of Richland, Marion, Hardin, Allen, and Mercer Counties, thus including the northwestern part of the state. During this Joint Synod convention the pastors in the newly designated district held a meeting May twenty-seventh and effected a temporary organization, electing George Cronenwett president and J. J. Beilharz secretary.[108] The first regular convention of the Northern District was held at Perrysburg, September 8 and 9, 1851. Nine pastors and three lay delegates were present, four pastors were absent. This time Beilharz was chosen president and Cronenwett secretary.[109]

With the continued growth of the body the conventions of the Joint Synod increasingly became a problem. The number of pastors, lay delegates, and visitors attending conventions reached the hundred mark and was still growing. Many parishes could not entertain a convention of that size. Recognizing this fact, the English District authorized its president in 1845 to correspond with other district presidents suggesting the appointment of a committee to prepare a plan for conventions of delegates of districts. But the correspondence failed of its purpose.[110] In 1848 Henry Heincke, the president of the Joint Synod, proposed that the body meet annually, instead of every third year, and that it consist of delegates from the districts, but his suggestion was rejected.[111] However, three years later a committee was authorized and appointed. The report of the committee as a proposed re-

108 *Minutes* of the Joint Synod, 1851, pp. 28, 35.
109 *Minutes* of the Northern District, 1851, p. 5.
110 *Minutes* of the English District, 1846, p. 5.
111 *Minutes* of the Joint Synod, 1848, pp. 8, 13.

vision of the constitution was first made to an extra session held in 1853 and was adopted at a regular convention the next year. It specified that each district would be entitled to two delegates, one clerical and one lay, for every six pastors and congregations until the total convention delegation was fifty. A regular convention would be held every second year.[112] The first delegate convention was held November 9 to 14, 1854, at Greensburg, Pennsylvania.

Meanwhile, however, the Joint Synod was losing the majority of its small English District. When a secession had occurred in 1840 a few pastors had remained faithful to the Joint Synod, thereby continuing the English District. Even the language troubles at the Seminary and the Zanesville resolution of 1844 were not sufficient to shatter their loyalty. The District declared,

> *Resolved,* That we deeply regret that a resolution was passed at the extra session of the Joint Synod of Ohio at Zanesville which does not meet the general approbation of the Church; but that we have full confidence in the brethren with whom we have cooperated for years; and that we will continue our connection with them, with the assurance that all have equally the general interest of the Church at heart.[113]

Moreover the pastors of this District held conservative views in matters of Lutheran doctrine and practice.

By 1850 this small District numbering fourteen pastors was beginning to feel the strain of being outnumbered by the three German districts. Some revision of the constitution of the Joint Synod at a previous convention was considered not well suited to the English District, and a committee was appointed to report the matter to the next Joint Synod convention. The outcome of this matter does not appear in the published proceedings, and was soon overshadowed by a more serious concern.

When the preparatory department of the Seminary was elevated to college status, becoming Capital University in 1850, the first president was Dr. William M. Reynolds, whose brother-in-law, Professor A. Essick, became a member of the faculty. Reynolds became a member of the Western District, Essick of the English. The Reynolds administration was not successful in satisfying the aims of the majority of the Joint Synod. Whereupon both Reynolds and Essick resigned.

The English District espoused the cause of these two men. At the convention of 1854 James Manning in his presidential report expressed his distress over the situation as well as his doubt as to the possibility of continuing amicable relations with the Joint Synod. A series of resolutions was presented. Promptly adopted were the first four which deplored the events at the University, expressed confidence in Reynolds and Essick, viewed the future of the school as dark, and reaffirmed the truly Lutheran position of the District. The fifth resolution, sharply critical of the Joint Synod, was rejected. In its place was prepared a lengthy preamble to the sixth resolution reviewing the dissatisfactions and declaring that connection with the Joint Synod was "no longer profitable or agreeable." A seventh resolution proposed severing the ties, and an eighth proposed joining the General Synod. Action on these last four resolutions was deferred until after the next convention of the Joint Synod because "brethren who had associations of twenty years' standing found it hard to have them severed." [114]

A month later the Joint Synod held its delegate convention at Greensburg, Pennsylvania. A committee reported on the minutes of the English District, saying, "They accuse this convention of intolerance, oppression and inconsistency, as well as of pursuing a ruinous policy with regard to our Church Institution." Such deplorable resolutions awaken groundless suspicions.

> Further intercourse on the part of the English District with the members of this Synod would clear away the misapprehensions, apparently written under the influence of wounded feelings.
> *Resolved,* That we herewith assure the English District of our continued fraternal feeling toward them and entreat them prayerfully to consider whether their best interests and those of the Church do not require them to leave the tie, which has hitherto bound us together, unbroken.[115]

A committee was appointed to carry these sentiments to the English District, but it was ominous that the vote on the resolution was ten to seven.

When the English District met in adjourned session at Wooster, April 12, 1855, it was in no mood to listen to the Joint Synod representatives, W. F. Lehmann and M. Loy. By a vote of thirteen to eight it decided to secede. Next to be adopted was a resolution to follow the example of the Ministerium of Pennsylvania and join the General Synod. Twelve pastors and five laymen voted in favor of the resolution, three pastors and two laymen against it. After this decision was made, the three pastors who voted in the negative—A. S. Bartholomew, D. Rothacker, and P. J. Buehl—asked for honorable dismission from the body, which was granted.[116] Later in

---

[114] *Minutes* of the English District, 1854, pp. 7 f.
[115] *Minutes* of the Joint Synod, November 9–14, 1854, p. 8.
[116] *Minutes* of the English District, April 12, 1855, pp. 4 f.

the year this body was admitted to membership in the General Synod at its convention in Dayton.

Nothing in the record seems to indicate that the issue was one of Lutheran doctrine and practice. There were personality considerations, as Lehmann and Loy reported to the Joint Synod. Essick was present and served as secretary of the District during these sessions. Beyond that was the fact that the District had built its hopes on Capital University becoming a successful college of the type developing in this country. Members of the District were exasperated that the Joint Synod was determined to preserve a strong German flavor at the school. This exasperation was severe enough to induce James Manning, who was the first president when the District was organized in 1836 and president again at its reforming in 1840, to lead the movement of secession. As further evidence that the difficulty focused on educational policy there may be cited a resolution adopted at Wooster to direct students to attend Wittenberg College. Thus "The English Evangelical Lutheran Synod and Ministerium of Ohio and Adjacent States" ceased to be a district of the Joint Synod, and went its independent way.

SALEM SYNOD

An extreme instance of contention and personal grievance which led to secession appeared in a splinter body with a brief existence at this time. Minor concerns were inflated into divisive issues. Separation and secession were not uncommon in American religious life.

A few dissatisfied pastors of the Miami Synod held a conference at which it was agreed to set a date for the organization of a new synod. The nature of the dissatisfaction is not stated but seems to have been one of personality. Accordingly the group met September 15, 1854, in Salem Church near Ridgeville, Warren County, Ohio. Five pastors and four lay delegates were present. The constitution of the Miami Synod, with suitable adjustments, was adopted. Officers were John Surface president, George Shafer secretary, and Adam Surface treasurer.[117] The editor of *The Evangelical Lutheran,* in the issue of October 5, 1854, printed the report of the convention without correcting the misspellings of the reporter.

The Salem Synod appointed a delegate to the next convention of the Kentucky Synod, but the latter body was unwilling to be an ally. It regretted

117 Manuscript minutes of Salem Evangelical Lutheran Synod of Ohio and adjacent States, in the Archives of the Ohio Synod of the Lutheran Church in America.

the formation of a new body, declaring itself unable to recognize the Salem Synod as a regularly organized Lutheran synod. The Kentucky Synod said that it opposed all such "disorderly, schismatic and fanatical movements," and advised the Salem group to disband.[118]

The Miami Synod expressed its disapproval of the new Synod. The president wrote to John Surface protesting that the proceedings of his group were contrary to good order. Surface, in reply, gave as one of the reasons for his Synod's existence the need in the church for "some ministers who are not college bred." Yet the Miami Synod could not tolerate his "disorderly and un-Lutheran proceedings." It both suspended him from the ministry, and warned the laymen he had ordained to desist from their ministerial activity.[119]

The second convention of the Salem Synod was held March 28 to April 1, 1855, and the third convention May 7 to 11, 1856, both at Salem Church, Warren County, Ohio. The Synod recommended *The Lutheran Observer, The Evangelical Lutheran,* and Wittenberg College to its congregations. It endorsed revivals, Sunday Schools, temperance, and S. S. Schmucker's *Lutheran Manual.* It reached its maximum size in 1856 with six ordained ministers, three licentiates, and two catechists, but thereafter diminished rapidly in size. Therefore, at the 1857 convention, the Synod voted to disband.

In October of that year, Surface wrote to the Miami Synod asking for reinstatement. This was denied him for two years, until he appeared in person and made formal confession of his wrong, as well as a repudiation of his acts. He continued in the Miami Synod until his death in 1866.[120]

SYNODICAL LEADERS

The diversity of trends evident in these synods which to some degree overlapped geographically was to be seen also in the persons who were prominent in these synods. It has been customary to think of these men in terms of the degree of their loyalty to the Lutheran confessional writings. However, motives and influences were complex. Intertwined with confessional loyalty was an attitude toward adaptation to the American scene,

---

[118] *Evangelical Lutheran,* July 20, 1855.

[119] *Minutes* of the Miami Synod, 1854, p. 7; 1855, pp. 5, 9, 21.

[120] *Minutes* of the Miami Synod, 1856, p. 17; 1857, p. 21; 1858, p. 19.

the two sometimes being antitheses. There were synodical loyalties also, to say nothing of differences in personality.

At one end of the spectrum was Wilhelm Sihler (1801–1885). He was born in Germany where his studies culminated in the degree of Doctor of Philosophy. He passed through a period of rationalism to one of strict confessionalism, and thereby encountered difficulties with the church authorities. Encouraged by the Dresden Missionary Society, he came to America in 1843. His connection with the Joint Synod of Ohio and his separation from it have been noted. His career as a teacher at Fort Wayne and his leadership in the Missouri Synod were notable. His publications were numerous. While a member of the Joint Synod of Ohio his insistence upon a distinctly Lutheran formula of distribution in the Communion indicated his vigorous confessionalism, and his protest against introducing English into the Seminary revealed his resistance to adjustment to American ways.

There were three influential men in the Joint Synod who sympathized with Sihler's views in many ways but who were unwilling to carry the matter to the point of schism. They were C. G. Schweizerbarth, W. F. Lehmann, and M. Loy.

Johann Gottlieb Christian Schweizerbarth (1796–1862)[121] was born in Stuttgart, Germany, and studied at the University of Tübingen. After coming to America he studied theology at New York under the direction of Dr. Frederick William Geissenhainer, Sr., a pastor loyal to the Lutheran Confessions. He was ordained by the Joint Synod of Ohio in 1826. For more than a quarter of a century he was pastor at Zelienople, Pennsylvania. When services in English were desired he consented to an amicable division whereby a separate English congregation was organized. At the time of the language problem at the Seminary in Columbus he voted with the majority to permit English lectures. Yet his preference was for German. He not only participated in the founding of the Seminary but supported it loyally. He exercised vigorous leadership in the Eastern District of the Joint Synod, helping to keep congregations in Western Pennsylvania within that body when others, including the English Church in Zelienople, were joining the Pittsburgh Synod.

William Frederick Lehmann (1820–1880) during his lifetime was easily the most outstanding member of the Joint Synod. Brought from Germany

---

121 So the name appears in the obituary account in Peter & Schmidt, *op. cit.*, p. 175. Usually the synodical roll gives the initials "C.G." though at times " G.C." He is "Johann" in the Zelienople church record.

to Philadelphia at the age of four, he had his early education in that city and studied theology in the new Seminary in Columbus. Within the Joint Synod of Ohio which ordained him he devoted his extraordinary talents to his work as pastor, professor in the Seminary, professor and president of Capital University, president of the Synod, and recognized leader in his church. He served several terms as president of the Synodical Conference. For many years he was editor of the *Lutherische Kirchenzeitung* and provided translations of German works for the columns of *The Lutheran Standard*. His facility in both languages was a distinct asset. Without being hostile to English he recognized that the Joint Synod would continue to be a German-speaking body during his lifetime and that the policies of the Synod must reckon with that fact. Some adjustment to American life would indeed be necessary but not at the expense of Lutheran doctrine and practice. His was a staunchly conservative Lutheran position.

Matthias Loy (1828–1915), a native of Pennsylvania, was a student and later a colleague of Lehmann at the Seminary. Of the two men he was more sympathetic with the position of the Missouri Synod. For over a quarter of a century he was editor of *The Lutheran Standard,* meanwhile serving terms as president at Capital University and of the Synod. Several books came from his pen. Though he preferred to speak English rather than German, and though he was thoroughly American in his manner of life, he nonetheless gave his first loyalty to his Synod and Seminary committed vigorously to confessional Lutheranism. By voice and pen he energetically promoted such confessionalism. Adaptation to the American scene was a minor consideration.

There were two men who displayed their loyalty by important service to the Joint Synod of Ohio but who found its policies to be increasingly rigid and unsatisfactory. James Manning (1800–1897), born at Dover, Delaware, was instructed in theology by Andrew Henkel and was ordained by the Ohio Synod in 1829. He was the first president of the English District, and after the schism in 1840 was president of the district which continued its connection with the Joint Synod. He steadily encouraged the use of English. With the collapse of the Reynolds administration at Capital University, he was among the majority of the English District which withdrew from the Joint Synod, though he returned to its membership shortly before his death. The other man was Emanuel Greenwald (1811–1885) who was born in Frederick, Maryland, and there was instructed in theology by his pastor, David F. Schaeffer. He was ordained by the Joint Synod of

Ohio, ministering to parishes in New Philadelphia and in Columbus. He was secretary of the first English District, continuing with the Joint Synod section after 1840. He was the first editor of *The Lutheran Standard* and a member of the board of directors of Capital University. Later he was pastor at Easton, and then at Lancaster, Pennsylvania. The author of many books, he found the spirit of the General Council more congenial to his taste.

There were others to whom the idea of Lutheran exclusiveness seemed to be the antithesis of the American spirit. They believed that faithfulness to Lutheran doctrine did not preclude participation in community life. Such a person was Charles Frederick Schaeffer (1807–1879). He was born in Philadelphia and his collegiate education was received at the University of Pennsylvania. He was trained in theology by his father, F. D. Schaeffer, and his brother-in-law, Charles R. Demme, developing a firm commitment to the doctrinal position of the Lutheran Confessions. In this his sympathies lay in a different direction from those of his brother-in-law, S. S. Schmucker at Gettysburg. From his pastorate at Hagerstown, Maryland, he was called to be professor in the Theological Seminary at Columbus, being urged to accept by Pastors Manning and Greenwald. When trouble arose he promptly resigned. Later he was theological professor at Gettyburg and finally at Philadelphia. Though he was the English professor at Columbus, he had an appreciation of German theological literature, translating numerous works into English. In spirit he was more pietistic than polemical. His cousin, David Porter Rosenmiller (1809–1880), though a graduate of Gettysburg Seminary, shared his conservative theological position. Rosenmiller preached to his Dayton congregation in English but could use German. He was at first a member of the Western District of the Joint Synod of Ohio but was a leader in the formation of the Miami Synod in which he exerted a conservative influence along with Schaeffer. In the Pittsburgh Synod it was William Alfred Passavant (1821–1894) who provided this kind of theologically conservative, sympathetically Americanizing leadership.

In this matter of adjustment, inclusiveness, and liberalism there were some who were at the other end of the spectrum from Sihler. Such a person was Francis Jacob Ruth (1805–1884), the first president of the Wittenberg Synod. He was born in Frederick, Maryland, and there studied theology under David F. Schaeffer. He became a member of the Ohio Synod when he came to this state in 1831. His participation in the English District and its secession indicated his linguistic interest. He was among the first to introduce "new measures" into parish practice in the areas around Ashland

and Mansfield. Much more influential was another native of Maryland, Samuel Sprecher (1810–1906). He was heartily in accord with the viewpoint of his teacher and brother-in-law, S. S. Schmucker. As president and theological professor at Wittenberg for many years, he guided the doctrinal position and the church practices of a majority of the General Synod pastors in the state in the direction of fraternizing with other Protestant denominations. He was the author of a substantial volume in systematic theology as well as of numerous magazine articles. The keenness of his mind and the breadth of his scholarship were widely recognized.

7 / INSTITUTIONS AND ACTIVITIES

THOUGH ORGANIZED RELIGIOUS ACTIVITIES are not the essence of the Christian religion, they nonetheless provide the records and the data needed for historical narratives. Unless there are diaries or journals revealing the thoughts and inner experiences of individuals, it is only the record of corporate activity which is available for historical interpretation. The few personal accounts which have survived deserve attention, and the findings from such memoir sources must be correlated with data derived from a scrutiny of synod minutes and church papers. Thus attention must be given to the worship and work, the theology and the attitudes of Lutherans in Ohio.

EDUCATION

As worship is a primary activity of the Christian fellowship, so the leadership in worship is a matter of great concern in that fellowship which is the church. An important facet in the history of the ministry is its function in public worship, even though questions of rank, authority, induction, and power too often monopolize the discussion.

Lutherans in Ohio inherited a tradition that those who led public worship, preaching the Word and administering the sacraments, should be men properly trained and certified. Though there were difficulties involved, certification could be accomplished even on the frontier, for synods could soon be formed. But training was a much more difficult matter. It was for the primary purpose of training pastors that the Lutheran educational institutions in Ohio were founded. Other purposes were subsidiary.

The Theological Seminary at Columbus, founded exclusively for this primary purpose, had great difficulty, however, in gaining support from the congregations. During the first quarter century of its existence it survived largely through the generosity of its underpaid professors. Though Schmidt had agreed to teach without salary, the Synod voted him $150 a year. Then the Directors sold him four acres of land for $400 to be paid for in four annual installments deducted from his salary. No wonder the Synod requested all correspondents writing to the professor to send all their letters postpaid! In addition to his other duties he was given the task of soliciting funds for the Seminary.[1]

A decade later there was a proposal that aid be solicited from the Ministerium of Pennsylvania which had an interest in theological education in the German language. Pastors M. J. Steck and Christian Spielmann went to a convention of that body asking for aid and offering the privilege of naming four members of the Board of Directors. The Ministerium accepted the proposal and elected four directors, none of whom, however, came to a Board meeting. Meanwhile the Joint Synod secured from the Ohio Legislature an amendment of the Seminary charter permitting the increase in the size of the Board, but this needed the approval of the Joint Synod in regular convention—the next one being at Lancaster in 1845. In the interval the Ministerium chose other directors, two of whom attended the extra convention at Zanesville in 1844. Somehow they misunderstood the situation so that on the basis of their report the Ministerium annulled its agreement on the grounds that the Joint Synod had failed to keep its part of the proposal. News of this action came as a surprise to the Joint Synod. Likely it was an impractical proposition at best, considering the many miles separating the two synods and the poor means of travel at the time.[2]

Fresh prosperity came to the Seminary when William F. Lehmann began his long career as professor. His work was made easier by the settlement of the language question. Uncertainty about the location of the school was removed in 1848 by the decisive defeat of efforts to take it away from Columbus. Lehmann, an alumnus of the Seminary, had the confidence of the Joint Synod for his ability, his loyalty, and his devotion. He avoided extremes in the excited church debates of the day, seeking to preserve the strength of the Synod and the growth of the Seminary by moderation. His long and constructive service deserves the gratitude of both.

Elected as theological professor, Lehmann began instructing students June 21, 1847, in his parish at Somerset until he could close his ministry there. In October he moved to Columbus, reopening the institution there.

---

[1] *Minutes* of the Joint Synod, 1832, pp. 16 f.; 1833, p. 17.

[2] Accounts of these negotiations appeared in *The Lutheran Standard;* news of the Ministerium's action in the issue of June 11, 1845; Editor Stephen A. Mealy gave the Ministerium's position in the July 23, 1845, issue; accounts by the Board and by Spielmann were printed in the issue of August 13, 1845.

The following spring the Board reported to the Joint Synod that there had been twenty-one students during the winter, that instruction was given in both German and English languages, and that the Seminary was free of debt. To demonstrate the quality of the academic work being done, six seminary students gave a performance in the courthouse in which they presented original essays and poetry in German and English.[3] The future looked bright.

The education of candidates for the ministry was a concern of the independent English synods also. Their resources were even more slender than those of the Joint Synod, but the persistence of those promoting the project brought Wittenberg College with its theological department through difficult times. Ezra Keller at first had hopes of uniting the two theological schools in Ohio and by such union relieve the financial problems to some degree. With this in mind he attended the tense Zanesville convention of the Joint Synod in 1844. There he was able to assess the real situation. Concerning his impression he wrote,

> It was a question with me when I entered the West whether it was not possible by conciliatory measures and mutual concessions to reunite the brethren in the Columbus Seminary. . . . I found it would be unwise as well as useless to prosecute the effort. . . . The Columbus Seminary does not and will not answer the wants of the English portion of the Church. And this portion is already more than half of the Church and rapidly increasing. . . . It will also appear . . . that the English language can never obtain prominence in that institution without disturbing its peace and the peace of the Church.[4]

He was aware also that the English Synod's views on doctrine and "new measures" with which he concurred would likewise make impossible the uniting of the two theological schools.

Keller's brief tenure as theological professor and president was sufficient to get the institution started at Springfield and to impart to it a character of evangelistic zeal and piety. He did as much as it was possible to do to equip men for the ministry by a one-year course of theological study. His untimely death December 29, 1848, was a shock to the institution. Among the tributes paid to Keller was an editorial, probably by E. Greenwald, in *The Lutheran Standard* which said:

> He was a man of indomitable energy and perseverance; and of whose Christian virtues and piety those who know him intimately speak in the highest

---

3 *Minutes* of the Joint Synod, 1848, pp. 10 f., 14.

4 "The Church in the West," *Lutheran Observer*, XII, 18 (January 3, 1845).

terms of praise. Our personal acquaintance with him was but partial, yet slight as it was, we respected and esteemed him as a Christian and scholar.[5]

Samuel Sprecher was Keller's successor, beginning his long teaching career in 1849. The next year he was joined by Frederick William Conrad who for five years shared with him the responsibilities of teaching theology. Both of these men belonged to the theologically liberal wing of the General Synod at the time, although they later became more conservative. Both of them rendered outstanding service to the Church.

The training of ministers by no means exhausted the educational interests of Lutherans in Ohio. One factor in the situation was that candidates for the ministry needed academic training as preparation for theological study, and when classes were begun in academic subjects they were opened to non-theological students as well. A second factor was the frank desire to provide collegiate education under church auspices to aspiring young people in the congregations. Both factors inspired the founding of Lutheran colleges.

Wittenberg College was established to meet this larger need from its very beginning. If Ezra Keller had ever believed that a theological seminary was all that was needed, he soon changed his mind. He recorded these observations:

> In my travels during the summer I found some of our youth in almost every academy, high school and college with which I became acquainted. In most neighborhoods where I preached in reference to our contemplated College I found young men in our congregations who desired a liberal education and parents who were willing and able to educate their sons as soon as they obtained the opportunity at a convenient distance and under the supervision of some of our ministers.[6]

All this simply confirmed the design of erecting a collegiate and theological institution as a dual project. Students in the collegiate department always outnumbered those in theology. The first commencement was held in 1851 when the first degrees were conferred. Wittenberg College was on its way, even though many lean financial years lay ahead. Its continued existence meant that the English synods were committed to a program of general and theological education for an indefinite future.

[5] *Op. cit.*, VI, 24 (January 17, 1849), p. 3. For biography, cf. M. Diehl, *Biography of Rev. Ezra Keller, D.D.* (Springfield, 1859); Herbert W. Veler, *A Life of Ezra Keller, D.D.* (unpublished thesis, Chicago Lutheran Theological Seminary) 1951.

[6] *Lutheran Observer*, XII, 22 (January 24, 1845), p. .1

Within the Joint Synod there was an abortive effort to start a college in eastern Ohio. The location was Jefferson (Germano) in Harrison County. With the backing of members of the English District, over $4500 had been collected and a two-story brick building to house the professor and classes was nearly finished early in 1847. Amos Bartholomew was president of the Board at the time a charter was secured. In accordance with public announcement, classes in the preparatory department were begun the next October fourth. The Reverend August Bernhard Bierdemann, A.M., M.D., Ph.D., was in charge. A scale of tuition fees was announced. The school was given the name Muehlenberg College. An effort was made to have half of the English District's subscriptions to the Seminary diverted to this school. On June 20, 1848, at the end of the school term there was a public exhibition of the work of the school in which there had been thirty-six students. But by the time winter arrived the project had been abandoned.[7]

Success in the collegiate field was achieved in 1850 when Capital University was established at Columbus in connection with the Theological Seminary and with the support of all the districts of the Joint Synod. It fulfilled hopes which had been held for many years. From the beginning of the Seminary it had been necessary to include some collegiate subjects in the theological training, such as the classical languages and logic. Such courses were open to non-theological students. Moreover, the constitution of the Seminary contained paragraphs espousing general academic education.

Six months before the death of Professor Schmidt, the Joint Synod adopted a resolution to erect as soon as the means were available a literary institution connected with the Seminary. Three years later the Synod observed that there were still no funds for a college, but renewed its determination to found one. Early in 1843 the General Assembly of Ohio (the Senate in January and the House in March) enacted a bill to incorporate Germania College to be connected with the Evangelical Lutheran Theological Seminary.[8] The troubles involving Professors Schaeffer and Winkler delayed the plan. Meanwhile, C. Jucksch for a short time taught languages and literature.

Among the recommendations of the Board of Directors of the Seminary to the Joint Synod in 1845 were several calling for the establishment of a

[7] *Lutheran Standard,* February 2, April 28, August 4, and December 8, 1847; July 1 and December 20, 1848. *Lutheran Observer,* April 28 and July 21, 1848. *Minutes* of the Joint Synod, 1848, p. 23.

[8] *Minutes* of the Joint Synod, 1842, p. 10. *Lutheran Standard,* I, 14 (January 18, 1843), p. 3; I, 21 (March 8, 1843), p. 3.

college with its own faculty, finances, and curriculum. But again it was the case that the support of the Seminary exhausted the funds contributed by the congregations, so that action was deferred.

During the winter of 1849–50 a more aggressive spirit appeared in the Board of the Seminary. If the Synod could not by its own resources establish a college, perhaps with the aid of the community it could be done. There was consultation with leading citizens of Columbus and a solicitation of help. From the General Assembly of the State a new charter was secured. The plans for Germania College were laid on the shelf, and an ambitious program for a university with the name Capital was promoted. There was to be an affiliation with a medical college already in operation, and a law school might be started. The Seminary would be the school of theology of the University. An enlarged Board of Directors would provide ample representation for the city.

The recurrent desire for a college thus found fulfillment in Capital University. The fresh enthusiasm led to prompt action. Within a few months the Board elected a president, Dr. William M. Reynolds of Gettysburg, and chose some teachers. A new property was purchased to which the Seminary was moved. Classes began in September. Both the Synod and the city rejoiced.

President Reynolds, however, was not successful in satisfying the ambitious program devised for his administration. The multi-school university structure was not attained. College and Seminary was the most that could be developed. The membership of the Synod had no enthusiasm for more than that. There was the impression that the aims of the University were too secular, too much slanted toward the non-Lutheran, English-speaking community. Though Reynolds in the General Synod was a conservative, he was not sufficiently so for the Joint Synod. The dissatisfactions accumulating in four years led to his resignation and that of Professor Essick. He was followed in the presidency by Christian Spielmann who better understood the spirit and temper of the Joint Synod. Nonetheless Capital University faced a future full of difficulty. The decisive issue, however, was that it was to be a church-related college, not a secular university.

The quality of the education received in the middle of the nineteenth century in these Lutheran institutions is difficult to assess. Evidently the college curriculum was classical in the sense that there was heavy emphasis on Latin and Greek. Much the same character prevailed in the theological schools. This is indicated not only by the announced curricula but also by the demands made by synodical examining committees of candidates for the ministry. Applicants in one group of the English Synod were examined in their knowledge of the Greek New Testament, natural religion, biblical theology, and church history. The result of the examination was not fully satisfactory, "yet the great destitution of the church in the West requires that we should give them license and place them under the care of the neighboring brethren to prosecute their studies." [9]

The Miami Synod wrote into its constitution the specifications of the educational and spiritual attainments expected of candidates.

> III. The examination shall embrace at least the following subjects: *viz.*, personal piety and the motives of the applicant for seeking the holy office, the Greek and Hebrew Scriptures, the evidences of Christianity, Natural and Revealed Theology, Church History, Pastoral Theology, the rules of sermonizing, and Church Government.
>
> IV. The Ministerium shall not, in any case whatever, license an individual whom they do not believe to be hopefully pious.[10]

Later the Wittenberg Synod incorporated this Section III *verbatim* in its Constitution. With these requirements it was presumed that the applicant knew Latin and Greek. That was expected of applicants in the Joint Synod from the time of its organization.[11]

Financial assistance to students was another aspect of the educational problem. Even theological students who did not have tuition to pay needed funds for living expenses. Prospective students for the ministry without such resources could be encouraged to prepare themselves for pastoral service if money was available to help them. This need was recognized quite early, and steps were taken toward meeting it. As was usual in those days when special tasks were undertaken by the formation of special societies such as Bible societies, missionary societies, humane and temperance societies, a Parent Education Society was formed to give financial aid to needy students.

Emanuel Greenwald, reporting in 1836 for a committee authorized by the Eastern District the year previous, presented to the Joint Synod a proposed constitution for an education society. The Synod adopted the report authorizing the immediate formation of the society with branch societies in each congregation.[12] From that date the Education Society

---

9 *Minutes* of the English Synod, 1841, p. 22.

10 *Minutes* of the Miami Synod, 1845, p. 39.

11 *Minutes* of the Joint Synod, 1818, p. 6; 1819, p. 14.

12 *Minutes* of the Joint Synod, 1836, pp. 15 f., 21 ff.

served a useful purpose in the Joint Synod. Jacob Leist was for many years a director and president of the Society. In 1848 it reported receipts of $149.92 which included fifty-nine one dollar gifts from pastors.[13] The Society soon was having an income of almost a thousand dollars a year. In 1854 the treasurer reported receiving in the previous three year period the sum of $2924.07, three dollars of which were counterfeit.[14] Though authorized by the Synod, holding its meetings at the conventions of the Synod, and publishing its proceedings in the Minutes of the Synod, the Society was an independent organization with its own treasury.

The English synods also were concerned with assisting ministerial students, conducting the work through a committee instead of by an independent organization, and handling the funds in the synodical treasury. Because the amount of aid received by students depended upon the size of contributions earmarked for that purpose, there was at first no guaranteed amount per student. Thus in 1852 the English Synod divided the $149.32 it had received among four students. But three years later it decided to give each beneficiary $100 a year, to be increased to $120 during his senior year.[15] The Miami Synod divided $185 among six students in 1848, increasing the amount to fifty dollars per student the next year, and in 1851 making the sum seventy dollars each. This money was a loan rather than a gift. At graduation a student was expected to sign an interest-bearing note. Repayment of the principal was not demanded unless he demitted the ministry. One half of the contributions of his congregations for education was to be applied to reducing the indebtedness until it was repaid. For a time the student funds were placed in the hands of the Wittenberg faculty to be disbursed at its discretion to the students. Among the beneficiaries in 1853 were L. A. Gotwald and J. H. W. Stuckenberg.[16] The Wittenberg Synod in 1850 was granting each student seventy-five dollars a year.

WORSHIP AND LITURGY

Some degree of liturgical formality was found in the public worship of Lutherans in Ohio from early days. Pastors migrating to the state brought with them copies of liturgies used in the east. William Forster used his copy of the Service Book (*Kirchen Agende*) issued by the Ministerium of

[13] *Minutes* of the Joint Synod, 1848, pp. 39 f.
[14] *Minutes* of the Joint Synod, 1854, p. 20.
[15] *Minutes* of the English Synod, 1852, p. 22; 1855, p. 11.
[16] *Minutes* of the Miami Synod, 1848, pp. 5, 8; 1849, pp. 15 f.; 1853, pp. 6 f., 13.

Pennsylvania and printed in Philadelphia in 1786. His hymn book was one printed in 1791 at Frankfort-am-Main in Germany.[17] In the first decades it was considered sufficient if each pastor had a copy of the liturgy, none being provided for the members of the congregation. This fact makes intelligible the decision of the Ohio Synod in 1819 to purchase two dozen copies of the Church-Order of the Ministerium of Pennsylvania.[18] Twenty years later in the report of President Steck attention was called to the lack of copies of a printed liturgy in German. Newly ordained pastors either wrote out copies of books owned by older pastors, or simply composed formularies of their own. A committee was appointed to deal with the problem.[19]

In that same year the Ministerium of Pennsylvania appointed a committee to revise and republish its liturgy, inviting other synods to share in the undertaking. The New York Synod accepted the invitation, as did also the Joint Synod of Ohio which named Professor William Schmidt and Pastors John Wagenhals and J. J. Fast to the committee. The death of Professor Schmidt ended his participation, but the names of the others appear at the end of the Foreword dated March 8, 1842. The book appeared in print that year.[20] Since it made no provision for responses by the congregation, it was not a service book to be placed in the pews. Instead, it merely provided prayers and forms for the pastor to read on Sundays, on special church festivals, and at occasional services such as baptisms and confirmations. An appendix listed the Gospels and Epistles for the church year.

The formula for administering the elements to communicants read, *"Jesus spricht: Nehmet hin und esset, das ist mein Leib,* etc." (Jesus said: take and eat, this is my body, etc.) This is the formula to which Dr. Sihler and his associates objected. Moreover, it is the formula preferred by union congregations, i.e., Lutheran and Reformed. It is somewhat surprising that the Joint Synod consented to this formula, since the English liturgy it had published in 1830, as we shall see, provided only the Lutheran formula. This *Liturgie und Kirchenagende,* however, reflects the predominant weight of the sentiment in the eastern synods. Further evidence of the union mood of the book may be seen in an alternate form for the Lord's Supper in which is included an invitation to "all who confess Christ as their Saviour," telling them that "you are welcome at this feast of love."

---

[17] These books are in the Archives of the Synod of Ohio at Springfield.

[18] *Minutes* of the Ohio Synod, 1819, p. 9.

[19] *Minutes* of the Joint Synod, 1839, p. 8.

[20] *Liturgie und Kirchenagende für die Evangelisch-Lutherischen Gemeinden in Pennsylvanien, Neu York, Ohio und den benachbarten Staaten.* Philadelphia, 1842. 264 pages.

A description of the worship of that day is given in the Preface; it will be quoted presently in English translation. It suggested that a sermon should not exceed one hour in length. The Joint Synod of Ohio officially approved the new book and urged its use by all its pastors and congregations where German was spoken.[21]

A decade later the Ministerium of Pennsylvania was again interested in a revision of the liturgy, and again invited the participation of the Joint Synod of Ohio. Dr. C. R. Demme came from Pennsylvania to bring the invitation in person to the Ohio convention in 1853. A committee appointed to confer with him reported that it approved the revision in general, but desired in the liturgy that the formula for distribution in Communion should read, "Take and eat, this is the body of Christ . . ." since a majority of the pastors in the Synod used it. Synod approved the report and the appointment of a committee to present these views to the corresponding committee of the Ministerium of Pennsylvania. Appointed to this task were Wagenhals, Lehmann, and Greenwald.[22]

The new edition issued in 1855 is a volume of 449 pages. In addition to the materials in the earlier edition this book contains collects and introits for the church year, the Augsburg Confession, and a large section of family prayers. It was recommented for use in all German Lutheran congregations.[23]

Meanwhile the needs of English-speaking congregations were not overlooked. In 1828 a committee was appointed to publish an English "liturgy arranged according to the spirit and doctrines of our Church." Members of the committee were David Schuh, Samuel Kämmerer, Charles Henkel, John Wagenhals, and James Manning. These five pastors, together with seven laymen, had met as a Special English Conference at Zanesville the previous October when it was resolved to bring the need of an English liturgy and other matters to the attention of Synod. Two years later the manuscript prepared by the committee was approved by Synod. Henkel and Wagenhals were authorized to supervise the printing of not less than 200 nor more than 300 copies. The book was recommended to the congregations.[24]

[21] *Minutes* of the Joint Synod, 1842, p. 25.

[22] *Minutes* of the Joint Synod, 1853, pp. 9, 18, 23 ff.

[23] *Liturgie und Agende: ein Kirchenbuch für die Evangelisch-Lutherische Kirche in den Vereinigten Staaten.* New York, 1855. For a description of the liturgies issued by the Ministerium of Pennsylvania and used in Ohio see L. D. Reed, *The Lutheran Liturgy* (Philadelphia, 1947), pp. 168 ff.

[24] *Minutes* of the Ohio Synod, 1828, pp. 7, 12 f.; 1830, p. 8.

The title page of the book reads: *"Liturgy or Formulary for the Use of Evangelical Lutheran Churches.* Compiled by a committee appointed by the Synod of Ohio and ordered to be printed. Lancaster, Ohio. Printed by John Herman. 1830." This volume of 120 pages contains two orders for public worship, sixteen other orders for such services as baptism, confirmation, etc., a table of Epistle and Gospel lections, as well as morning and evening prayers. The price was seventy-five cents bound, fifty cents unbound. Chief credit for the work was given to Charles Henkel, translator,[25] who was to receive twenty-five copies as evidence of the gratitude of the Synod. Like the other liturgies in use in America at that time, this made almost no provision for responses by the congregation. Instead it provided merely formulas and prayers to be used by the pastor. It suggested that "an ordinary sermon should not exceed an hour." The formula for distribution in the Communion reads, "Take and eat, this is the body of Christ . . ." The text of the Apostles' Creed includes the words, "the holy Catholic Church."

The English District of 1836 used this liturgy. Probably some of its pastors continued to use it after the District became an independent synod. Soon, however, the publications of the General Synod were in use in the English Synod, especially the liturgy in the Hymn Book of 1832. Ezra Keller later was a member of the committee that prepared *A Liturgy for the Use of the Evangelical Lutheran Church,* Published by Order of the General Synod of the Evangelical Lutheran Church in the United States. Baltimore, 1847. This also did not provide services with congregational responses. Though its text of the Apostles' Creed includes the phrase, "the Holy Catholic Church," its formula of distribution in Communion reads: "Take and eat, said Jesus, this is my body . . ." According to the preface this book was simply a translation, with some slight editing, of the 1842 *Liturgie und Kirchenagende* published jointly by the synods of Pennsylvania, New York, and Ohio already noted.

The worship of the day is described in the preface thus:

> The minister rises and pronounces a benediction, or some other devotional passage of Scripture, and then gives out the hymn that is to be sung. After the singing he goes to the altar, and calls upon the congregation to confess their sins, or reads one of the general prayers for Sunday. The prayer is followed by the reading of a portion of Scripture, such as the Gospels, the Epistles, or some other suitable passage. After this the minister announces a hymn adapted to his sermon, and whilst it is sung, ascends the pulpit.

[25] *Minutes* of the Ohio Synod, 1831, p. 15.

After the close of the hymn he prays, preaches, and prays again; whereupon the congregation, having sung another hymn, is dismissed with the benediction.

This translation agrees with the German original except that the sermon should be limited to three-quarters of an hour.

It was the custom both in the congregations and also at the synodical conventions to hold a preparatory service on Saturday evening preceding the Communion service on Sunday morning. The record reads quaintly that the service was held "in the evening at early candle-light." As further evidence that the liturgical forms were read by the liturgist without responses by the congregation, the Minutes of the English District in 1836 record that the "ordination service was read by the President." Later "the ceremony of licensing was then performed before the whole Ministerium. The President read the Form prescribed in the Liturgy."

Criticism of the General Synod liturgy was aimed not at its inadequate structure but rather at its fullness. A Miami Synod committee appointed to evaluate the liturgy expressed the judgment that while the language of the forms was chaste and classical, a plainer, shorter style would have been preferred. But the committee's recommendation that a request be made to the General Synod for a liturgy with "more perspicuity in its language and more brevity in its forms" was laid on the table.[26]

Within the Joint Synod, however, criticism was in the opposite direction. The English District in 1843 was of the opinion that "the English liturgies in use among our Ministers are very defective, and no standard liturgical forms are found in our church." The District adopted a resolution recommending a translation of the German liturgy of 1842. Pastor E. Greenwald was appointed the District's representative to confer with the other districts.[27]

The first hymnals used by Lutherans in Ohio were in German, such as the one used by Forster and that of the Special Conference already noted. Another one that has been preserved is a copy of the Marburg hymnal printed in Germantown, Pennsylvania, by Christoph Saur in 1770.[28] Books in English appeared also. It is impossible to determine the extent of the use of any of these in the state. The most that can be said is that copies of

26 *Minutes* of the Miami Synod, 1850, p. 16.

27 *Lutheran Standard*, I, 34 (June 7, 1843), p. 3.

28 The title page reads: *Vollständiges Marburger Gesang-Buch zur Uebung der Gottseligkeit in 649 Christlichen und Trostreichen Psalmen und Gesangen Hrn. D. Martin Luther und andrer Gottseliger Lehrer. . . .*

the hymnals in the following list were in the possession of Lutherans in Ohio. Only books published in America will be included.

Of the hymnals in German the one edited by Paul Henkel found acceptance in Ohio.[29] Published in New Market, Virginia, in 1810, it contained 246 hymns. Another hymnal brought to Ohio was the 1826 revision of the one prepared by the Ministerium of Pennsylvania.[30] The preface of the first edition of this work had been written by H. M. Muhlenberg in 1786. This revised edition contained 746 hymns, with an appendix of prayers for morning, evening, and other times. A hymnal authorized by the General Synod and prepared by a committee of that body contained 415 hymns suited for use in either Lutheran or Reformed congregations.[31] In 1849 a hymnal containing 710 hymns was published in the name of the Ministerium of Pennsylvania, the Ministerium of New York, and the West Pennsylvania Synod.[32] A committee appointed by the Joint Synod of Ohio to examine this book reported favorably on it, suggesting that the Synod recommend the hymnal to the congregations as the Eastern and Western Districts had already done. Some congregations had already adopted it. The committee considered it desirable that all Lutheran congregations should use the same book.[33]

Two hymnals in English found acceptance in Ohio, one issued by the New York Synod, the other by the General Synod.[34] The New York book contained 520 hymns arranged by topic, not according to the church calendar, together with 153 pages of liturgy including prayers, benedictions, and occasional services.[35] Prepared while Frederick H. Quitman was presi-

---

[29] *Das Neu eingerichtete Gesang-Buch bestehend aus einer Sammlung der besten Liedern zum Gebrauch des öffentlichen Deutschen Gottesdiensts und andern Uebungen zur Gottseligkeit in den Vereinigten Staaten von Nord-America.* Published by Ambrosius Henkel & Co., 1810.

[30] *Erbauliche Lieder-Sammlung zum Gottesdienstlichen Gebrauch in den Vereinigten Evangelisch-Lutherischen Gemeinen in Pennsylvanien und den benachbarten Staaten.* Gesammlet, eingerichtet und zum Druck befördert durch das hiesige Deutsche Evangelisch-Lutherische Ministerium. Germantown, 1826.

[31] *Evangelische Lieder-Sammlung genommen aus der Liedersammlung und dem Gemeinschaftlichen Gesangbuch zum bequemeren Gebrauch in den evangelischen Gemeinen.* Gettysburg, 1834.

[32] *Deutsches Gesangbuch für die Evangelisch-Lutherische Kirche in den Vereinigten Staaten.* Philadelphia, 1849.

[33] *Minutes* of the Joint Synod, 1851, p. 20.

[34] *Lutheran Standard*, I, 37 (June 28, 1843), p. 2.

[35] *A Collection of Hymns and A Liturgy for the Use of Evangelical Lutheran Churches to which are added Prayers for Families and Individuals.* Published by Order of the Evangelical Lutheran Synod of the State of New York. Philadelphia, 1817.

dent of the Synod, this volume concentrated on hymns of English origin, neglecting German hymnody. The General Synod hymnal had the words *Lutheran Hymn Book* stamped on the spine and therefore was known by that name instead of the one on its title page. [36] It contained 965 hymns and included "A Liturgy for the Use of the Evangelical Lutheran Churches. Published by order of the General Synod of the Evangelical Lutheran Church in the United States." The second edition, issued in 1852, increased the number of hymns to 1024. The price of the first edition had been seventy-five cents per copy, but was reduced in 1843 to six dollars per dozen cash or $6.25 per dozen on six months' credit. The hymns included were largely of English origin, though the second edition listed thirty of German derivation. Three Ohio pastors, W. G. Keil, J. H. Hoffman, and W. H. Harrison, were members of the committee that prepared the 1852 edition.

Within the Joint Synod of Ohio dissatisfaction with these two hymnals became vocal in 1843. One group of pastors felt that a new book using the best out of the earlier hymnals was desirable, and even expressed the hope that in a new German collection there might be hymns which could be sung to English tunes.[37] This latter proposal met with disfavor among pastors in the Pittsburgh area who felt that the sedate German mind and worship needed the German tunes. "The exciting English church singing would be calculated to promote mere animal excitement in our congregations." To introduce English melodies would be a step toward expelling "the German mother language out of our congregations." [38]

The English District felt that a new collection of English hymns, similar in arrangement to the General Synod book but available at lower cost, was greatly needed.[39] A joint committee representing the three districts was appointed. The result two years later was a volume with *Lutheran Hymns* stamped on the spine containing 458 hymns, to which were appended "Prayers for the Use of Families and Individuals" reprinted from the New York book.[40] The preface declares that the committee had followed the instructions to make the General Synod book the basis of this collection "so that the books might be used conjointly." Some of the hymns were from

[36] *Hymns Selected and Original for Public and Private Worship.* Published by the General Synod of the Evangelical Lutheran Church. Baltimore, 1832.

[37] *Lutheran Standard,* I, 23 (March 22, 1843), p. 2.

[38] *Ibid.,* I, 30 (May 10, 1843), p. 2.

[39] *Ibid.,* I, 34 (June 7, 1843), p. 3.

[40] *A Collection of Hymns and Prayers for Public and Private Worship.* Published by order of the Evangelical Lutheran Joint Synod of Ohio. Zanesville, 1845.

the New York Synod book, and others were from the Book of Common Prayer. Apparently this *Collection* was not a success. When the 1852 revision of the General Synod book appeared it was recommended by the English District for use in the Joint Synod on the ground that it was the best available, that it was priced below any book the Joint Synod could publish, and that English congregations of the Synod were adopting it.[41]

CHURCH PAPERS

Within Ohio there were usually some subscribers to religious periodicals published in the East. For instance, the Ohio Synod recommended *The Lutheran Intelligencer* as an excellent religious paper for members of the congregations.[42] Before long, however, it was felt that a paper published in Ohio would better serve the needs of this area.

A committee appointed to devise a plan for publishing a monthly paper offered a proposal copied from the Synod of West Pennsylvania. The paper, to be named *Die Evangelisch-Lutherische Stimme vom Westen*, was to be published under the auspices of the Synod in the German language, the subscription price of the monthly to be one dollar. Jacob Leist, Charles Henkel, and Samuel Kaemmerer were named the publishing committee.[43] But the paper failed to appear. When it was reported that the number of subscribers was insufficient to support the paper, the Synod decided to postpone publication.[44] When the Synod of West Pennsylvania proposed that the two synods publish a paper jointly, the offer was politely declined. The committee which reported the matter suggested this action:

> *Resolved,* That the signs of the times, and the prevailing spirit of the religious papers—which either advocated the cause of new measures and fanaticism, or vacillated like Lot's wife between Sodom and Zoar, between the inventions of men and the old way laid down in the Word of God—make it necessary that we establish a religious paper under the exclusive control of this Synod.

This expressed the sentiment of the Synod well enough, yet it was voted to postpone publication for a year in the hope that there might be room

[41] *Minutes* of the English District, 1853, p. 9.

[42] *Minutes*, 1828, p. 19. The *Evangelical Lutheran Intelligencer,* edited by D. F. Schaeffer, was published monthly at Frederick, Maryland, 1826–1831 as a family magazine for English-speaking Lutherans.

[43] *Minutes*, 1829, pp. 15 f.

[44] *Minutes*, 1830, p. 15.

for a printing press in the new Seminary building.[45] These hopes were not realized, and the paper continued to be postponed.

The Western District of the Joint Synod adopted a series of resolutions in 1841 calling for the immediate establishment of a semi-monthly English religious paper. A committee consisting of C. F. Schaeffer, J. Wagenhals, and D. P. Rosenmiller was authorized to circulate a prospectus and subscription list. It was instructed to negotiate with the other districts and with the Synod of the West seeking their cooperation in publishing and financing the paper, as well as sharing in naming the paper, the editor, and the place of publication. [46]

Though this plan did not work out as anticipated, it was sufficient to stimulate the Joint Synod into action the next year. That body *"Resolved, That this Synod publish a weekly religious paper in the English language to be entitled The Lutheran Standard* which shall be the property of the Board of Directors of the Theological Seminary at Columbus." A publication committee to function under the direction of the Board was authorized. In order to have funds for buying equipment, the pastors were to ask their congregations for loans in amounts of five dollars or more for a period of five years with "legal" interest. E. Greenwald was chosen editor at a salary of $300 to be paid from profits. Publication was to be at New Philadelphia, and the price was to be two dollars a year in advance.[47]

The paper thus authorized has continued to the present. The issue of Volume One, Number One is dated Wednesday, September 21, 1842. Besides the advance subscription price, the subscribers were offered the option of paying $2.50 after six months or $3.00 at the end of the year.

The editorial policy was announced in the first issue.

> In the pages of the Lutheran Standard the doctrines of the Evangelical Lutheran Church, as taught in the Bible, and exhibited in the Augsburg Confession of faith, will be explained and defended, and those venerated usages will be upheld which our pious forefathers loved and practised. In doing so, however, the Editor will seek to combine mildness of spirit with firmness of principle, and to comply with the Scriptural precept to "speak the truth in love." As mere theoretical orthodoxy without practical piety is insufficient, therefore the Lutheran Standard will be made the medium through which to preach "repentance toward God, and faith in the Lord Jesus Christ."

This moderate conciliatory spirit had been typical of the major part of the

---

[45] *Minutes* of the Ohio Synod, 1832, pp. 13, 17.
[46] *Minutes* of the Western District, 1841, pp. 14 f.
[47] *Minutes* of the Joint Synod, 1842, p. 24.

Joint Synod, but it was to be sorely tried in the next few years. The mood of this statement together with the fact that the paper used the English language looked toward the Americanizing influences in the Joint Synod, a circumstance which was to produce some misunderstandings between the editor and his readers. There was no uncertainty, however, about the *Standard's* opposition to "new measures"; editorials made that abundantly clear.[48]

Greenwald completed two volumes as editor. Stephen A. Mealy followed him in office, beginning with issue Number One of Volume Three, December 11, 1844. Zanesville became the place of publication. But trouble arose at once. Mealy resigned two months later, effective the following October. The issue of October 8, 1845, was the last under his editorship. He was a member of the Ministerium of Pennsylvania and did not transfer his membership to the Joint Synod. When the Ministerium was considering the proposal to join in the maintenance of the Seminary at Columbus it was largely Mealy's interpretation of events which led the Ministerium to withdraw. Moreover, Mealy had some misunderstandings with the Joint Synod leaders.

Publication was resumed at Somerset, November 8, 1845, with Christian Spielmann as editor. He continued for two and a half years until ill health forced him to resign. With the issue of July 18, 1848, Greenwald was again in charge. Greewald continued as editor until October, 1854.

The financial management of the paper was a continual problem. When it was handled by the Seminary Board it was a responsibility which came at a very difficult time for the Seminary. In 1845 the Joint Synod approved the formation of a stock company with a capital of $500 in shares of ten dollars each and with its own board of directors in full control. This plan failed. Meanwhile the paper had accumulated a debt of $1800. Three years later the responsibility for publishing was transferred from the Seminary Board to a committee of the Joint Synod. An increase in the number of subscribers had reduced the debt to $700.

The synods connected with the General Synod also were interested in having a church paper published in Ohio. They felt that *The Lutheran Observer* did not adequately represent the ideas in this area nor did it advance their projects with sufficient zeal, since its interests and focus were in the East. This feeling was somewhat unfair; the *Observer*, depending for its news and articles on voluntary contributions, printed all that was contributed from Ohio. An example was the series of articles about Wittenberg College submitted by Ezra Keller. Yet the feeling of neglect continued.

---

[48] Issues of September 21, 1842, and December 11, 1844.

Suggestions that these synods undertake the publication of a paper failed to produce action, since the energies of these bodies were consumed in establishing themselves and their congregations. Though the English Synod concurred in the plan of the Synod of the West to publish a *Western Lutheran Observer,* nothing materialized.[49] When a paper did appear it was the project of a few individuals, who, however, had the endorsement of the Ohio synods of the General Synod.

The paper was named *The Evangelical Lutheran.* It was published in Springfield, Ohio, with Victor L. Conrad as editor. It carried as a banner the words of Peter Meldenius: "In Essentials Unity, In Non-Essentials Liberty, In All Things Charity." Its aims were to spread religious knowledge, to provide items for profitable conversation, to help the religious training of the young, to advance the cause of education, to stimulate liberality and piety, and to promote the work of the Church. The first issue, June 16, 1853, was intended as a specimen. The subscription price was two dollars a year for single subscribers, a dollar and a half in clubs of five or more to one address, and one dollar to pastors and theological students. Pastors who sent prepaid club subscriptions of twenty or more were to receive the paper free. The paper was to be devoted to the position of the General Synod on doctrine, characteristics, and usages, but it did this more moderately than *The Lutheran Observer* and therefore was less colorful.

The cost of publication was always greater than the income, even though there was a continual appeal for subscribers. The synods as they considered the problem felt that it was better for them to own the paper. Accordingly they appointed members to a joint committee with power to act. In this the Olive Branch Synod cooperated with the three synods in Ohio. For the second half of 1854 the paper had a deficit of about $800. Though there were 1400 subscribers, the income was less than half the expenses. Besides, the country was in "hard times" and there had been crop failures.[50] A year later, though there were 1650 subscribers, the expected deficit for the year was $300. No solution was found.

The demise of the paper came about, however, for another reason. Editor Conrad felt he could not support the decision of some of the synods in the controversy over the *Definite Synodical Platform.* Lack of confidence in him began to reduce the number of subscriptions, and he resigned. The last issue published was dated March 21, 1856. The subscription list was sold

[49] Cf. p. 126.
[50] Issue of December 29, 1854.

to *The Lutheran Observer* which promised to include in its issues a "Western Department" edited by Dr. Sprecher. The remaining debt of $275 was assumed in equal parts by the four synods.[51]

The failure of *The Evangelical Lutheran* made it clear that eager enthusiasm was no adequate substitute for skill and experience in the publishing business. Religious publications have a high mortality rate. Moreover, it became apparent that the resources of the synods concerned were inadequate to support a paper of the size published. Synodical subsidies apparently were out of the question. In addition it was recognized that sectional interest was not sufficient reason for publishing a separate paper. *The Lutheran Observer,* which served all parts of the General Synod, was in a better position to survive. The articles and the general news in *The Evangelical Lutheran* virtually repeated what the *Observer* printed, and the space given to local news was not increased enough to justify the cost. For the time being, sectional interest in publication was overcome by national interest.

A church paper in the German language was a necessity in Ohio also. Indeed, it is surprising that the predominantly German Joint Synod concentrated first on a paper in English. Likely the reason lay in the fact that a paper published in Pennsylvania had considerable circulation in Ohio. It was the *Lutherische Kirchenzeitung,* edited and published by Frederick Schmidt at Easton, 1838–40, while he was a professor there, and then at Pittsburgh, 1840–46, where he was pastor. It favored a strongly Lutheran position in opposition to revivals. It therefore was acceptable in the Joint Synod, but rejected by the English Synod.[52] Financial difficulties caused it to be discontinued in June, 1846.

Another periodical with Ohio subscribers was the *Lutherische Hirtenstimme* edited in Baltimore, 1842–47, by C. G. Weyl. The theological position espoused was essentially that of *The Lutheran Observer* and thus was recommended to the members of the English Synod.[53] When Schmidt's *Lutherische Kirchenzeitung* ceased publication, Weyl proposed to the Western District of the Joint Synod that it associate with him in publishing a new paper to be named *Lutherische Kirchenzeitung und Hirtenstimme* into which his paper would be merged. But the Western District declined the offer on the grounds that the *Lutherische Hirtenstimme* did not display the proper Lutheran viewpoint.[54] Soon afterwards Weyl's paper was taken over

[51] *The Lutheran Observer,* April 11 and 18, 1856.
[52] *Minutes* of the English Synod, 1841, p. 20.
[53] *Minutes* of the English Synod, 1843, p. 11.
[54] *Minutes* of the Western District, 1847, p. 9.

by the Ministerium of Pennsylvania and renamed the *Lutherischer Kirchenbote.*

It was in 1846 that the Western District of the Joint Synod actively concerned itself with the problem of a German periodical. It appointed John Wagenhals and J. J. Beilharz to correspond with the other districts about the project.[55] Meanwhile *Der Lutherische Botschafter* entered the picture in January, 1848. A. B. Bierdemann of Canton was indicated as editor. The Eastern and Western Districts urged pastors to support it. After a committee recommended it in 1848, the Joint Synod also resolved to urge the pastors to support it with articles, letters, and subscribers.[56] An advertisement inside the back cover of the *Minutes* described it as a magazine devoted to the pure doctrine and usages of the Lutheran Church according to the Symbolic Books; not sectarian but concerned with true religion for all Christians; fifty cents a year; soon to be semi-monthly at one dollar. It discontinued in December, 1849, for lack of support.

The report of the Joint Synod Committee on Church Papers in 1851 declared that the *Lutherischer Kirchenbote* of the Ministerium of Pennsylvania had no decided commitment to Lutheran doctrine, and therefore was not recommended. *Der Lutheraner* of the Missouri Synod was considered too harsh. *Der Lutherische Herold,* edited in New York by Henry Ludwig beginning in 1851, was considered not intolerant, yet faithful to the Lutheran confessional writings, and hence was to be recommended. *The Evangelical Review,* a theological journal begun in 1849 at Gettysburg with W. M. Reynolds and later C. P. Krauth as editors, was approved, even though it printed both sides of theological issues.[57]

STEWARDSHIP

As the work of the synods in Ohio increased in size and complexity, the need for regular and larger support became more pressing. It soon became apparent that a program of systematic contributions to the benevolent activities of the synods was highly desirable. Once colleges were founded and obligations for student aid were incurred, there had to be something better than sporadic offerings. Out of this necessity arose efforts at stewardship.

[55] *Minutes* of the Western District, 1846, p. 13.

[56] *Minutes* of the Joint Synod, 1848, pp. 27 f.

[57] *Minutes* of the Joint Synod, 1851, pp. 12 f. Cf. F. G. Gotwald, "Pioneer American Lutheran Journalism," *Lutheran Quarterly,* vol. 42 (April, 1912), pp. 161 ff.

The problem was to find or to develop a suitable system. The English Synod recommended that its congregations adopt a cent-a-week plan as likely "the most successful way of raising funds for benevolent purposes." [58] For the most part responsibility in this matter rested on the pastors rather than on the laymen. They were expected to preach on the subject, calling attention to First Corinthians 16:2. Pastors who had collected little or nothing during the year for the synodical treasury were earnestly requested to give attention to this matter. Resolutions were adopted calling on all church members to subscribe to benevolent causes, and requesting each pastor to solicit his members individually so that the funds would be gathered by the time of the annual convention.[59] The next step was to ask the pastors to commit themselves individually by pledging in advance the amount each one thought could be raised in his congregations for the support of the synodical projects.[60] Pastors who did not fulfill their pledges were at first expected and later required to present their excuses and give their reasons for not having done so.[61] This practice was in effect for many years.

The most ambitious program was developed by the Miami Synod. A committee appointed to devise a plan reported to the 1850 convention. It suggested both the publication of stewardship literature and the inauguration of a system of gathering offerings. The literature was to be in the form of a "circular" printed in the church papers and to be read to the congregations. It was to stress the themes: "Giving is an essential element of all true religion. God has recorded many precious promises for the encouragement of liberality. He asks us to give proof of our love to Him by the extent of our benevolences." On the practical side it suggested the regular giving of a definite part of one's income, e.g., in a family of seven, the father might give five cents for each working day, the wife two cents, and each child one cent, a total of $37.44 a year. In each congregation there should be a committee of ladies to explain the plan, encourage the giving, and collect the funds.[62]

The plan sounds somewhat naive. It set standards greatly beyond the actual giving of that day, which was far less than a dollar a year per com-

58 *Minutes* of the English Synod, 1845, p. 23.

59 *Minutes* of the Wittenberg Synod, 1850, p. 17.

60 *Minutes* of the English (East Ohio) Synod, 1852, p. 32.

61 *Minutes* of the Wittenberg Synod, 1851, p. 13.

62 *Minutes,* 1850, pp. 13 f.

municant for benevolences. No evidence has survived to indicate how widely the plan was adopted, but there was marked improvement in the Miami Synod's benevolent funds. Up through 1850 the giving to benevolences ranged from nine to sixteen cents per capita of the communicant membership, an indication that many people gave nothing to benevolences during a whole year. The next year the contributions had increased to almost twenty-eight cents per member, which was still far from the plan's ideal, but improving.

In 1853 the Miami Synod was ready to take a step further. On the promotional side, each pastor was urged to instruct his people more fully on the subject of stewardship. On the practical side, the Synod was to provide each pastor with a "small blank book in which to receive subscriptions for Beneficiary Education, Home Missions, Foreign Missions, and Bible Distribution; and that, at the meeting of the next Synod each return his book as his report on the several subjects mentioned." [63] The following year the plan was reaffirmed. Pastors were urged to preach about the benevolent objects separately to cultivate interest. Reports showed that during the year five pastors had followed the plan, five others had done so in part, two merely took collections, one did not follow the plan, and one received no blank book. Thus the majority believed the plan practicable and good.[64]

The result was that the Miami Synod greatly surpassed its sister synods in funds raised for benevolences. While recognizing the fact that statistical standards of that day lacked certain precision, it still is clear that the Miami Synod was far in the lead. The number of communicants reported in 1855 was approximately 3500 in the English Synod, 2700 in the Miami Synod, and 2000 in the Wittenberg Synod. The English Synod reported benevolent offerings of $400. the Miami Synod $1400, the Wittenberg Synod $560. In per capita terms this was eleven cents for the English Synod, fifty-one cents for the Miami Synod, and twenty-seven cents for the Wittenberg Synod. Thus whether in the total of funds raised or in per capita, the Miami Synod contributed more than the other two synods combined, though all of them were feeling the effects of the economic depression of that time.

The stewardship situation in the Joint Synod is not entirely clear. At the 1851 convention the parochial reports covered a period of three years. They indicated that in the three districts there were 237 congregations with

[63] *Minutes,* 1853, p. 13.
[64] *Minutes,* 1854, pp. 7, 15.

23,529 communicants. The total contributions to education, home and foreign missions, and the synodical treasury were $2,324.55, or about ten cents per communicant.[65]

MORAL AND SOCIAL ISSUES

Concern with matters of personal morals appears more frequently in the synods belonging to the General Synod than among other Lutherans in Ohio. Being more Anglicized they felt more strongly the currents derived from revivalism and Puritanism. Persons who possessed "vital religion," or "experimental religion," were expected to show it by strictness of life.

Among other things this included "Sabbath observance." There were repeated resolutions adopted calling the people to stricter observance of the day, and urging the pastors to preach on the subject repeatedly. A conference of the Miami Synod considered it to be inconsistent with good morals for church members to attend a circus. A pastor who attended a circus explained that deceptive advertising had led him to believe he was attending a menagerie; he asked the pardon of the Synod, promising to avoid such offense in the future.[66] The use of tobacco was pronounced disgusting and offensive to "serious, wise, and pious people." Apparently the use of tobacco was a problem in church, for the resolutions decried it as especially offensive in the house of God. Lotteries were condemned as a species of gambling injurious to public and religious life. The English District of the Joint Synod felt that persons engaging in lotteries were proper subjects for church discipline.[67]

The problem of alcoholic drinks received special attention from the temperance movement common in American Protestantism and influential among Anglicized Lutherans in Ohio. *The Lutheran Observer,* which regularly supported the movement, began weekly series of articles with its third issues under the captions, "The Difference that Whiskey Makes," "Ardent Spirits Do Not Increase Strength," "American Independence Secured Without Rum," "Rum Drinking Minister, Read This!" Beginning with the fifth issue it had a regular "Temperance Department." *The Lutheran Standard,* while Greenwald was editor, carried frequent articles with such titles as "The Drunken Mother," "Drunken Physicians," and "The Antidote to

---

[65] *Minutes* of the Joint Synod, 1851, pp. 36 f.

[66] *Minutes* of the English Synod, Extra Session, October 20, 1853, p. 5.

[67] *Minutes* of the English District, 1853, p. 15.

Rum." Editor Mealy published an article entitled "Intemperance and Crime."

When a proposal to support the temperance movement first came before the English Synod in 1837 at the instance of a lay delegate, that body expressed its opposition to intemperance but declined to commit its members to the movement.[68] Two years later the Synod by resolution rejoiced in "the onward march of the Temperance Reformation" and encouraged support of it. A decade passed before expression of sentiment on this matter became energetic. By mid-century when the temperance movement was beginning to have some success in having liquor-control laws enacted, there was a flurry of optimistic support. The Miami Synod expressed its "deep interest in the advancement of the temperance reformation." The Wittenberg Synod, after reciting the evils of the traffic in alcoholic liquors, urged its people to "exert themselves for the discouragement and final overthrow of this horrid business." The English (East Ohio) Synod considered the traffic in intoxicating liquors "a hindrance to the progress of the Gospel and one of the direst curses of the world."

There soon appeared the conviction that action beyond preaching and teaching temperance was needed. In 1852 it was recommended that pastors and laymen "patronize temperance taverns in preference to those who sell intoxicating drinks." In addition to this boycott there was suggested "the use of political influence until this River of Death be stayed." The English Synod was convinced "that the success of this cause imperatively demands the enactment of a law in the State of Ohio similar to that now in force in the State of Maine designed to prohibit the sale of intoxicating liquors as a beverage."[69] In view of this sentiment all Christians were encouraged to vote for such legislators as were pledged to enact a prohibition law. The English District of the Joint Synod joined "in the hope that ere long the traffic in intoxicating liquors as a beverage will cease, that prohibition will be established as the law of the land, and that intemperance will no longer harass and vex the church."[70]

The ideas thus expressed before 1855 were to continue to be the sentiments held for many years to come. They were somewhat incidental interests of Lutherans whose chief concerns were the founding and strengthening

---

[68] Letter by G. W. Keil, *Lutheran Observer*, V, 14 (November 24, 1837), p. 55. There is no mention of this in the printed Minutes.

[69] *Minutes* of the English Synod, 1853, p. 18.

[70] *Minutes* of the English District, 1853, p. 13.

of congregations and institutions. Yet they indicate attention to matters that certainly were problems.

The problem of the Negro, whether freed or enslaved, also drew the attention of Ohio Lutherans. As early as 1827 the Ohio Synod was invited to support a society which proposed to settle free Negroes in Africa. Though approving the purpose of the society, the Synod declined to commit itself as a body financially but left the matter to the discretion of the individual members.[71] As for freeing the slaves, Editor Greenwald of *The Lutheran Standard* felt that the abolition movement, headed by extremists, had "thrown back the emancipation of the slave at least fifty years. Whilst the movements of abolitionists have convulsed the country with excitement and even threatened the dissolution of our happy Union without accomplishing anything whatever as to the practical abolition of slavery . . ." a moderate means was needed.[72]

Among the English synods more vigorous expression appeared, at times in rather florid language. In the Wittenberg Synod slavery was branded a "great national evil and an abomination in the sight of God." The English Synod called slavery "a system of oppression and high-handed injustice, and entirely contrary to the spirit of the Gospel of Christ." One of its pastors, William G. Keil, had moved from the South in order to live "on the free soil of Ohio." Christians were urged to pray for guidance in finding a solution to the problem. They should deplore the efforts made to "extend and perpetuate this stupendous evil." They were to sympathize with both slave and slave-owner who found themselves enmeshed in a system for which they had found no completely just and satisfactory correction. More than this, it was resolved,

> That we consider it the duty of all our ministers and members North and South to seek and to communicate more light on this momentous question; and to use their influence to free the Church from the reproach of participating in the crime of perpetuating oppression, and by all fair and Christian means to aid in delivering the oppressed out of the hands of the oppressor.[73]

It might be expected that the English-speaking Lutherans in Ohio, who thus by implication were fully Americanized, would so insist upon the separation of church and state as to leave entirely alone the political aspects of the slavery problem. Instead it was the German-speaking sections which

---

[71] *Minutes* of the Ohio Synod, 1827, p. 7.
[72] *Lutheran Standard,* I, 21 (March 8, 1843), p. 2.
[73] *Minutes* of the English Synod, 1853, pp. 18 f.

were silent, in keeping with the state-church tradition in which churchmen carefully refrained from dealing with political issues. During the days when there was a struggle in Congress over whether new areas in the West should be slave or free the English synods in Ohio were swept along in the public agitation. When Congress enacted legislation establishing Kansas and Nebraska as territories in which slavery might be legal the Wittenberg and the English (East Ohio) Synods passed resolutions of deep disapproval.[74] From this attitude toward public affairs they were not to recede.

DOCTRINAL POSITIONS

Out of the tensions of the times appeared more decided statements concerning the doctrinal position of the various synods. The issues were debated by S. S. Schmucker and W. M. Reynolds, as noted in an earlier chapter. The problem became acute in the discussion over the *Definite Synodical Platform* which will be discussed in a later chapter. At this point it will suffice to review the statements made previous to 1855.

As early as 1833 the Joint Synod of Ohio had adopted a model constitution for congregations, which specified one of the duties of pastors to be that of "proclaiming the Word of God according to the doctrine of the Symbolical Books of the Evangelical Lutheran Church." [75] This ideal would not prove to be troublsome unless an effort were made to enforce it strictly upon the older pastors unaccustomed to subscribing the Confessional Writings, or upon other pastors who fraternized with the Reformed in union congregations. Three years later the Joint Synod was asked if it intended to take this position seriously and to insist that its pastors adhere strictly to Lutheran doctrine. In reply the following resolution was adopted:

> *Resolved,* That this Synod strictly adhere to the Augsburg Confession of faith, and admit no one to membership in its body who shall deny any part thereof; and that all congregations within its Synodical boundaries be advised to receive no one as teacher [pastor] who does not fully adhere to this confession.[76]

When the first English District became an independent synod the discussion that ensued touched upon the question of loyalty to the Augsburg

---

[74] *Minutes* of the English Synod, 1854, p. 31. The action of the Wittenberg Synod reported in *The Evangelical Lutheran,* October 20, 1854.

[75] *Minutes,* 1833, pp. 18, 27 f.

[76] *Minutes,* 1836, p. 8.

Confession. Pastors in the English Synod were not required to subscribe to that document. Delegates of that body to the General Synod in 1853 were instructed to oppose the introduction or adoption of a "doctrinal basis" for the General Synod.[77] The following year when a pastor declared that he held to the Augsburg Confession in so far as it was "substantially correct" according to Scripture, his statement went unchallenged into the minutes. There were limits, however, to the tolerance of the English synods. A pastor in Zanesville was suspended from the ministry by the Miami Synod in 1854 "for the crime of publishing fundamental error"—in this case, universalism.[78]

Within the Joint Synod the pastors became increasingly sensitive to questions of doctrine. When the General Synod catechism omitted two questions: "Do you believe that the true Body and Blood of Christ are in the Lord's Supper?" and "What induces you to believe this?" the members of the Eastern District of the Joint Synod considered the doctrine omitted one characteristic of the Lutheran Church. They therefore called for the publication of an unmutilated catechism in English.[79]

Four years later the Eastern District expressed itself again. A circular letter, written in 1845 by a General Synod committee headed by S. S. Schmucker and sent to German churchmen, favored the position of the United Church in Germany. It contained the statement "that Luther's peculiar view on the bodily presence of the Lord in the Eucharist had been given up long ago by the great majority of our preachers." In contrast, the Joint Synod was thinking of requiring candidates for ordination to pledge themselves to Lutheran doctrine. The Eastern District expressed itself as favoring such a requirement and declared that it could not "recognize as genuine Lutheran preachers" those who denied the Lutheran doctrine of the Lord's Supper.[80] The unanimous decision of the Joint Synod the next year reads:

> *Resolved,* That the Ministerium herewith adheres to the Symbolical Books of the Evangelical Lutheran Church, and pledges itself to teach accordingly because they correctly declare the doctrines of the holy Scripture; and that in the future all applicants and ordinands will be examined therein and obligated thereto.[81]

77 *Minutes* of the English Synod, 1853, p. 18.
78 *Minutes* of the Miami Synod, 1854, pp. 4, 18. *Lutheran Observer,* December 1, 1854.
79 *Minutes* of the Eastern District, 1841, p. 12.
80 *Lutheran Standard,* IV, 25 (February 3, 1847), p .3.
81 *Minutes* of the Joint Synod, 1848, p. 36.

This decision must be seen, however, in the light of the desire of the Joint Synod to steer a course between the General Synod on the one side and the Missouri Synod on the other. This moderate spirit was expressed by Editor Spielmann in *The Lutheran Standard* in these words:

> We have no desire on the one hand to advocate *ultraism,* nor on the other to indulge in *supercilious invective* on *hyper-orthodoxy* and *exclusiveness;* for we have very little affection for the *vague* and *indefiinite spirit of latitudinarianism* which is palming itself off as genuine Lutheranism. There is, we think, a golden mean between, in which the genuine Lutheran may stand with the Symbols of the Church in his hand.[82]

Something of the same spirit is revealed in Article II of the Constitution of the Joint Synod of 1853 which speaks of "the doctrines of God's Word according to the testimony of all the Symbolical Books of the Evangelical Lutheran Church, or at least as they are set forth in the Unaltered Augsburg Confession and Luther's Small Catechism."

CHURCH PRACTICES

Though Lutherans were neighbors to persons of other church bodies whose practices in administering the sacraments were different, the available evidence indicates that Lutheran customs were continued. When the question of the propriety of baptism by immersion was raised in the English Synod, the answer was "that we see no reason for our ministers to deviate from the general custom of the Lutheran Church on the mode of baptism." [83] Among the German-speaking Lutherans there was enough aversion to the German Baptists to prevent any influence from that direction.

The Communion vessels of that day that have been preserved were usually of pewter or similar metal, and were of simple design. The chalice was a plain cup without a handle. The flagon was a pitcher with straight sides and sometimes without a lid. The question of admitting non-Lutherans to the Communion was troublesome, the Joint Synod tending toward a stricter practice, the other synods toward open Communion though insisting that only baptized persons were to be admitted. As for the quality of the wine to be used, it was the opinion of one synod that often the wines on sale at public places were adulterated with drugs or liquors and that therefore the congregations should make or buy pure wine for sacramental purposes.[84]

[82] *Lutheran Standard,* III, 51 (February 4, 1846), p. 2.
[83] *Minutes* of the English Synod, 1852, p. 31.
[84] Action of the Wittenberg Synod, *Evangelical Lutheran,* October 20, 1854.

The title by which pastors were to be addressed was a topic of discussion for a few years. On the grounds that in the New Testament the clergy were called "bishops" it was decided by the English Synod that its pastors should "be addressed by that apostolic name" beginning in 1842. Three years later the practice was abandoned. The Wittenberg Synod and the Eastern District of the Joint Synod also experimented with the title for a few years, and then discarded it.

Catechetical instruction presented difficulties when the congregations were small and scattered, and when catechisms were scarce. In response to these needs both the General Synod and the Joint Synod published catechisms for their congregations. For the most part catechetical instruction continued to be the practice, even in the congregations that had adopted "new measures." That there was some negligence in this matter is indicated by the fact that both the Joint Synod and the independent synods from time to time reasserted the conviction that catechetical instruction was part of every pastor's task. In the congregations where "new measures" were in vogue, catechetical instruction was combined with those measures. In some instances those who received instruction were expected to attend a protracted meeting and there give evidence of earnest Christian faith. As they phrased it, they regarded catechetical instruction "as a means of leading sinners to an experimental knowledge of God." In other instances the catechetical instruction occurred after the protracted meeting and was given to persons who had been converted.

The majority of the congregations of the independent English synods used these "new measures." It was this fact buttressed by a pietistic theology and a demand for the use of English that led to their independence. With a few exceptions, the English-speaking pastors who opposed "new measures" remained within the Joint Synod during the 1840's. That body blamed the division of Lutherans in Ohio upon the introduction of "new measures." [85] Its congregations were cautioned against such practices by both the Joint Synod and *The Lutheran Standard*. Editor Mealy wrote that though "new measures" have the appearance of usefulness, "all experience has shown them to be rather adapted to promote mere physical excitement and the diffusion of a morbid sympathy than the power of genuine religion." [86] Editor Greenwald complained that the "new measure" men by dishonorable means intruded into well established parishes, producing

[85] *Minutes* of the Joint Synod, 1842, p. 25.

[86] *Lutheran Standard*, III, 1 (December 11, 1844), p. 2.

factions and splitting congregations which even when united were scarcely large enough to support a pastor.[87] The criticism of revivals received fresh force when John Nevin's book, *The Anxious Bench,* was published in 1844. It was translated into German by A. B. Bierdemann and in that form was approved by the Eastern District of the Joint Synod the same year.

In view of this criticism the pastors of the English Synod were cautioned to conform "as much as possible where practicable to the customs, manners, forms and usages of our fathers without injuring the cause of vital godliness." Though things should be done "decently and in order," yet efforts must be made "to awaken sinners and bring them to the knowledge of truth as it is in Christ." [88] Such efforts were made, though spasmodically, pastors assisting each other in conducting protracted meetings. Apparently there were times when the revival spirit lagged. The editor of *The Lutheran Observer* complained in 1849 that "there has rarely been a period within the past ten years when there were so few revivals as at the present time."[89]

The question of membership in secret societies appeared in the 1840's. The Wittenberg Synod in 1847 considered such membership, either for pastors or laymen, "to be highly injurious to the peace and prosperity" of the Church, naming the Masonic Order and the Society of Odd Fellows in particular.[90] The next year the English Synod took similar action for "the peace and harmony" of the Church, limiting itself to forbidding membership by pastors and naming no societies.[91] In 1852 it reaffirmed this resolution. That this action was merely for advice and not for discipline is indicated by the fact that the next year John Hamilton wrote an excuse for his absence from the convention including the notice that he could not serve a parish that year because he was busy as Grand Master of the Grand Lodge of Ohio.[92]

On the question of secret societies it was the Western District of the Joint Synod that first expressed itself. It admonished its members to join no society whose basic position is opposed to the spirit of the Evangelical Lutheran Church.[93] Two years later the Joint Synod voiced its disapproval of societies, especially secret ones, whose aims usurped the functions of the

[87] *Lutheran Standard,* II, 32 (May 31, 1844), p. 2.
[88] *Minutes* of the English Synod, 1842, p. 14.
[89] *Lutheran Observer,* XVII, 48 (November 30, 1849), p. 2.
[90] *Lutheran Observer,* XIV, 45 (July 9, 1847), p. 1.
[91] *Lutheran Observer,* XVI, 21 (May 26, 1848), p. 1.
[92] *Minutes* of Extra Session of the English Synod, 1853, p. 6.
[93] *Minutes* of the Western District, 1852, p. 22.

Christian Church and whose spirit was likely to produce indifference, if not actual hostility, to Christianity. It resolved "that in future we will admit no one into our connection who belongs to said societies." Two pastors, A. Henkel and H. Heincke, gave notice of their negative vote.[94] The next year in the Western District there was raised the question whether this action was constitutional. The District voted to refer the question to the Joint Synod. The prolonged struggle with this problem must be described in a later chapter.

Sunday Schools were part of the program of most of the congregations in Ohio from early days. The Joint Synod at its first convention in 1818 urged all pastors to establish such schools, German being the language most commonly used. A decade later the resolution was renewed and an extensive plan for school operation was devised. Though the number of schools increased rapidly, recommendations for establishing them in all congregations continued to be made.

Literature for the schools began to appear. In 1843 the Western District of the Joint Synod expressed its thanks to Pastor F. Schmidt of Pittsburgh for samples in German of Luther's Small Catechism with additions, a book of ninety-two songs, *Der Meerstrom* (a beautiful Christian story for youth), and an A-B-C book. Literature for Sunday Schools of the English Synods was available from sources connected with the General Synod. Evidence is lacking that any was published in Ohio.

MISSIONS

From the beginning of Lutheranism in Ohio, missionary work was conducted under the plan of "traveling preachers." The synod appointed a pastor to tour a neglected area for a specified time, usually a month. For this service he was paid out of the treasury of the synod. Tours were made westward into Indiana, north and west in Ohio, and on at least one occasion into Canada.[95]

A typical tour was that made by Joseph A. Roof from November 12 to December 16, 1836, in the northwestern counties of Ohio. He was appointed to this task by the English District which agreed to pay him fifteen dollars. He reported to the next convention that he had traveled 486 miles, preached thirteen times, baptized four, confirmed thirteen, administered the Lord's

---

[94] *Minutes* of the Eighth Session of the Joint Synod, June, 1854, pp. 13 f.

[95] Missionary trip by J. D. Nonnenmacher; *Minutes* of the Joint Synod 1848, p. 16.

Supper to 125 communicants, attended four funerals and collected $5.37½.[96] Apparently he had spent on the average about four hours a day in the saddle, traveling fourteen miles, and the offering received averaged forty-one cents each time he preached.

The English District felt that a more systematic and better organized approach to the work was needed. Therefore it recommended that the Joint Synod as a whole organize itself as a missionary society. Apparently this proposal failed to gain support. But when the English District became independent in 1840 it proceeded to adopt the plan for its own operation.[97] In accordance with this program every pastor was expected to be a missionary exploring adjacent areas and giving such pastoral service as was possible to neighboring congregations without a pastor. Occasionally an exploring missionary was sent to farther areas.[98] In special instances a new congregation was given financial support, as was the case when the English Synod appropriated $100 to the English Lutheran mission in Cincinnati.[99] Soon the Home Missionary Society of the General Synod was giving financial aid to pastors of new congregations in Ohio. In 1849 aid was given to A. Helwig at Urbana, and Jacob Schauer at Upper Sandusky; in 1850 to James Cather at Panama, Defiance County, L. C. Barnes at Lock, Knox County, and Philip Locker at Greenville. [100]

The plan of operation whereby the whole synod constituted the missionary society meant that the same persons were members of both organizations, each of which had its own officers, treasury, meetings, and reports. The persistence of such a plan of parallel organizations is indicated by the fact that in 1849 the English District of the Joint Synod constituted itself a missionary society and adopted a "Plan for Missionary Operations." [101] The Western District took similar action. By this time, however, the independent synods were beginning to discard the dual organization plan and to incorporate the missionary work into the synodical structure. The English Synod in 1845 was the first to do so.[102]

[96] *Minutes* of the English District, 1837, p. 12.

[97] *Minutes* of the English District, 1838, p. 13. *Minutes* of the English Synod, 1840, p. 13.

[98] John Surface, exploring missionary in Indiana, reported to the Miami Synod in 1848. *Minutes,* p. 10.

[99] *Minutes* of the English Synod, 1843, p. 12.

[100] *Lutheran Observer,* XVII, 25 (June 22, 1849), p. 1. *Minutes* of the General Synod, 1850, pp. 46 f.

[101] *Minutes* of the English District, 1849, p. 14.

[102] *Minutes* of the English Synod, 1845, p. 21.

Though this missionary activity resulted in a considerable increase in the number of congregations and in membership, it also produced an unavoidable and deplorable rivalry between the independent synods and the Joint Synod. Since most of the congregations of the Joint Synod were opposed to "new measures" and entrenched themselves behind the German language, the synods favoring "new measures" and English had to decide whether or not to establish new congregations of their kind in areas where congregations of the other kind already existed.

Occasionally it happened that in a congregation of the Joint Synod there was a faction so sympathetic to "new measures" and English that it withdrew and formed a new congregation. The other synods, facing the question of whether or not to give encouragement to such a faction, decided to give that encouragement by accepting it as a congregation in their fellowship. This action was justified on the grounds that revivals were needed for true piety, that English was necessary for the growth of Lutheranism, and that if the faction were rejected it would turn to some other denomination and thus be lost to the Lutheran Church.[103] Good will between the synods always suffered in such instances.

Active interest in foreign missions was first aroused by correspondence from missionaries and by publications describing the pathetic conditions in heathen lands. From India J. C. F. Heyer, missionary of the Ministerium of Pennsylvania, wrote often about his work. His letters were printed in the church papers which circulated in Ohio. On one occasion he told of the need of $2000 for the mission. In 1843 Pastor J. G. C. Schweizerbarth, in his report as president of the Eastern District of the Joint Synod, called attention to Heyer's plea. He recalled the fact that the District had established a Foreign Mission Society in 1837, but that practically nothing had been done. He suggested that the District pledge itself to pay $100 annually to the India mission. The decision of the District, however, was to request each pastor to take an annual collection for missions, the funds to be divided equally between home and foreign missions.[104]

The mission in India was known also by those in Ohio who were part of the General Synod. Any contributions to that work came from individuals and congregations rather than from synods. At Wittenberg College missionary interest appeared quite early. A Missionary Society was organized on August 3, 1847, following a preliminary meeting July 16. It was composed of theological students, fifteen of whom signed the constitution. Their

103 *Minutes* of the English Synod, 1842, pp. 9, 20.
104 *Minutes* of the Eastern District, 1843, pp. 8, 12, 14.

aims were to inform themselves on foreign and domestic missions so as to promote the cause.[105]

The following summer Ezra Keller wrote that one of the "fruits of the revival last winter" was a

> missionary spirit which now so strongly possesses our pious students. Besides the monthly meeting and exercises on the subject of missions in the church and Institution, the students hold a missionary prayer and conference meeting every fortnight. And we have the pleasing anticipation that before many years our Wittenberg will preach the precious Gospel in heathen lands. The Lord grant us the joy of realizing this anticipation.[106]

About the same time a student who used the pen-name "Andrew" wrote a series of thirteen articles under the title, "Our Brother's Cry," in which he described the work of foreign missions in such a way as to appeal for funds and volunteers. His articles show maturity and considerable acquaintance with foreign mission literature.[107]

Further interest was created when a graduate of the theological department of Wittenberg College, William Isaac Cutter, was ordained by the Miami Synod in 1851 to be a missionary appointed by the Foreign Missionary Society of the General Synod. The ordination service conducted in Springfield made a profound impression. Here was the first person to go from Ohio to the foreign field as a Lutheran missionary. Soon afterwards in Seward, New York, an impressive service was held in connection with his wedding before he and his bride set sail for the mission field in India. By the end of 1855, however, Mrs. Cutter's health was such that they had to return to America.

About the same time another Wittenberg graduate, Morris Officer, aroused further missionary interest by his pleas for and commitment to work in Africa.[108] Since there was no Lutheran society prepared to support work there, he accepted appointment in 1852 by the American Missionary Association.[109] That year he preached on the subject at the convention of the English Synod. A resolution was introduced to invite him "to present the claims of this noble cause" to the congregations. Unwilling to commit

---

[105] *Minutes Book of the Missionary Society of Wittenberg College.*

[106] Letter in *The Lutheran Observer*, XVI, 28, July 14, 1848, p. 111.

[107] Articles in *The Lutheran Observer* beginning April 28, 1848, and a supplement October 20, 1848.

[108] See Alexander J. Imhoff, *The Life of Rev. Morris Officer* (Dayton, 1876).

[109] This was a Congregationalist organization which arose out of anti-slavery sentiment, came to include interest in settling ex-slaves in Africa, and finally focused on missionary work among ex-slaves and other natives in Africa.

itself that far, the Synod, after voting hearty approval of his decision to be a missionary, gave him the undefined assurance that it "will in every appropriate way assist him in the prosecution of his noble purpose." [110]

Morris Officer reached Africa the following February. Correspondence from him concerning the work there produced in the English Synod a more generous mood, so that it resolved to "cordially invite him on his return to his native country to visit our congregations to present the spiritual wants of that people and their claims upon the Church." [111] A year later he had returned. His account of conditions in Africa was listened to with great interest. A pamphlet written by him entitled, "A Plea for a Lutheran Mission in Liberia," [112] was circulated effectively. At every opportunity he urged his proposal.

The founding of a mission in Africa required resources larger than the English synods in Ohio could supply. They decided to request action by the General Synod to be convened in Dayton in June, 1855.[113] The way in which that request resulted in the establishment of the mission in Liberia will be described in a later chapter. At this point it is enough to note that the Miami Synod joined in the request. It proposed that the General Synod appoint a committee of five to establish a training school for Negroes who would be sent to Africa as missionaries. It would be the duty of the committee to purchase property and to appoint a General Agent who would seek Negro candidates, supervise their training, and solicit funds. The Miami Synod decided further that if the General Synod did not start a mission in Africa it would undertake to do so. Morris Officer was nominated as General Agent, and a tentative committee of five was appointed.[114] It was this same Synod that had encouraged its congregations in 1853 to offer prayers, provide funds, and supply missionaries for the work in Guntur, India.[115]

Missionary work among the American Indians was resolved upon by the Northern District of the Joint Synod in 1851. Then it was referred to the Joint Synod which appointed a committee to conduct the work.[116] But by 1855 nothing definite had been accomplished.

110 *Minutes* of the English Synod, 1852, pp. 18, 25, 27.
111 *Minutes* of the English Synod, 1853, p. 20.
112 Published in Baltimore, Md., 1855, price ten cents; printed serially in *The Lutheran Observer*, May 11 and 18, 1855.
113 *Minutes* of the English Synod, 1854, pp. 20, 23.
114 *Minutes* of the Miami Synod, 1855, pp. 10, 18.
115 *Minutes* of the Miami Synod, 1853, pp. 16 f.
116 *Minutes* of the Joint Synod, 1853, p. 34.

THE WAY THINGS LOOKED

Lutherans in Ohio in the 1830's and 40's needed more pastors. Virtually every synodical convention had before it requests from vacant congregations for pastoral service. In addition there were communities in which Lutherans had not been organized into congregations. A pastor seeing this need wrote, "I hope that some of our young brethren will ere long cross the mountains and come to our assistance." [117] A letter from "a much respected and pious layman residing in Ohio" declared that if a Lutheran pastor able to preach in German and English would come to their community a congregation large enough to support him could be organized. "I and my family would have joined the Methodist connection long ago if we had not cherished the pleasing hope of having a minister of our own some day." [118] A correspondent in 1839 stated that "In Richland County, Ohio, there are about twelve congregations vacant." [119]

The shortage of ministers created a situation in which unworthy clergymen and clerical impostors could appear. A missionary in 1839 reported that

> the Lutheran Church in Ohio is bleeding at every pore in consequence of ungodly men who assume the clerical office among them, and by their impious conduct have well nigh ruined the church. I fear our synods are not strict enough in the investigation of the character of those persons who apply for license.[120]

Another correspondent, noting that such men of bad character "invariably held collections and not infrequently spend it for the liquid poison," observed that they were few in number and usually were men expelled from other synods.[121]

James Manning in his report as president of the English District in 1837 said:

> It is to be deplored that the character of the church in the West has been so much injured by straggling imposters who represent themselves to be Lutheran ministers, when it is notorious that they are without any license or standing in any Synod, and who by their immoral and frequently outrageously vile conduct utterly destroy the hopes and prospects of our church in many places. It is to be regretted, too, that our members in many instances

[117] Letter by A. S. Link, *Lutheran Observer*, VII, 28 (March 23, 1840), p. 3.
[118] *Lutheran Observer*, II, 37 (May 8, 1835), p. 147.
[119] *Lutheran Observer*, VI, 23 (January 25, 1839), p. 3.
[120] Letter by R. Weiser, *Lutheran Observer*, VI, 48 (July 19, 1839), p. 3.
[121] Letter signed "Ohio," *Lutheran Observer*, VII, 3 (September 6, 1839), p. 2.

are not more careful in admitting men into their churches as preachers; for in every instance where a stranger appears among them and represents himself as being a Lutheran minister, they should first require him to produce his certificate of Licensure or Ordination or other well authenticated testimonial of regular standing in some Lutheran Synod.[122]

Another writer complained that clergymen who had gotten into trouble in Germany were encouraged to come to America to reform their morals. Such a man usually "brought an open letter in which he was recommended for his talents, learning, eloquence and many other external good qualities, and at the same time a *sealed* letter in which the same writer bid us beware of him,—that he was guilty of this and that transgression."[123]

The synods in Ohio exercised such discipline as they could. When accusations were made there were investigations, and when the evidence justified it a pastor's name was removed from the clerical roll. In other instances a man's name disappears from the roll with no reason being given, but leaving the impression that his life and work as a pastor had not been satisfactory. Such instances of discipline were few but painful.

It is certain that the salaries paid to pastors were not large enough to attract many impostors. Joshua Crouse wrote: "My salary for preaching the first year [1844-45] all told was seventy-five dollars, and I preached nine years before my support from the people amounted to three hundred dollars a year." [124] D. P. Rosenmiller in Dayton wrote that "many of our western ministers are very meagerly supported." [125] Edward Hengstenberg's account of salaries in America was:

> Whilst the salary of American clergymen in the country generally among Episcopalians, Presbyterians and Congregationalists amounts to from $600 to $800, and among the Methodists . . . from $400 to $500, we find that, with the exception of the old and well endowed congregations in the large seaports, the income of German clergymen varies from $150 to $350. . . . The lowest sum necessary for even a tolerable support is from $350 to $400.[126]

For Lutheran pastors in Ohio this description was likely true, though the English congregations seem to have provided more adequately. When Solomon Ritz was engaged as district missionary by the Miami Synod in

122 *Minutes* of the English District, 1837, p. 5.
123 Letter signed "Americus," *Lutheran Observer*, X, 48 (August 4, 1843), p. 2.
124 Typed copy of *Autobiography of Rev. Joshua Crouse*, p. 72.
125 *Lutheran Observer*, XIII, 1 (August 29, 1845), p. 2.
126 *Lutheran Observer*, XVI, 10 (March 10, 1848), p. 1.

1851 his salary for the year was set at $500. Salaries increased as congregations grew, but living costs advanced also. Congregations were urged to increase salaries "in proportion to the advancement of the prices on the necessaries of life," and pastors were advised to preach on the subject.[127]

It was during these years that the federal government was struggling to stabilize its money and to provide adequate coinage. There was a struggle over control of banks and bank notes, some of which were not accepted at face value. In 1839 *The Lutheran Observer* published this notice: "We must request our agents in Ohio and farther west to suspend their remittances for the present, or else send us better money. The postage and discount on a five dollar Ohio note amounts to one dollar, and this is more than we can afford to pay." [128]

By 1855 some synods were discussing plans for aiding aged or incapacitated pastors. They asked the congregations to gather an offering each year for such a fund. The English Synod had before it a plan for a Preachers' Aid Society to give assistance to pastors "worn-out, afflicted or dying while active in the Evangelical Lutheran Church," but it deferred action. To the fund of the Society each pastor was to give one dollar a year and to transmit the offerings gathered in his congregations. It was hoped that the aid would amount to $100 a year for each needy pastor, a hundred for his wife or widow, and twenty dollars for each child under fifteen years of age.[129] The Miami Synod was studying a similar plan the same year, though it expected to conduct the program through a committee instead of an auxiliary society. The proposed scale of benefits differed in that the wife would receive fifty dollars, a widow seventy-five dollars, and children between the ages of ten and fifteen ten dollars each.[130]

Descriptions of the general religious conditions of the day were colored by the mood of the reporter and the purpose of the report. If he wanted to encourage his audience, he would point to gains being made. Thus in the report on "the state of the church" made to the General Synod in 1850 it was said that in the Miami Synod "the churches are generally in a prosperous condition." [131] Of three pastors of the English Synod reporting in 1846, one thought there had been a decline in zeal and evangelism, a

---

[127] *Minutes* of the English Synod, 1853, p. 12.
[128] Issue of November 22, 1839, p. 2.
[129] *Minutes* of the English Synod, 1855, pp. 12, 37 f.
[130] *Minutes* of the Miami Synod, 1855, pp. 13 f.
[131] *Minutes* of the General Synod, 1850, p. 33.

second said, "My charge is in a tolerably prosperous condition," and the third reported sixty converts made in recent revivals in his parish.[132] If the reporter looked at the community around his congregation he might give a gloomy account. It was said of Zanesville in 1839, "the state of religion there is deplorable beyond description in consequence of the prevalence of Infidelity, Universalism, and irreligion generally." [133] D. P. Rosenmiller wrote that in Dayton,

> men forget eternal interests in the amusements of the world. Sometimes political excitement will be the all-engrossing subject, sometimes the mania of speculation will turn men's brains away, and now to make money by close dealing and speculate upon the probability of a war with Mexico seems to be the all-engrossing theme. In the meanwhile but few seem deeply concerned for the cause of Christ.[134]

As far as the statistics may be trusted the indication is that there was Lutheran growth. In 1833 there were thirty-seven pastors, 159 congregations, and 13,252 communicants. As reported in 1855 there were in the Joint Synod (consisting of four districts) 103 pastors, 194 congregations, and 19,439 adult members; in the three English synods there were sixty-four pastors, 173 congregations, and 8,324 adult members. This was a total of 167 pastors, 367 congregations, and 27,763 members. It includes some congregations in Pennsylvania, but does not include Missouri Synod congregations in Ohio. It indicates that in two decades Lutheran membership had doubled. It is noteworthy also that in 1833 the average number of communicants per congregation was eighty-three, and the average parish had four congregations. In 1855 the average number of adult members per congregation was 100 in the Joint Synod, but forty-eight in the English synods. Average parish size had declined to slightly less than two congregations in the Joint Synod, and less than three in the English synods. There were fifty-six Sunday Schools in the Joint Synod, and 133 in the three English synods.

During these decades when population was increasing in the state, the means of communication and travel were improving. Roads through the state both brought new settlers into it and also conveyed others out of it to the West. A missionary in 1839 considered Ohio delightful country with good soil, equal to the best in Maryland; land could be bought in Colum-

---

[132] *Lutheran Observer*, XIV, 16 (December 11, 1846), p. 1.

[133] *Minutes* of the English District, 1839, p. 8.

[134] *Lutheran Observer*, XIII, 4 (September 19, 1845), p. 2.

biana and neighboring counties for twenty-five to thirty dollars an acre, but the price was declining because people were moving farther west.[135] Ezra Keller found areas in which virgin timber was standing majestically, but the roads that were cut through were very muddy in wet weather. To keep them passable, logs were laid across the road making a continuous though uneven covering. A Lutheran visitor to the state in 1835 wrote:

> We entered Steubenville on the Ohio and proceeded thence to Cadiz through a broken country over a rough road. They do not seem to understand the value of turnpikes in this state,—they have *rail roads* in abundance, but they are not like yours at Baltimore, constructed of iron, but really and literally of *rails* or *logs,* and those laid across the road. I advise all dyspeptics to take a jaunt on the rail roads of Ohio, and if they out-live the operation they will certainly be cured. From Cadiz (where we paid but 37½ cts. for a most sumptuous supper, clean bed and excellent breakfast) we went to New Philadelphia where we got among our German countrymen.[136]

Jacob Crigler, after years of pastoral service in Boone County, Kentucky, moved to Portsmouth, Ohio, a few years before he died, and from that point went to preach to congregations in the country. He wrote:

> As I have no horse here, they have promised to fetch me, which they do in their plantation wagons . . . and those without any covering. . . . In these I set on my chair and take the weather as it comes. Sometimes while I am travelling over those rugged roads I am tossed to and fro from one side of the wagon to the other, and if my hold happens to break I have fallen flat on my back in the wagon.[137]

Yet these were the days when an extensive system of canals was built in the state and railroad trains were beginning to haul passengers. Three articles entitled "Notes of Western Travel," likely written by W. M. Reynolds, the first president of Capital University, when he came to occupy that position, give an interesting account of a trip westward over the mountains to Pittsburgh by stage coach, by steamboat to Cincinnati, and by railroad to Xenia and Columbus.[138]

In 1854 residents of Dayton were rejoicing in railroad connections whereby they could get to New York or Baltimore in thirty-six hours for a fare of ten dollars. The second half of the nineteenth century was a time

---

[135] R. Weiser, *Lutheran Observer*, VI, 48 (July 19, 1839), p. 3.

[136] *Lutheran Observer*, III, 4 (September 18, 1835), p. 15.

[137] Letter in *The Lutheran Observer*, X, 42 (June 23, 1843), p. 2.

[138] *Lutheran Standard*, VIII, 9 (June 19, 1850); 10 (July 3); and 12 (July 31, 1850).

of greatly improved transportation with important consequences for the marketing of Ohio grain and livestock. Railroads affected church life both by improving communications and by increasing general economic prosperity in the state.

Though by mid-century Ohio was a generation removed from a life of frontier subsistence, its population was still predominantly rural. Education in the country schools was brief and elementary. Clergymen or church bodies ventured to begin academies and colleges in many localities. What Lutherans were doing in education was typical of the activity displayed by religious denominations generally and often earlier. In publishing church periodicals Lutheran synods were attempting to supply for their constituents a literature comparable to that arriving in Methodist or Presbyterian homes. Hymnals were commonly used by those Protestants who were literate.

In facing the second half of the century Lutherans as well as other Christians had an awareness of undertakings well begun, but of great tasks in education and missions still awaiting attention. Meanwhile on farms and in villages concern for church activities was being distracted by political excitement related closely to the question of slavery.

8 / SCHISM AT THE SUMMIT
1855-1881

AMONG THE FACTORS which brought the American nation into the lamentable conflict of the Civil War, two are usually given special attention: sectionalism (differences in local loyalty) and slavery (differences in theory and practice). The military decision of the war did not resolve these differences; it simply prevented their manifestation in secession and involuntary servitude.

The conflicts in which Ohio Lutherans were engaged in this period were also sectional and ideational, though the latter, as it concerned doctrine, was much more prominent. Lutherans were involved in decisions affecting theology and fellowship, and the conflicts produced heated feelings and strong words. The result as seen after 1881 was a pattern of separation still apparent among Lutherans in America.

There are some issues that cannot be endlessly postponed. They must be faced. Doctrine has been such an issue among Lutherans. When a controversy arose the opponents promptly were aligned as contending parties. The calculating efforts of either side to gain ground met resistance. Either party endeavored as a defensive measure to become more deeply entrenched. Each party accused the other of being the aggressor. Presently there arose the conviction that a victory must be gained whatever the cost to unity or fellowship. So the conflict was on.

"AMERICAN LUTHERANISM"

The first conflict in this period occurred within the General Synod, although the Joint Synod of Ohio indicated clearly where its sympathies lay. In Ohio the four synods having membership in the General Synod were East Ohio (the name taken by the English Synod in 1857), Miami, Wittenberg, and the English Synod and Ministerium (which had just seceded as an English District from the Joint Synod). These were the synods which were directly concerned with the effort to make dominant in the General Synod the modified doctrinal system known as "American Lutheranism" and advocated by Schmucker, Kurtz, and Sprecher.

As is often the case, the issue was complicated by other factors. Preferences in language, in practice, and in liturgy were involved. Yet the sharpest conflict was in the area of doctrine. Specifically the question was whether to accept the Augsburg Confession in its full or in a modified form. Those who accepted the Unaltered Augsburg Confession without reservation were denounced by their opponents as intolerant "Symbolists," "Old Lutherans," or simply "foreigners" who held to antiquated, unreasonable, and un-American ideas. Members of the other party considered themselves up-to-date, tolerant, American, and at the same time as truly Lutheran as was Melanchthon. But since these were men who accepted only the "fundamental" doctrines of the Augsburg Confession, and who permitted dissent in doctrines considered "non-fundamental," they were accused of being un-Lutheran and latitudinarian. Perhaps the term "Melanchthonian" best designates them.

It will be remembered that from the beginning Lutheranism in Ohio contained two trends. One of these, led by John Stough, was strongly pietist, greatly concerned about the devout life of individual Christians, but giving less attention to matters of doctrine. The other, represented by the Henkels, was congenial to the strong doctrinal emphasis found in the Tennessee Synod. Both parties were hostile to the rationalism that previously had been so prominent in American religion. The General Synod had been organized to provide fellowship between Lutherans of both kinds, as well as to present a united front against rationalism. The achievement of these goals required a policy of toleration by each party of Lutherans for the other. The Joint Synod of Ohio by 1855 had come to consider such toleration a concession to error, so that membership in the General Synod was unthinkable. In this it followed the leadership of Lehmann and Loy. The Ohio synods of the General Synod, especially those influenced by Sprecher, favored the policy of toleration. At the same time it must be recognized that in all these Ohio synods there were varying shades of opinion on this matter.

The tolerant spirit within the General Synod was soon to be challenged from both sides. The one party whenever possible secured the adoption by Synod of a constitutional article accepting the Augsburg Confession, and of a regulation requiring canditdates for ordination to pledge themselves to preach in accordance with it. The other party as far as possible kept doctrinal statements out of synodical constitutions and avoided confessional pledges by ordinands. But some in this party recognized that theirs was a weak position which ought to be strengthened by a firm declaration of views—a declaration which might be adopted by the General Synod and district synods.

The call for a declaration containing only "fundamental" doctrines marked a basic change in strategy from the earlier policy of making no doctrinal statements. Typical of the new trend was a series of articles in *The Lutheran Observer* beginning November 13, 1852, signed "Sander." Their basic assumption was that the actual doctrinal basis of the General Synod was a qualified acknowledgment of the Augsburg Confession, omitting such doctrines as that of the real presence of Christ in the Lord's Supper. "Sander" wrote, "I am decidedly of the opinion, sir, that the time has come when our church in connection with the General Synod ought to adopt a confession of faith. Let it be the Augsburg Confession so modified as to obviate the difficulties already spoken of." It should define doctrines on which all should agree, allowing freedom on other doctrines. Thus it would meet the need for "a clear, unequivocal and veracious declaration."[1]

As if in response to this demand, pastors of the General Synod in the late summer of 1855 received an anonymous publication called the *Definite Synodical Platform*.[2] It contained a proposed constitution for synods and an "American Recension of the Augsburg Confession" which rephrased articles alleged to contain error.

The document received a much less favorable reception than its authors anticipated. Those who were loyal to the Augsburg Confession rejected the *Platform* vigorously. The first mention of it in *The Lutheran Observer* is a letter supporting it and also a hostile letter which said, "It is the embodiment of the rankest partyism, urging the condemnation of the great Reformers and a large portion of the Lutheran Church, and which, if pressed, must become a wedge of deep disruption . . . I would therefore beseech our Synods not to touch this fatherless revolutionary platform."[3]

There were many other pastors who agreed with the doctrinal views of the *Definite Synodical Platform* but were opposed to the strategy which

[1] *Lutheran Observer*, November 13 and 19, December 31, 1852, and January 21, 1853.
[2] So stamped on the cover. The title page reads: *Definite Platform, Doctrinal and Disciplinarian, for Evangelical Lutheran District Synods; Constructed in Accordance with the Principles of the General Synod*. Philadelphia: Miller & Burlock. 1855.
[3] Unsigned letter, *Lutheran Observer*, XXIII, 38 (September 21, 1855).

produced it. They stood on the principle of toleration. They insisted that agreement in doctrine was not necessary for united work in the General Synod. They believed that the adoption of any doctrinal statements whether conservative or liberal, would wreck the General Synod. Therefore they opposed the document.

Those who favored the *Platform* believed that adopting it was both necessary and honest. It would mark the end of indecisiveness. It would be an action both frank and forthright, specifying publicly the kind of doctrinal position they held. If it led to division in the General Synod, then at least there would be an end of the struggle then going on.

> If adoption of the American Recension of the Augsburg Confession cannot be adopted without dividing the church, let the division take place in fact, for it now virtually does exist. The breach cannot be much enlarged. The symbolic men have made a breach and we cannot close it without the sacrifice of everything we hold dear as free independent American Lutherans.[4]

The outcome was that the *Platform* was either rejected or ignored by an overwhelming majority of the members of the General Synod.[5] Such a defeat was an unexpected disappointment for its supporters, chief of whom were S. S. Schmucker, Benjamin Kurtz, and Samuel Sprecher. Schmucker soon acknowledged his part in the preparation of the *Platform*.[6] In writing the document he had conferred with the others. Kurtz as editor of *The Lutheran Observer* espoused and defended the *Platform* in his paper with all possible vigor. Sprecher used his influence at synod conventions. But outside of Ohio their efforts met with little success.

Their aim by this bold move was to counteract the growing confessionalism among Lutherans in America. Within the Ministerium of Pennsylvania, which after a separation of thirty years had rejoined the General Synod, there had developed strong loyalty to the Lutheran confessions. In an effort to increase the confessional party in the General Synod, the Ministerium urged the Joint Synod of Ohio to join that body. It was to offset just such a development and the influences coming out of the Missouri Synod that the "American Lutheranism" party acted. "Nativism" as well as doctrinal considerations were at work. Thus it was stated that a critic of the *Platform* in the *Lutherischer Herold* was "evidently a foreigner." Such foreigners do not "know how to appreciate the liberties of America,

---

[4] Letter by "A True Lutheran," *Lutheran Observer*, XXIII, 39 (September 28, 1855).
[5] See the extended treatment in Virgilius Ferm, *The Crisis in American Lutheran Theology* (New York, 1927).
[6] *Lutheran Observer*, XXIII, 41 (December 7, 1855).

either civil or religious, so imperfectly do they understand the liberal principles of the General Synod with which this Definite Platform is in entire harmony." [7]

Two of the English synods in Ohio affiliated with the General Synod adopted the *Platform,* largely through the influence of Samuel Sprecher. A third partly endorsed its doctrinal position without adopting it *in toto.* A fourth synod rejected it emphatically.

The first of these synods to convene after the *Platform* appeared was the Wittenberg Synod, which met in Bellefontaine September 6 to 12, 1855. Sprecher was a member of that synod. The committee of which he was chairman recommended the adoption of the *Platform* for it "supplies a great want in our church." It accordingly was adopted.[8] A year later, when it was clear that the *Platform* had met with little approval generally, the president, Joshua Crouse, noted that the other synods had accused the Wittenberg Synod of hasty action. But it renewed its affirmation of the previous year, modifying its position only to the degree that it left the question open as to whether or not the Augsburg Confession contained the errors alleged by the *Platform.*[9]

The East Ohio Synod convened in Shanesville October 18 to 23, 1855. Sprecher was present and was granted the privileges of an advisory member. The *Platform* was "adopted to be the Platform of this Synod," and its text was printed in full in the minutes.[10]

The English Synod and Ministerium of Ohio held its convention at Uniontown, October 25 to 29, 1855. Since loyalty to the Augsburg Confession was a characteristic of this Synod, the *Platform* was certain of rejection. The Synod took this action:

> *Resolved,* That this Synod regrets exceedingly the appearance of such a production, and hereby enters its most solemn protest against it, believing that it is not only subversive of all that is peculiar in Lutheranism, but that it is also in the highest degree unjust to her past history, incorrect and uncandid in the representation of her doctrines, injurious to her character as a church, dangerous to her peace, and utterly uncalled for by anything in the condition of the church in the west.[11]

[7] *Lutheran Observer,* XXIII, 52 (December 21, 1855).

[8] *Minutes,* Wittenberg Synod, 1855, pp. 20 ff.

[9] *Minutes,* Wittenberg Synod, 1856, pp. 17 f.

[10] Pp. 14-25.

[11] *Proceedings of the Nineteenth Annual Convention of the English Evangelical Lutheran Synod and Ministerium of Ohio and Adjacent States,* 1855, p. 10.

By the time the Miami Synod met, May 30 to June 3, 1856, the fate of the *Platform* was evident. A minority within the Synod was influential enough to prevent an unconditional acceptance of the the *Platform*. When that document came before the convention there was a majority and a minority committee report. The majority report, after being amended, was adopted. In the spirit of the *Platform* it declared: "We reject, 1. The approval of the ceremonies of the Mass; 2. Private confession and absolution; 3. The denial of the divine obligation of the Christian Sabbath; 4. Baptismal regeneration; 5. The Real Presence of the Body and Blood of the Saviour in the Eucharist." But it went on to say,

> We also reject the Preamble, Resolutions and Disclaimer accompanying what is commonly called the "Definite Synodical Platform," and receive the Original Augsburg Confession of Faith, so far as it is consistent with the foregoing five articles of rejection relating to the Mass, Confession, Christian Sabbath, Baptismal Regeneration, and the Real Presence.

The minority report would have left open the question as to whether or not the Augsburg Confession teaches these five things in the sense "that Baptism is of necessity attended with an internal spiritual change 'from the mere outward performance of the act,' " or that in the Eucharist there is "the gross and material presence of the body and blood" of Christ.[12]

Ultimately, however, it was the minority statement concerning baptism and the Eucharist which was adopted. At the 1857 convention it was asserted that the 1856 action in effect amended the synodical constitution, but in an unconstitutional way. Therefore a proposal to amend the constitution in proper order was made, final action to be taken a year later. The proposal would insert in the constitution a list of nine "fundamental doctrines" typical of evangelical Protestantism. Concerning the five rejected doctrines, it was proposed to say: "We do not believe that the following errors are taught in the Augsburg Confession." But this was changed to read: "We utterly repudiate and abhor the following errors." And the statements on baptism and the Eucharist were those of the minority report of 1856. The proposed amendment was adopted in 1858.[13]

In the synods outside Ohio, except in the Olive Branch Synod, the *Definite Synodical Platform* went down to defeat. It failed to accomplish its aim of establishing "American Lutheranism" as the official position of the General Synod. The Minutes of the 1857 convention of that body make

---

[12] *Minutes* of the Miami Synod, 1856, pp. 13 ff.

[13] *Minutes*, 1857, pp. 14 ff.; 1858, pp. 9 f.

no mention of the *Platform*. Its cause was hopelessly lost, and no effort was made to revive it.

Its failure was in part due to a mistake in strategy. Because the *Platform* was written privately without authorization by the General Synod, and was published anonymously, it was received with suspicion by some persons. The method was too secretive, too underhanded. At the same time it proposed uniform action in all the synods whereby all of them would adopt the identical text of the *Plaform*. In this plan it was too restrictive; the independence and liberty of the synods was jeopardized. For both reasons the strategy backfired.

The fate of the *Platform* made apparent the fact that in the General Synod an extreme group could not hope to win the whole body. This would be true whether the extreme group was of the left or of the right. The dominant spirit was to be one of toleration. This was the interpretation given by Charles Porterfield Krauth in 1857. Concerning Articles Two and Ten of the Augsburg Confession, he said, the General Synod

> leaves brethren in absolute liberty . . . to accept or reject such parts. . . . No man who desires freedom of conscience can ask more than this. . . . The Augsburg Confession with liberty in non-fundamentals, the whole Augsburg Confession, and nothing but the Augsburg Confession will be the basis of union for our church in this country. If she cannot unite on that, she cannot unite on anything.[14]

It was apparent also that there was a strong determination to preserve this spirit of toleration in the General Synod as the only policy capable of uniting Lutherans in America. The party of "American Lutheranism" and the synods in Ohio which adopted the *Platform* were regarded with some disfavor and suspicion. They were looked upon as a party of strife, placing the worst possible interpretation upon the position of the confessionalists. For example, when there was court action between the English and the German Lutheran congregations at Circleville, Ohio, a report signed "Vindex" alleged that the German congregation testified in court to believing the five doctrines alleged by the *Platform* to be errors.[15] John Wagenhals, pastor of the German congregation, replied that "Vindex" had entirely misrepresented the court testimony and had charged the confessional Lutherans with teaching views they did not hold.[16]

[14] *Missionary*, May 14, 1857.
[15] *Lutheran Observer*, April 20, 1860.
[16] *Missionary*, May 17, 1860.

Within the Joint Synod of Ohio there was distinct aversion to the proponents of "American Lutheranism." The charge by the *Platform* that the Augsburg Confession contained errors was quite distasteful. At that time it was customary at every synodical convention to have a committee report on the published minutes received from other synods. In 1856 the Joint Synod *"Resolved,* that in the future we consider only the proceedings of such synods as at least avow the unaltered Augsburg Confession in the spirit and sense of the collected symbolical creeds of the Evangelical Lutheran Church." [17] Under such circumstances no union of Lutheranism in Ohio was possible, nor could fellowship be expected.

Neither the Joint Synod of Ohio nor its Districts could be directly involved in the proposed plan of the *Definite Synodical Platform* since they were not part of the General Synod. But *The Lutheran Standard* gave considerable attention to it. The first mention occurred in the issue of October 19, 1855, where there are reports of the unanimous adoption of the *Platform* by the Wittenberg Synod, and unanimous rejection by the East Pennsylvania Synod. The editor had not yet seen a copy, but in his judgment "the convulsions of death have come upon *American* Lutheranism." The point which was stressed in this and subsequent issues of the paper was that the *Platform* evidently was marked by a sectarian spirit. The charge that the Augsburg Confession contains errors was obviously an absurdity.

For many months the readers of *The Lutheran Standard* had been receiving a steady flow of articles interpreting sympathetically the doctrines of confessional Lutheranism. Beginning in December, 1853, and continuing for the next three years, there was published serially "A Popular Exposition of the Augsburg Confession. From the German of Lehmann & Schnabel, by M." Steady readers of this series would have found the allegations of the *Platform* preposterous. No letters or articles approving the *Platform* appeared in *The Lutheran Standard;* instead, it became a means of expressing the opposition felt even by members of the General Synod. *The Lutheran Standard* gave full publicity to the published refutation of the *Platform* by W. J. Mann and J. N. Hoffman. It also quoted the criticisms which appeared in *Lehre und Wehre.*

Though the editorials and articles in *The Lutheran Standard* were not without partisanship and bias, for the most part they were calm and clearheaded enough to detect three serious defects in the program of the *Definite Platform.* The first had to do with the question of the authority and reliability of the Augsburg Confession. The "Recensionists," as the supporters of

---

[17] *Minutes* (German), Joint Synod, 1856, p. 5.

the *Platform* were called in the *Standard,* made charges of error in the Augsburg Confession which were simply unfounded. It was hard to understand how the authors of the *Platform* could have such a mistaken understanding of the Augsburg Confession. The *Platform* must be the evidence of an un-Lutheran spirit which would down-grade and disparage the standard confessional statement of Lutheranism.

In the second place, the writers of *The Lutheran Standard* considered the *Platform* disruptive and sectarian. Its preparation and publication was a calculated effort to enforce "American Lutheranism" upon the whole General Synod and narrow that body to its point of view. Pastors of confessional loyalty must either surrender or withdraw. In order to avoid the charge of being disruptive, the "Recensionists" made the accusation of schism against those they called "symbolists" who, they said, were already dividing Lutheranism in America. It was apparent to *The Lutheran Standard* that the "Recensionists" had abandoned a policy of inclusive Lutheran unity in America and had committed themselves to separation.

As a third item, and underlying the others, was a basic misunderstanding of the nature of the Church. The General Synod for practical purposes had followed a policy of toleration. This is basically a political concept and necessity, providing a condition in which citizens of differing views can live together amicably under one government. Part of it is the right of private judgment. These were precisely the views of the "Recensionists" carried over into the church where they did not fit. Within the association of Christians in the church, specifically of Lutherans in the Lutheran Church, there should be such unity and agreement in the truth historically proclaimed by the Church that toleration is superfluous. Inconsistently the party of "American Lutheranism" urged tolerance, yet was intolerant of the "symbolists."

The tumult in the General Synod stirred up by the *Definite Synodical Platform* soon subsided, though reverberations continued for some time. The tolerant inclusiveness of the General Synod remained in force, the situation being a kind of truce. Yet there were definite limits to the toleration practiced in that body. The "American Lutheranism" of some of its synods was tolerated as long as it did not seek by a *Platform* to exclude others. A decade later the General Synod policy was put to another test and strained to the point of rupture.

At the 1864 convention one of the two synods applying for admission was the Franckean Synod, a body notorious for its "American Lutheranism," and having no formal acceptance of the Augsburg Confession in its constitution. The General Synod voted to admit the Franckean Synod as soon as it amended its constitution in this matter. The delegates of the Synod contended that in voting to apply for admission their body had understood that it was accepting the doctrinal position of the General Synod. In view of this the General Synod changed its action and by a majority vote decided to admit the Franckean Synod at once, but with the request that it should amend its constitution at its next convention. In this decision the delegates of the East Ohio, Miami, and Wittenberg Synods voted with the majority. The English Synod and Ministerium of Ohio delegates voted against the motion.

The delegates of the Ministerium of Pennsylvania entered a protest that the action was unconstitutional. In accordance with a provision accepted when it joined the General Synod in 1853, the delegates of the Ministerium, after entering the protest, formally withdrew from the convention to report to their own body. Their action in reality was doctrinal as well as practical.

The 1866 convention of the General Synod, held at Fort Wayne, Indiana, was to be crucial. In the two intervening years there had been much discussion of the question whether the withdrawal of the Pennsylvania Ministerium delegates in 1864 had or had not been secession. At Fort Wayne the president ruled that until that question had been answered the delegates from the Ministerium of Pennsylvania could not be recognized, and a majority of the convention sustained his ruling. The delegates of the East Ohio, Miami, and Wittenberg Synods, except L. A. Gotwald, voted with the majority. The delegates of the English Synod and Ministerium of Ohio voted against the ruling.

The aim of the majority was to compel the Ministerium of Pennsylvania to cancel the provision requiring its delegation to withdraw from a convention in protest. That provision smacked of intolerance. After the president's ruling was sustained, there once again was a formal protest, this time by delegates of several synods. The Pennsylvania Ministerium delegates declared themselves illegally excluded, and once more went home. Soon afterward the Ministerium of Pennsylvania officially withdrew from the General Synod, and a number of other synods, including the English Synod and Ministerium of Ohio, did the same. The seceding synods, and some others, the next year organized the General Council. Since they had constituted the party in the General Synod interested in cultivating cordial relations with the Joint Synod of Ohio, the General Synod and its affiliated synods in Ohio were thereafter much further removed from fellowship with the Joint Synod. Such were the results of this schism at the summit.

THE FOUR POINTS

The second disagreement during this period took place within the General Council, deeply involving the Joint Synod of Ohio. The basic issue was Lutheran unity. Since it was evident that the General Synod after its rupture would likely never include more than a minority of Lutherans in America, there was an impulse to unite the others in some organizational pattern. Once again the Joint Synod of Ohio was invited to leave its isolation and become part of a national federation. The conduct of its English District, and four questions involving the expression of doctrine in practice, made the acceptance of the invitation impossible.

As was recounted in Chapter VI, the Joint Synod for a second time had lost its English District by secession, the loss occurring in 1855. Two years later the minority that had opposed seceding organized an English District for the third time, as authorized by the Joint Synod.[18] At the first convention, held in Circleville, Ohio, August 26 to 28, 1857, Jacob Leist presided. Nine pastors signed the constitution. Its doctrinal position was that it accepted the "doctrines of the Word of God as set forth in the Unaltered Augsburg Confession and Luther's Smaller Catechism and in the sense and spirit of the other Symbolical Books." [19] It declared that "our body considers itself a branch of the Joint Synod of Ohio, and intends to remain in connection with the same like the other districts." [20]

Tension between the English District and the Joint Synod, however, quickly arose. Irritations arose over the question of secret societies, and related to that was the problem of the jurisdiction of the Joint Synod over its districts.

In 1865, in his report as president of the English District, Daniel Worley gave a long review of the difficulties. He complained that the District had always been distrusted within the Joint Synod. He called attention to the fact that "unchurchly societies" had been a problem in the Joint Synod five years before the District was organized. After the Joint Synod had expressed itself in opposition to secret societies, Andrew Henkel in 1855 published a *Protest* which in Worley's judgment "was not proper and regular." The following year a report on secret societies, prepared by W. F. Lehmann and M. Loy, was accepted by the Joint Synod and published in *The Lutheran Standard*, March 18, 1857. In reply Henkel published a "Defense

[18] *Minutes* (German), 1856, p. 9.
[19] *Minutes* of the English District, 1857, p. 4.
[20] *Minutes* of the English District, 1858, p. 18.

against the frivolous and unchristian attack of the Joint Synod of Ohio upon Secret and other Societies." This reply, in Worley's judgment was "very unfortunate both in the harsh words used in the title and the language employed." All this occurred while Henkel was a member of the Western District, which received no censure.

When the English District was formed with Henkel as a member it felt that it was unfairly held responsible for events occurring before its founding. P. Eirich, a pastor of the Joint Synod, continued to press for action against Henkel. In 1859 Henkel published "A Short Review, etc." which was less objectionable in tone and spirit. Eirich issued a sharp reply shortly before he transferred to the Missouri Synod. The Joint Synod at its extra meeting in November, 1859, took notice of these publications and advised the English District to investigate. The secretary of the Joint Synod failed to send word of this action to the English District which in the absence of official notification took no action. This sequence occurred the next year for a second time, though on this occasion the English District advised pastors to examine their membership in secret societies, and if found unchurchly to resign.

The difficulty reached a new phase when the Joint Synod voted to censure the English District for laxity, and also Henkel for continued offense. The action of the Joint Synod was:

> *Resolved,* That this Synod herewith reprove the English District for their dereliction of duty and loose proceedings in this matter. For the public interest of the church always requires to remove open scandal; and Pastor Henkel surely has given and yet gives open scandal by his connection with a secret society. To have that scandal removed both the interest of the church and the honor of God demanded.
>
> *Resolved,* That the Rev'd President of this body is hereby requested to exhort the English District in regard to their conduct which has here been rebuked, and to explain to them their duty by the Word of God and the usage of the Church.

A protest by D. Worley and Enoch Smith was entered against these resolutions on the ground that the English District had fulfilled its duties and that these resolutions were unjust.[21]

Resenting this censure, the English District at once raised the question of the constitutional authority of the Joint Synod over any of its districts. The English District

[21] Minutes of the Joint Synod in *Lutheran Standard*, January 1, 1863.

Resolved, That for the sake of the peace, harmony and prosperity of the church, This District Synod will take no further notice of the matter, at the same time reminding the Joint Synod that its relation to the District Synods is only that of an advisory body, and therefore the resolutions of the Joint Synod are not considered binding upon us until adopted by this body.[22]

Worley alleged that the Joint Synod's resolution was marked by distrust and suspicion. The Joint Synod called for discipline when lodge membership led to indifference, estrangement, or infidelity; in special cases it allowed for action in keeping with conscience and Scripture. He affirmed that the English District had acted faithfully in accordance with Joint Synod action.[23]

Nonetheless the odium of laxity came to be attached to the English District. The Eastern District alleged that some pastors transferred to the English District for reasons other than language, namely to escape discipline. It suggested that the Joint Synod take action to prevent transfer to the English District except for reasons of language, and that such transfers be only by the authority of the Joint Synod. It suggested also that the Joint Synod amend its constitution so as to have jurisdiction over the districts. The English District protested that the Eastern District was guilty of "captious interferences and unjustifiable and unconstitutional judgments upon our actions." [24]

Included in all this was the reluctance of the English District to discipline one of its senior pastors. Andrew Henkel had been born in New Market, Virginia, October 21, 1790, and therefore was of advanced years when these events took place. He was nearly eighty years old when he died on April 23, 1870. By his death the central figure of the controversy was removed, but by that time the schism had become a fact.

Though the Joint Synod had declared itself unwilling to admit to membership pastors who were members of secret societies, the English District stated that it would require of new members no test which would justify discipline of old members. Yet all members should examine societies with Scripture and the Confessions and when convinced they were wrong should resign.[25] In 1866 Professors Loy and Lehmann came as a committee of the Joint Synod to improve relations between the two bodies and had consider-

---

22 *Minutes* of the English District, 1863, p. 15.
23 *Minutes* of the English District, 1865, pp. 4-14.
24 *Minutes* of the English District, 1864, pp. 16 f.
25 *Minutes* of the English District, 1865, pp. 32 f.

able success. At that time the English District unanimously adopted a statement—the "Westmoreland Resolutions"—which called for peace and harmony. It promised to endeavor to persuade members of secret societies to withdraw therefrom; it requested the Joint Synod and the other districts to disclaim intrusion; and it urged mutual forgiveness.[26]

This left unresolved the question of the relation of the districts to the Joint Synod. Had the issue been only one of secret societies, the relaxed tensions might have been completely removed. The English District was claiming an independence somewhat foreign to the structure of the Joint Synod. By claiming that it must ratify Joint Synod actions before they were in force, the English District asserted its complete autonomy over its internal affairs. The Joint Synod, on the other hand, asserted that its right of jurisdiction over the districts was both indirectly implied and directly specified in its constitution; [27] there must be no rejection of its right to review the actions of districts and to admonish them for derelictions of duty. This difference in viewpoint soon led to a crisis.

The General Council, of which mention has already been made, came into existence following a preliminary meeting at Reading, Pennsylvania, in December, 1866. A committee authorized by the Ministerium of Pennsylvania had sent out a "Fraternal Address" and made the necessary arrangements. Confessional Lutheran synods were invited to send delegates for the purpose of considering plans for a new general body which would aim at including all Lutherans not affiliated with the General Synod.

The Joint Synod accepted the invitation to the meeting at Reading. M. Loy and W. F. Lehmann were appointed as delegates. An editorial by Loy thought that the projected new organization "may lead to lasting results for good. . . . We look upon this as an important movement and one which has our most cordial concurrence." Yet he had small hope of its success. "For ourselves we must confess that we are not very sanguine in our expectation of immediate great results. . . . We see difficulties which must and can be overcome." [28] It was Loy, however, who preached the opening sermon at the Reading convention. In it he advocated a doctrinal unity based upon three points: God's revealed truth; a commitment to the Lutheran Confessions; and agreement on issues not confessionally defined. Both Loy and Lehmann participated actively in the convention and its com-

[26] *Minutes* of the English District, 1866, pp. 18 f.
[27] Minutes in *Lutheran Standard*, March 1, 1865.
[28] *Lutheran Standard*, July 1, 1866.

mittees. They seemed willing to let their hopes overcome their misgivings.

The organizing convention of the General Council was held in 1867 in the same church in Fort Wayne, Indiana, where the rupture of the General Synod occurred the year before. The delegates of the Joint Synod were Pastors G. Cronenwett, F. A. Herzberger and G. Baughman. These delegates presented a paper which declared that though the Joint Synod did not have a copy of the proposed constitution in time for action it did desire union on the doctrinal basis which had been prepared. However, it saw practical difficulties in the fact that "un-Lutheran doctrine and practice" were to be found in some synods which were accepting the doctrinal basis. The paper asked, "What relation will this venerable body in future sustain to Chiliasm? Mixed Communion? The exchange of pulpits with sectarians? Secret or unchurchly societies?" These were the famous "four points." The paper added,

> Especially would we earnestly desire a decided answer with regard to the last item, inasmuch as the Joint Synod, for years already, in view of certain relations in one of its District Synods, has had its difficulties in consequence of four pastors belonging to Secret Societies, and would not, therefore, again burthen its conscience.[29]

The General Council replied that nothing in its "Fundamental Principles" or its Constitution left any doubt but that decisions on these four points "will be in harmony with the Holy Scripture and the Confessions of the Church." Evidence of un-Lutheran practice would be dealt with according to the Constitution, but it must be remembered that the General Council had advisory, not legislative, power over congregations. Pulpit and altar fellowship with non-Lutherans was condemned. Discipline should "be exercised toward those who are members of secret societies.[30] This answer did not seem to be decisive enough to suit the Joint Synod.

There was another matter which was distasteful to the Joint Synod; namely, the presence at the Fort Wayne convention of a delegation from the English District consisting of three pastors and two laymen who took active part in the organization of the General Council. Pastor C. Albrecht became a member of the English Hymnbook Committee, and Pastor G. W. Mechling a member of the German Hymnbook Committee. The third pastor was Daniel Worley, formerly editor of *The Lutheran Standard*. In the eyes

[29] *Minutes of the General Council,* 1867, p. 12. *Minutes* of the Joint Synod, 1867, pp. 10 ff.

[30] *Ibid.*

of the Joint Synod the English District was not entitled to a separate delegation. The delegates of the Joint Synod were said to represent all the districts. The representatives of the Joint Synod at Fort Wayne first presented
a protest, then withdrew it. The net result was that the Joint Synod declined
membership in the General Council, preferring to continue as an independent body. The hope of the General Council to unite all the confessional
Lutheran synods in America was frustrated by this schism at the summit
in which other German synods shared also.

W. A. Passavant represented the General Council at the 1868 convention
of the Joint Synod. He tried to reassure that body that the General Council
did not want to evade the four points, but would make a fuller statement.
He argued that the General Council could not refuse to receive the English
District when the Joint Synod delegates had withdrawn their protest. But
he accomplished nothing.[31]

Of the "four points" the one concerning chiliasm was least troublesome
and soon dropped from sight in the General Council. The questions concerning pulpit and altar fellowship were much more troublesome in view
of the fact that the Ministerium of Pennsylvania contained many union
(i.e., Lutheran and Reformed) congregations where intercommunion occurred. Within the Joint Synod the question had been discussed since 1850.
A vigorous effort had been made to eliminate all union congregations,
Lutherans separating completely from the Reformed. The prevailing view
was that "members of other denominations which do not recognize the
confession of the Lutheran Church cannot be admitted to communion since
this would be disloyal to doctrine." [32] The committee report on the subject,
which was adopted by a vote of thirteen to seven, further declared that
"A Lutheran minister may not administer to United Congregations without
denying his faith as a Lutheran Pastor." [33] Nor could exchange of pulpits
with pastors not united in doctrine and practice be permitted, since it is
contrary to Scripture and the Confessions to permit the preaching of heresy.[34]

The difference between the Joint Synod and the General Council on these
points was between a rigorous and a moderate enforcement, between a disciplinary and an educational approach. The English District expressed
itself thus:

[31] *Minutes* of the General Council, 1868, p. 29.
[32] *Minutes* of the Joint Synod, 1856, pp. 12 f.
[33] *Lutheran Standard,* October 31, 1856.
[34] Theses adopted by the Joint Synod (*Minutes,* 1874, pp. 13 f.) represented the practice in force for some years.

1. That, as it is the duty of every minister to see that no error is preached from his pulpit and to protect his people against it, exchange of pulpits with those of a different confession is not, in the judgment of this Synod, consistent with that care which every pastor should exercise over the souls of those committed to his charge; and this Synod therefore heartily condemns it..

But our confessions do not teach that there may not be some circumstances in which some persons who are not fully Lutheran in faith and doctrine may with proper foresight and care on the part of the pastor be admitted to our pulpits.

2. As the Holy Supper of our Lord is the most solemn mystery of the Christian Church, and is intended for none but true believers, it should be carefully guarded against the approach of unworthy persons.

The practice of indiscriminate communion is, in the judgment of this Synod, unwarranted by our Confessions, opposed to the Scriptures, and has a tendency to promote disregard for holy things and indifference to sound doctrine.

According to I Cor. 11:26-29 and Luther's Small Catechism none should be invited to the Lord's Table except such as examine themselves and discern the Lord's body, i.e., those who are truly penitent for their sins and take the Lord at His word when He says, "this is my body and blood given and shed for you for the remission of sins." [35]

This discussion, which continued over a decade in the General Council, seemed to men in the General Synod to be strange and unrealistic in the pluralistic American scene. An editorial by J. H. W. Stuckenberg in *The Lutheran Evangelist* expressed the following views:

We are not in favor of indiscriminate pulpit and altar fellowship (i.e., no preaching of heresy should be permitted, but denominations having so much in common can have exchange of pulpits on fundamental doctrines.) If absolute freedom from error were the condition of pulpit fellowship then many of our Lutheran brethren might have to be excluded from their own pulpits.

We advocate no indiscriminate communion. Nor do we think that invitations to members of other churches ought to be extended as a matter of courtesy. But we believe that Christians of evangelical churches in good standing ought to be invited.

The discussion [in the General Council] is only of secondary importance to us. . . . If it is the mission of others to spend their strength in wrangling over pulpit and altar fellowship while Romanism is extending it borders and infidelity is attacking the very heart of the Gospel, let them accomplish their mission. It is evidently our mission to do something else. . . . We are of course abused for our position. Because we favor fraternal relations with other denominations we are treated in a most unfraternal manner.[36]

---

[35] *Minutes* of the English District, 1868, pp. 11 f.
[36] *Lutheran Evangelist*, October 5 and 12, 1877.

There remained the problem of the relation of the English District to the Joint Synod, its parent body. This was a question within the area of organization and polity. Ignoring the fact that the Joint Synod had established its districts as administrative subdivisions, the English District considered the Joint Synod as a federation of the districts as synods. Hence it declared that "The formation of new ecclesiastical relations has not been entrusted by the District Synods to the Joint Synod, but is from the very nature of the case a matter which particularly and directly belongs to the District Synods alone." [37]

The Joint Synod considered itself a unit—a complex unit, to be sure, but nonetheless such a unit that the affiliation of any of its districts with another body constituted a separation from the Joint Synod. For a district to act in variance with the parent body was secession. This was the view expressed at the 1868 convention of the Joint Synod. That body warned the English District that if it persisted in its membership in the General Council it by that fact severed its connection with the Joint Synod. It further warned that the minority in the English District which desired to belong to the Joint Synod instead of the General Council would be recognized as the true English District.

This was the state of affairs confronting the English District at its convention in 1869. President Worley in his report, noting that the District was charged with unfaithfulness and willful resistance to the Joint Synod, suggested that the District consider its relation both to the Joint Synod and the General Council. He raised the question whether the District should not accept the Joint Synod's ultimatum and take steps to sever their connections. He noted in passing that heretofore the minority in the District had concurred with the majority in electing delegates to the General Council.[38]

The decisive moment was the adoption by the District of his suggestion that members of other districts seeking admission to the English District by certificate be required "to give assurance . . . that they are in full sympathy with our present churchly position." [39] This was intended to exclude applicants hostile to the General Council. Following this there was presented a minority protest signed by twelve pastors and five laymen affirming loyalty to the Joint Synod, and labeling the position of the majority a usurpation of power. A reply to this document charged that the guilt lay upon the

[37] *Minutes* of the English District, 1867, p. 6.
[38] *Minutes* of the English District, 1869, p. 5.
[39] *Op. cit.*, p. 8.

Joint Synod which was actually the body usurping power. It was claimed that the English District had always fulfilled its obligations.[40]

A committee was authorized and appointed to study the relation of the District to the Joint Synod and report next year. Meanwhile the minority party withdrew and organized itself as the English District loyal to the Joint Synod, eleven pastors thus leaving the older group. The 1869 convention at Lima, Ohio, was thus the dividing one. A year later the committee reported that separation from the Joint Synod was a fact. It recommended that a committee prepare a revision of the constitution conformable to the General Council. The revised constitution in proper form was adopted in 1873. This body, which later dropped the word "English" from its name, is to be known hereafter as the District Synod of Ohio.

With two Synods in Ohio belonging to the General Council, there remained the problem of their relation to each other. The English Synod and Ministerium of Ohio, which had been the Joint Synod's English District until 1855, and the District Synod of Ohio were small bodies whose territories overlapped. The English Synod and Ministerium joined the General Council in 1867, being represented at Fort Wayne by two pastors, J. A. Roof and John Rugan, and a layman. Even before that time a joint committee had been examining the possibilities of uniting the two synods. The report of the joint committee stated that there were no differences between the two bodies in doctrine or practice, including the District's "Westmoreland Resolutions" on secret societies. The report was unanimously adopted by the English Synod and Ministerium, but the District Synod, while approving its findings, postponed action on the grounds "that, in accordance with the Constitution and previous action of this Synod we could not receive them as a Synod but only as individuals." [41] With this answer the union activity seems to have stalled. The English Synod and Ministerium was a small body of about a dozen pastors, not over thirty small congregations, and less than twenty-five hundred communicants. In 1871 the president, J. A. Roof, wrote to the District Synod expressing regret over his inability to attend that body's convention to discuss union, but indicating that for the present he must continue with his own Synod. Yet two of his pastors, James Manning and Jacob Singer, transferred to the District Synod that year, and others transferred to other bodies, reducing his Synod to five pastors. By 1872 it had completely disbanded.

[40] *Op. cit.*, pp. 10 ff.
[41] *Minutes* of the English District, 1867, p. 15.

PREDESTINATION

What relation the Joint Synod should have to the Missouri Synod was a problem during this period. Two possibilities were available to the Joint Synod, either to be independent or to join one of the larger constellations of Lutherans in America. To some minds independence had somewhat schismatic overtones, whereas fellowship with other Lutherans was theologically and practically desirable. To stand alone meant to be misunderstood on all sides. Thus an editorial in *The Lutheran Standard* said: "It is the misfortune of the Ohio Synod to be placed between two bodies, which, however antagonistic in other respects, unite in opposing us. On the one hand we are assailed for not renouncing our faith in the well-established doctrines of the church; on the other because we will not commit ourselves to a violent and exclusive system of church government." [42]

The ill will involved in the withdrawal from the Joint Synod in 1845 of men who joined in organizing the Missouri Synod continued to appear in the journals of the two bodies. For example, in the March 4, 1851, issue of *Der Lutheraner* Dr. Sihler of Fort Wayne criticized the Western District of the Joint Synod for unionism, since it refused to forbid its ministers to serve congregations of Lutherans and Reformed or to withhold communion unless the communicants disavowed non-Lutheran doctrine. The harshness of Sihler's attack was deeply resented in an editorial in *The Lutheran Standard* of April 9th. Partisan references to this event continued to appear in these journals for several months.

Defections from the Joint Synod to the Missouri Synod usually perpetuated the ill will. Two such instances appeared at the time of the difficulties over secret societies. *The Lutheran Standard* spoke of "the shameful and disorderly reception of Messrs. Eirich and Buehl by the Missouri Synod when these men went out from us in open contempt of every principle of Christian order and decency." [43] The action of the Joint Synod was: "*Resolved,* That we feel constrained most emphatically to disapprove the reception [of Eirich and Buehl] into the Missouri Synod without honorable dismission; and this resolution be sent to that Synod, their sin be represented to them, and they be admonished to repent." [44]

A few months later an editorial entitled, "The Missouri Synod," sarcastically remarked, "The Doctors of the Missouri Synod have spoken, and

[42] *Lutheran Standard,* July 16, 1851.
[43] *Lutheran Standard,* November 9, 1860.
[44] Minutes in *Lutheran Standard,* January 18, 1861.

it is therefore becoming that all the earth should stand in awe and tremble."
It added that Prof. Walther "had been guilty of grave misdemeanors and
sins by secretly aiding and counseling malcontents in the Ohio Synod."[45]
Later that year Dr. Walther published a defense of Missouri's reception of
a student expelled at Columbus. Again editorial displeasure was expressed:

> The only reply we can make to this worthy who . . . justifies the ungodly
> reception of the expelled student . . . into the Missouri Seminary is that his
> short and characteristic article contains at least a half dozen slanders, misrepre-
> sentations and absolute falsehoods. One would suppose from the "Lutheraner"
> that the Missouri Synod, with Mr. Walther as Pope or Captain, was entirely
> composed of theological pirates; they seem to have their hand against every
> man and every man's hand against them. May the Lord speedily have mercy
> upon them and deliver them from their delusion and sins.

The editor would thus speak of the Missouri "Synod which is not only
founded upon schism but which is and always has been exhibiting the
most deadly enmity towards the Ohio Synod." [46]

Yet within a very few years an entirely different attitude appeared.
The Missouri Synod, which in 1860 had sixteen voting and four advisory
pastors in Ohio, began to appear in a more favorable light. The change in
part reflected the total Lutheran situation in America. The Joint Synod of
Ohio found itself holding common ground with the Missouri Synod both
in the repudiation of the General Synod and later in dissatisfaction with
the General Council. In contrast with the large issues of confessional loyalty
and disciplinary practice, the irritations of defecting pastors seemed distinctly minor. Moreover, the departure of the District Synod removed from
the Joint Synod such men as Daniel Worley who as editor of *The Lutheran
Standard* spoke sharply of the Missouri Synod, leaving in control such men
as Matthias Loy who had friends among Missouri Synod pastors.

Much more influential was a series of four free conferences which
brought together members of confessional Lutheran synods. Such a conference was proposed in the January, 1856, issue of *Lehre und Wehre* and
published in translation in *The Lutheran Standard* of February 8. This
called for a free conference of members of Lutheran synods "who without
any reservation recognize and confess the unaltered Augsburg Confession
of 1530 to be the pure and true expression of the doctrine of the Holy
Scriptures." The *Standard* continued to publish a cumulative list of persons
endorsing the project.

[45] *Lutheran Standard*, February 15, 1861.
[46] *Lutheran Standard*, December 6, 1861.

212 / A Century of Lutherans in Ohio

The first conference met in Columbus on October 1 to 6, 1856. Fifty-four pastors and nineteen laymen attended, members of the Pennsylvania Ministerium, New York, Missouri, and Ohio synods. Prof. W. F. Lehmann was chosen president and M. Loy was one of the secretaries. A beginning was made in discussing the Augsburg Confession article by article. All those present agreed on these doctrines. It was proposed that another meeting be held a year later. *The Lutheran Standard* reported that "a bond of brotherly union and communion has been cemented. . . . Our personal impression of the brethren East and West were of the most happy character and far different from what in some of them at least we had anticipated." [47]

The second meeting of the conference was held in Pittsburgh, October 29 to November 4, 1857, Again W. F. Lehmann was president. Discussion of the articles of the Augsburg Confession continued. W. A. Passavant, who observed the meeting, noted that most of those present were from the Midwest. He described these "old Lutherans" as soundly Protestant, candid, and impartial, but strict.[48] The third convention was held in Cleveland, August 5 to 11, 1858, and the fourth meeting was in Fort Wayne July 14, 1859.[49] Members of midwestern German synods for the most part constituted the attendance at the later meetings. Suspicion gave way to understanding and mutual respect; doubt was replaced by confidence. Even though these conferences were unofficial, in no way committing the synods whose members attended, they generated good will among the pastors who conferred with each other. This good will was a force struggling to overcome the prejudice still current in the synods concerned.

After the failure of the General Council to win the approval of the Missouri Synod and the Joint Synod of Ohio, these two bodies again began examining the possibilities of fellowship or union. Indeed, in 1867 when the General Council was forming, representatives of the Missouri Synod came to Columbus to discuss union with the Joint Synod. The agreement reached, both as to doctrine and practice, was ratified by the Missouri Synod. In the Joint Synod there was unanimous acceptance of the agreement, but with the understanding that the discussion of the doctrine of the ministry which was not yet completed by the Joint Synod should not be discontinued. The Missouri Synod misunderstood this action, interpreting it as indicating a lack of full agreement. It therefore voted to postpone union with Ohio. But in

---

[47] *Lutheran Standard,* October 17, 1856. A sarcastic account of the conference appeared in *Lutheran Observer,* November 7, 1856.

[48] *Missionary,* November 12, 1857. Cf. *Lutheran Standard,* January 6, 1858.

[49] *Lutheran Standard,* October 1, 1858; November 11, 1859.

1870 the Joint Synod completed discussion of its theses on the pastoral office, and ratified the articles of agreement with the Missouri Synod without qualification.[50]

The Joint Synod appointed a committee to complete negotiations. This committee met twice during 1871 with representatives of the Missouri, Wisconsin, Illinois, and Norwegian synods, preparing a proposed draft of an organization. When the proposal was accepted by the synods concerned, their representatives met at Milwaukee, July 1 to 16, 1872, and formally organized the Synodical Conference. C. F. Walther was chosen president and W. F. Lehmann vice president. Thus the Joint Synod participated in the formation of a confederation of synods predominantly German and committed to strictly confessional doctrine and practice. The Synodical Conference came into being for purposes of consultation and fellowship rather than for organizational merger.

The 1876 convention, under Missouri Synod leadership, proposed further consolidation. In order to remove the difficulties inherent in overlapping territories, the Synodical Conference discussed a plan of reorganization in the form of synods with the geographical boundaries of states. Under this plan all the Synodical Conference congregations within a state would belong to the synod of that state. The state synods thus constituted would be combined in three larger groups or "general synods": (1) East, to include all state synods east of Indiana; (2) Northwest, the synods of Michigan, Wisconsin, Minnesota, Dakota, and westward; (3) West, the synods west and south of the other two. English synods would be district synods within their area general synod.[51]

Proposed consolidation included also a plan of combining seminaries. All the theological seminaries would be merged into one to be located in or near Milwaukee. Alternate sites, if the Norwegian Synod was not included, would be St. Louis, Columbus, or Richmond, Indiana. The plan called for making the Practical Seminary at Springfield, Illinois, and the Normal School (Teachers' Seminary) at Addison, Illinois, common property of the Synodical Conference.[52]

These imaginative proposals, which could have profoundly affected the development of Lutheranism in America, evoked little sympathetic response in Ohio. Congregations were asked to express their opinion. At the 1880 convention of the Joint Synod a roll call showed that only a small number

[50] *Minutes* of the Joint Synod, 1870, pp. 28 f.
[51] *Minutes* of the Joint Synod, 1880, p. 13.
[52] *Ibid.*

of congregations favored both proposals, a slightly larger number favored state synods but not a merger of seminaries, a still larger number opposed both, and the large majority had shown so little interest as to make no decision at all. "Synod derived the impression that the time had not yet come for final action." [53]

Though appreciating the values of the Synodical Conference it was not clear to the Joint Synod that the proposals increased these values. "This indeed appeared to constitute the true reason why the Synod could not decide to take action in favor of the union." [54] The Joint Synod "*Resolved, That* the report of the committee comprising the propositions of the Synodical Conference be and are herewith laid on the table, and that this synod hereby declares that at present it is not prepared to decide in favor of the formation of state synods and a consolidated seminary." [55] Thus was displayed a congregational inertia satisfied with the synodical structure and seminary then in existence. The contacts at the summit had slight significance for them. There was more loyalty to the familiar structure of the Joint Synod than to the remote configuration of the Synodical Conference. Into this situation marked by apathy there suddenly dropped a sharp theological controversy which aroused strong feelings and became disruptive of the Synodical Conference. The topic of the controversy was predestination.

The theological meaning of predestination had been discussed from time to time within the Missouri Synod. There were occasional articles in *Lehre und Wehre* through the years. At a convention of the Northern District of the Synod in 1868 when Walther was present a statement was made that election in view of faith (*intuitu fidei*) is unfortunate terminology since it seems to place a condition upon God's sovereign will. Nine years later the topic was on a program of the Western District where Walther presented theses in which predestination was defined in terms of God's eternal will. Dissatisfied with these theses, which did not follow the pattern of the eight points in the Formula of Concord, Pastor H. A. Allwardt dissented. Prof. F. A. Schmidt of the Norwegian Synod concurred in this dissent. Thus began the controversy on predestination in the Synodical Conference.

Walther and Schmidt came to Columbus in 1879 to discuss the matter with the leaders of the Joint Synod. When no agreement was reached, a

[53] *Op. cit.*, p. 14.
[54] *Op. cit.*, p. 15.
[55] *Op. cit.*, p. 16.

colloquium to be held the next year seemed to offer some hope of a peaceful solution. Meanwhile Allwardt, who stated his views at a pastoral conference of the Northwestern District of the Missouri Synod, found the majority opposed to him. At the Western District of that Synod Walther so expressed himself on the doctrine that those who dissented considered themselves attacked and ridiculed.

In January of 1880 appeared the first issue of *Altes und Neues* published by Schmidt to voice his side of the controversy, Allwardt adding his voice on the same side in the second issue. Walther elaborated his position in the columns of *Der Lutheraner*. He defined the issue as being whether salvation is of God or of man—a definition which his opponents felt falsified the issue. Walther published his views in a long article running through five numbers of *Lehre und Wehre*. In Ohio Loy editorially called attention to *Altes und Neues,* saying, "The occasion of its appearance is one that causes sorrow rather than rejoicing. It forebodes trouble." [56]

At the 1880 convention of the Joint Synod the report of Vice President C. H. L. Schuette (in the absence of the president who was ill) suggested that the Synod discuss the doctrine at an early date. By action of the Synod, Pastor C. H. Trebel was appointed to prepare theses on the doctrine of predestination and election as given in the Formula of Concord so that "the true doctrine as contained in our Confessions which are based on the Word of God shall be maintained . . . and . . . numerous false doctrines shall be rejected." It was resolved to hold a free pastoral conference to discuss his theses.[57] In Ohio there was sympathy for Schmidt's insistence that Walther's formulation of the doctrine was not in tune with the Formula of Concord, but that it introduced a new tone which had a Calvinistic sound. Loy published a series of editorial articles in *The Lutheran Standard* insisting that predestination must be connected with foreknowledge and faith. This was significant in view of Loy's vigorous support of the Synodical Conference through the years.

Any attempt to state briefly the elements of the controversy is bound to do injustice to its complexity.[58] The interest of Dr. Walther and his col-

[56] *Lutheran Standard,* January 17, 1880.

[57] *Minutes* of the Joint Synod, 1880, pp. 1, 27 f. Trebel's theses appeared in *The Lutheran Standard* July 16, 1881, expressing the Ohio view. The conference was called to meet in Wheeling in September.

[58] No scholarly, dispassionate account of the controversy has yet been published. The position of the Joint Synod is given in *The Error of Modern Missouri,* edited by E. L. Tressel (Columbus, 1897).

leagues was to stress the fact that salvation is solely the work of God, both in the general plan of redemption accomplished by Christ's atonement and in the election of individual persons in whom faith is aroused. Walther's opponents considered this statement of the election of individuals as Calvinizing; they desired a declaration that election took into consideration the fact of the faith of individuals as foreseen by God. Walther insisted that such a formulation made faith a condition of election, and therefore was synergistic. His opponents asserted that election cannot be unconditional; instead it is conditioned by the fact that man can reject God's grace. Thus the positions seemed to be irreconcilable.

The controversy was unfortunate on several grounds. When the party on one side was accused of "Calvinizing," and the party on the other side was called "synergistic," deep wounds and resentment resulted on both sides. Amid such heavily emotional conditions an atmosphere developed in which agreement and understanding were virtually impossible to achieve. Moreover, this controversy tended to injure the cause of Lutheran confessionalism in America. The claim that the Lutheran Confessions can be a firm basis for unity was damaged when confessionalists sharply disagreed in interpretation. An editorial by Prof. S. A. Ort of Wittenberg College in *The Lutheran Evangelist* said: "That prominent doctrines of the Word of God have not been clearly settled by the Formula of Concord is surprising. And yet the latter appears now to be the case if the present controversy has any meaning." [59]

The controversy both intrenched and dislocated the conviction that an intellectual apprehension of truth can be final and static. Both sides insisted that theirs was the final answer, and this insistence was unyielding. In Ohio it was said that the Missouri Synod had fallen into error by holding a doctrine contrary both to the Bible and the Confessions of the Lutheran Church. The Missouri Synod, on the other hand, charged that its opponents were "those who have vilified the doctrine of God's Word and of our Confession by pronouncing it Calvinism." [60]

Those who were outside the controversy were more than ever convinced that election is really a mystery which may be variously apprehended. A stiff, fruitless dogmatic quarrel was all the more tragic at a time when the Lutheran Church needed to face forward to the difficult intellectual problems of the American religious scene. While Lutherans were writing at great length on the nuances of election as discussed in the sixteenth and seven-

[59] Issue of March 18, 1881.
[60] Quoted from *Der Lutheraner* in *Lutheran Standard*, July 30, 1881.

teenth centuries, they had no time to say anything significant about the nineteenth-century problems of Marxism, theological liberalism, social gospel, science, and evolution. Persons interested in such matters left the Lutheran Church to find elsewhere a church alert to the modern scene.

The critical year of the controversy was 1881. The Missouri Synod at its convention in Fort Wayne, May 11 to 21, adopted a series of thirteen propositions phrased in terms favorable to its point of view. It also adopted a statement that opponents of this viewpoint, who charged the Synod with Calvinism, must repent if they were to remain in fellowship with the Synod lest they be disciplined and excluded. This decision of the Missouri Synod to discontinue church-fellowship with her critics brought matters to a head. In Ohio it seemed that the Missouri Synod "preferred to push the matter in hot haste and cut off all hope of coming to any agreement on the vexed question." [61]

The Joint Synod held an extra convention at Wheeling, September 8 to 13, following the pastoral conference. President Loy stated the issues:

> In the first place, we must decide whether we must refuse or welcome into our midst as brethren such pastors and congregations as can no longer remain in that synod and apply for admission among us. In the second place, we must decide in what relation we stand to that body after she has instructed her delegates to the Synodical Conference not to sit and confer with those who have raised against her the accusation of Calvinizing tendencies." [62]

Six sessions of the convention were devoted to a discussion of theses on predestination and election. Resolutions were placed before the convention and substitutes for the resolutions were offered. The first decision was the adoption of the following statement, the vote being 109 pastors and thirty-three lay delegates in favor, nineteen pastors and three lay delegates opposed.

> We again herewith confess the doctrine of election as it is contained in the Formula of Concord, and also as it has in accordance therewith been always taught on the whole by the great teachers of our church; especially do we hold the doctrine of our fathers, that the ordination of the elect to eternal life took place in view of faith, i.e., in view of the merits of Christ appropriated by faith, to be in accord with the Scriptures and our Confessions; Therefore,
> *Resolved,* That in the future as in the past the doctrine here anew confessed be alone authorized in our institutions, schools, publications and churches.[63]

[61] *Lutheran Standard,* July 30, 1881.
[62] *Minutes* of the Joint Synod, 1881, p. 7.
[63] *Ibid.,* p. 40.

Those who voted in the negative entered their written protests. It was charged that the adoption of this resolution both changed the doctrinal position formerly held by the Synod, and by binding its pastors to this interpretation was un-Lutheran and oppressive of consciences. Questions were raised as to whether fellowship was to be denied those who taught that election is "unto faith" or is "through, in and to faith." The Synod answered that the use of these phrases with proper qualifications was not in opposition to its declaration and therefore was not church-dividing. Those who were not fully satisfied were invited to a conference with the members of the theological faculty.

The next action was to sever connection with the Synodical Conference by adopting the following:

> *Resolved:* That the Joint Synod of Ohio and other states, much as it regrets the step, herewith separates itself from the Synodical Conference of North America, because the honorable Synod of Missouri, which, as is known represents the great majority of the Synodical Conference, has,
>
> 1. Set forth and definitely adopted (last May) a doctrine concerning election which we cannot accept; and
>
> 2. Has definitely declared that it cannot confer with the majority of the delegates our districts have elected this year, because they have felt it to be their duty publicly to declare that the above-mentioned doctrine is Calvinizing.[64]

Seventeen pastors who voted against this action entered in the record a declaration of the reason for their negative vote. Though they acknowledged that during the controversy some expressions used by members of the Missouri Synod gave a Calvinistic impression, they could not agree that the thirteen theses adopted by the Missouri Synod at Fort Wayne contained the leaven of false doctrine. Hence the Joint Synod had no doctrinal ground for withdrawing from the Synodical Conference. The declaration of these dissenters, however, in no way changed the firm decision of the overwhelming majority.

Here again was schism at the summit which was to remain until the present day. The hope of combining in one federation all the strictly confessional (and also predominantly German) synods was frustrated. Some other solution would have to be found for unity among Lutherans in America. The search for precise, completely correct theological formulae was to be a will-of-the-wisp which, though at times almost within reach, continu-

[64] *Ibid.*

ally became unattainable by the rise of new problems. The break in 1881 produced sufficient disillusionment to generate pessimism concerning the possibility of Lutheran unity in America for at least a generation.

SUMMARY

The vigorous emotions connected with slavery and secession had their counterpart in Lutheran disagreements. The state could compel conformity by force; religious problems yielded to no such facile treatment. Therefore the divisions which appeared among Lutherans could not be healed at that time.

The disruption in the General Synod occurred because the basis of its organization was challenged. Toleration of differing opinions, praised as the American way, had been the policy from the beginning. The migration to America of "old Lutherans" intensely devoted to the doctrinal declarations of the Reformation seemed to constitute a threat to the American pattern of toleration. Some appreciation of the truly Lutheran heritage began to appear in the General Synod.

On the other hand, the partisans of "American Lutheranism" espoused a modified Lutheranism. They issued the *Definite Synodical Platform* as a uniform pattern for the synods of the General Synod. The *Platform,* by accusing the Augsburg Confession of error, was in effect a frontal attack on the "symbolists" firmly attached to the Lutheran Confessions.

The defeat of the *Platform* meant that the extreme left wing of the General Synod was discredited. The supporters of the *Platform,* in opposing what seemed to them to be intolerance, were in turn accused of intolerance. This left wing party exposed its lack of Lutheran catholicity. It became clear that toleration must be limited by truth. In the aftermath, when there was a contest over a parliamentary technicality, a considerable part of the conservatives within the General Synod withdrew and participated in the formation of the General Council. Ohio Lutherans of all synods were affected by these separations.

While the struggle over "American Lutheranism" involved the identity of Lutherans doctrinally, the discussions on the "Four Points" concerned Lutheran identity in practice. Chiliasm, pulpit and altar fellowship, and secret societies had doctrinal implications to be sure, but the contest for the most part was not at that level. Fellowship, either with non-Lutherans in worship or with non-Christians in secret societies, was officially disavowed in the General Council, but not everywhere strictly observed in practice. The Joint Synod of Ohio desired that declaration be joined to discipline. When this did not seem to be achieved, the Joint Synod refused to participate further in the General Council, losing the majority of its English District in the process. Implicit in the contest was the question of the nature of the unity to be expected within Christian fellowship.

The controversy over predestination was primarily a theological debate between the leaders of the Missouri Synod and their opponents in other parts of the Synodical Conference. Yet it, too, involved the question of the nature of unity. Dr. Walther stated the Missouri position as one which gave all the glory to God when describing predestination. The representatives of Ohio insisted that the doctrine must be so defined as to take faith into consideration. The Missourians were accused of a subtle Calvinism, the Ohioans of synergism.

The demand for complete agreement in a doctrinal formulation was not realized, with the result that fellowship was disrupted. Dogmatic uniformity was required of all members of the Synodical Conference. Both parties in the controversy agreed in rejecting adaptation to the American scene at the expense of clear-cut Lutheran doctrine. However, the schism within the rigorously confessional part of Lutheranism in America was evidence that there was more than one way for such Lutheranism to express itself. The denial of such variety could lead only to schism. Once more Lutherans in Ohio were involved in the separation.

9 / *MISSION AND MESSAGE*

THE QUARTER CENTURY indicated in the previous chapter was marked by development as well as by schism. The simplicity of church life in previous decades gave way to increasing complexity. Both on the parish level and in the area of synodical activity more things were undertaken and programs became more involved. All this was part of the adaptation of Lutherans to the life of the world about them in Ohio. In some respects the adaptation was more marked among English-speaking Lutherans, but even those who used German could not escape the influences about them. As Americanization advanced, adaptation increased.

It is the aim of this chapter to survey the public manifestations of Lutheranism in Ohio during the years in which there was growth in population and economic development as well as involvement in the Civil War and periods of financial distress.

THE STATE OF RELIGION

During these decades religion had to compete with increasingly powerful forces and public developments. Political campaigns, the problem of slavery, and the excitement of war tended to distract attention from church activity. Meanwhile the state was undergoing an extensive alteration in its economic life. Agriculture, the occupation of most of the citizens, was profoundly changed by the introduction of farm machinery. The raising of livestock was encouraged when railroad transportation replaced driving herds on foot over the mountains to eastern markets. These years saw also the rapid increase of manufacturing industries whose total income surpassed that of agriculture. Such secular concerns easily became a substitute for interested activity in religion.

In the late 1850's, when the excitement of revivals had dimmed and the country was in the midst of a financial recession, churches found it difficult to maintain zeal and show progress. The war years were especially distracting, though not without compensations. A report in 1864 said, "Some of the brethren speak despondingly of the religious condition of their charges, but the larger number are encouraged in their work." [1] Amid the distractions following the close of the war, another report indicated increases in church attendance, in membership, in liberality, and especially in Sunday schools. "Many church edifices are being erected. Old ones are too small." [2] Other observers were less optimistic, seeking answers to the question, "What is the cause of so little progress aggressively in our Synod?" [3] The only solutions suggested were those which called for greater zeal and for renewed efforts. It was clear that indifference to religion would not disappear of itself.

The synodical statistics for the period, though deficient in accurate parochial reporting, give sufficient approximations to indicate trends which show relation to public events. The population of Ohio in 1850 was almost two million people. This had increased by 1880 to almost 3,200,000, a growth of 60 per cent. The number of German-born people in the state in 1850 was over 111,000. In 1880 this number was over 192,000, an increase of about 73 per cent.

Between 1855 and 1881 the number of communicant members of the synods in Ohio (some with congregations in neighboring states) increased from 27,763 to 73,584, an increase of 165 per cent—over twice the rate of growth of the population. Though the rate of increase in Lutheran membership was more than double that of the German-born population, it would appear that only slightly more than a third of these Germans were in Lutheran congregations in 1880. Meanwhile Lutheran church membership in the United States had grown from about 200,000 to over 800,000, a four-fold increase, due largely to German and Scandinavian immigration into the midwestern states.

The number of pastors in the Ohio synods increased from 167 to 337— a gain of about 100 per cent. The increase in the number of congregations was from 367 to 575—better than fifty per cent. This indicates an improvement in the supply of clergymen as well as a decrease in the number of congregations constituting the usual parish served by one pastor.

The following table lists the figures reported in 1881.

[1] *Minutes* of the Miami Synod, 1864, p. 18.
[2] *Minutes* of the Wittenberg Synod, 1866, pp. 23 f.
[3] *Minutes* of the Miami Synod, 1868, p. 12; 1869, p. 4.

Synod	Pastors	Congregations	Members	Members per Congregation
Joint Synod	186	325	47,550	146
District	31	66	7,017	106
Wittenberg	37	65	6,016	93
East Ohio	47	70	5,148	73
Miami	26	35	3,059	87
Augsburg	10	14	1,850	132
TOTAL	337	575	73,584	

Obviously the Joint Synod was still by far the largest synod both in membership and size of congregations. The Wittenberg Synod grew rapidly with the development of the northwestern part of the state. The German Augsburg Synod was but five years old in 1881.

Though rejoicing in this progress, Lutherans realized that they still had a large task ahead of them, especially in winning the great number of Germans of recent immigration. Contrary to the assumption of some historians that the Germans who came to Ohio in this period were ultra-conservative "Old Lutheran" in viewpoint, the fact was that many of them were radical and rationalist in temper. The earlier immigrants had been largely farmers with limited education. Among the newer arrivals were persons of culture and university education. Many of these persons were "Forty-eighters"— exiles or refugees from the abortive revolution in Germany in 1848 and 1849. They were responsible for starting numerous periodicals devoted to political radicalism and to rationalism in religion. Cincinnati in particular was a center of their activity.

A contemporary account noted that whereas the earlier immigration was Protestant and pious the new immigration was more likely to be marked by Romanism and infidelity. It continued:

> There are at least fifty thousand Germans in and around Cincinnati, and what are they doing? Why they have their *Turnvereine* by the dozen, their Theaters, their Reading-rooms, their Beneficial Societies, societies of *Freimaenner, Rothmaenner,* Odd Fellows, any number of beershops, and half a dozen Rationalistic churches. The Romanists also, of course, have churches for all who profess their faith, and also a large and skilfully conducted German newspaper, and so have the Methodists several congregations and here Dr. Nast edits the *Apologete*. The German Reformed have likewise a German and an English congregation (worshipping in the same house, and with

the same pastor, I believe), and the Lutherans—were not the fact notorious I should be ashamed to publish it—yes, the Lutherans have *two* German preachers, one preaching to a handful of Lutherans of the Missouri school scarcely known as one of the religious elements of the city, the other in a house in which Lutheranism is not acknowledged as having any peculiar rights of possession.

The article asserted that no "church exerts any serious influence or makes any important impression" on the population. What was needed was a supply of German preachers of such high education and culture as to command attention and respect, men who were skilled in German and in theology and philosophy; and the church should support them.[4]

In one of the rare instances in which Lutherans gave attention to this problem *The Lutheran Standard* spoke of "the host of German infidel papers which flood our land, poisoning the minds and subverting the happiness of thousands." The editors were described as "political renegades, who were no longer tolerated in their fatherland because opposed to all established order in Church and State. . . . Their poisonous shafts are directed against Christianity and Christ himself as well as against his ministers and followers."[5] The *Standard* in the issue of February 22, 1854, carried an editorial entitled, "The German Infidel Press," and in the same issue reprinted from *The German National Democrat* of Washington an editorial, "Liberty or Audaciousness" by Frederick Schmidt, former editor of the *Lutherische Kirchenzeitung,* attacking the rationalism of the German-language newspapers.[6]

The presence of so many persons of German birth in the state could not be ignored. In the Civil War there were whole regiments of them, specifically the Ninth, Twenty-eighth, Thirty-seventh, and Sixty-seventh Ohio Volunteer Infantry Regiments, as well as German companies in other regiments, e.g., Company H of the Forty-fourth O.V.I. In some instances translations of public documents were published in German, such as the report of the Adjutant General for the year 1862.[7]

Lutheran synods no less than the state were concerned about these Germans. Though efforts in the Cincinnati area were largely fruitless, some

[4] Article, "Our German Population," by "R" (Reynolds), *Lutheran Standard,* April 5 and 19, 1854.

[5] *Lutheran Standard,* February 8, 1854.

[6] See chapters five and six of *The German Language Press in America* by Carl Wittke, (University of Kentucky Press, 1957).

[7] *Jährlicher Bericht des General-Adjutanten an den Gouvernör von Ohio für das Jahr endend 31 Dezember, 1862.* Printed at Columbus, 1863.

results were obtained in other areas. The Miami Synod in 1864 resolved to undertake work among Germans, especially in the Cincinnati area, and authorized the formation of a German Conference. Later it sought young Germans to prepare for the ministry, and it authorized the distribution of an abstract of the synod proceedings in German. These efforts were unsuccessful.[8]

In the East Ohio Synod there was sufficient success to produce a new synod. For five years, beginning in 1869, a German translation of the minutes was published. In 1873 four German pastors were admitted by transfer from the Evangelical Synod. The next year eight pastors requested honorable dismissal in order to form a German synod. The request was approved, provided the new body would have at least eight pastors and would adopt the position of the General Synod.[9] After an abortive effort to join the German Maryland Synod, the German Augsburg Synod of the Evangelical Lutheran Church was formed at Millersburg, Ohio, May 10, 1876. The East Ohio Synod dismissed six pastors to this body, though only five were present. An extra session of the Augsburg Synod was held at North Georgetown, Ohio, June 20, 1876, at which three men were ordained.[10] In the following years the Augsburg Synod had a small but steady growth extending into states other than Ohio.

The District Synod in 1875 and 1876 appointed J. P. Hentz as German Secretary and authorized the printing of 400 to 600 copies of the minutes in German. Before and after those dates it provided for an abstract of the minutes in German to be published either in the *Lutherische Zeitschrift* or the *Lutherische Herold,* three or four hundred copies of the abstract to be distributed.

Though the story is one predominantly of growth and expansion, it was true also that some rural congregations were not able to maintain themselves and became defunct. In some instances the names of congregations disappear from the rolls without any explanation. At other times an accounting is given, particularly if a sale of property is involved. In 1869 the East Ohio Synod, noting that Mt. Olivet Church, Harrison Township, Carroll County, was no longer used for worship, decided to sell the property and use the proceeds for church extension. This set a pattern for dealing with

8 *Minutes of the Miami Synod,* 1864, pp. 15 f.; 1870, p. 21.

9 *Minutes* of the East Ohio Synod, 1874, p. 15.

10 *Minutes* of the East Ohio Synod, 1876, p. 7. *Lutheran Observer,* May 26, June 16, and July 7, 1876. Slightly different data are given in *Lutheran Cyclopedia* (Concordia), p. 68, and J. N. Lenker, *Lutherans in All Lands* (Milwaukee, 1896), pp. 811 f.

other defunct churches, though the synod did not always receive the proceeds. In 1876 and 1877 the Miami Synod took notice of seven congregations that had gone out of existence. Small rural congregations were having increasing difficulty maintaining themselves. The future lay with the congregations in towns and cities.

PARISH AND MINISTRY

The gradual improvement in the economic level of the state was reflected in the parishes. New and larger buildings were erected. Old buildings were renovated and enlarged. For example, in 1859 the interior of the church at Ashland was painted and papered, and fixtures for lighting with gas were installed—an improvement over oil lamps.[11] Congregations became affluent enough to purchase organs, either reed or pipe. The New Philadelphia congregation advertised in 1861 for a "good second-hand organ." The First Lutheran Church of Dayton installed a pipe organ during 1863–64. Whether or not this was the first pipe organ in an Ohio Lutheran church has not been determined. St. Paul's of Dayton had an organ in 1869.

Public worship continued to develop in orderliness and dignity. Efforts were made to secure uniformity in the practices of congregations. For example, the East Ohio Synod recommended that standing for prayer be the posture in all congregations.[12]

The text of the liturgy continued to be a problem. The 1855 *Liturgie und Agende* of the Ministerium of Pennsylvania was viewed with something less than complete favor by the Joint Synod. From a committee appointed to evaluate the liturgy came a minority report approving it and a majority report asserting that the work was not quite true to the Lutheran Confessions, though acknowledging that it was being used by a majority of the pastors. The Joint Synod's action was:

> *Resolved,* That for the sake of uniformity in the services of the church a committee be appointed to point out in the Pennsylvania Synod's Liturgy those formulas which Synod recommends its ministers to use.
>
> *Resolved,* That this Synod ask the Pennsylvania Synod to leave out in a new edition of their liturgy those formulas of which we do not approve.
>
> *Resolved,* That if this request be not granted we will then take measures to publish a new liturgy more consistent with the confessions of the Church.[13]

[11] *Lutheran Observer,* April 29, 1859.
[12] *Minutes* of the East Ohio Synod, 1862, p. 19.
[13] *Verhandlungen,* 1856, pp. 6, 8 ff.; translation in the *Lutheran Standard,* October 31, 1856.

The list of desired emendations was prepared by the committee and approved by the Synod.

The points of dissatisfaction rested upon doctrinal rather than liturgical grounds. Even on the latter basis the Ministerium of Pennsylvania *Liturgie* of 1855 has been characterized as "far from satisfactory." [14] It was defective in form and in adequate provision for congregational participation. The Joint Synod, however, was dissatisfied with phrases which reflected Reformed or union influences.

Meanwhile the English District appointed a committee to draft a liturgy in English. The committee in 1857 decided to postpone work when it heard of the proposed new liturgy by the Ministerium of Pennsylvania. Though the District approved that English liturgy when it appeared, there was fresh action in the Joint Synod which superseded the District's approval.[15] A committee appointed in 1860 to gather liturgical formulas in accord with the Synod's position made its report two years later. It was then directed to take such parts of the liturgy of the Ministerium of Pennsylvania as had been approved by the Joint Synod and add other soundly Lutheran items, and to submit the result to a pastoral conference which would have the power of decision.[16] When this liturgy appeared in print in 1864 the Joint Synod let it be known that it expected its pastors to use it rather than others. The Synod also authorized the committee to issue a musical supplement which church members could use in singing the responses.[17]

Several hymnals were published for use in the Joint Synod. *The Cantica Sacra* appeared in 1855, containing music for the hymns in both languages together with chants and a liturgical service.[18] In 1864 the Joint Synod voted to publish "a purely Lutheran hymn book of unaltered and unadulterated text," if possible in cooperation with the Ministerium of Pennsylvania.[19] The committee appointed for the task found that the qualities specified were unattainable because an unadulterated text was difficult to find, and

---

[14] Luther D. Reed, *Op. cit.*, p .171. Cf. A. Spaeth, "History of Liturgies . . .," *Lutheran Church Review*, XVII, 93 ff. The title of the German liturgy has already been given on page 159. The English edition, translated and edited, was *A Liturgy for the Use of the Evangelical Lutheran Church, by authority of the Ministerium of Pennsylvania.* Philadelphia, 1860.

[15] *Minutes* of the English District, 1861, pp. 7 f., 15.

[16] *Minutes* of the Joint Synod, 1862, p. 14. *Lutheran Standard,* January 1, 1863.

[17] *Minutes* of the Joint Synod, 1864, pp. 9, 26.

[18] *The Cantica Sacra.* A collection of church music embracing, besides some new pieces, a choice selection of German and English Chorals, Set Pieces, Chants, etc., from the best European and American authors; adapted to the various meters in use; with the text in German and English. by J. J. Fast, Ev. Luth. Minister, Canton. Ohio. Hudson, Ohio.

[19] *Minutes,* 1864, pp. 14 f.

also because change in language through the years made some editing necessary. Proof-sheets were presented to the convention of 1867, a few additional hymns were approved the next year, and the *Gesangbuch* came from the press in 1870.[20] It contained 532 hymns, the liturgy, lections, a Passion history, and prayers. The need for a better English hymnal was noted, and authorization for its preparation was given in 1874. In print six years later, it bore the title, *Evangelical Lutheran Hymnal.*

The General Synod had a committee making studies in the liturgy and hymns. The result was the *Book of Worship.*[21] It was the book used by the synods of that body in Ohio for the next half century. Besides a liturgy (the so-called Washington Service) and hymns, it contained Luther's Small Catechism, the Augsburg Confession, the Formula for Government and Discipline, and the Constitution of the General Synod. For German congregations there was the *Formel Buch für Ev. Luth. Gemeinden* issued by J. D. Severinghaus in 1870 at Cincinnati. For the congregations of the General Council there was the *Church Book*[22] which contained liturgical forms, 588 hymns, eighteen doxologies, the Augsburg Confession, and Luther's Small Catechism.

During these years increasing attention was given to the festivals of the church year, especially Christmas. A Christmas tree was used in 1855, evidently not for the first time, at the Orphans Home and Farm School at Zelienople, Pennsylvania, and there is note of one the next year in St. Paul's church of that town.[23] About the same time Christmas trees appeared among Lutherans in Dayton, and Americans were reminded of interesting customs in Germany.[24] In 1864 there was a tree and gifts for each child in the Sunday school at Bellefontaine, where there had been "a Christmas festival for the past three or four years." The English church in Springfield had a tree for the first time that same year.[25] About the same time the Lutheran periodicals began publishing editorials and articles concerning Christmas, Lent, and Easter. Observance of the Festival of the Reformation was stimulated by the occasion of the three hundred fiftieth anniversary of the posting

[20] *Gesangbuch für Gemeinden des Evang.-Lutherischen Bekenntnisses.* Herausgegeben von der Allgemeinen Ev.-Luth. Synode von Ohio und anderen Staaten. Columbus. 1870.

[21] *Book of Worship.* Published by the General Synod of the Lutheran Church in the United States. Philadelphia. 1870.

[22] *Church Book for the Use of Evangelical Lutheran Congregations.* By Authority of the General Council of the Evangelical Lutheran Church in America. Philadelphia. 1868.

[23] *The Missionary,* January 2 ,1856; January 1, 1857.

[24] An address of Dr. H. Borchard to the Berlin Missionary Society translated by John Hinderer serially in the *Lutheran Observer,* September 4 to October 23, 1863.

[25] *Lutheran Observer,* January 27, 1865.

of the Ninety-five Theses. The synods urged that special services be held on or near October thirty-first, 1867, and that offerings for benevolent causes be received.

Vestments were frowned upon in the General Synod, pastors usually wearing long black coats instead of gowns. Within the Joint Synod the use of the gown was encouraged. Against the accusation that the gown is Romish it was said: "If it has any peculiar associations at all they are mainly with Lutheranism. . . . We love the good old Church gown and hope to see the day when all Lutheran churches will restore it to its proper place." [26]

Public worship in the congregations of the English synods had an evangelistic note more clearly evident than in congregations using German. But during this period the emphasis upon revivals declined. In the 1850's the reports of synodical presidents encouraged renewed activity in the use of revivals, but by 1881 this emphasis had largely disappeared. It was during these years that revivalism in much of American Protestantism was on the wane until renewed by D. L. Moody.

Emphasis upon stewardship, however, was increasing among Lutherans in Ohio. The burden of raising funds rested upon the pastors. With the increasing needs of educational institutions and of home mission work there was pressure for larger financial support from the congregations. Under such circumstances the pastors were exploring ways both of increasing benevolent giving and of easing the strain upon themselves. The latter aim was accomplished more easily than the former. In the Miami Synod the section in the constitution which required each pastor at Synod to state the amount of money his parish would contribute that year to benevolences, and the following year to report how nearly the goal had been reached, was repealed. About the same time the Wittenberg Synod discontinued publishing lists of contributors and amounts given as reported by each pastor.

Committees which studied the problem brought in reports urging more preaching on the subject of stewardship. They recommended that every member of the church be impressed with the duty to give, that the giving should be regular (probably weekly), and that it should be proportionate to the giver's means.[27] The significant change was in the fact that at the beginning of this period giving was thought of in terms of an annual donation, whereas toward the end of the period there was more likelihood of

[26] Editorial, *Lutheran Standard*, April 1, 1862.

[27] *Minutes* of the Wittenberg Synod, 1870, p. 16. *Minutes of the East Ohio Synod*, 1870, p. 19.

weekly contributions. In 1871 the Wittenberg, East Ohio, and Miami Synods adopted the General Synod's plan of the "Lord's Treasury" whereby members had small boxes in which to place weekly gifts for benevolences and which were brought to church quarterly. But some congregations used offering envelopes, some used the "Lord's Treasury" boxes, and some used the "old system." [28] The Joint Synod approved the suggestion of its president, W. H. Lehmann, that "the ancient apostolic usage of Sunday collections" should be revived in the congregations, but it is not clear what was done about it in actual practice.[29]

Toward the end of this period two other aspects of stewardship are to be noticed. One was the growing practice of individual subscriptions to benevolent causes. Each member was encouraged to pledge a weekly amount for this purpose. The other aspect was the plan of apportionment whereby the congregations were expected to pay one dollar per member into the benevolent treasury of synod. This was the plan of the General Synod. While such ideals of giving were encouraged, the use of fund-raising bazaars and suppers was disparaged. True stewardship "is not that of appealing to men's carnal appetites and desires, and putting the profits accruing from their gratification into its treasury." [30]

The stewardship of Ohio Lutherans was put to the test by two economic recessions, one near the beginning and the other near the end of this period. At the time of the financial difficulties during 1857 and 1858 Ohio Lutheranism was largely rural and therefore escaped its most disastrous results. Sharp effects were felt when there were obligations to banks, or when funds were deposited there. An instance may be seen in the case of the treasury of the Wittenberg Synod. Its funds were deposited in a bank at Plymouth, Ohio, which became involved in the failure of larger finance houses. When settlement could be made, the Synod received thirty-three per cent in cash and was promised the remainder in four equal annual installments.[31]

The recession of 1873 to 1878 was felt more keenly because there were more Lutheran congregations, especially missions, in towns and cities whose members were employed in industry. The income of rural areas was likewise reduced. During these years the reports of synodical presidents re-

[28] *Minutes* of the East Ohio Synod, 1871, p. 10.

[29] *Lutheran Standard,* January 18, 1861.

[30] Editorial, "How to Raise Money for Church Work," *Lutheran Standard,* October 11, 1879.

[31] *Minutes* of the Wittenberg Synod, 1858, p. 10.

peatedly refer to the "general financial depression among our people." A typical statement is this:

> Almost all branches of industry have been languishing; labor has been poorly rewarded, and multitudes of men have been without employment. As was to be expected, the various enterprises of the Church have suffered the consequences of these adverse circumstances. The means of carrying forward the work of the Church came largely from the laboring classes, and when these are partially or wholly deprived of remunerative employment, they find it impossible to exercise the wonted liberality.[32]

The church periodicals took notice of conditions also in such words as these:

> The financial crisis through which we are passing is seriously embarrassing some of our churches. Many of them find it exceedingly difficult to meet their obligations, while others are contracting debts. In some cases pastors' salaries are reduced, and in others the amounts promised are not promptly paid. In these times weak charges and churches with heavy debts resting on them find it hard work to maintain themselves.[33]

Another aspect of parish life was the effort to guide practices in directions which were truly Lutheran. This was the continuing problem of adaptation to American life. For the English-speaking congregations there was the temptation to adopt the usages of the denominations surrounding them. Among the congregations using German there was the struggle to define parish practices in terms which conformed to the Lutheran confessions strictly understood.

Several extreme instances illustrate the problem among the English congregations. On two occasions, once in 1861 and later in 1872, the East Ohio Synod censured pastors and congregations for baptizing by immersion, insisting that the usual Lutheran mode should be used. In 1858 the Wittenberg Synod expressed the judgment that it is un-Lutheran for elders or deacons instead of the pastor to distribute the elements of the Lord's Supper. Among the German congregations the problem was that of pastors ministering both to Lutherans and Reformed. Though there was a struggle with this question, as early as 1856 the Joint Synod declared that a Lutheran pastor was denying his faith when he administered Communion to members of other denominations. This was adopted by a vote of thirteen to seven.[34]

[32] Report of President G. W. Mechling, *Minutes* of the District Synod, 1877, p. 6.
[33] *Lutheran Evangelist*, February 9, 1877, p. 4.
[34] *Lutheran Standard*, October 31, 1856.

It was commonly recognized that improvement in parish practice depended upon faithful catechetical indoctrination. The synods periodically urged careful catechetical instruction upon pastors and congregations. The Committee on the State of the Church reported to the Miami Synod in 1864 that only a minority of the pastors had catechetical classes. Likewise the president of the Wittenberg Synod in 1880 noted that few pastors reported such classes. Within the Joint Synod there was greater faithfulness in this matter.

During these years the synods endeavored to establish regular standards for the ministry. Within the Joint Synod attention was given especially to the theological aspects, so that it adopted a set of theses on the pastoral office in 1870 specifying the Synod's understanding of the Lutheran doctrine of the ministry. The English synods were more concerned about establishing regular standards for the practical aspects of ministerial life. When some congregations wanted to require their pastors to be re-elected every year, the synods insisted on permanent pastorates, declaring that pastorates are not limited except by the ability of pastors to serve. Thus the District Synod in 1870 published a set of theses concerning the call of a pastor.

The annual salary of Lutheran pastors in Ohio during these years is not reported generally, but data from the Wittenberg Synod may be fairly representative. In 1857 the average salary was $379, in a range from $200 to $500. For several years the figure increased, then declined slightly during the war years but increased to $589 in 1865, the maximum salary being $1050. The climb increased through 1874 when the average was $816, one pastor receiving as much as $2000. During the panic years a decline again set in, the average reaching a low of $702 in 1880, after which a rise occurred. These figures are somewhat better than those occasionally reported by the East Ohio or the District Synod for corresponding years. During the war years, when living costs were rising, appeals were made by synods to the congregations to increase salaries proportionately, but it is not clear that such appeals were effective. There was some relief for pastors, however, in the increase in the number of parsonages. And when attending synod conventions the pastors were given either free return tickets or reduced rates by the railroads, or even free passes. The typical synodical minutes of the 1860's and 1870's contained a resolution of thanks to the railroads concerned.

The financial pressure upon pastors with inadequate salaries was such as to induce a man here or there to engage in secular work either part time or full time. In such instances the synods encouraged the man either to give his full time to the ministry or to demit it. The East Ohio Synod had a provision in its constitution forbidding pastors to engage in secular work. Men who violated this provision were first reproved, and if they did not heed the reproof were suspended from the ministry. In the Wittenberg Synod pastors without parishes were required annually to give their reasons for not being active in the ministry. Two licentiates of the Miami Synod who took up the practice of law had their licenses revoked. A pastor of the District Synod, who during the panic of the 1870's became a county treasurer, was admonished to resume his ministry. That Synod adopted a series of theses on the subject of secular work of pastors, one of which read: "A minister who evinces a sordid, coveteous, avaricious or penurious spirit should be promptly deposed or suspended from his office." [35]

There were other reasons for disciplining pastors, either by suspending them temporarily from performing ministerial functions or deposing them permanently from the ministry. In many instances the suspension became permanent. The most frequent accusation was contempt of synod, meaning that the person involved refused to abide by the regulations or decisions of the synod. This might mean chronic non-attendance at synod conventions, or, in case of a dispute, the pastor's refusal to accept the synod's decision. Another frequent accusation involved immorality or unministerial conduct. Occasionally there was discipline for un-Lutheran doctrine or practice. In one instance the accusation was breach of promise to marry, in another it was divorce. The total number of discipline cases was not large.

There were instances in which a pastor who had been deposed by one synod was accepted by another. This, of course, caused irritation between the synods concerned. An instance in which the Missouri Synod accepted men disciplined by the Joint Synod of Ohio has previously been noted. Pastors at odds with the District Synod and under sentence of discipline by it were deemed faithful by the Joint Synod. Men in disfavor in the Joint Synod found acceptance in an English synod. For example, Joel Swartz, pastor at Circleville, was deposed by the English District of the Joint Synod for un-Lutheran doctrine and practice. The Miami Synod to which he applied regarded him as a Lutheran in doctrine and practice according to its standards and therefore admitted him. With proper wisdom this action of the Miami Synod was editorially criticized by W. A. Passavant on the grounds that it contributes to schism and disorder. "One district synod is not a court of appeal from another. . . . Lutheran synods are bound to respect each other's actions." [36]

[35] *Minutes* of the District Synod, 1880, p. 9.
[36] *Missionary,* June 23, 1859.

Financial assistance to aged pastors or their widows received increasing attention. Sometimes there were special appeals on behalf of certain individuals. The Miami Synod resolved "that each minister take up a collection for Father [Abraham] Reck on Whitsuntide." [37] A member of the District Synod was authorized to solicit aid for Mrs. Konstantine Koeberlin and her children. The four hundred dollars collected was used to buy a small house and lot for her.[38]

As early as 1857 the synods of the General Synod were inspired by that body to organize a synodical Pastor's Fund Society. In the East Ohio Synod a committee appointed to prepare a constitution for such a society finally reported in 1861. Upon the acceptance of the report trustees, three pastors and two laymen, were elected. At the first meeting of the trustees, August 21, 1861, officers were chosen and a sum of twenty-seven dollars was voted to Rev. C. C. Gunther.[39] Members of the society contributed annual sums up to ten dollars and therefore were to receive preferred consideration when in need. During the years through 1881 the society paid to aged pastors or widows sums ranging from twenty-five to seventy-five dollars—rather pitiful annual amounts. The Wittenberg Synod had a Pastor's Fund Society during the years 1861 through 1872. The Miami Synod seems to have had such a society also.

The Joint Synod in 1864 resolved to establish a fund for "our superannuated ministers, pastor's widows and orphans" to be administered by a committee of three.[40] That this fund became of considerable size is indicated by the fact that in 1876 one widow was to receive one hundred fifty dollars and another three hundred dollars.[41]

Lutherans began giving attention to life insurance. The East Ohio Synod at one point recommended a certain insurance company for ministers to its pastors. At another time the Miami Synod called attention to a ministers' mutual association in which the annual cost was twenty dollars per member. But opposition to insurance companies appeared in the Joint Synod. "That the so-called Life Insurance Companies are institutions entirely opposed to the teachings of Holy Scripture seems so evident that it has not been deemed necessary to write much about it," said one writer.[42]

---

[37] *Minutes* of the Miami Synod, 1861, p. 11.

[38] *Minutes* of the District Synod, 1876, p. 21; 1879, pp. 17 f.

[39] *Record Book of the Pastor's Fund Society,* now in the Archives of the Synod of Ohio.

[40] Minutes in the *Lutheran Standard,* April 1 and 15, 1865.

[41] *Minutes* of the Joint Synod, 1876, p. 31.

[42] Article, "Life Insurance," *Lutheran Standard,* April 22, 1876. In the issue of October 28, 1876, appeared an article, "Why a Christian cannot participate in Life Insurance."

The membership of pastors in secret societies became a matter of vigorous concern in these years. The difficulties in this area which were involved in the separation of the District Synod from the Joint Synod have already been noted. Through the years numerous articles hostile to secret societies appeared in *The Lutheran Standard*. Editor Loy continued to press the charge that the District Synod was favorable to Freemasonry, whereas that Synod declared its opposition to all secret societies. On one occasion the Eastern District of the Joint Synod called the roll asking each pastor to state whether or not he was a member of a secret society, and when one such was revealed he was induced to promise to resign from it forthwith. There was opposition to secret societies by pastors outside the Joint Synod as well. W. G. Keil of the East Ohio Synod wrote of Freemasonry that it was "an evil that every Christian man should not only shun and renounce, but denounce and destroy as far as possible." [43]

SYNODICAL ACTIVITY

The maintenance and expansion of their educational institutions continued to occupy the attention of Lutherans in Ohio during these years. At the end of the period both Wittenberg and Capital had larger enrollments and resources than at the beginning. The Civil War and the economic recessions made temporary pauses in this progress. While these two institutions grew, others were failures.

Samuel Sprecher continued as president at Wittenberg until 1874. When his successor, John B. Helwig, took office the institution owned thirty-three acres of land and was free of debt. A campaign for funds had secured enough cash and pledges to increase the endowment to $200,000. The economic recession of the next few years made many pledges worthless, making some retrenchment necessary in 1876. Women students were admitted for the first time in 1874. The theological department was closed during the 1872–1873 academic year. When it reopened, its course of instruction was expanded to cover two years. In 1881 Wittenberg had an income of $13,400, which was slightly more than its expenditures. There were 181 students in all departments. An appeal being made in Springfield for funds to erect a second building was having difficulty, but was soon to be successful.

Capital University had had its first commencement June 29, 1854, when eight students were graduated with the degree of Bachelor of Arts. Though

[43] *Lutheran Evangelist,* July 2, and 9, 1880.

an army camp was set up near the campus in 1861, the institution continued to function during the war years. In 1876 it was moved to its present site in suburban Bexley. William F. Lehmann succeeded Christian Spielmann in the presidency in 1857, continuing in office until his death in 1880. His was a successful administration in spite of great difficulties. At the commencement in 1880 the jubilee of the seminary was observed with speeches and contributions of money. The main building, though not free of debt, was evidence of the growing strength of the institution. Annual expenditures were about $8000. Matthias Loy became president in 1881.

The possibility of establishing academies for a time occupied the interest of Lutherans. In Dayton the Cooper Female Seminary was in operation for a short time. Two pastors who were brothers, Victor L. and Frederick W. Conrad, directed the school. There were 161 pupils in the academic year 1859–1860. Both the Miami and the Wittenberg Synods recommended the institution. A few years later the East Ohio Synod recommended "Grove Female Institute of Wooster, Ohio, under the control and management of Mrs. E. M. Pope, widow of the late Rev. Benjamin Pope, to the confidence and support of those who have daughters to whom they desire to give a liberal education." [44] Two years later the three synods appointed a joint committee to plan for a female seminary in Ohio. The committee offered to locate the institution in any city that would donate $50,000 for this purpose. But no offers were received, either for that sum or at a lower figure, and the plan was dropped.

The District Synod in 1873 appointed a committee to plan for an academy for boys. The citizens of Germantown were willing to donate land and erect a building if the Synod would operate the school. Instruction in Germantown Institute began September 8, 1875, though the building was not ready for use until a year later. From the beginning the income from tuition was insufficient to pay salaries, and the Synod was unwilling to cover the deficit. Disagreements between the trustees and the citizens of Germantown soon arose. The building was sold to satisfy a mechanic's lien. The Synod renounced all further responsibility for the institution in 1877. [45]

Financial aid to students increased just as living costs increased. Beneficiaries of the East Ohio Synod in 1855 each received $100, increased to $120 in the senior year in college. In 1863 the top figure in the Wittenberg Synod was $150. By 1873 the Miami Synod was granting $175, and the District Synod $200. By that time the synods were requiring the

[44] *Minutes* of the East Ohio Synod, 1864, p. 27. It closed in 1865.
[45] *Minutes* of the District Synod, 1880, pp. 23 f.

beneficiaries to sign notes promising to repay with interest the sums advanced if they left the Lutheran ministry.

The establishing of parochial schools was advocated at this time. The District Synod in 1874 declared that "wherever practicable, congregational schools, providing for the thorough moral and religious and intellectual culture of the children and youth of the Church should receive hearty encouragement." [46] Evidence that this advice was heeded is lacking. That same year, M. Loy, in his report as president of the Joint Synod, recommended such schools. This desire came to be expressed in the Constitution which specified that pastors and congregations "must also promise, as it is the duty of Christians, to provide their children with Christian schooling, and for this reason to labor zealously for the establishment and maintenance of Christian parochial schools." [47] The development of this ideal came in the years that followed.

Ohio synods took an interest in books and pamphlets written by their members. A treatise on baptism by Andrew Henkel met with approval, as did also *The Groundwork of a System of Evangelical Lutheran Theology* by Samuel Sprecher. J. H. W. Stuckenberg had written *Ninety-five Theses* as well as a *History of the Augsburg Confession*. Works by Matthias Loy were: *Life and Deeds of Luther, Luther's House Postil,* and *Justification.* Pastors as well as professors wrote articles for *The Evangelical Review.* A complete list is too long for this space.[48]

There was development also in the area of periodicals. *The Lutheran Standard* continued to be published. It was edited by a committee through February 3, 1860. Daniel Worley was the editor beginning with the issue of February 17, 1860, and ending with that of March 15, 1864. Matthias Loy was editor of the magazine beginning with the issue of April 15, 1864, and continuing through this period. Its pages were devoted chiefly to doctrinal articles and reports, little space being given to church news. The Joint Synod in 1859 authorized the publication of a bi-monthly periodical in German which would conform to the confession and interests of the Synod. Edited by a committee, the first issue of the *Lutherische Kirchenzeitung* bore the date of January 1, 1860.

Among the synods of the General Synod there was renewed agitation in 1874 for a church paper in the Ohio area. The synods were unwilling to assume financial responsibility for such a paper, but they urged that it be

---

[46] *Minutes* of the District Synod, 1874, p. 15.
[47] Article III, Section e, *Minutes* of the Joint Synod, 1880, p. 18.
[48] For the titles see John G. Morris, *Bibliotheca Lutherana,* Philadelphia, 1876.

a private enterprise. A beginning was made when the first issue of *The Evangelist* appeared July 7, 1876. This was to be a weekly paper published at Bellefontaine with A. R. Howbert as proprietor and J. Steck as editor. The presses and type were owned by the proprietor who did much of the work and was prepared to print or publish other things as well. This was quickly replaced by *The Lutheran Evangelist*, the first issue dated January 5, 1877. It was published at Bellefontaine and Springfield with J. H. W. Stuckenberg as editor and was financed by an association of stockholders. W. H. Singley was editor beginning October 31, 1879, and was succeeded by S. A. Ort whose first issue was dated March 11, 1881. This paper represented General Synod sentiments and contained many news items.

At Columbus the *Theological Magazine* made its appearance in February, 1881, with M. Loy as editor. A monthly *Lutheran Child's Paper*, edited by C. H. L. Schuette, began about 1875.

In doctrinal position there was virtually no change by the synods during this period. Throughout these years the Joint Synod adhered fervently to the confessional writings ("Symbolical Books") contained in the Book of Concord. This view is expressed in the statement, "Annihilate the Symbolical Books and you annihilate the *Lutheran* Church." [49] The constitution of the Joint Synod 1880 contained the statement: "Synod accepts all the canonical writings of the Old and New Testaments as the written Word of God and the only rule and guide of faith and life, and also all the Symbolical Books of the Evangelical Lutheran Church as the pure and unadulterated explanation and exposition of the Word of God" [50] Synods of the General Council said the same.

This doctrinal affirmation encountered some criticism within the General Synod. An editorial by W. H. Singley asked, "If we must accept the convictions and opinions of any uninspired man as 'the pure, unadultreated explanation and exposition of the Word of God,' how can we submit ourselves to that Word as our only infallible judge in matters of faith and life?" [51] General Synod views on this matter were far from uniform. The most common position was acceptance of the Augsburg Confession but with an assertion of liberty in matters deemed non-fundamental. When it was proposed that the General Synod adopt a constitutional amendment accepting "the Augsburg Confession as a correct exhibition of the fundamental doctrines of the Divine Word," the synods in Ohio approved, though with

---

[49] Letter signed "Staupitz," *Lutheran Standard*, February 26, 1851.
[50] *Minutes* of the Joint Synod, 1880, p. 17.
[51] *Lutheran Evangelist*, November 5, 1880, p. 4.

some reservations by those who had adopted the *Definite Platform*.[52] Nevertheless, the amendment turned the tide against those who charged the Augsburg Confession with error. Yet a published sermon said: "We teach that the body and blood of Christ are truly present and are dispensed to the communicants in the Lord's Supper. Not in the gross, material sense, however, but that in a spiritual sense we as communicants partake of Christ." [53] The doctrines of synods of the General Synod tended to be guided by a popular understanding of the Bible more than by the Confessions.

Despite these theological disagreements there was virtually no difference in the attitude taken toward the new sciences.

> Science has become haughty and arrogant. Reason usurps the place of faith. . . . The attacks made upon the Church and her doctrines by the Darwins, Huxleys, Spencers, Tyndalls of our day are the oppositions of science falsely so called. . . . It is not facts which they oppose to the Scriptures but false theories illegitimately deduced from facts.[54]

Man is not "a highly developed beast, related to the gorilla and ourangoutang." [55] "He, then, who reads nature aright reads what the finger of God has written there; but God did not write one thing in nature and its opposite in the Bible. Correct scientific investigation will therefore inevitably result in coincidence with God's Word." [56] An article entitled "Darwinian Theology" asserted that the Genesis account is literal history and is opposed to Darwinian evolution.[57] An editorial by W. H. Singley said, "The modern discussion of the relation of science to religion is producing most gratifying results. The evidence of the truthfulness of the Bible is becoming stronger just in proportion to the clearness obtained in science." [58] Of the Reverend J. A. Hall, who gave a lecture on geology, it was said, "Like every true conservative scientist, he maintained the perfect harmony of revelation with thoroughly established scientific truth." [59] Such statements indicate that Lutherans had not yet felt the full impact of successful scientific method based on materialistic assumptions.

Of the missionary work increasingly occupying the attention of the synods the missions in the home field, being close at hand, received the

[52] E.g., *Minutes* of the East Ohio Synod, 1868, p. 9.
[53] Sermon by G. W. Miller, *Lutheran Evangelist,* July 16, 1880.
[54] *Lutheran Standard,* October 1, 1872.
[55] *Op. cit.,* August 9, 1873.
[56] *Op. cit.,* July 15, 1876.
[57] *Op. cit.,* April 6, 1878.
[58] *Lutheran Evangelist,* March 26, 1880.
[59] *Op. cit.,* November 14, 1879.

greater notice. Yet the synods were groping for a program for promoting this work and for funds to advance it. The Miami Synod had a section in its constitution specifying that the officers of the Synod should constitute a committee on missions. Failing to make the desired progress, the Synod authorized the appointment of a Cooperating Committee on Home Missions.[60] At the same time it was proposed that the synods related to Wittenberg College form a Home Missionary Union and employ a missionary; but this plan was abandoned when the General Synod assigned Morris Officer to direct mission activity in Ohio. In 1865 the Wittenberg Synod set up an Advisory Board of Home Missions to cooperate with the General Synod Board, and four years later the East Ohio Synod did likewise. The District Synod, following a different pattern, established the office of Missionary President in 1869. Four years later it expressed the opinion that mission work would advance more satisfactorily if all the mission activity of its constituent synods were transferred to the General Council. The General Council, however, thought otherwise. Within the Joint Synod the work was directed by Commissioners for Home and Foreign Missions as specified in the by-laws.[61]

In 1881 the East Ohio Synod had six missions: Orrville, Loudenville, Salem, Alliance, Leetonia, and Cleveland. The Miami Synod had one: Circleville. The Wittenberg Synod had two: Bryan and Upper Sandusky. The District Synod had eight: Ada, Alliance, Columbus, London, Middle Point, Paulding, Pawnee, and Cleveland. It is noteworthy that none of these were in the Ohio Valley or the southern counties.

The inadequacy of the program for home missions interacted with the insufficiency of funds. In 1859 the East Ohio Synod urged that contributions for this work be doubled. The total amount received for home missions reported in 1881 by the three synods of the General Synod was $1979.65. That year the treasurer of the District Synod reported the mission expenditure of $904.57, most, if not all, of which apparently was for home missions.

Foreign missions received increasing attention during these years. When the proposed mission in Liberia, Africa, was approved by the General Synod, a committee was appointed and Morris Officer was named superintendent. The three synods in Ohio endorsed the project, inviting Officer to visit their congregations. He had considerable success in raising funds. There was no success, however, in finding Negroes to train for missionary work in Africa,

60 *Minutes* of the Miami Synod, 1864, pp. 14 f.
61 By-Law I, B, 5. *Minutes* of the Joint Synod, 1880, p. 53.

so the plan for a training school was abandoned. Officer, assisted by Henry Heigerd, went to Liberia and broke ground for a mission station in 1860. When the work was organized he returned to America to promote this missionary project. He found considerable response in Ohio. Synods urged pastors to preach on foreign missions and to gather funds.

The mission in India received attention also. Missionaries on furlough from that field addressed Ohio congregations. In 1872 an appeal was made for funds to erect a chapel in the Guntur mission. Since Sunday schools were deemed appropriate places for cultivating missionary interest, Children's Missionary Societies were formed and A. D. Rowe, the children's missionary in India, was invited to visit congregations in Ohio in 1873. Lemon L. Uhl was ordained by the East Ohio Synod in 1872 for service in India, reaching his mission station the following March.

In subsequent years extended reports of foreign mission work were made at the conventions of synods. According to reports made at the 1881 conventions, the total sum received for foreign missions by the East Ohio, Miami, and Wittenberg synods was $1845.36.

During these years the Joint Synod had no foreign mission work. A proposal of the English District in 1864 that the Joint Synod establish a foreign mission was rejected on the grounds "that this body has already enough to do within its own limits before establishing an independent mission, and would move that the monies collected for foreign mission be sent to Past. Harms at Hermannsburg or to Leipzig" [62] That this latter suggestion was followed is evident from the reports of the treasurer. For example, for the biennium 1872 to 1874 he remitted $1,840 to Th. Harms for the Hermannsburg Mission, $163 to J. Hardeland for the Leipzig Mission, and $278.90 for travel expense and student support at Hermannsburg.

Missionary work was fostered by Women's Home and Foreign Missionary Societies. As proposed by the General Synod there was to be such a society in each congregation, as well as an organization comprising all the congregational societies within a synod. The plan was approved by the synods in 1877 and committees were appointed to put it in operation. Within two years about a third of the congregations had formed societies and preparations were made for a synodical organization. Wives of pastors usually were the leaders in the societies. The first convention of the Miami Synod society was held at Tipp City in 1879 with Mrs. J. F. Shaffer as

[62] Minutes of the Joint Synod in *Lutheran Standard*, April 1, 1865.

president. In the Wittenberg Synod Mrs. S. F. Breckenridge was president of the first convention held in 1881 at Carey, though organized the year previous.

Inner mission activity in America owes its development to the vision and zeal of William Alfred Passavant. Though he was a member of the Pittsburgh Synod, the appeal and interest of his institutions crossed synodical lines. An orphanage begun in April, 1852, with two children, was located in Zelienople, Pennsylvania. At the cornerstone-laying, July 4, 1854, the main speaker for the ceremony was F. W. Conrad of Springfield, Ohio, and the event was noted by the Joint Synod.[63] After the schism of the eighteen-sixties the Passavant institutions were the special interest of the General Council, and therefore in part of the District Synod of Ohio. Dr. Passavant addressed the District Synod convention in 1866 telling of the institutions under his care. In expressing sympathy for this care of the sick and the orphans the Synod endorsed contributions to such institutions.[64]

There was also an isolated instance of J. M. Straeffer, a layman in Cincinnati, who spent part of his time as city missionary visiting a Widows' Home, the Asylum, the county jail, and the Commercial Hospital, as well as doing street preaching.[65]

Within the Joint Synod there was a proposal in 1856 by the Northern District that there be established an "asylum" which likely meant an orphanage. But the Joint Synod considered the time not yet favorable. Twenty years later there was renewed interest in having an orphans' home. The Joint Synod adopted a resolution in favor of beginning such an institution without delay and appointed a committee to prepare plans. The committee suggested that the orphanage be erected near Capital University, and it presented a tentative set of regulations.[66] Funds available for it amounted to $814.15. As it turned out, however, the Joint Synod's institution became Wernle Orphans' Home and Asylum for the Aged at Richmond, Indiana. On February 24, 1879, the housefather, Rev. J. Dingeldey, was installed. When the building was dedicated, May 4, 1879, there were fifty-eight orphans being cared for.[67]

Beyond the educational and missionary activities of the synods was the necessary concern to preserve the constituency and organization of each

[63] *Lutheran Standard,* July 28, 1854.
[64] *Minutes* of the District Synod, 1866, p. 14.
[65] Reports in *Lutheran Observer,* April 25, 1856, May 8, 1857, April 16, 1858, April 29, 1859.
[66] *Minutes* of the Joint Synod, 1876, p. 23.
[67] *Minutes* of the Joint Synod, 1880, p. 38.

synodical body. Each synod was eager to preserve the loyalty of its member pastors and congregations, and therefore resisted any effort to dislodge the loyalty of such members. The English synods, in order to avoid misunderstandings, agreed on geographical boundaries. This was particularly true in this period of the District Synod, which accepted the state line as a boundary between it and the Pittsburgh Synod on the east and the proposed synod of the General Council in Indiana on the west. There were repeated difficulties, however, with the Pittsburgh Synod.[68] The boundary between the East Ohio and the Wittenberg Synods involved some difficulty also. The East Ohio Synod disapproved the action of one of its pastors who formed a congregation in Wittenberg Synod territory.[69]

Trouble was more frequent where synods occupied the same area. This was especially the case with the English Synod and Ministerium of Ohio, which had congregations in the same territory as the East Ohio Synod. Occasionally a pastor or congregation of either synod would seek to evade responsibilities or discipline by transferring to the other body. At other times a congregation without a pastor would seek the services of a pastor of the other synod and be transferred to it. Instances of this sort occurred at New Philadelphia, New Pittsburgh, and Newcomerstown.[70] There were protests also when a pastor was accepted by one synod without having been dismissed officially by the other.

At times the difficulty lay, not between synods, but between parishes within the same synod, particularly if a parish or "charge" consisted of several congregations. If a pastor of a neighboring parish performed ministerial acts in one of the congregations which might be at odds with its sister congregations of the parish, that pastor would be accused of intrusion or interference.

The synods generally supported good order, ministerial courtesy, and equitable dealings. The Joint Synod "*Resolved,* That we hope and desire that no other synods of the Lutheran faith, whatever their names may be, will receive any minister or congregation of our connection without having previously entered into correspondence with our Synod and paying due regard to our rights." [71] The East Ohio Synod expressed its good will toward the English Synod and Ministerium, declaring that in disputes between them it would accept the decision of a two-thirds majority vote in

[68] *Minutes* of the District Synod, 1871, p. 18; 1874, p. 28.
[69] *Minutes* of the East Ohio Synod, 1862, p. 14.
[70] *Minutes* of the East Ohio Synod, 1859, p. 13; 1862, pp. 5 f., 13 f.
[71] *Lutheran Standard,* October 31, 1856.

244 / A Century of Lutherans in Ohio

any congregation.[72] Encroachments by pastors upon other parishes were disapproved and directed to be discontinued. Interference in other congregations was deplored; ministers were warned to avoid it. Breaches of ministerial courtesy were declared to be grounds for synodical censure. Usually such declaration by synod was sufficient to correct the case at issue.[73] To protect congregations from having rival congregations established near them the East Ohio Synod adopted a by-law forbidding the organization of a congregation within five miles of another congregation without the latter's consent.[74]

The English synods took increased interest in Sunday Schools in the latter part of this period. The East Ohio Synod ordained Levi Ricksecker in 1860 to become an agent of the American Sunday School Union. In the next decade synodical Sunday School associations were organized: of the Wittenberg Synod in 1875, of the Miami Synod in 1876, of the East Ohio Synod in 1877. Delegates from Ohio attended the National Lutheran Sunday School Convention at Johnstown, Pennsylvania, in November, 1874, and at Wooster, Ohio, in 1875. Such conventions discussed methods and materials, urging the use of Lutheran literature such as the *Augsburg Sunday School Teacher*.

Typical of the Sunday School development was that of the Wittenberg Synod for the twenty years preceding 1875. The number of schools increased from forty-six to fifty-seven. At the earlier date half of the schools were union, whereas all but seven were Lutheran in 1875. The number of scholars had increased from 1,147 to 5,725. Formerly the literature and supplies were those prepared by the American Sunday School Union, but Lutheran materials were being used increasingly. Most schools used the International Lessons. The quality of instruction was improving. The schools cultivated interest and support for benevolent causes.[75]

The synods were concerned also with the problem of unity, either among Lutherans or among evangelical Christians in general. Lutherans could be united, according to the view held in the General Synod, if they permitted some freedom in doctrinal opinion and if they tolerated differences in nonfundamentals. Other synods believed that agreement in doctrine was necessary for unity. The Free Lutheran Conferences of 1856 to 1859 mentioned

[72] *Minutes* of the East Ohio Synod, 1866, p. 13.

[73] *Minutes* of the Miami Synod, 1859, pp. 13 f.; *Minutes* of the East Ohio Synod, 1862, pp. 18, 21; 1863, p. 6; *Minutes* of the Wittenberg Synod, 1865, p. 12.

[74] *Minutes* of the East Ohio Synod, 1867, p. 13.

[75] Address by Joshua Crouse, *Minutes* of Wittenberg the Synod, 1876, pp. 22 ff.

in an earlier chapter insisted that a return to the Lutheran Confessions was "the first requisite for the attainment of true unity." [76]

This latter position involved the repudiation of union churches in combination with the Reformed, as well as exchange of pulpits with non-Lutherans. The Joint Synod in 1856 took the position that Lutheran pastors could not serve union congregations. Ten years later the District Synod protested against building union churches. The Joint Synod in 1874 adopted a series of theses which rejected any exchange of pulpits by ministers not united in doctrine, the reason being that such practice is opposed both to Scripture and the Confessions. In the Constitution of 1880 was this section:

> They [pastors and congregations] must renounce all kinds of unionism and syncretism, such as: pastoral ministrations to heterodox or mixed congregations as such; exchange of pulpits and altar-fellowship with errorists; participation in the worship and sacramental acts of such congregations; taking part in the missionary and tract operations of errorists and unionists, and also secret societies and the like.[77]

Within the General Synod, however, there was a disposition to fraternize with non-Lutherans. On Sundays during conventions it was customary for Lutheran pastors to preach in most of the churches in town. Fraternal visitors were exchanged with other denominations. The Wittenberg Synod exchanged delegates of this kind with the Congregationalists in 1867, the Reformed Synod of Ohio in 1871, and the Methodist Protestant Conference in 1879. The Miami Synod exchanged visitors with the Congregationalists for five years beginning in 1867. The East Ohio Synod expressed itself in 1869 as desiring to cultivate Christian fellowship and sympathy with the Congregationalists; but when the latter understood this to mean organic union the Synod by resolution stated specifically that it had no intention of abandoning Lutheranism for Congregationalism.[78]

Cooperation of the sort encouraged by the Evangelical Alliance (an association formed in 1846 for mutual assistance among Protestants) appeared among these synods also. Special notice was given to the "Union Doctrinal Basis of the Evangelical Ministerial Association of Cincinnati" prepared at a time when a Lutheran, W. H. Harrison, was the secretary. This document of twenty-one articles is evangelical in a broad sense; it is

[76] *Lutheran Standard,* November 14, 1856. See also E. L. Lueker, "Walther and the Free Lutheran Conferences of 1856–1859," *Concordia Theological Monthly,* XV, no. 8 (August, 1944), pp. 529–563.

[77] *Minutes* of the Joint Synod, 1880, p. 18.

[78] *Minutes* of the East Ohio Synod, 1870, p. 12.

definitely not unitarian, universalist, or Romanist. Its statement on free will and the Lord's Supper would not be acceptable to confessional Lutherans. It was not intended as a basis for church union but only for cooperation. The Miami Synod endorsed it.[79] Five years later this synod adopted a resolution proposed by J. B. Helwig in accord with General Synod resolutions on Christian unity. This called for an ecumenical spirit and for measures designed to heal the divisions in Christendom.[80]

ISSUES

The problem of slavery and its abolition received increased attention through the years of the Civil War. Pastor R. D. Emerson, who returned to Ohio after living in Missouri for three years, said, "Missouri has cured me of my former pro-slavery sentiments." A few pastors resisted the abolitionist tide. At the convention of the East Ohio Synod in 1864 there was considerable agitation when Pastor John Hamilton dared to ask for biblical evidence that slavery is sin. The Synod interpreted his position as teaching that slavery is authorized by the Word of God. Agitated by this, the Synod adopted a statement which stigmatized slavery as "belonging to the same category of sins with theft, adultery and licentiousness," and which utterly disavowed Hamilton's position.[81]

The Lutheran Observer, which was read by General Synod Lutherans in Ohio but which also had subscribers in the southern states, kept the discussion of slavery out of its columns in the 1850's, so that from its pages one could get no impression of the controversy in progress. With the approaching political campaign of 1860 the *Observer* lamented the fact that election excitement diverted attention from religion. In the issue of July 13, 1860, it reprinted a Presbyterian interview with Henry Clay in which abolitionism was called fanaticism. It declared that divisions in the churches on this subject boded ill for the nation.

This was not the predominant view of the *Observer's* readers in Ohio. The Wittenberg Synod, which saw the abolition of slavery as one of the expected results of the war, hailed "with unmingled delight the prospect of the final and utter end of slavery on this continent, and the establishment of truth, justice, benevolence and freedom in its stead." [82] Four pastors

---

[79] *Minutes* of the Miami Synod, 1863, p. 11. The text is given on pages 20 f., and the *Lutheran Observer,* June 19, 1863.

[80] *Minutes* of the Miami Synod, 1868, p. 18.

[81] *Minutes* of the East Ohio Synod, 1864, pp. 27 f.

[82] *Minutes* of the Wittenberg Synod, 1862, p. 22.

and four laymen voted against the resolution as being "incendiary, fanatical and unwise."

The Emancipation Proclamation of President Lincoln was greeted with approval and delight. With this went a sense of responsibility for the ex-slaves and a concern for their future. The Wittenberg Synod *"Resolved, That it is the duty of the Lutheran Church, as well as all others of our land, to exert itself for their religious instruction and salvation."* [83] At the end of the war the Synod declared "That it is the duty of the Government to extend to the disenthralled colored race all the rights and protection due to Freemen." [84] And when the general agent of the American Missionary Association explained the work of his organization among the Freedmen the Synod resolved that "we hereby heartily endorse the Association as the most efficient organization now prosecuting this most necessary and noble work, and we commend the Association to the confidence and liberality of our churches." [85]

When the war began the Lutheran churches had to consider what their action should be: to endorse it, or oppose it, or ignore it. There is no instance on record in which a Lutheran synod in Ohio took a position of opposition to the war, though a few pastors and congregations did. The usual course was either to approve the policy of the Federal government, or to insist that this was a political matter with which the church independent of the state should have nothing to do.

Two weeks after Fort Sumter surrendered, the Miami Synod at its convention adopted a vigorous loyalty declaration. After a long preamble with five "whereas" sections, it was

> 1. *Resolved*, That we . . . declare it to be a Christian as well as a civil duty to support the Government in its constitutional efforts to punish treason, and put down rebellion by all the means within our power.
> 2. *Resolved*, That we call upon all our people to lift up holy hands in prayer to the God of battles. . . .
> 3. *Resolved*, That we deeply sympathize with all loyal citizens and Christian patriots in the rebellious portion of our country.

This statement was unanimously adopted by a rising vote.[85a] It was the first declaration of its kind by any Lutheran synod. There was no further expression of sentiment by the Miami Synod, except that President Jeremiah

---

[83] *Op. cit.*, 1863, p .13.
[84] *Op. cit.*, 1865, p. 20. Negro franchise in Ohio came in 1869.
[85] *Op. cit.*, 1867, p. 20.
[85a] *Minutes* of the Miami Synod, 1861, p. 14.

Geiger in his report in 1862 said, "We are now in the midst of a bloody, but on our part, holy war. It becomes our duty to implore God . . . to give success to our army and navy . . . until this unholy rebellion shall be subdued and peace restored to us as a nation." [86]

The East Ohio Synod in August of 1861 adopted with one dissenting vote the same resolutions which the Miami Synod adopted in April. Two years later, though three pastors declined to vote, it adopted the resolutions of the Allegheny Synod including this: "*Resolved,* That we, as ministers in Synod assembled, do pledge our hearty support to the President of the United States for the suppression of this most atrocious rebellion. . . ." [87] The next year it adopted the resolutions of the General Synod including one which recognized "the sufferings and calamities of war as the righteous judgment of a just God visited upon us for our transgressions." [88]

The Wittenberg Synod, meeting in August, 1861, also expressed its moral judgment of the war. A preamble affirmed that since civil governments are ordained of God who has blessed our nation, the states which seceded are united in "treasonable conspiracy" and in "formidable rebellion." Therefore it was

> *Resolved,* That we, in the capacity of an ecclesiastical body, do most cordially approve of the prompt and efficient measures adopted by the President. . . .
>
> *Resolved,* That in the national contest of right against wrong . . . we will earnestly and devoutly betake ourselves to the God of battles and implore His divine succor. . . .
>
> *Resolved,* That we deeply sympathize with all loyal citizens who are subject to the reign of terror inaugurated by a few politically corrupt and aspiring demagogues. . . .
>
> *Resolved,* That in compliance with the appointment of the President we will recommend to the congregations belonging to this Synod the general observance of the 26th of September as a day of national fasting and prayer. . . .[89]

These sentiments were reaffirmed in 1862 and 1864.

Expressing the same loyalty to the Federal government and the same moral condemnation of the Confederacy, the English Synod and Ministerium approved this statement:

[86] *Op. cit.,* 1862, pp. 4 f.
[87] *Minutes* of the East Ohio Synod, 1863, pp. 22 f.
[88] *Op. cit.,* 1864, p. 28.
[89] *Minutes* of the Wittenberg Synod, 1861, pp. 21 f.

Resolved, That we hold the righteousness of the cause in which our government is engaged, and that we will labor and pray that it may be successful in speedily crushing to the earth and burying forever in future the misguided and Satanic rebellion raised against it.[90]

The Joint Synod made no formal declaration concerning the war, but the view of the Eastern District was expressed in these sentences:

God's Word teaches plainly that it is the duty of every Christian to obey the lawful government of the country in everything which is not against the word of God. We must therefore heartily regret that so great a number of our Southern brethren have been so far misguided as not only to resist the constitutional government of our country, but even to attack it by force of arms.[91]

Elsewhere in the Joint Synod it was felt that the Church should keep silent on political matters. There is no mention of the war in the *Minutes* of the English District during the years of conflict. Daniel Worley, a member of this district and editor of *The Lutheran Standard,* in an editorial, "Temper Judgment with Mercy," called for calmness during the crisis. In his view, "It is greatly to be regretted that our people are about to suffer the fruits of ungodly ambition, national pride and sectional prejudices; and that by our forgetfulness of God in our national affairs." [92] Another editorial, "The Closing Year," in the issue of December 20, 1861, felt that the conflict was the result of the stubbornness and rashness on both sides. It had hoped for a peaceful settlement before war began, and now yearned for peace. After the war ended Worley as president congratulated the District upon its dispassionate stand during the conflict on the ground that "as congregations, as ministers of the Gospel, and as Synods we have nothing whatever to do with the affairs of civil government." [93]

Support of the Federal government was indicated by the service of men as well as by adopting resolutions. The following Lutheran pastors served as chaplains in the Ohio Volunteer Infantry regiments indicated: George A. Exline, 46th; Abraham R. Howbert, 84th; Thomas Hill, 114th; W. A. G. Emerson, 120th; Jeremiah Geiger, 167th; A. R. Brown and A. R. Smith of whose regiments no record has been found. These pastors had member-

[90] *Minutes* of the English Synod and Ministerium of Ohio, 1861, p. 11.

[91] Quoted in the *Lutheran Standard,* March 1, 1862.

[92] *Lutheran Standard,* April 26, 1861. The editorial, "Temper Judgment with Mercy," was in the issue of August 30, 1861.

[93] *Minutes* of the District Synod, 1865, p. 4.

ship in synods of the General Synod.[94] Other pastors served as soldiers. J. B. Brandt was a captain for over two years in the 114th O.V.I. Abram F. McConaughy of the Wittenberg Synod, a private in the 49th O.V.I., died of wounds in Georgia July 30, 1864. Daniel Worley was absent from the 1863 convention of the English District because of military service.

There were several German regiments of Ohio in the Civil War, such as the 9th, the 28th, the 37th, and the 107th. The chaplains of these regiments were not Lutheran.[95]

An editorial, "The Conscription of Ministers," in the Lutheran Standard, expressed regret that ministers were not exempt from military service. Of course, a conscript could be released by paying $300, but since few pastors could pay that amount it was proposed that the Joint Synod provide a fund for this purpose.[96] The suggestion seems to have produced no result.

The Christian Commission, which carried on religious and welfare work among the troops, received some support from Ohio Lutherans. In three years the Wittenberg Synod contributed over $500 to its fund. A pastor of that synod, Thomas Atkinson, was employed by the Commission for its work. Later he was an agent for the National Homestead for Soldiers' Orphans. Pastor S. S .Lawson of the English Synod and Ministerium also was employed by the Christian Commission.

There were a few instances in which sharp disagreements over war issues produced division in a congregation. When members opposed to the war refused to support or attend church, the English Synod and Ministerium resolved that such persons after proper admonition and trial should be suspended from membership.[97] A small congregation near Logan, which had made a promising beginning as a mission, was disastrously disrupted by political discord.[98] In Guernsey County some congregations declined in membership when some persons resented "political preaching," i.e., favorable to the war and abolition.[99] In Dayton the First English Lutheran Church was divided when the pastor, D. Steck, and a faction opposed to

[94] Lutheran Almanac, 1863, p. 37. W. D. Allbeck, "Alumni in the Civil War," Wittenberg Bulletin, Hamma Digest Number, May, 1957, pp. 5 ff.

[95] The Lutheran Observer, February 21, 1862, mentioned Adolphus Gerwig, chaplain of the 37th, as pastor of St. Paul's Lutheran Church in Cincinnati. He was a German Evangelical minister.

[96] Lutheran Standard, April 1, 1863.

[97] Lutheran Observer, December 2, 1864. That Synod had difficulty with congregations critical of pastors loyal to the Federal Government. Minutes, 1863, pp. 4 f.

[98] Minutes of the Miami Synod, 1865, p. 11.

[99] Lutheran Observer, September 15, 1865.

war and abolition withdrew to form St. John's Church, aided, according to report by C. L. Vallandingham.[100] W. C. Barnett, a pastor with similar political views, led a faction out of First Church in Wapakoneta to form St. Mark's. The Wittenberg Synod condemned this schism and directed that union be restored. It refused St. Mark's admission to Synod, and a year later removed Barnett's name from the roll of ministers.[101]

At the end of the war some would concur in the exclamation: "Thanksgiving and praise for the overpowering blow which has crushed the life out of rebellion, and left the monster bleeding, gasping and dying." [102] The Wittenberg Synod adopted a series of five resolutions prepared by T. T. Titus which said in part:

> Whereas, The efforts of the national authorities to suppress the slaveholders' rebellion in the Southern States have been crowned with success, and peace has returned to our beloved land, therefore,
> 1. *Resolved,* That we sincerely rejoice in the triumph of our arms over treason and traitors, and in the emancipation of four millions of bondmen in our borders; and we hereby express our profound gratitude to Almighty God for these results.[103]

The rejoicing was swiftly muted by the death of President Lincoln. Said the *Lutheran Standard,* "The country has been shocked by the sad announcement that the President of the United States was assassinated on Good Friday last. It is truly a calamity that has befallen the land, and we do not wonder that the nation mourns now which was jubilant with joy before in the hope of a speedy restoration of peace." [104] The Miami Synod, lamenting "the fiendish assassination of our late beloved President, Abraham Lincoln, and the most brutal and murderous assault upon our Secretary of State," resolved to renew its devotion to the nation and its "support of its Chief Executive, Andrew Johnson, in whose ability, integrity and patriotism we have undivided confidence." [105]

Similar sentiments were expressed sixteen years later when President James A. Garfield was assassinated. A typical statements reads: "It is scarcely necessary for us formally to express the deep feeling which per-

[100] *Lutheran Observer,* January 27, 1865. *Minutes* of the Miami Synod, 1865, pp. 16 f.
[101] *Minutes* of the Wittenberg Synod, 1865, pp. 15 ff.; 1866, pp. 17 ff. *Lutheran Observer,* September 15, 1865.
[102] *Lutheran Observer,* April 7, 1865.
[103] *Minutes* of the Wittenberg Synod, 1865, pp. 19 f.
[104] *Lutheran Standard,* May 1, 1865.
[105] *Minutes* of the Miami Synod, 1865, p. 24.

vades our breasts. . . . By this writing we wish to express our sympathy, and give assurance of our readiness to support all honest efforts of our civil authorities in all work of righteousness and the suppression of the ways of wickedness." [106]

Aside from the concerns of the Civil War the one issue which aroused the most spirited agitation was that of temperance. The Ohio Legislature in 1854 made into law "An Act, To provide against the evils resulting from the sale of Intoxicating Liquors in the State of Ohio." [107] It prohibited the sale of intoxicating liquors for drinking on the premises where sold, or to minors, or to intoxicated persons or to those having the habit of getting intoxicated. It penalized intoxicated persons. It made legal any damage suit brought by a person injured by someone intoxicated. This law indicates the fact that there was public concern with the problem.

During these years Lutherans in Ohio knew of the Maine Law enacted in 1851 which prohibited the manufacture and sale of alcoholic beverages. Public disgust with the corruption and drunkenness common in the years following the Civil War was used by temperance advocates to advance their cause. Francis Murphy, a reformed drunkard from Maine, became famous as an evangelist and temperance lecturer. He urged conversion and signing a pledge rather than political measures, and his devout sincerity and temperance evangelism were highly respected. Women's organizations were formed. The Women's Temperance Crusade, begun at Hillsboro, Ohio, in 1873, was successful, by means of prayer-meetings held at the doors of saloons, in inducing the owners to close up shop and destroy their liquor stock. The first Ohio State Temperance Union meeting was held in Springfield, October 4, 1874. That same year the Women's Christian Temperance Union was formed at Cleveland. Meanwhile on the political front the Prohibition Party was organized in 1869.[108]

Lutherans of General Synod connection took great interest in this issue. Numerous resolutions were adopted. These dealt with one or more of four matters: total abstinence; business, i.e., manufacture and sale; propaganda; and legislation.

In earlier decades the protest was against drunkenness from the use of whiskey or other spiritous liquors. The temperance movement advanced

---

[106] *Minutes* of the District Synod, 1881, p. 28. See also *Minutes* of the Miami Synod, 1881, p. 30; *Minutes* of the East Ohio Synod, 1881, pp. 23 f.

[107] The text is given in the *Lutheran Standard*, August 25, 1854.

[108] See "Ohio" and other articles in *Standard Encyclopedia of the Alcohol Problem*, E. H. Cherrington, ed., Westerville, Ohio, 1929. 6 vols.

to include opposition to all drinks with alcoholic content, even used temperately as a beverage and without drunkenness. A typical statement reads: "That we regard the use, in any form as a beverage, of all spiritous and malt liquors, whether made in the home or manufactory, as inconsistent with Christian, and especially ministerial character." [109] In other instances it was alleged "That the habitual moderate use of alcoholic liquors as a beverage is a sin. . . . All church members who use alcoholic drinks as a beverage in this enlightened age are false to their profession and guilty in the sight of God." [110] An effort was made to discourage the use of alcoholic liquors under every circumstance, even for medicinal purposes, and to encourage personal total abstinence.[111]

The business of making and selling such beverages was frowned upon also. Church members were advised to avoid renting property for such purposes. Those who did so were hurting both the church and the community. Any Christian who participated in this business in any way was involved in the guilt of contributing to drunkenness.

The propaganda of the churches included sermons, the distribution of temperance literature, and the organization of temperance societies.[112] Encouragement and aid were given to temperance organizations on the state and national level. The Woman's Temperance Crusade and the "Murphy Christian Temperance Movement" were approved.[113]

Legislation was looked upon as a major aspect of the solution of the problem of intemperance. Hope was expressed for prohibitory legislation similar to the Maine Law.[114] When this hope was not realized the next strategy was to urge that church members should vote only for such candidates as were favorable to prohibition. Ministers were to secure signatures to petitions asking for appropriate legislation favorable to the temperance cause.[115]

Within the Joint Synod there was criticism, rather than endorsement, of the temperance movement. An editorial, "The New Temperance Move-

[109] *Minutes* of the East Ohio Synod, 1867, p. 17.

[110] *Minutes* of the Wittenberg Synod, 1868, p. 11.

[111] *Minutes* of the Miami Synod, 1869, p. 15.

[112] Cf. *Minutes* of the Wittenberg Synod, 1866, p. 26; 1867, p. 26; 1872, p. 25. *Minutes* of the East Ohio Synod, 1870, p. 20.

[113] *Minutes* of the Miami Synod, 1874, p. 23. *Minutes* of the Wittenberg Synod, 1877, p. 21.

[114] *Minutes* of the East Ohio Synod, 1867, p. 17. *Minutes* of the Wittenberg Synod, 1867, p. 26.

[115] *Minutes* of the Wittenberg Synod, 1870, p. 16; 1872, p. 25; 1873, p. 20. *Minutes* of the East Ohio Synod, 1870, p. 20.

ment," discussed the practice of temperance women praying in front of saloons. Though condemning drunkenness and approving prayer the editorial said,

> It is a wrong just as grievous to burden consciences by leading them to the belief that touching or tasting intoxicating liquors is a sin because drunkenness is condemned. It is making additions to God's Word. . . . It is wrong to interfere with men's business in such an officious way. . . . It is not necessary that our women should constitute themselves legislators.[116]

An article, "The Christian Church and Temperance Societies," said,

> It is a lamentable fact that in working against vice and public crime . . . the Church and the State are too often . . . mingled together, and matters are thus made worse instead of better. [The Church] has no right to use any other weapons or means for the conversion and moral reformation of man [than the Word of God]. . . . The Church should have nothing to do with temperance societies.[117]

Later there was the editorial comment that the movement begun by Francis Murphy was more sane and successful than others; but it tended to drain off Christian energy from the proper work of the church, using unscriptural methods and involving unionism.[118]

A few other issues appeared fleetingly. The use of tobacco was considered so harmful physically and spiritually that pastors and beneficiary theological students were expected to abstain therefrom.[119] Extravagance in dress was criticized on the ground that it was an import from corrupt European cities, that it aroused pride in church and alienated the poor. Pastors' families should set an example in simplicity and modesty.[120] Sabbath observance was a matter of concern also. The traditional quiet of Sunday was being disturbed by "the rattling of car wheels and the whistling of engines." Men were being required to work on that day, and people were being encouraged to travel. Efforts were being made to make Sunday something else than a day of worship, and the Sunday laws were in danger of repeal. So Sabbath observance was encouraged and the International Sabbath Association endorsed.[121]

116 *Lutheran Standard*, February 14, 1874.

117 *Op. cit.*, August 15, 1874.

118 *Op. cit.*, June 2 ,1877.

119 *Minutes* of the East Ohio Synod, 1868, p. 17. *Minutes* of the Wittenberg Synod, 1868, p. 17; 1869, p. 19; 1870, pp. 16 f.; 1871, p. 17.

120 *Minutes* of the Wittenberg Synod, 1871, p. 16.

121 *Minutes* of the Miami Synod, 1867, p. 8; 1869, p. 15; 1878, p. 26. *Minutes* of the Wittenberg Synod, 1871, p. 17. *Minutes* of the East Ohio Synod, 1877, p. 19.

The question concerning reading a portion of the Scriptures in the public schools brought this action:

> Whereas, There is in our country a large class of our population consisting of Catholics, Jews and Infidels who are endeavoring to remove the Bible from our common schools altogether, and,
>
> Whereas, It is the judgment of this Synod that the hope of the nation and the church depends upon a most thorough and general knowledge of God's Word, therefore,
>
> *Resolved,* That we as a Synod will not only do all in our power to have the Bible retained in our public schools as it now is, but also to have its principles faithfully enforced.
>
> *Resolved,* That we, too, will make use of the political arena to meet on their own ground these enemies of the church and the nation.[122]

On the problem of capital and labor the solitary voice raised was that of J. H. W. Stuckenberg. In an editorial, "What can the Church do for the Laboring Classes?" he wrote, "Many [laborers] feel that the church has deserted them. . . . [They must] be made to realize that the church is their true friend. . . . Whiskey, tobacco and improvidence are among the workingman's greatest foes. But they also have real grievances. . . . Some of them are almost hopelessly doomed to poverty." The church should promote their culture with lectures, it should make worship popular, and it should cultivate friendly contacts.[123]

A discriminating judgment of social issues is to be found only after 1880. The Social Gospel movement reached its vigor after that date. Before that time only a few solitary voices had been raised to call attention to social injustices. For the most part Lutherans were outside the movement. The few instances which have been cited are nothing more than incidental comments without a coherent framework. A systematic approach would come later.

Where disagreements appeared among Lutherans in Ohio on these issues there were indications both of theological and sociological differences. It is not clear which was more influential.

Theologically it has been the traditional Lutheran view that the task of the church is to preach the Gospel and administer the sacraments. This removes the church from the arena of politics. Though Luther spoke vigorously against social injustices, Lutherans in Germany in later times were subservient to the state. The church concerned itself almost exclusively with doctrines found in the Bible and the Lutheran Confessions. To claim insights

---

[122] *Minutes* of the Wittenberg Synod, 1871, p. 17.

[123] *Lutheran Evangelist,* August 23, 1878, p. 4.

for issues beyond the Scriptures was considered fanaticism. The result has been to leave Lutherans uninformed and unmoved by social injustices. On the other hand, the few persons who became concerned about such evils were usually weak theologically and confessionally. They quoted and interpreted Scripture to suit their convictions, rather than shape their views strictly by the Bible. For such social reformers theological considerations were secondary.

Sociologically the difference represented a variation in the degree of adaptation to the American scene. Lutherans vigorously involved in these issues were thoroughly Anglicized. They completely identified themselves with their nation. Though they might have been expected to stress the separation of church and state, their involvement in American life committed them to espouse religiously what seemed to be most salutary for the nation. Those on the other side, being closer to their migration to America, had made less progress in adaptation. Whether in Europe where the church was subservient to the state, or in America where separation existed, it was believed that the church should be silent on public matters. This, as well as language, was an obstacle to thorough involvement in American life. Here is a curious paradox: those Lutherans who were more advanced in adaptation to American ways were less concerned about complete separation of Church and public issues.

Ohio Lutherans in 1881, in reviewing the previous twenty-five years, could observe very significant growth in membership, in the number of pastors, and in resources. Part of this increase could be attributed to immigration, part to missions and evangelism. This gain was made despite the vigorous rationalism and the larger proportion of Roman Catholics among the immigrants.

Increased size involved greater complexity of function. At the parish level was to be found more satisfactory equipment for worship in such matters as buildings, liturgies, and hymnals. The stewardship of the laity improved so that larger funds were available for church purposes. The congregations were not only able to secure pastors more easily, but were capable of providing better salaries as well as of contributing to the support of superannuated clergy.

On the synodical level progress was made in educational institutions whereby seminaries and colleges were enlarged, though experience with academies was less satisfactory. Literature, both in the form of books and of periodicals, made its appearance on the territory of the synods. Home missions advanced, foreign mission interest was cultivated especially in the English synods, and a beginning was made in inner mission work. Meanwhile the synods dealt with the problems of overlapping boundaries and mutual relationships.

The Civil War brought with it the inescapable question of slavery, military activity, and concern for the welfare of soldiers. In general more anti-slavery sentiment and greater enthusiasm for the war policy of the Federal government was expressed in the English synods, whereas sympathy for the soldiers was widespread. Opposition to the Federal war program produced schism in a few congregations. Temperance was the other issue that attracted much attention in the English synods. On the problems of social injustice, particularly within industry, virtually the only voice raised was that of Stuckenberg—a voice that went largely unheeded.

10 / ERA OF EXPANSION

IN THE THREE AND A HALF DECADES from the predestination controversy to American participation in World War I the most prominent aspect of Lutheranism in Ohio was that of expansion. Doctrine and practice were less in the forefront, not because they were neglected or unimportant, but because differences in these matters were taken for granted and were less in active controversy. Acrimonious divisions began to give way to instances of inter-Lutheran conversation. By the end of this period there could be the beginnings of cooperation, and, in part at least, the prospect of unity. All this, however, was incidental to growth in membership and increase in resources. The developing strength was used to undertake enlarged responsibilities. Moreover, expansion was inevitably accompanied by increase in complexity both of work and of organization.

All this ran parallel to similar developments on the Ohio public scene. There was marked increase in population, part of which was due to immigration from Europe. Rapid development of industries was accompanied by the growth of cities. Industrialization and urbanization were to bring difficult problems both to civic and to religious bodies. Other increases on the public scene significant for the churches were in wealth, the standard of living, travel, and communications.

With the end of this period Lutheranism in Ohio had passed a century of organization on the congregational level, and was completing a century on the synodical level. It could contemplate as well as celebrate its history. It could begin to discern its direction for the future so as to plan to follow it with strength. Just as the first stage of a rocket fires and falls away leaving the second stage to exert its propulsion, so Lutheranism's first century put it into position to thrust forward strongly into the next century.

Transplantation, adaptation, expansion—these are the three overlapping aspects of Lutheran existence in America. In Ohio during this period the first two continue to be evident. Transplantation characterizes the appearance in the state of Norwegian, Swedish, Latvian, Slovak, and Hungarian, as well as German, congregations. Adaptation appears in the steady swing toward the use of English and the greater consciousness of being involved in American life. For the partly or completely Anglicized portions of Ohio Lutheranism expansion was the chief feature. In the overall view this predominated.

This chapter therefore will review the events of the period from this point of view.

CENSUS OF OHIO

In 1880 the population of Ohio was 3,198,062. The state ranked third in the nation, being surpassed only by New York and Pennsylvania. Thirty years later the population was half again as large—4,767,121. Then the state ranked fourth, having been passed by Illinois. During these years the number of foreign-born persons in the state increased from about 400,000 to nearly 600,000, but the proportion remained about the same, namely 12 per cent. The number of persons coming from Lutheran countries in Europe, however, decreased. During these decades the majority of Germans and Scandinavians had been going to the Mississippi valley and the Northwest. The German-born in Ohio in 1880 were enumerated at 192,597. By 1910 this had decreased to 175,095. The number of Scandinavians had grown from about 2,000 to over 12,000, but this was a mere trickle compared to the Northwest.[1]

Though the growth in population was rather general throughout the state, the greatest increase was in the industrial areas along Lake Erie, in the Cleveland-Pittsburgh axis, and the Ohio River valley. Cincinnati in 1880 was the largest city in the state with 255,139 inhabitants. Thirty years later it had grown at almost the same rate as the state to almost 364,000. But Cleveland had surpassed it, increasing from 160,000 to 560,000 in round numbers. Toledo had spread from 50,000 to 168,000, and Columbus had expanded at nearly the same rate from 52,000 to 182,000. Smaller cities experienced population growth related to industrial expansion also, so that the city of Springfield, for example, increased from 21,000 to 47,000, a rate more than double that of the state at large. Yet, curiously enough, between

[1] The statistics by nations for 1880 and 1910 are: Denmark 642 and 1,837; Norway 178 and 1,110; Sweden 1,186 and 5,522. Finland is not listed in 1880, but in 1910 was the native country of 3,988 persons.

these two dates the percentage of foreign-born persons in these cities was cut almost in half—a matter of linguistic interest for the churches.

Ohio during these years continued to be important in agriculture, even though the total product of larger western states became much greater. However, it was industrial expansion that was most marked. Even in 1880 the industries of Ohio were important, having an invested capital of almost two hundred million dollars. Thirty years later this was over 650 per cent larger. During the same period the gross value of industrial products quadrupled reaching almost a billion and a half dollars. In this Ohio ranked fifth in the nation.

NEW RESIDENTS

There were Lutherans among the European laborers who came to be the working force in the new industries. They arrived in most cases with little money. Physical hardiness was their greatest asset. They were willing to work hard while living on an economic level not greatly above subsistence. Until they learned English they might find themselves imposed upon by unscrupulous predators. Struggling to establish themselves economically, they had only meager resources which could be drawn upon for establishing and maintaining congregations of their language. There were instances in which individuals received aid from the American Evangelical Lutheran Immigrant Missionary Society of which J. N. Lenker was the president.[2]

The coming of these immigrants meant that transplantation continued. The new congregations perpetuated as far as possible the customs, liturgical forms, and religious patterns as well as the language of the old country. The religious life thus imported had to struggle for existence in a free church society where there were no government funds to erect church buildings or to pay the salaries of pastors. Occasionally aid could be secured from Lutheran bodies well established in America, but such aid was small. For the most part the transplanted Lutherans were on their own resources.

The number of Slovaks and Hungarians, of Swedes and Norwegians, settling in Ohio was small. The number of Finns was scarcely greater. Much more numerous were the Germans arriving from a unified Germany. Representatives of all these nationalities made their homes in Ohio during the 1880's and the decades following. Therefore the order in which they are to be treated is quite arbitrary.

[2] *Minutes* of the East Ohio Synod, 1884, pp. 24 f. *Stall's Lutheran Year Book*, 1886, pp. 102 f.

From Austria-Hungary, where their economic status was so depressed as to be virtually hopeless, there came the Slovaks and the Hungarians to work in the mines or the steel mills. Their American neighbors had difficulty distinguishing between them, and were further confused when the Hungarians were called Magyars or the Slovaks were designated as Slavonians. Though they had been under the same monarch in Europe, they were determined in America to maintain their separate identity in language and tradition. So they remembered their ancient rivalry.

The first Slovak congregation in Ohio was Holy Trinity Evangelical Lutheran Church, founded in Cleveland, December 5, 1892. With it was established also a parochial school.[3] A few years later the Joint Synod directed its Board of Home Missions to consider work among Slovaks (Slavonians) in Youngstown and elsewhere.[4] In response to a request from St. Paul and St. Peter Church in Cleveland, the Board secured as pastor A. Havel who had studied at Martin Luther Seminary in St. Paul, and had been working in the Pittsburgh Synod.[5] When he left Cleveland the work there came to a halt. Meanwhile L. Coffman, a pastor at Massillon, learned the Slovak language so as to provide some ministry to scattered groups of Slovak people.[6]

As early as 1884 Pastor Cyrell Droppa of Streator, Illinois, called the attention of the General Council to the need for work among the Slovaks. Accordingly a Mission Committee was appointed. Nothing much was done until 1903 when there was authorization for correspondence with officials in Europe for the purpose of securing pastors. The following year there was one mission pastor working in Pennsylvania, and two students from Europe had arrived.[7]

Dr. Martin Luther Slovak Evangelical Lutheran Church in Cleveland was founded in 1910.[8] Its pastor, Karol Salva, ministered also to missions in Barberton and Gypsum.[9] A later pastor was Albert D. Dianiska who included Akron in his parish.[10] A Detroit pastor, Samuel Placko, held services for Slovaks in Toledo, Lima, Dayton, Middletown, Port Clinton,

[3] Eleanor E. Ledbetter, *The Slovaks of Cleveland* (Cleveland, 1918), p. 16.
[4] *Minutes* of the Joint Synod, 1898, pp. 90 f.
[5] *Ibid.*, 1902, p. 48.
[6] *Ibid.*, 1906, pp. 49 f.
[7] *Minutes* of the General Council, 1905, p. 20.
[8] Ledbetter, *op. cit.*, p. 23.
[9] *Minutes* of the General Council, 1911, p. 155.
[10] *Ibid.*, 1917, p. 89.

and Byesville.[11] A. L. Ramer, the superintendent of the General Council's Slav Mission Board, reported that he had preached at Barton and Piney Fork, Ohio. The most prosperous of these congregations was Dr. Martin Luther Church in Cleveland which dedicated a $35,000 building November 25, 1917.[12]

Hungarian immigration, which had been small before 1900, increased greatly after that date. About 194,000 Hungarians came from the depressed condition of the old country to America in 1907.[13] The "good" Hungarian usually expected to make some money quickly and return to Europe. Hence he had little interest in establishing a congregation. The "bad" Hungarian was lawless and irreligious. In either case the church had difficulty. When return to Hungary proved impractical the immigrant turned to the church for support in an alien environment, using it as "an instrument in keeping his children from becoming strangers in the parental home." [14]

In Cleveland about thirty Hungarian families held a meeting October 9, 1905, and appealed to the Bishop of Hungary for a pastor, being meanwhile supplied with ministerial services by Rev. Julius Csernecky. Stephen Ruzsa became their pastor in September, 1907, and formally organized them as a congregation. A church and parish house, bought for $8,200, were dedicated December 1, 1907.[15] At Martins Ferry in 1906 a congregation with 110 heads of families met in the German church under the pastoral care of Csernecky and later of Ruzsa.[16]

It was to the same industrial areas that Swedes came. The first congregation was Capernaum Church at Ashtabula, founded in 1881, which led the others in size. Other congregations were Bethlehem in Cleveland, established in 1885, Bethany in Akron and Bethel in Youngstown, both begun in 1888, and Zion in South Euclid, 1900.[17] They became the Cleveland District of the New York Conference of the Augustana Synod. A pastor named G. Nelsenius was the mission organizer in this area.

Norwegians and Danes have been less numerous in Ohio and their congregations have been smaller than those of the Swedes. They have had three congregations, all in Cleveland, whose names and dates of founding are:

11 Ibid., 1916, p. 25; 1917, p. 88.

12 Ibid., 1918, p. 11.

13 Emil Lengyel, Americans from Hungary (Philadelphia & New York, 1952), p. 124.

14 Ibid., p. 179.

15 E. B. Burgess, op. cit., p. 750.

16 Minutes of the General Council, 1907, p. 32; 1911, p. 156. Minutes of the Pittsburgh Synod, 1907, pp. 57, 59.

17 Referat of the Augustana Synod, 1902.

First Scandinavian, 1880; Our Saviour's, 1884; Immanuel Danish-Nor-
wegian, 1894.[18] These three are now merged.

Finns began settling at Ashtabula Harbor in 1874.[19] Soon they were
locating in neighboring areas as well. Some of the congregations which
were established became members of the Finnish Evangelical Lutheran
Church (Suomi Synod); others joined the Finnish National Evangelical
Lutheran Church. Besides Ashtabula, congregations were organized at Fairport Harbor, Conneaut, Cleveland, and Warren. Two laymen visited the
settlers in 1889 to provide temporary religious service, but permanent work
awaited the coming from Finland in 1891 of Pastor A. Kivioja who organized the congregations in Ashtabula and Fairport Harbor that year.

There was a small group of Latvians in Cleveland before 1900. Hans
Rebane (1863–1911), a pastor who came to America in 1896, visited the
Latvians in Cleveland and organized Immanuel Church with fifty mem-
bers, June 13, 1897. From his home in Boston he made regular tours to
Cleveland and other cities where Latvians were located. After his death,
his successor in Boston, Eduards Jurevics, continued the regular visits to the
Cleveland congregation until 1917 when Pastor Karlis F. Buchrots took
charge.[20]

Though the number of German-born persons in Ohio declined between
1880 and 1910, they were numerous enough to be important both as members and as prospective members of Ohio Lutheran congregations. The
English synods made only a few efforts among these people. In Toledo the
District Synod organized two congregations in 1890, Zion Church which
was German, and bilingual Martin Luther Church. Rationalist Germans,
especially in Cincinnati, continued to be hostile to religion. Many others were
indifferent. Some with mild doctrinal convictions joined union congregations or became members of the Augsburg Synod. Such Germans as were
"old Lutheran" in viewpoint affiliated with congregations of the Joint
Synod, the Iowa Synod, or the Missouri Synod, all of which made membership gains in the state in these decades.

Among the Germans were the Siebenburger Saxons who had lived in
Transylvania in southeastern Hungary since the twelfth century. They had
remained German, yet with traits sufficiently distinct that they did not asso-

---

[18] *Minutes* of the Norwegian Lutheran Church, 1923, p. 476.

[19] John I. Kolehmainen, "Founding of Finnish Settlements in Ohio," *Ohio State Archaeological and Historical Quarterly*, XLIX, 1940, pp. 150 f.

[20] Talivaldis Gulbis, "The Story of the Latvian Lutheran Immigrants in the United
States of America," unpublished manuscript, pp. 17, 47.

ciate with other Germans in the United States. Those who settled in Ohio were ministered to by George Schuster who had been ordained by the Pittsburgh Synod in 1909. His first congregation was organized at Youngstown the next year. Other mission points where he preached were Salem, Niles, Alliance, Cleveland, Lorain, Columbus, and Martins Ferry.[21]

The First World War created much difficulty for foreign language congregations, especially German. Not only was immigration halted, but social, and sometimes legal, pressure was exerted to compel the use of English. A foreign-language church not only could not be reinforced by fresh immigration, but suffered losses as the younger generation, extremely sensitive to public attitudes, insisted upon being members of English-speaking congregations. In some mission localities where preaching points had been hopefully established or even where congregations had been organized, the work had to be abandoned. Unless the foreign-language population was fairly large, or adaptation was accepted, the congregation was not likely to survive.

NEW AMERICANS

During these decades Lutherans who were of a second generation or more were undergoing the stage of adaptation, a process which was to be greatly accelerated by the First World War. As has been noticed in earlier chapters, the process includes both a change to the use of English and a greater awareness of being part of American life. This involves a breakdown in the factors producing isolation, and also a willingness to converse with those who are outside one's own synodical group. A more irenic spirit replaces the polemic attitudes of the period of doctrinal controversies.

The increase in the use of English is indicated by evidence of several kinds. In 1882 the Joint Synod published 2500 copies of its German minutes and 1000 of the English. In spite of large growth in western German-speaking districts, the trend toward English was great enough to preserve relatively the same proportion of German to English in the Joint Synod. English steadily gained ground on German in the educational institutions and periodicals of the Joint Synod. During World War I the transition became rapid. In 1916 the Jubilee Committee reported that it had published 50,000 German and 65,000 English tracts on the Reformation. Two years later the figure stood at 34,500 German and 106,000 English tracts.[22]

---

21 *Minutes* of the General Council, 1911, p. 157; 1915, pp. 168 f.
22 *Minutes* of the Joint Synod, 1916, p. 99; 1918, p. 54.

The transition to English removed one of the causes for rivalry between synods, for the English synods felt justified in starting missions in localities where the only Lutheran services were held in a foreign tongue. It was under such circumstances that the District Synod began a mission in Hamilton. But when the German congregations there introduced English services, the District Synod decided to discontinue its rival mission.[23]

Another aspect of adaptation was increasing willingness to accept religious pluralism as a characteristic feature of American life. This entailed a broader view in which Lutherans recognized themselves as part of the pluralistic society. Instead of the older position which considered the views of one's own synod as completely and exclusively correct, and therefore to be maintained in isolation, there were increasing instances of courtesy toward those in other church bodies. Hostility gave way to civility, even friendliness. There was a decline in the practice of designating all non-Lutherans as sects and "errorists." This did not mean a weakening of doctrinal conviction nor a unionizing in practice. For example, in 1910 the District Synod in convention declined an invitation of the local ministerial association to join in a Memorial Day observance.[24] But the mood was more generous and less censorious.

Toward other Lutherans the attitude became increasingly fraternal, and ways were found to remove causes of friction and ill-will. Boundary lines between synods were one difficulty. A realignment was easily agreed upon by the East Ohio, Miami, and Wittenberg Synods in 1901. The District and the Pittsburgh Synods, both in the General Council, experienced some tension for many years following the transfer of some Westmoreland County, Pennsylvania, congregations in 1882 in a way that the District Synod considered irregular. By 1900 it was agreed that the state line should be the boundary, but Pittsburgh Synod congregations in Ohio were slow in making the transfer before 1918. Another source of difficulty had been instances in which a pastor in discipline by one synod was accepted by another synod without formal dismissal or certificate of transfer, but cases of this kind became increasingly rare.

Since the territory of the District Synod was identical with that of the three synods of the General Synod in Ohio, there was ample opportunity for increasing good will to express itself. The Miami Synod and the District Synod agreed to a plan whereby weak rural congregations of both synods might be combined in self-supporting parishes, though no actual combina-

[23] *Minutes* of the District Synod, 1905, p. 45.
[24] *Ibid.*, 1910, pp. 23, 38.

tions seem to have been effected.[25] The East Ohio Synod, however, did act on such a program, voting to approve the transfer of two pastorless congregations to the Adamsville parish of the District Synod.[26] In another evidence of good will the Miami Synod decided to sustain a disciplinary action of the District Synod. A Dayton mission of the latter body came under criticism for accepting as pastor a man whose ordination had been annulled. The mission disbanded, but some of the people organized again and applied to the Miami Synod for admittance. The District Synod made a protest. The matter was settled amicably when the Miami Synod refused to admit the congregation until the members involved signed an apology acceptable to the District Synod.[27]

A similar spirit prevailed between the District and the Wittenberg Synods. The latter body came into the possession of the deed and records of a nearly defunct congregation. But when it was learned that the congregation belonged to the District Synod the documents were promptly surrendered.[28] Beginning in 1916 there was an exchange of fraternal delegates between the two synods. At that time a similar exchange was arranged between the Wittenberg Synod and the English District of the Joint Synod.

During these years there was a noteworthy change in the attitude of the Joint Synod toward negotiations with other Lutheran bodies. Earlier efforts at comity failed. A joint committee of the Pittsburgh and Joint Synods reached an agreement on troublesome instances of transfers of congregations from one synod to the other. But the Joint Synod rejected the agreement made by its representatives, since agreement implied a doctrinal unity which did not exist.[29] Similarly, when it was proposed that there be cooperation between Lutheran bodies in matters of home mission and foreign mission comity, as well as a decrease in polemical articles in periodicals, the Joint Synod replied that cooperation without unity in doctrine and practice is contrary to Scripture and the position of the Synod.[30]

A different mood soon began to appear. Prof. G. H. Gerberding, D.D., representing the General Council, came to a convention of the Joint Synod bringing "hearty and friendly greetings." The chairman "welcomed the

25 *Minutes* of the District Synod, 1905, pp. 15, 41; 1906, p. 11. *Minutes* of the Miami Synod, 1905, pp. 13 f., 29.

26 *Minutes* of the East Ohio Synod, 1908, pp. 15, 28.

27 *Minutes* of the District Synod, 1891, p. 34; 1898, pp. 22, 25; 1899, pp. 9 f.; 1900, p. 15; 1901, p. 11. *Minutes* of the Miami Synod, 1900, p. 25.

28 *Minutes* of the Wittenberg Synod, 1910, pp. 13, 37; 1913, pp. 28 f.

29 *Minutes* of the Joint Synod, 1886, pp. 53 f.

30 *Ibid.*, 1894, pp. 132 f.

worthy Doctor in a fitting speech." [31] A few years later the Rev. G. Doering, the Emigrant Missionary of the General Council, addressed a convention of the Joint Synod. Since some members of congregations of the Joint Synod had been assisted by this missionary and the Emigrant Home, the Joint Synod recommended the work.[32] In 1912 President C. H. L. Schuette of the Joint Synod said to his body,

> The present state of aloofness characterizing our Lutheran synods does not comport with normal conditions, and is in many respects more of a hindrance than a help to the great cause we are enlisted in; so that, if not a union, at any rate a more friendly relation between these bodies is imperatively called for. That this be effected, plain duty bids us to pray and labor. and not to falter therein.[33]

To accomplish this he urged an irenic spirit in the Lutheran periodicals, the holding of free conferences, and the formation of intersynodical committees for amity. Implementing this last suggestion, the Joint Synod voted to authorize the selection of a committee on amity and to notify all other Lutheran bodies of the fact.[34]

The greatest success so far as the Joint Synod was concerned was achieved in negotiations with the Iowa Synod. The story of this success has been told with competence and in detail by Professor Fred W. Meuser in his book, *The Formation of the American Lutheran Church*.[35] Following some informal discussions, the Joint Synod in 1886 took the initiative. In the interest of unity it voted to invite the Evangelical Lutheran Synod of Iowa to hold colloquiums to inquire as to "whether we might not with good conscience recognize each other as orthodox." [36] But difficulties arose due to the fact that a pastor who had been highly critical of Iowa Synod leadership sought to transfer his membership to the Joint Synod of Ohio, and no colloquium was held. Correspondence between the presidents of the two synods resulted in preserving a friendly atmosphere in spite of dissident minorities, with the result that in 1892 committees on negotiations were appointed.

The colloquium was held in 1893 in Michigan City, Indiana. The discussion led to agreement expressed in a set of theses which were considered

31 *Ibid.*, 1898, p. 123.
32 *Ibid.*, 1906, p. 119.
33 *Ibid.*, 1912, p. 5.
34 *Ibid.*, p. 119.
35 Published by the Wartburg Press, Columbus, 1958.
36 *Minutes* of the Joint Synod, 1886, pp. 54 f.

sufficient grounds for cooperation between the two synods. Yet neither synod adopted the theses. In the Joint Synod of Ohio a minority party objected to the Michigan City Theses as being insufficient doctrinal unity for cooperation. Hence the Joint Synod postponed action.[37] The ex-Missourians in the Joint Synod who advocated complete agreement in all doctrinal details as a prerequisite for fellowship distrusted Iowa Synod's position on "open questions" (differences of opinion which do not disrupt fellowship) and were in turn regarded with suspicion by the Iowa Synod. In its attitude toward full agreement in doctrine the Joint Synod seemed closer to Missouri than to Iowa.

The major part of the Joint Synod favored fellowship with Iowa, but was content to bide its time as it grew in strength. In 1906 the Joint Synod approved the "wish that an attempt be made to come to an agreement with Iowa on doctrine and practice. We propose to Joint Synod that steps be taken to bring about such a consummation with Iowa." At the same time it could be reported that at the Seventy-fifth Jubilee service of the Seminary in Columbus letters of congratulation were received from the theological faculty of Wartburg Seminary and from the President of the Iowa Synod.[38] As a result a colloquium was held in 1907 at Toledo where theses again were affirmed. Iowa promptly accepted the Toledo Theses. The Joint Synod approved them also despite some dissent, yet declined to declare fellowship until Iowa's relation to the General Council was clarified. The erection of opposition altars in home mission areas as well as all interference in parishes of the Iowa Synod was renounced.[39] To clarify its position the Joint Synod in 1914 formally adopted the Toledo Theses. Four years later, after the Iowa Synod had severed all connection with the General Council because of the latter's decision to merge into the United Lutheran Church in America, the Joint Synod officially pronounced pulpit and altar fellowship with Iowa.[40]

Impulses toward union were felt in the English synods in Ohio also. It was proposed that members of the General Synod hold a meeting to discuss the issues. The assembly was held in Springfield, June 3, 1896, and a second one convened a year later. Such a spirit of fellowship was cultivated that other meetings were recommended.[41] No more were held in Ohio, probably because the Ohio synods were heartily involved in the free conferences

[37] *Ibid.*, 1894, p. 132.

[38] *Ibid.*, 1906, pp. 116, 119.

[39] *Ibid.*, 1908, pp. 9 ff., 132.

[40] *Ibid.*, 1918, pp. 140 ff.

[41] *Minutes* of the East Ohio Synod, 1895, pp. 27, 35; 1896, p. 29. *Minutes* of the Wittenberg Synod, 1896, p. 33; 1897, p. 33.

held in 1898, 1902, and 1904 in which members of the General Synod, the General Council, and the United Synod in the South participated. The speakers at the conferences favored more sympathetic understanding, greater cooperation, and the cessation of polemics.[42] The conferences aided in creating an atmosphere in which merger of the three general bodies in the United Lutheran Church in America was possible in 1918, a union in which all four of the English synods in Ohio unanimously concurred.

Meanwhile there was an abortive effort at forming an inter-Lutheran organization to be a united front against external forces. C. H. L. Schuette, who had prepared a statement designed to represent the position of the Joint Synod on matters of Lutheran unity, gave the substance of it in his president's report in 1914. He said,

> We recommend that an effort be made to institute a federation of all Lutheran synods of our land with the purpose in view to defend the interests of the Lutheran Church over against the influences of the world and the sects, that the Honorable President of Joint Synod be authorized to communicate with other Synods to this effect, and that report be made on this matter to Synod two years hence.[43]

The Synod gave its approval.

When Schuette received over sixty favorable replies from presidents of synods and general bodies, he called a meeting which convened in Toledo April 14, 1915. He was chosen president, and V. G. A. Tressler, professor in Hamma Divinity School, became vice president. The constitution suggested by Schuette was approved with slight amendments. The influences against which this Lutheran Federation was to protest were: the effort to place the name of God and Christ in the Constitution of the United States and thereon to base legislation on religious matters; the pernicious political activity of the Roman Catholic Church; the teaching in tax supported schools of things subversive of true religion; the official attendance at church services by "public servants." [44]

There were no further meetings of the Federation. The Joint Synod found that the major response had been from synods of the General Synod. The General Council objected to representation by district synods and virtually boycotted the Federation. The largely negative program of the

---

[42] The record is found in *The First General Conference of Lutherans in America. Proceedings, Essays and Debates.* 1898. *The Second General Conference* etc. 1902. *The Third General Conference etc.* 1904. The Free Lutheran Diets at Philadelphia, 1877 and 1878, involved no Ohio pastors.

[43] *Minutes* of the Joint Synod, 1914, p. 126.

[44] *Ibid.,* 1916, p. 9.

Federation was overshadowed by the events of the First World War, by the urgent work of the National Lutheran Commission for Soldiers' and Sailors' Welfare, and by the merging activities of the bodies forming the United Lutheran Church.[45] The East Ohio, Miami, and Wittenberg synods had been officially involved, the District Synod unofficially.

Lutheran cooperation found some expression also in plans for celebrating the Quadricentennial of the Reformation, though this joint effort, too, took second place to merger plans. The East Ohio Synod adopted a memorial to the General Synod in 1908 urging plans for a celebration, though the General Synod thought the time too early for a beginning.[46] Yet the General Council began making plans in 1909 and the Joint Synod in 1912. A committee appointed in the latter year reported its plans to the General Synod in April, 1913, and secured the adoption of a resolution asking other Lutheran bodies to cooperate in preparing the celebration. In September of the same year the General Council adopted a similar resolution following the report of the president that he had instructed their official visitors to other bodies to suggest such a plan. The Joint Synod gave its theological faculty at Columbus power to act on the invitation for a joint planning of the celebration.[47]

Within this general pattern each body made its own plans for services and for raising funds, the Joint Synod $250,000, the General Synod $1,000,000, and the General Council $2,000,000. The Miami and Wittenberg Synods held their 1917 conventions in Springfield and united in a mass meeting in Memorial Hall on October 18. The Joint Synod voted that eight of its districts should hold their conventions in Columbus in September, 1917, and unite in a Jubilee Mass Meeting.[48] The districts, however, decided otherwise.

The entry of the United States into World War I provided another occasion for Lutheran cooperation. The Miami Synod in 1917 voted to select a pastor to minister for six months to Lutherans in Camp Sherman at Chillicothe. It determined to raise $1200 for the purpose, and invited others to cooperate. A thousand dollars was pledged on the floor of synod.[49] When the Wittenberg Synod agreed to the proposal, a joint committee arranged details and persuaded Chalmers E. Frontz to accept the appoint-

---

[45] For a detailed account see Meuser, *op. cit.*, pp. 139 ff.

[46] *Minutes* of the East Ohio Synod, 1908, p. 33. *Minutes* of the General Synod, 1909, p. 120.

[47] *Minutes* of the Joint Synod, 1914, p. 145.

[48] *Ibid.*, 1916, p. 125.

[49] *Minutes* of the Miami Synod, 1917, pp. 28 ff.

ment. He began work November 1, 1917. The East Ohio, District, Joint Ohio, and Pittsburgh Synods were invited to participate, and all but Pittsburgh did. This led to the suggestion that there be Lutheran pastors assigned to all camps, with the resultant formation of the National Lutheran Commission for Soldiers' and Sailors' Welfare in which the Joint Synod asked to be included.[50] The Wittenberg Synod provided two camp pastors: Frontz, who later was at Camp Merritt, New Jersey, and Alvin E. Bell at Camp Hancock, Augusta, Georgia. Gerhard Lenski of the Joint Synod was called to be camp pastor at Camp Sherman, Chillicothe, and R. E. Golladay at Fort Oglethorpe, Georgia.

GROWING ORGANIZATION

In describing synodical growth during this period, geographical expansion was most typical of the Joint Synod. To the southeast, in Virginia and beyond, was the Concordia English District which had officially become part of the Joint Synod in 1877. In the opposite direction a group of sixteen pastors and five congregations that had withdrawn from the Missouri Synod in the predestination controversy asked for admission to the Joint Synod as a Northwestern District and were so received.[51] This district expanded so greatly that it had to be subdivided. The Joint Synod came to include congregations in Texas and California, and even in Australia. There was a home mission activity in all the districts. Besides this there was a ministry of modest proportion to Jews and to Negroes.

In the thirty-five years following 1882 the English synods had grown to two and a half times their earlier size in communicant membership. In 1882 the combined total was slightly over 20,000; in 1917 it was reported as well above 50,000. The baptized membership was not reported in 1882, but in 1917 it was more than 68,000. In the later years the caption "communicant" was changed to "confirmed" members.[52] The number of congregations in these synods had increased from 237 to 295. About the end

[50] *Ibid.*, 1918, p. 26. *Minutes* of the Joint Synod, 1918, pp. 8, 122.
[51] *Minutes* of the Joint Synod, 1882, pp. 17 f.
[52] The actual figures are given in the following table:

	Communicant		Baptized
	1882	1917	1917
District Synod	6,456	13,355	18,469
East Ohio Synod	4,853	9,871	15,997
Miami Synod	2,920	10,686	13,858
Wittenberg Synod	5,952	16,404	19,851
Total	20,181	50,316	68,175

of the decade there were approximately 165,000 Lutherans in Ohio in 711 congregations of various synodical bodies.[53] Though strictly comparable figures are not available, the indications are that in this period Lutheran membership increased at about three times the rate of the growth in population.

The increase, both in the number of congregations and of members, was chiefly in the cities. The reports of directors of home mission activities continually pointed to the cities as the places where work was urgently needed. The lists of reported mission stations after 1900 rarely contain the names of rural localities. It is worth noting also that the cities listed are in the northern half of the state, except for Dayton, Middletown, and Cincinnati. The rural congregations had difficulty maintaining themselves. Some that survived were among the earliest in the state and could celebrate a centennial, as did New Hope, Adamsville, and Holy Trinity, Stark County, in 1911, and Israel's, Amanda, in 1912. Much more frequently there appears the notice of a defunct congregation whose property was sold for a small sum. Mt. Union church near Tarlton was sold for thirty-five dollars. The Kleffecker church in Darke County brought the unusually large sum of $650.[54] The Fairview church in Butler County was given to a man on the condition that he would keep the cemetery fence in repair.[55] Notices concerning defunct congregations appear much more frequently after 1900, but it is not clear whether disbandings became more numerous or whether synods became more alert to the equities involved.

The marked increase in wealth in the state due largely to industrial development during these decades contributed to the strength of the city churches but worked to the disadvantage of small country congregations. By the same token the financial depression of 1892 and the years following created acute problems for mission churches in the cities engaged in a building program.

An aspect of urban development was increased means of communication and transportation. Electric car lines expanded. W. G. Dressler, Missionary President of the District Synod, said, "The modern trolley sys-

---

53 *The Lutheran World Almanac* for 1921, page 548 ff., gives the following statistics of "members" which may be for 1918 or 1919: United Lutheran Church, 61,645; Joint Synod, 59,309; Iowa, 8,752; Immanuel, 602; Augustana, 1,305; Norwegian Lutheran Church, 392; Suomi, 1,997; Finnish National, 580; Synodical Conference, 30,233; total, 164,824.

54 *Minutes* of the Miami Synod, 1884, p. 6.

55 *Ibid.*, 1904, pp. 13 f.

tem of transportation and travel brings our isolated missions closer together, and we sincerely urge the consolidation of our smaller missions into self-sustaining parishes." [56] A convention of the Miami Synod in 1901 first accepted and later declined an invitation from the Street Railway Company to view the sights of Columbus. But automobiles were more of a novelty and the Synod did accept the offer of an auto ride around "the historic city of Marietta" provided by the men of St. Luke's Church.[57] At a convention of the East Ohio Synod "An invitation by the citizens of Millersburg was given for an auto ride at four o'clock. The invitation was accepted by the Synod." [58] But the tragedy of speed appeared also. John Knauer, pastor at Middle Point, was killed when his automobile was struck by a train November 6, 1914.[59] And it was recognized that easy transportation facilitated worldliness. Among the influences operating against the church were enumerated "Picture Shows, the Automobile, and Baseball, Tennis and all forms of amusement." [60]

Increased prosperity was reflected in stewardship. The churches made a more vigorous effort to cultivate a generous spirit among their members and to plan for systematic giving. Contributions for the work of the church at large were given special attention. The need for the cultivation of stewardship and the support of synodical objects was recognized quite early. "Financially we are in a bad shape," Theodore Mees told the Joint Synod in 1884, noting that many congregations contributed little or nothing to the synodical treasury.[61] He urged a reorganization of their financial systems to be administered by a General Treasurer, and his suggestions were adopted. In some instances synods recommended tithing. In other cases the use of special offering envelopes for benevolent contributions was successful. By the end of this period it was common practice for congregations to conduct an annual every-member canvass, and for members to use weekly duplex envelopes. Wherever this was done it was reported that contributions were larger.

Because information concerning per capita income in the state is not available before 1906, it is not possible to compare contributions with income

[56] *Minutes* of the District Synod, 1907, p. 54.
[57] *Minutes* of the Miami Synod, 1901, pp. 11, 28; 1916, p. 21.
[58] *Minutes* of the East Ohio Synod, 1913, p. 23.
[59] *Minutes* of the District Synod, 1915, p. 7.
[60] *Minutes* of the East Ohio Synod, 1915, p. 23.
[61] *Minutes* of the Joint Synod, 1884, pp. 21 f

during this period. Where data are available it appears that Lutheran per capita contributions did not increase as rapidly as per capita income.[62] Nonetheless the finances of the synods increased greatly. At the beginning of this period the usual per capita apportionment for synodical objectives was fifty cents. By the end of the period several of the synods had raised this to over two dollars.[63] Though the synods did not receive the full amount apportioned, there were benevolent contributions also to unapportioned objects, so that the per capita benevolence contributions of the four English synods increased from eighty-nine cents in 1882 to $2.53 in 1917, and the per capita total offerings for all purposes was raised from $7.25 to $13.82.

The rise in the economic level is reflected also in the salaries of pastors. In 1892 the president of the East Ohio Synod suggested that the minimum annual salary be $700 and parsonage. By 1909 the synods were recommending a minimum of $1000 and parsonage. The average salary in the East Ohio Synod in 1910 was nearly $900, but by 1917 it was $1,210, the largest salary paid any pastor being $2,400. During this period it became customary also for the congregation to pay the expenses incurred by the pastor and lay delegate in attending conventions of synod.

The synods found themselves in better position to give aid to disabled pastors and to widows of pastors. The East Ohio Synod in 1882 was still giving such pitiful annual amounts as fifty dollars to a pastor and twenty-five dollars to a widow. In 1885 the District Synod was considering the possibility of forming a beneficial society for Lutherans but abandoned it in favor of a plan to establish a Disabled Pastors' and Pastors' Widows Fund financed by offerings gathered in the congregations. Later when a bequest was received it was voted to establish an endowment to be called the Elizabeth A. Notestein Fund for this purpose, the bequest to be supplemented to make a total endowment of $10,000. The Fund was assisted by payments from apportioned benevolence.[64] In accordance with a recommendation of the Joint Synod its districts adopted a plan whereby each pastor and teacher would give one per cent of his salary to the "Pastors' and Teachers' Widows' and Orphans' Fund," and that congregations make an annual offering for this purpose. Participation by pastors and teachers was voluntary, not com-

[62] George Herman Ulrich, "Economic Stewardship of Lutherans in America: A Fifty-year Study, 1906–1956," an unpublished study.

[63] The figures are: District Synod, $1.27; East Ohio Synod, $2.20; Miami Synod $2.26; Wittenberg Synod, $2.14.

[64] *Minutes* of the District Synod, 1885, p. 10; 1892, pp. 14 f.; 1894, pp. 17 f.; 1909, pp. 27 f.

pulsory. A list of suitable classes of beneficiaries was composed, a board of trustees was provided, and a set of rules of procedure was enacted.[65]

THE PARISH

The increase in membership meant larger congregations on the average. In general it seems that English congregations grew more rapidly than those using a foreign language. At the beginning of this period the German congregations were on the average much larger than the English ones; at the end of the period they were only slightly larger. The statistics available in 1921 giving the figures for two or three years earlier indicate 232 baptized members per congregation in Ohio. For the Ohio congregations of the Joint Synod the figure was 246; for the English synods, based on reports in 1917, it was 235.[66]

The greater strength represented by the increase in members manifested itself in better church buildings more comfortably equipped. In 1895 congregations were reporting new structures which cost four or five thousand dollars to erect.[67] Twenty years later the figures were much larger, partly due to increased prices. Old structures were renovated with frescoes, paint, carpet, new furniture, furnaces, and lights. For a time gas light or acetylene lights were used. The church in Troy had electric lights in 1893, the church in Germantown in 1900, and other congregations in rapid succession thereafter. In the English congregations toward the end of this period there was a return to architectural design which included a chancel with altar, pulpit, and lectern. Typical of this was Trinity Church, Canton, dedicated April 18, 1910, and Trinity Church, Akron, dedicated December 13, 1914.

Prominent in the changing pattern of parish activity was the organization of auxiliary societies for women, young people, and men. At the beginning of this period only a limited number of women's societies existed. By the end of the period a parish program was not considered complete unless it included active organizations for young people and for men as well as for women. All such auxiliary societies meant greater activity by laymen.

[65] *Minutes* of the Joint Synod, 1900, p. 56; 1902, pp. 45 ff.

[66] For other bodies the average baptized membership per congregation was: Synodical Conference 315, Suomi 333, Augustana 261, Iowa 230, Finnish National 193, Norwegian 98. Statistics based on the *Lutheran World Almanac,* 1921, pp. 584 ff. As reported in the minutes of the English synods in 1917 the averages were: District 201, East Ohio 222, Miami 257, Wittenberg 258.

[67] Millerburg, $5,000; New Franklin, $3,500; St. Paul's, Akron, $4,000; Washingtonville, $3,500; South Akron, $5,300; Alliance, $5,000. *Minutes* of the East Ohio Synod, 1895, p. 11; 1896, p. 9.

The women's missionary societies which made their appearance in the late 1870's increased in size and activity. The minutes of the synodical society were published with the minutes of the East Ohio Synod beginning with 1886, and other synods began to do likewise. The Miami Synod, typical of others, "*Resolved,* That as a Synod we not only approve of the ladies' work, but will continue to support and encourage their work in all our churches." [68] The District Synod, which urged every congregation to have a Woman's Mission League, had a Committee on Woman's Work, which in 1889 reported only eight societies comprising 212 members. Three years later the name was changed to Woman's Missionary Society, a constitution being provided for congregational and district organizations. At the turn of the century a synodical society was proposed, which was organized at Lima, May 29, 1901, with Mrs. E. M. Potts as president. At that date the total membership of the congregational societies had passed the thousand mark. [69]

The first impulses toward organizing young people's societies came from non-Lutheran sources, but Lutherans soon adapted the idea to their own practices. In 1889 both the Miami and the Wittenberg Synods adopted this statement:

> *Resolved,* That we regard with favor the organization of Young People's Societies of Christian Endeavor in our churches as an aid to the spiritual work of the pastors, as also a most helpful assistance both to their growth in grace and in Christian confidence and ability on the part of the young members of our churches in the exercise of their public religious duties. [70]

About this time the name "Luther Alliance" began to be used for some organizations, and after 1895 "Luther League" was the increasingly preferred term. In that year every congregation except one in the East Ohio Synod had a young people's society; thirty-four were Christian Endeavor, four were Luther Alliance, one was Luther League, and five were missionary. [71] In general it was in the town and city congregations where young people's organizations were formed. The synods expressed special interest in Luther Leagues, rather than Christian Endeavor.

[68] *Minutes* of the Miami Synod, 1887, p. 30.

[69] *Minutes* of the District Synod, 1887, p. 30; 1889, p. 14; 1892, pp. 19 f.; 1900, p. 42; 1901, p. 13.

[70] *Minutes* of the Miami Synod, 1889, p. 32. *Minutes* of the Wittenberg Synod, 1889, p. 37.

[71] *Minutes* of the East Ohio Synod, 1895, p. 10.

The next step was to form organizations on a regional and a national level. On the basis of a recommendation adopted in 1892, a young people's society of the Miami Synod was formed the next year at Springfield, which included ten parish societies, either Christian Endeavor or Luther Alliance. Others were expected to join.[72] At the suggestion of other synods this organization gave way to a state federation, The Luther League of Ohio, organized at Wittenberg College, June 3, 1896.[73] When the Luther League of America was organized at Pittsburgh, October 30 and 31, 1895, there were delegates present from all the Ohio synods. The Joint Synod, however, retained its own organization, which was formed at Pittsburgh, October 31, 1894.

Whereas the pastors of the General Synod accepted this youth movement largely from practical considerations, the District Synod and the Joint Synod were determined to evaluate it from the standpoint of Lutheran doctrine and practice before endorsing it. Though the District Synod in 1898 had fifteen Luther Leagues among its congregations, it was not until six years later that the Synod gave its endorsement, "as long as the Luther League operates in proper lines, respects proper church authority, considers and seeks the church's welfare, and maintains an unquestioned loyalty to our Lutheran Zion." [74] The Joint Synod first referred the question to the districts. The report of the president in 1898 specified seven items to be taken into consideration among which were these: the Luther League must be subordinate to the congregation and the synod and must consent to supervision; it should avoid "unionism" with those not in fellowship with the Joint Synod; and its organization should be confined to districts.[75]

Societies for women and young people had long been flourishing before any such auxiliary organizations for men were formed. In 1906 the Miami Synod authorized a committee to consider the possibility of such organizations in congregations and the synod, and to present the matter to the General Synod.[76] The proposal met with favor in the General Synod which recommended the organization of a Lutheran Brotherhood in each congregation and on a national level. The East Ohio, Miami, and Wittenberg Synods endorsed the plan. During the next decade men's organizations were

---

[72] *Minutes* of the Miami Synod, 1892, p. 29; 1893, p. 13.
[73] *Ibid.*, 1896, p .16.
[74] *Minutes* of the District Synod, 1898, table after p. 32; 1904, p. 33.
[75] *Minutes* of the Joint Synod, 1896, pp. 113 f.; 1898, pp. 16, 113 f.
[76] *Minutes* of the Miami Synod, 1906, p. 40.

formed in most of the congregations, though sometimes a men's Bible class was substituted for a brotherhood. The program of the Lutheran Brotherhood of America received the endorsement of the general Lutheran bodies, including the Joint Synod.[77]

Meanwhile there appeared a Laymen's Movement, in part co-ordinate with the Lutheran Brotherhood, but with special emphasis on stewardship. Authorized by the General Synod in 1907, it was endorsed by the Ohio synods of that body and accepted by a majority of the congregations. Its aim was to convince laymen of their responsibility for the financial management of the congregation. It urged the plan of the every-member canvass and the use of the duplex envelope. In the District Synod approval was given in 1912 for a synodical men's organization which would meet as part of the convention of Synod. It took the name, "The Laymen's Association of the District Synod." [78]

The Sunday School was another part of the parish activity. As an organization it became in effect one of the auxiliary societies, with officers, business meetings, and treasury. Within synodical boundaries the Sunday School leaders met periodically for conference. Lutherans knew something of the literature of the interdenominational movement wherein aims, methods, and problems were discussed. Three matters received more than casual treatment at conferences of Lutherans. The first was better training for Sunday School teachers. Second was the use of Lutheran instructional materials, since the interdenominational publications failed to satisfy Lutheran doctrinal interests. The preparation and publishing of such Sunday School literature became the task of the general bodies. The Lutheran Book Concern at Columbus, as will be noted later, supplied the needs of the Joint Synod of Ohio for study booklets and hymnals. A third concern was curriculum. Some congregations for a time used the International Uniform Lessons. By the end of this period, when interdenominational groups had developed a graded series of lessons, Lutherans were interested in following the same ideal.

EDUCATION

During this period the colleges and seminaries at Columbus and Springfield enlarged their facilities, increased their resources, added faculty members, and broadened their programs. All this meant that they were more

---

[77] *Minutes* of the Joint Synod, 1918, p. 122.
[78] *Minutes* of the District Synod, 1912, p. 21; 1913, pp. 37 f.; 1916, pp. 83 f.

permanently established in their respective locations. Moreover, the church was in a better position to show its appreciation of the service they were rendering.

The Seminary at Columbus continued to be the chief theological school of the Joint Synod. To some degree its fortunes fluctuated with those of Capital University and shared the same buildings. In 1881, following Lehmann's death, Loy was moved up to the position of First Professor, teaching systematic theology. That same year F. W. Stellhorn began teaching history and exegesis in the Second Professorship, and C. H. L. Schuette in the Third Professorship instructed in practical theology. There were thirty-seven students in the academic year 1881–1882.[79] By an act of the General Assembly of the State of Ohio, dated May 12, 1902, the name was changed from "The German Lutheran Seminary of the German Lutheran Synod of Ohio and adjacent States," to "The Theological Seminary of the Evangelical Lutheran Joint Synod of Ohio and other States." That year Loy, because of ill health at the age of seventy-four, was made professor emeritus with full salary, with the right of voice and vote in the faculty, and with "the privilege of doing such work in the school as may be agreeable to him." [80] He lived almost thirteen years longer, the "grand old man" of the Seminary who recounted the experiences of his life in his autobiography.[81] He with his associates and their successors faithfully fulfilled their task of training pastors, meanwhile adding to their duties by teaching college courses and by completing synodical assignments. There were considerable fluctuations in the size of the student body, but by the end of this period it was definitely on the way up. There were fifty-three students in the 1917–1918 academic year, and sixty-three the year following. By this time the faculty was larger, the courses offered were more numerous, and a seminary building was in prospect.

Capital University meanwhile went through critical years. The problem of finances was almost always acute. Between 1890 and 1910 the student enrollment was down, due to several factors: a stricter control of beneficiary aid; the continued use of German in the classroom; the insistence of the Synod that the University must educate for the Church rather than for secular professions; the general impression that the college courses were primarily pre-theological; the lack of adequate facilities and of accreditation. This affected seminary enrollment also.

[79] *Minutes* of the Joint Synod, 1882, pp. 32 f.
[80] *Ibid.*, 1902, p. 22.
[81] M. Loy, *op. cit.*

But by 1918 things were definitely looking better. President Otto Mees had begun his long and successful tenure. Recitation Hall, the multi-purpose Loy Auditorium, and the Rudolf Library had been added to the campus equipment, together with modernization of Lehmann Hall. At the urging of the alumni, science courses were added and expanded, modifying the character of the predominantly classical curriculum. The course of instruction was raised to full college level. The library was expanded to include other than theological works. After extended discussion of coeducation and over the opposition of some western German districts, it was voted by the Joint Synod in 1918 to admit young ladies to the liberal arts course, with the limitation that there be no more than twenty-five of them. But once the girls got a foot in the door the limitation was quietly ignored. An effort in 1912 to move Capital from Columbus was defeated. After the First World War the University experienced large advance.[82]

On the Wittenberg campus additions were made to the theological faculty, so that in 1889 the theological department was recognized as Wittenberg Seminary. Since 1907 it has been called Hamma Divinity School, in recognition of a large bequest by the Reverend Michael Wolfe Hamma, D.D. A seminary building, which contained both dormitory and classrooms, was erected in 1889. It burned in 1900 but was rebuilt and later enlarged. A classroom building was constructed in 1915. There were twenty-nine students during the academic year 1917–1918. Meanwhile the faculty was enlarged and relieved of teaching in the college. Most important was the fact that the professors held a theological position loyal to the Confessions, in marked contrast to the Sprecher era, and they helped lead the General Synod in that direction.

There was expansion in Wittenberg College also. An ample recitation hall, a Carnegie science hall, a library building, a women's dormitory, and a small athletic building were added to the campus. In spite of financial discouragements there continued to be additions to the faculty and to the curriculum. After World War I Wittenberg entered a period of great progress.

The District Synod encouraged its students to attend the institutions of the General Council. Thus the theological students went to Philadelphia. A proposal in 1882 to establish a college and seminary of the General Council in or near Ohio failed to produce action. After the Chicago Lutheran Seminary was founded, the District Synod became interested in that school, voting in 1904 to raise $1500 annually for the salary of a professor

[82] For details see *These Hundred Years,* the centennial history.

there. Because there were difficulties gathering the money year after year, it was decided in 1914 to provide an endowment of $50,000, the Synod to have the right thereupon of nominating the professor when a vacancy occurred. By 1918 nearly half the sum was raised. The District Synod had an interest also in Thiel College, Greenville, Pennsylvania, accepting membership on the Board of Trustees in 1917.

The German Theological Seminary at Chicago, an institution of the General Synod, received some funds from the Miami and Wittenberg Synods during the thirteen years of its existence. The founder and president was J. D. Severinghaus, a Wittenberg alumnus.

It should be noted that the Joint Synod for a time operated two practical seminaries outside of Ohio, one at Hickory, North Carolina, (1887–1910), and the other at St. Paul, Minnesota, (1883–1928).

Lutherans in Ohio made several ultimately unsuccessful attempts to establish schools of academy or normal level in the state. Greentown Academy at Perrysville, Ohio, attempted to secure the support of the Wittenberg and East Ohio Synods in 1885, but after investigation both synods declined the invitation. A North West Ohio Normal School at Middle Point, Ohio, was offered to the District Synod in 1900, but after inquiry this, too, was declined. At Lima a Lutheran Educational Association operated a normal school with the name of Lima College, which had been begun by members of the English District of the Joint Synod. An effort was made in 1896 to secure the endorsement of the Joint Synod, but that body was reluctant to do so for fear of damage to the interests of Capital University, and perhaps also because Lima was coeducational. The next year a similarly unsuccessful offer was made to the District Synod. Overtures to the Joint Synod were renewed in 1900, and four years later definite proposals were exchanged between the Association and the Synod on which no agreement was reached. With failure there, the Lima authorities turned again to the District Synod, which held a special convention in 1908 to consider the matter. The Synod was willing to accept the property, but, remembering its painful experience with Germantown Academy, very carefully limited the extent of its financial responsibility. Within a year the property had been sold to the Lima Public School Board and the effort ceased. Thereafter the District Synod turned its attention to proposals from Weidner Institute, Mulberry, Indiana, though action was incomplete in 1918.

The Joint Synod had more success with Woodville Teachers' Seminary, later renamed Woodville Normal and Academy. Begun by the Northern District, it was accepted by the Joint Synod in 1882. Though the building was destroyed by fire March 16, 1892, a new structure was erected, the dedication occurring October 8, 1893. A proposal at that time to admit girls as students was rejected, but in 1904 was accepted. The school by 1918 was having a modest growth, training teachers for the parish schools of the Joint Synod.

Though the synods continued to give financial aid to students for the ministry, there was a trend to administer such aid more strictly. The East Ohio Synod, for example, committed this responsibility to a board which required students to fill out an application form giving data concerning life, habits, preparation, resources, etc.[83] Within the Joint Synod where the assistance had been generous enough to include room and board it seemed that this generosity was being abused. Therefore more limitations were imposed, a condition which contributed to the decline in enrollment around the turn of the century. The amount of aid granted to any student by any of the synods reached a maximum of $150—an increase not commensurate with rising living costs.

Besides concern for institutions, Lutherans joined in the public interest in training church workers and informing the laity. In 1899 there was a proposal to establish a Lutheran Chautauqua in Ohio, and though encouragement for such a project continued for a decade, nothing was accomplished. Somewhat more successful was the plan of a Summer School for Sunday School Workers. Proposed first by the District Synod, the school was held on the Wittenberg campus, August 2 to 8, 1909, and a second one August 7 to 15, 1910. Thereafter the program lapsed, though referred to the conference of Sunday Schools. Another successful program was the Pastors' Institute held at Hamma Divinity School, May 4 to 6, 1915, aimed at providing intellectual stimulus and inspiration for men in the ministry.

INNER MISSION INSTITUTIONS

The first Lutheran orphanage in Ohio was begun in the early 1860's in Toledo by Pastor John Doerfler and members of Salem Church of the Iowa Synod. The first inmates were Civil War orphans. Though this was not a synodical institution, it derived its support from members of the Iowa Synod who organized a society for its maintenance. The property consisted of a building and about forty acres of land in what then was called East

[83] *Minutes* of the East Ohio Synod, 1886, p. 15; 1898, pp. 28 f.

Toledo. In 1896 there were sixty-four children in the home.[84] Before long provision was being made there for the care of the aged. As reported in 1913, the District Synod had attempted without success to negotiate a plan for sharing in the institution. Part of the problem was that the home was largely German. Later it was learned that District Synod pastors in Toledo might become members, and even trustees, of the supporting society, and they were encouraged to do so. Property value had reached $75,000, annual expenditures were $10,000, and there were forty-five children inmates.[84a]

The Joint Synod continued to support Wernle Home in Richmond, Indiana, and presently added another institution in Pennsylvania. The Eastern District in 1893 dedicated at Pittsburgh a home for the aged staffed by two deaconesses. Three years later St. John's General Hospital was begun on the grounds. Authorized to relocate outside Pittsburgh and to receive orphans, the Home dedicated a new building at Mars, July 12, 1903. There it continued to expand.

Members of the General Synod had to look outside Ohio for inner mission institutions also. Beginning with 1881 the East Ohio Synod shared in the maintenance of Tressler Orphans' Home, Loysville, Pennsylvania. Somewhat later a desire was expressed for an orphanage in Ohio. In 1901 the Wittenberg Synod proposed that a joint committee be appointed to consider the matter, and both the East Ohio and the Miami Synods accepted. This committee received authority to incorporate and receive funds. From the estate of Mrs. Amelia Oesterlen in Findlay came funds for an orphanage. The synods joined in electing a board of trustees. A site near Springfield was selected. Reverend and Mrs. A. J. Kissell were chosen to be superintendent and matron. The dedication took place June 10, 1904, and five days later five children were received. The congregations were urged to receive Children's Day offerings for the support of the Home. An additional building was erected, dedication services being held September 20, 1911. Oesterlen Home continued to have the hearty interest and support of the synods concerned in its founding.

These same synods had an interest in a home for the aged. The will of Miss Sarah Feghtly of Tipp City gave her entire estate, valued at $75,000, to the General Synod to establish a home for widows and "indigent maiden ladies." A board of trustees, consisting of an equal number of men and

---

[84] Johannes Deindoerfer, *Geschichte der Evangel.-Luth. Synode von Iowa und anderen Staaten* (Chicago, 1897), pp. 115 f., 188, 323.

[84a] *Minutes* of the District Synod, 1914, p. 45; 1917, pp. 35 f.; 1918, pp. 29 f.

women of the Miami Synod, operated the institution in Tipp City beginning in 1906.[85]

Pastor Stephen Ruzsa and the members of the First Hungarian Lutheran Church in Cleveland saw the need for an institution for orphans and the aged who were bewildered when compelled to live in institutions where English was used. A building was erected and a house purchased in 1913, the first inmates being admitted April 14, 1914. Pastor and Mrs. Ruzsa were in charge. In addition to support by the congregation, contributions were received from the District and the Pittsburgh Synods. A day nursery was operated in connection with the institution, which had the name Hungarian (Magyar) Orphans' Home.

FOREIGN MISSIONS

Through the years the Joint Synod expressed its missionary interest through its financial support of the Hermannsburg Mission in East India to the extent of several thousand dollars a year. It almost succeeded in having a mission of its own by 1918. The first person to respond to the need abroad was E. Schulz, pastor at Celina, Ohio, who in 1898 accepted a call to be a teacher of English in the mission in India. The Joint Synod heartily approved.[85a] That same year Mr. D. Shabatz from Persia, a graduate of Philadelphia Lutheran Seminary, asked to be sent to his homeland. The Synod voted to recommend him to the Hermannsburg Society for appointment to Persia, and to include his work in the synodical contributions to Hermannsburg.[86] Four years later Baba N. Shabaz, a 1901 graduate of the Seminary in Columbus, went as missionary to Persia with the support of Christ Lutheran Church, Columbus, and other friends. By 1910 he had died.[87]

In 1900 there was a divided committee report, the majority recommending a modest beginning by taking over one mission station, the minority wanting more aggressive action by sending a missionary and adopting a field adjoining the Hermannsburg mission. But Synod postponed action. Two years later it was voted to invite a representative of Hermannsburg to attend the next convention of the Joint Synod at Synod's expense to

---

[85] *Minutes* of the Miami Synod, 1906, p. 10.
[85a] *Minutes* of the Joint Synod, 1898, p. 123.
[86] *Ibid.*, pp. 90 ff.
[87] *Ibid.*, 1902, p. 20; 1910, p. 127.

negotiate a program. Such representative came in 1904 and reached an agreement whereby the Joint Synod would have special interest in some stations. Within four years the Hermannsburg Society worked out a plan whereby it would sell part of its India field to the Joint Synod to be supported and directed from America. But though $13,384 had been contributed for foreign missions in the 1906–08 biennium, and though a native pastor in India was being supported by professors and students at Capital, the Joint Synod again deferred action.

Affirmative action finally was taken in 1912. By a vote of forty-seven to twenty-six (later made almost unanimous) the Joint Synod agreed to the purchase of two stations in India with the understanding that the previous workers, program, confessional position, policy, and salaries would be continued. The Joint Synod paid $17,600 for the stations, and received additional area from the London Missionary Society. Jesse P. Pflueger, pastor at New Orleans, Louisiana, having accepted the call to be a missionary, was commissioned in Columbus, May 31, 1914. A student, William F. Schmidt, accepted the call to be the second missionary, and accordingly was ordained in his home congregation in Sandusky, December 5, 1915.

The many postponements in synodical action, delaying real work until the First World War had begun, meant that the decision came too late. By that time the British government was moving against German missionaries in India. Pflueger and Schmidt reached Ceylon, but were refused admission to India. Protests by way of the United States Department of State were unavailing. Assurances that these men were American-born and were not under the jurisdiction of any German society failed to shake the British decision. When the Hermannsburg missionaries were compelled to return to Germany, and Pflueger and Schmidt had come home, it was arranged that the mission be cared for by missionaries of the General Synod and the General Council, who with a committee of Englishmen guaranteed the loyalty of the mission to the government of India. Yet that government refused to sanction the transfer of the mission to the Joint Synod until later, specifying, however, that the parents of missionaries must also be American-born. Because the Joint Synod had no qualified candidates, it had to arrange with the General Synod to man and supervise the field.[88]

The Student Volunteer movement found response on the Wittenberg campus. A Band was formed there by April, 1891, with sixteen members. It continued through this period.

[88] *Ibid.*, 1900, pp. 78-85; 1902, p. 59; 1904, pp. 61 f.; 1908, pp. 12 f., 121 f, 65 f.; 1910, p. 126; 1912, pp. 37 f., 131; 1916, pp. 35, 37; 1918, p. 45.

The synods of the General Synod and the General Council shared in the missionary work of those bodies both by furnishing funds and by supplying workers. The names of L. L. Uhl, M. Edwin Thomas, John C. Finefrock, J. H. Harpster, Grover C. Leonard, and Ralph J. White were prominent in missionary records, as well as Mary Baer, M.D., and her sister Emma, Jessie Thomas, Katherine Fahs, and Mary C. Knauss. Others, who were not natives or residents of Ohio but who received their education and missionary inspiration at Wittenberg, were ordained by Ohio synods. They represented the zeal and missionary spirit of the General Synod.

PUBLICATIONS

During these years the increasing concern for publications resulted in the founding of a publishing house. Periodicals already established survived in strength. Some new ventures failed. Some journals were combined for greater effectiveness.

The publishing house was the Lutheran Book Concern of the Joint Synod. It was formed at a committee meeting, November 8, 1880, to publish at Columbus such almanacs, liturgies, hymnals, and magazines as the Joint Synod needed. Beginning quite modestly, it was a success from the beginning. It made such progress that a decade later it was authorized to purchase land, erect a building, and buy machinery. By 1892 it had a three-story building on East Main Street. Soon outmoded, that building was supplemented by a new structure in 1908. Not only did the Book Concern serve the Synod with an increasing amount of printed material, but it steadily increased its assets, meanwhile contributing out of its profits to the synodical treasury and building up an endowment for a professor of German at Capital University.

The Lutheran Standard continued through this period as the English periodical of the Joint Synod, as did the *Lutherische Kirchenzeitung* for the German-reading constituency. The *Theological Magazine* was joined by the *Theologische Zeitblaetter,* both published by the Book Concern but having a small list of subscribers. There was agitation to combine the two, success being achieved when the bilingual *Theologische Zeitblaetter - Theological Magazine* appeared beginning in January, 1911. The *Lutheran Child's Paper* was published for some years, as was also *Die Christliche Gemeindeschule* which had originally been started by the Northern District. Two other publications were the *Little Missionary* with E. Pfeiffer as editor, first published January 1, 1886, and *Kinderfreunde* edited by E. A. Boehme.[89]

Both *The Lutheran Observer* and *The Lutheran Evangelist,* representing the non-confessional spirit in the General Synod, continued to be circulated in Ohio. The theological faculty at Wittenberg began publishing a *Theological Monthly* in April, 1888. But C. H. Ehrenfeld soon became editor, changing the name at the end of the second year to *New and Old.* It was "American Lutheran" in character, being critical of the Common Service, growing liturgical practices in the General Synod, and the developing confessionalism at Wittenberg. It discontinued publication when Ehrenfeld left Wittenberg in 1892. To give voice to the conservative Lutheranism of the General Synod, *The Lutheran World* was published beginning March 3, 1892, with Ezra K. Bell as editor at Cincinnati. Several years and editors later it was moved to Springfield with David H. Bauslin, professor at Hamma, as editor beginning November 1, 1900, and so continued until 1912 when it was absorbed in the *Lutheran Church Work,* the official magazine of the General Synod.

The District Synod felt the need for a synodical publication. In 1901 it appointed a committee and appropriated fifty dollars. The next year the committee reported that *The Synodical Quarterly* was being issued. It continued for several years.[90]

The tone of these periodicals was definitely less polemical than in earlier decades. Though there were exceptions, there was a distinct disposition to think less harshly of other synods or general bodies. The older stereotyped opinions about the unpleasant character of other Lutheran groups was giving way to understanding, if not of sympathy. Harsh criticism was no longer welcome.

DOCTRINE AND PRACTICE

In the decades following the Predestination Controversy there was no decline in doctrinal interest among Lutherans in Ohio, though gradually a change in mood occurred. At the same time that there was an increasing distaste for the asperities of doctrinal controversy, there was a growing appreciation of the Lutheran confessional heritage whose uses were homiletical and pedagogical rather than polemical. The positions of the Lutheran confessions were held firmly and earnestly, but with less belligerence.

[89] *Ibid.,* 1888, p. 34.
[90] *Minutes* of the District Synod, 1901, pp. 35 f.; 1902, pp. 14, 38; 1904, pp. 38 f.

The most significant developments were in the General Synod, the Ohio members thereof concurring. The representatives of "American Lutheranism" with its accusation of error in the Augsburg Confession steadily declined in number and influence, though their opposition to confessional and liturgical developments persisted. In some instances those who held that point of view transferred to other denominations. Thus, when J. B. Helwig became a Presbyterian he gave as his reason "the constant tendency of the Lutheran Church to Catholicism and ritualism." The Wittenberg Synod affirmed that such a groundless accusation was made out of "the misconception of ignorance or the invention of malice." [91] The majority came to an appreciation of the importance of the Augsburg Confession and of traditional liturgies. Thus it was said, "We are pleased also to note that our dear church is becoming more and more loyal to her historic confessions and worship." [92]

The highwater mark of the opposition was reached in the trial of L. A. Gotwald. Early in 1892 articles appeared in *The Lutheran Evangelist* attacking the theological position of the Wittenberg Seminary. The following February three men preferred formal charges against Professor Gotwald on the ground that he accepted the Augsburg Confession and every article thereof as fundamental. It was charged that his views and teaching in the seminary were subversive of the position of the General Synod. These charges were presented at a special meeting of the Board of Directors in April, but were not sustained, Gotwald being unanimously acquitted.[93]

Meanwhile the General Synod had proceeded to a more definite confessional Lutheran position. In 1895 it reaffirmed its doctrinal basis, specifying particularly the "unaltered" Augsburg Confession as its standard. Six years later it repudiated the distinction between fundamental and nonfundamental doctrines in the Augsburg Confession—an earlier practice whereby those who disagreed on some doctrine could reject it as being non-fundamental. In 1909 it adopted a series of statements prepared by professors in Hamma Divinity School which not only affirmed loyalty to the Augsburg Confession but recognized the value of the other documents in the Book of Concord as well. On this basis the doctrinal article of the constitution was revised and submitted to the synods for ratification. The East Ohio, Miami, and Wittenberg Synods promptly ratified the proposed revision, expressing satisfaction that their theological professors had shared in

---

[91] *Minutes* of the Wittenberg Synod, 1891, pp. 22 f.

[92] *Ibid.*, 1909, p. 21.

[93] See *Proceedings in the Trial of L. A. Gotwald, D.D.*, Springfield, 1893.

composing the series of statements.[94] Approval within the Joint Synod was expressed by President C. H. L. Schuette, who said, "Thank God, that the great body known as the General Synod has at last planted itself fairly and squarely upon the unaltered Augsburg Confession historically interpreted, and hence may henceforth with greater right lay claim to the Lutheran name."[95]

Accompanying this doctrinal development was a corresponding improvement in Lutheran practice. The older unliturgical and revivalist usages gradually disappeared. A president's report noted "many evidences of growing loyalty to our Lutheran heritage."[96] Special meetings for the conversion of sinners gave way to greater stress on the regular preaching of the Gospel and to catechetical instruction. A committee reported: "We note with profound pleasure the manifest disposition to return in doctrine and methods to the old paths. The so-called revival method, for a time so popular in our churches, is being discarded, and an increased reliance is being placed upon the preaching of the Word and the catechization of the young."[97] Ministerial applicants from other denominations who did not approve of Lutheran practices were denied admission. In this spirit it was affirmed that "It is no longer an effervescent sentiment, but a profound conviction with many that sane and safe and distinctly Lutheran methods of Christianizing are the most scriptural and therefore the best."[98]

Parochial reports substantiate these statements. In the early 1880's many General Synod pastors neglected catechetical instruction. But with the passing of the years the proportion of those conducting such classes steadily increased. In the East Ohio Synod in 1901 less than half the parishes had classes in the catechism—"a strange report of a Lutheran custom in Lutheran churches," commented President Arthur H. Smith.[99] But the next year the proportion was more than half, and a few years later nearly every pastor reported having a class. The same development occurred in other synods. Indeed, it led to an intensification and improvement of the instruction so that there were classes for younger children as part of a catechetical program covering several years before confirmation. Moreover the program was expanded to include adult instruction for membership. To the ques-

[94] See their Minutes for 1911. Cf. J. L. Neve and W. D. Allbeck, *History of the Lutheran Church in America* (Burlington, Iowa, 1934), pp. 123 f.
[95] *Minutes* of the Joint Synod, 1912, p. 4.
[96] C. B. Etter in *Minutes* of the East Ohio Synod, 1910, p. 14.
[97] *Minutes* of the Miami Synod, 1894, p .30.
[98] *Minutes* of the Wittenberg Synod, 1907, pp. 15 f.; 1909, p. 20.
[99] *Minutes* of the East Ohio Synod, 1901, pp. 12 f.

tion, "Do you instruct adults before receiving them into the church?" eleven pastors in the East Ohio Synod in 1914 answered "yes," ten said "no," and sixteen gave qualified answers.[100]

Liturgical practice was another area in which there was also marked development. This centered particularly around the Common Service of 1888 prepared jointly by the General Council, the General Synod, and the United Synod in the South. In it the Lutherans of the separate bodies had a liturgy responsive in character and embodying traditionally Lutheran usages. One of the results was a fresh study of liturgical matters and a greater attention to the principles involved in worship. Articles on the subject were printed in the periodicals, and liturgical topics were discussed at conferences. In spite of some opposition the Common Service gradually won its way into the use of congregations in the English synods, and even in some of the English Districts of the Joint Synod.

The hymnals published in previous decades continued to be used in the revisions which appeared from time to time. These were the *Book of Worship* of the General Synod, the *Church Book* of the General Council, the *Gesangbuch* as well as the *Cantica Sacra* of the Joint Synod. The English District of the Joint Synod (named "First" English to distinguish it from the English Concordia District) appointed a committee in 1901 to prepare a new hymnal, which appeared seven years later. It contained a liturgy, 516 hymns, nineteen doxologies, the propers for the church year, a passion history, and indexes.[101] The congregations belonging to other synods, i.e., Missouri, Norwegian, Iowa, and Augustana, used hymnals sponsored by those bodies. The Swedish congregations, for example, had the *Koralbok* which the Augustana Synod had issued, and which was based on a Psalmbook of Sweden. The Finnish, Slovak, and Hungarian congregations used hymnals which were printed in Europe. In these instances, also, the liturgy of the hymnal used was the one in force in the congregation.

Part of the liturgical development in the English congregations was a recovery of the use of the church year. In addition to Christmas, Easter, and Pentecost, there came to be observances in Lent and Holy Week, and soon also other parts of the ecclesiastical calendar. By the time of World War I the church festivals were observed as usual practice. Vestments, usually a clerical gown, were being increasingly used.

100 *Ibid.*, 1914, p. 16.

101 *Evangelical Lutheran Hymnal.* Published by Order of the First English District of the Joint Synod of Ohio and Other Etates. With Music. Columbus, Ohio. Lutheran Book Concern. A.D. MCMVIII.

Changes had quietly been made in the Communion practices of congregations of the General Synod. Adherents of the temperance movement substituted unfermented grape juice for fermented wine in the sacrament. Congregations of other synods made no such change. The District Synod, for example, specified that at the synodical Communion "only pure wine and unleavened bread shall be used." [102] The fact that such a declaration was thought necessary is significant. A related matter was the common cup (chalice) or the individual cup. The latter was in use early in the present century in some congregations.[103] At Roseville the local Board of Health asked the churches to comply with a state rule abolishing the common cup. An attorney who made inquiry found that no such state regulation was in existence.[104]

There was improvement in practice also with regard to the ministry. The earlier custom of granting a license for performing ministerial acts to members of the senior class in the seminary came under stricter control and tended to be abandoned. It was found necessary to require such students to promise to finish their seminary training, or to have a call before licensure —a provision to enable them to serve a parish in the time between graduation in the spring and the synodical convention (and ordination) in the fall.

The synods frowned upon the annual re-election of pastors by parishes and largely eliminated the practice. It was insisted that the permanency of the pastorate was to be recognized, and that in every instance a service of installation be held. It was specified among the duties of the president of synod that he be informed of resignations and acceptances of calls, that he be consulted during vacancies, and that he officiate at installations—all this for the sake of good order and helpfulness.[105]

Membership in secret societies continued to be a problem. In the Joint Synod it continued to be a basis for exclusion from Communion and from church membership. Enforcement of this rule, which was not easy, was left to the discretion of the pastor. The temptation in mission congregations to ignore the rule was to be resisted. Home missionaries who did not earnestly oppose secret societies might find supporting funds from the synod discontinued.[106]

[102] *Minutes* of the District Synod, 1887, p. 23.

[103] E.g., at Arcadia. *Minutes* of the Wittenberg Synod, 1903, p. 14.

[104] *Minutes* of the District Synod, 1916, pp. 38 f.; 1917, p. 52.

[105] Cf. *Minutes* of the District Synod, 1895, p. 28; *Minutes* of the East Ohio Synod, 1907, pp. 49 f.

[106] *Minutes* of the Joint Synod, 1888, p. 53; 1892, pp. 127 f.; 1902, pp. 57 ff.

The District Synod continued to smart under the accusation that it approved secret fraternal societies. It discouraged its members from joining them and refused to admit pastors who were lodge members. It was averse to its pastors participating in public meetings of secret societies or secular or political organizations. But it was less likely to use disciplinary measures than was the Joint Synod.[107]

PUBLIC ISSUES

The concern with public issues continued to appear most often among Lutherans of the General Synod, though toward the end of this period the Joint Synod began to express its views. In part this difference was a matter of theology, in part it involved Americanization. Those who were in the General Synod were completely Anglicized. They felt most involved in the movements of the nation and like other Protestants felt the necessity of participating therein. To their minds public life quite properly should have the guidance of the Church. On the other side were those who were more European in outlook and language. They perpetuated the spirit of the church in Germany where the state was dominant and where the church confined itself to spiritual interests, avoiding political opinions. To their minds the sole task of the Church was to preach the Gospel and administer the sacraments.

During this period the temperance movement made great progress. It was considered "*schwaermerisch,*" unbiblical and unchristian by some members of the Joint Synod.[108] It was endorsed by members of the General Synod. Total abstinence was encouraged; legislative control of the liquor traffic was approved as a means of correcting obvious evils; prohibition of the manufacture and sale of intoxicating beverages was considered ideal. "While we are not visionary enough to believe that legislation will ever entirely cure this evil, we are equally positive that it may be kept in bounds; . . . we denounce the saloon as a common enemy." [109] The Anti-Saloon League, which was organized at Oberlin, Ohio, in 1893, and became a national organization two years later, had the endorsement of the East Ohio, Miami, and Wittenberg Synods. These synods generally approved the measures proposed by the Anti-Saloon League in the interest of tem-

---

[107] *Minutes* of the District Synod, 1884, p. 27; 1909, pp. 75 f.
[108] *Minutes* of the Northern District, 1885, p. 19.
[109] *Minutes* of the East Ohio Synod, 1898, p. 32.

perance. In one instance a pastor was in difficulty with his synod because he refused to support Anti-Saloon League measures.[110]

It was typical of the puritanic spirit of these synods that both tobacco and dancing were disapproved. Students for the ministry who were applicants for financial assistance were required to affirm that they did not use tobacco in any form. Social dancing was considered contrary to the spirit of the Gospel and harmful to the spiritual life.

In the same spirit these synods were concerned about "Sabbath observance." They passed resolutions recommending that factories be closed on Sundays. They viewed with alarm the growing tendency to turn Sunday into a holiday devoted to sports and pleasures. They deplored the legalizing of Sunday baseball games. Typical is this action: *"Resolved,* That the Sunday newspaper, Sunday picnics, unnecessary driving, visiting, and mere pleasure-seeking, as well as all unnecessary traffic upon railroads and public thoroughfares, are all hostile to the true intent of the Christian Sabbath, and must be strongly resisted." [111] These synods petitioned the managers of the Columbian World's Fair, held in Chicago in 1893, to close the exhibitions on Sundays. The District Synod, following the lead of the General Council, made a similar petition.[112]

The Miami Synod in 1884 endorsed the aims of the Ohio Divorce Reform League and urged pastors to preach on the sacredness of marriage. Following the pattern established in the General Synod, both the Miami and the Wittenberg Synods directed their pastors to refuse to officiate at weddings of divorced persons except when the divorce was for biblical reasons, and then only when innocent parties were involved.

The teaching of evolution in tax-supported schools was a matter of concern in the Joint Synod. A committee reported that most public school textbooks on science were based on the theory of evolution. The Synod urged that protests be made against teaching views fundamentally opposed to Scripture, and recommended the publication of anti-evolution literature.[113]

The issues of war and peace received attention also. The Miami Synod expressed gratitude for the "successful issue of the war with Spain in the interests of humanity." [114] The president of the District Synod noted the

---

110 *Minutes* of the Wittenberg Synod, 1909, pp. 11 f., 48; 1910, p. 12.

111 *Minutes* of the East Ohio Synod, 1887, p. 21.

112 *Minutes* of the East Ohio Synod, 1890, p. 30; Miami Synod, 1890, p. 21; Wittenberg Synod, 1890, p. 37; District Synod, 1892, pp. 21 f.

113 *Minutes* of the Joint Synod, 1914, pp. 65 f.

114 *Minutes* of the Miami Synod, 1898, p. 23.

end of the Russo-Japanese War and the defeat of Russia which "has led to a liberalizing of its government and to an enlargement of the civic and religious freedom of the people." [115] A request from the Presbyterian Church U.S.A. to sign a petition to all governments to settle issues by arbitration instead of war received this answer from the Joint Synod: "We are of the opinion that we cannot occupy ourselves with this matter." [116]

The First World War elicited resolutions from all the synods in Ohio. At its beginning the resolutions adopted were of a kind deploring the wretchedness of war and urging the settlement of international difficulties by arbitration.[117] After the United States entered the conflict the resolutions involved three matters: loyalty to the government; support of the Red Cross and other welfare agencies; prayer for peace. A typical statement was that of the Joint Synod.

> We see in the terrible war now raging the chastisement of God which is meant to turn all nations from the way of sin to Himself. . . . To us Lutheran Christians it is a matter of course that we owe love, obedience and loyal support to our Government. We therefore urge our people to do their full duty toward our Government in every way, and also to take an active part in the noble work of alleviating the suffering and want that are brought about by the war, and not to cease to pray the Lord for a just and righteous peace.[118]

No tabulation of the number of Ohio Lutherans in military service during World War I has been made, but thousands were so involved. In the parishes there were service flags indicating the members of the congregation who were in the armed forces as well as those who had lost their lives. Among the pastors who became army chaplains were Harvey E. Crowell, D. Bruce Young, and Ross Stover.

When disasters occurred there was response. The flood which devastated Johnstown, Pennsylvania, May 31, 1889, was the occasion for a collection of funds for flood sufferers. One hundred twenty-five dollars was collected in the Miami Synod and $287 in the Wittenberg Synod. The heavy rains in March, 1913, produced floods in Ohio, doing damage especially in Dayton and the Miami Valley. In other valleys it was families that suffered loss, but in Dayton churches sustained severe damage also. In Miamisburg the lower floor of the church and the parsonage were under eight feet of

---

[115] *Minutes* of the District Synod, 1906, pp. 6 f., 41.

[116] *Minutes* of the Joint Synod, 1900, p. 107.

[117] *Minutes* of the East Ohio Synod, 1914, p. 46; Wittenberg Synod, 1914, p. 50.

[118] *Minutes* of the Joint Synod, 1918, p. 121. Cf. East Ohio Synod, 1917, p. 44. District Synod, 1917, pp. 63 f. Miami Synod, 1917, p. 52. Wittenberg Synod, 1917, pp. 78 f.; 1918, pp. 56 f.

water, the pastor losing his entire library. The District Synod gave $1,861 for flood relief. The amount contributed in the Miami Synod was not speci-field, but in the Joint Synod it reached $25,161. There were appeals in the churches also in 1906 for contributions to relieve suffering in San Francisco after the earthquake.

On two occasions the Joint Synod raised its voice against injustice overseas. In 1896 it adopted a resolution of sympathy for Armenians suffering persecution by the Turks, asking the President of the United States "to use his gracious offices in their behalf." Eight years later, responding to a letter from the Massachusetts Commission for International Justice and a resolution of the General Conference of the Methodist Episcopal Church concerning the outrages perpetrated upon natives in the Congo Free State, the Joint Synod adopted a resolution asking Congress to investigate, and if the reports were found to be true, to intercede for the natives.[119]

ORGANIZATION

The increasing complexity of the program in the parish has already been noted. A similar complexity developed on the synodical level. Committees became more numerous and their reports longer. It became increasingly difficult to transact all the business within the allotted time. As early as 1894 the Joint Synod omitted the reading of reports at the convention, accepting them in the printed form. Questions inevitably were raised as to whether business was crowding spiritual matters out of the conventions. Holy Communion was administered at the end of the convention of many synods in the earlier years, but by the end of this period the trend was toward opening the convention with Communion.

Because of the size attained by the Joint Synod and its spread from coast to coast, it was proposed in 1890 that it return to the form of a delegate synod. This was adopted in 1892, and two years later the necessary amendment to the constitution was approved. The name was changed to Evangelical Lutheran Synod of Ohio and Other States by an act of the Ohio General Assembly February 17, 1898, but four years later the word "Joint" was inserted before "Synod."

The increasing volume of business impelled the synods in the direction of paid officers. At first there was only a small remuneration for the treasurer, the Miami Synod paying him one dollar a year beginning in 1887 (though occasionally giving him an honorarium for special work) and the East

119 *Minutes* of the Joint Synod, 1896, p. 122; 1904, p. 124.

Ohio Synod paying him fifteen dollars beginning in 1891. Remuneration for the secretary began in the Wittenberg Synod in 1893, the sum being fifteen dollars, other synods soon following this practice. In some synods the statistical secretary was paid, Miami Synod being first in 1899. Through the years the amount of remuneration was slowly increased for these part-time officers. By 1918 the largest payments were by the District Synod: the president $150, the secretary the same, the treasurer $300, the missionary superintendent $100.

Meanwhile some synods had arrived at the stage of having full-time salaried officers. The Wittenberg Synod chose a missionary superintendent at a salary of $900 and expenses, but this effort was premature, lasting only from January 1, 1891, to June 1, 1892, when C. S. Ernsberger held the office, and was not resumed. The East Ohio Synod decided to select a full-time "permanent secretary," later called "missionary superintendent," at a salary of $1500 and expenses. Ralph J. White occupied this office from June 1, 1911, to November 29, 1915. The salary of his successor was increased to $1800.

It was the Joint Synod, much larger in membership, that was able to have a full-time president. The proposal was defeated when first proposed in 1890, but four years later it was adopted, the remuneration being set at $1500 together with house rent and expenses. To this office of General President the Synod elected C. H. L. Schuette who served in this capacity for thirty years. There was loaded upon this officer not only the duties of a president who was expected to visit the districts, but also supervision of the educational and publication interests of the synod, the work of a missionary superintendent, and the task of soliciting bequests for the synod's institutions. This enormous burden Dr. Schuette carried faithfully. When it was proposed in 1906 to divide the work by electing a superintendent of missions, all the districts objected. The Synod found a way of solving the problem by authorizing the Board of Home Missions to employ an executive secretary who would perform the duties specified by the Board and be treasurer both of the mission fund and of the building fund. His salary was set at $1000 plus $300 for house rent and $100 from each treasury for his work as treasurer. Paul F. Hein was chosen for this post in 1910. Six years later his title was changed to that of General Superintendent of Home Missions.

Another indication of the expansion of these synods is the fact that all of them felt large enough to publish a history of their accomplishments. In 1894 appeared the *History of the Evangelical Lutheran Synod of Miami* by A. J. Imhoff—a tiny volume that included an historical address. The

Geschichte der Allgemeinen Evang.-Lutherischen Synode von Ohio und anderen Staaten by P. A. Peter and Wilhelm Schmidt, issued in 1900, traced the story by conventions. G. W. Mechling wrote the *History of the Evangelical Lutheran District Synod of Ohio*, 1911. *A History of the Wittenberg Synod* by C. S. Ernsberger, 1917, and *A History of the East Ohio Synod* by Arthur H. Smith, 1924, contained sketches of congregations. A centennial volume was the *History of the Evangelical Lutheran Joint Synod of Ohio and Other States* by C. V. Sheatsley, published in 1919. The publication of these volumes was evidence that these synods had advanced to the point where their resources were adequate to this undertaking.

SUMMARY

It is quite clear that Lutheranism in Ohio had made great gains between 1882 and 1917. Its membership was larger. Its resources were more ample. Its institutions were more firmly established. Its sense of Lutheran solidarity was greater so that there could be more cooperation and unity. Its program of work had expanded both in outreach and in complexity. While this period included some immigration and considerable Americanization, the dominant feature was expansion.

The outlook for the future was encouraging. With the problems of language and doctrine largely behind them, the synods could look forward with confidence to continued expansion in the future. Mergers in prospect would make available larger resources and a larger staff of full-time officers. While the union of all Lutherans in one church in America was still far in the future, it was now possible for all Lutherans in Ohio, whatever their synodical connection, to face the problem of evangelizing the unchurched with a sense of being both truly Lutheran and fully American.

BIBLIOGRAPHIC NOTE

Bibliographies of Lutheran history in America will be found in the general histories of that field as listed below. An early listing was John G. Morris, *Bibliotheca Lutherana*, Philadelphia, 1876. A recent treatment is the article, "Literature of Lutherans in America" by Herbert H. Schmidt in *Proceedings of the Twelfth Conference of the American Theological Librarians Association*, 1958.

Much source material is now available in microfilm. One such work is the *Microfilm Corpus of American Lutheranism*, edited by Robert C .Wiederaenders. Another important work is the *Microfilm Collection of the Concordia Historical Institute*.

The general history of Ohio is found in the work edited by Carl Wittke entitled *History of the State of Ohio*, Columbus, 1942. *A History of Ohio* (Columbus, 1953) by Eugene H. Roseboom and Francis P. Weisenburger is profusely illustrated. There are numerous histories of counties. Those consulted were:

Drury, A. W., *History of the City of Dayton and Montgomery County, Ohio*, Chicago-Dayton, 1909.

Graham, A. A., *History of Fairfield and Perry Counties*, Chicago, 1883.

History of Franklin and Pickaway Counties, Cleveland, 1880.

Mack, Horace, *History of Columbiana County*, Philadelphia, 1879.

The *Ohio Archaeological and Historical Society Publications* through the years include articles of Lutheran interest which are listed below under "Articles."

Among the general histories of Lutherans in America the following provided information:

Graebner, A. L., *Geschichte der Lutherischen Kirche in America*, St. Louis, 1892.

Hazelius, Ernest L., *History of the American Lutheran Church*, Zanesville, Ohio, 1846.

Jacobs, H. E., *A History of the Evangelical Lutheran Church in the United States*, New York, 1893.

Neve, J. L., and Allbeck, W. D., *History of the Lutheran Church in America*, Burlington, Iowa, 1934.

Wentz, A. R., *A Basic History of Lutheranism in America*, Philadelphia, 1955.

The published minutes of synods provided much of the data for this study. Titles are confusing not only because some synods changed their names but also because of a lack of uniformity in captions. The list in chronological order is:

Verrichtungen aller derer Conferenzen der Ev.-Luth. Prediger im Staat Ohio und Benachbarten Staaten 1812–1817 (a collection reprinted at Columbus, 1897). A typed translation by C. V. Sheatsley exists.

Verrichtungen (beginning 1828, *Verhandlungen*) *der Evangelisch-Lutherischen Synode von Ohio und den angrenzenden Staaten.* The title varies, beginning in 1818. In 1839 the word *Allgemeinen* was inserted. The English text is: *Proceedings* (sometimes *Minutes*) *of the Evangelical Lutheran Synod of Ohio and Adjacent States.* The word *Joint* was inserted in 1844. The English text begins with the 1827 convention. Minutes of the districts were published also.

Proceedings of the Evangelical Lutheran Synod of the West. This synod was in existence 1835–1846. Some printed minutes survive.

Proceedings of the Evangelical Lutheran Synod of Indiana. The synod dates from 1835 to 1859.

The East Ohio Synod was first an English District of the Joint Synod. *Minutes of the Synod and Ministerium of the English Evangelical Lutheran Church in Ohio and Adjacent States,* 1836–1840. *Minutes of the English Evangelical Lutheran Synod of Ohio and Adjacent States,* 1841–1857. *Proceedings of the East Ohio Synod of the Evangelical Lutheran Church,* 1858 to 1920.

Part of the English District remained in the Joint Synod until 1855; thereafter it was independent until it expired about 1871. *Minutes of the English Evangelical Lutheran Synod and Ministerium of Ohio and Adjacent States.*

Proceedings of the Evangelical Lutheran Synod of Miami, 1844–1920.

Proceedings of the Pittsburgh Synod of the Evangelical Lutheran Church, 1845–1867.

Minutes (sometimes *Proceedings*) *of the Wittenberg Synod of the Evangelical Lutheran Church.* Though the synod existed from 1847 to 1920, the first printed minutes were in 1850.

Proceedings (sometimes *Minutes*) *of the Olive Branch Synod of the Evangelical Lutheran Church of the State of Indiana,* 1848–1919.

Minutes (sometimes *Proceedings*) *of the Evangelical Lutheran Synod of Northern Indiana,* 1855–1919.

An English District, formed in 1857, became independent of the Joint Synod in 1869–1870. *Minutes of the English District of the Joint Synod of Ohio and Adjacent States,* 1857–1870. *Proceedings of the English Evangelical Lutheran District Synod of Ohio and Adjacent States.* Later the words "English" "and Adjacent States" were dropped from the name. The District Synod continued until 1920.

Proceedings of the Evangelical Lutheran General Synod in the United States of North America, 1820–1920. Later the words "of North America" were dropped.

Minutes of the General Council of the Evangelical Lutheran Church in North America, 1867–1920.

Public records of marriages or of deeds were consulted in the following counties: Columbiana, Jefferson, Montgomery, Perry, and Pickaway.

Periodicals furnished important information. A thorough search was made for data concerning Ohio Lutherans in the files of *The Lutheran Observer*, published 1831 to 1915; *The Lutheran Standard*, issued since 1842; *The Evangelical Lutheran*, 1853–1856; *The Lutheran Evangelist*, 1877–1909; *The Missionary*, begun in 1848, and *The Lutheran*, begun in 1856, which merged as *The Lutheran and Missionary*, 1861–1881, continuing thereafter as *The Lutheran*. Pertinent articles were located in *The Evangelical Review*, 1849–1870; *The Lutheran Quarterly*, 1871–1928; and in the *Concordia Theological Monthly*, published since 1930.

A few parish record books of an early date furnished some important information, especially the book of Zion Church, New Middletown, and Israel Church, Amanda.

Journals of Paul Henkel, John Samuel Mau, and John Stough were consulted, published as follows:

Clement L. Martzolff, "Rev. Paul Henkel's Journal," *Ohio Archaeological and Historical Publications*, XXIII, 162-218.

Allbeck, W. D., "A Journal of John Samuel Mau, 1794–1795," *Lutheran Quarterly*, XIII (1961), 155 ff.

Tappert, Theodore G., "The Diaries of John Stough, 1806–1807," *Lutheran Quarterly*, XII (1960), pp 44 ff.

Stough's autobiography in translation has been printed several times, notably in the histories by Burgess and by Sheatsley listed below.

Histories of synods used in this study were:

Baepler, Walter A., *A Century of Grace*, St. Louis, 1947.

Burgess, E. B., *Memorial History of the Pittsburgh Synod*, Greenville, Pennsylvania, 1925.

Defenderfer, C. R., *Lutheranism at the Crossroads of America*, published by the Indiana Synod, 1947?.

Deindoerfer, Johannes, *Geschichte der Evangel.-Luth. Synode von Iowa und anderen Staaten*, Chicago, 1897.

Documentary History of the Evangelical Lutheran Ministerium of Pennsylvania and Adjacent States, Philadelphia, 1898.

Ernsberger, C. S., *A History of the Wittenberg Synod*, Columbus, 1917.

Henkel, Socrates, *History of the Evangelical Lutheran Tennessee Synod*, New Market, Virginia, 1890.

Imhoff, A. J., *History of the Evangelical Lutheran Synod of Miami*, Philadelphia, 1894?.

Mechling, G. W., *History of the Evangelical Lutheran District Synod of Ohio*, published by the synod, 1911.

Meuser, Fred W., *The Formation of the American Lutheran Church*, Columbus, 1958.

Peter, P. A., and Schmidt, Wm., *Geschichte der Allgemeinen Evang.-Lutherischen Synode von Ohio und anderen Staaten*, Columbus, 1900.

Sheatsley, C. V., *History of the Evangelical Lutheran Joint Synod of Ohio and Other States,* Columbus, 1919.

Smith, Arthur H., *A History of the East Ohio Synod,* Columbus, 1924.

Spielmann, C., *Abriss der Geschichte der evangelisch-lutherischen Synode von Ohio und anderen Staaten . . . bis zum Jahre 1846,* Columbus, 1880.

Tedrow, W. L., *Our Church. A History of the Synod of Northern Indiana,* published for the synod, 1894.

Wagner, M. L., *The Chicago Synod and Its Antecedents,* Waverly, Iowa, 1909.

There are four histories of Lutheran educational institutions in Ohio:

Allbeck, W. D., *Theology at Wittenberg,* Springfield, 1945.

Lentz, Harold H., *A History of Wittenberg College, 1845–1945,* Springfield, 1946.

Owen, D. B., ed., *These Hundred Years. The Centennial History of Capital University,* Columbus, 1950.

Sheatsley, C. V., *History of the First Lutheran Seminary of the West,* Columbus, 1930.

The following articles are important:

Ahlstrom, Sydney E., "The Lutheran Church and American Culture: A Tercentenary Retrospect," *The Lutheran Quarterly,* IX, 4, November 1957, pp. 336 ff.

Allbeck, W. D., "Alumni in the Civil War," *Wittenberg Bulletin,* Hamma Digest Number, May 1957, pp. 5 ff.

Gotwald, F. G., "Pioneer American Lutheran Journalism," *Lutheran Quarterly,* vol. 42, April 1912, pp. 161 ff.

Johnson, Roy H., "The Lutheran Church and the Western Frontier 1789–1830," *Lutheran Church Quarterly,* III, 1930, pp. 225 ff.

Lueker, E. L., "Walther and the Free Lutheran Conferences of 1856–1859," *Concordia Theological Monthly,* XV, 8, August 1944, 529-563.

Maassel, George, "The Missouri Synod in Northwestern Ohio," *Concordia Historical Institute Quarterly,* XI, 4, January 1939, 101 ff.

Martzolff, C. L., "Lutheranism in Perry County, Ohio," *Ohio Archaeological and Historical Publications,* XXVIII, 375-395.

Pershing, B. H., "Lutheran Synodical Organization in Ohio before 1850," *Lutheran Church Quarterly,* IX, 1936, 402-418.

Prince, B. F., "Beginnings of Lutheranism in Ohio," *Ohio Archaeological and Historical Publications,* XXIII, 1914, 268 ff.

Spaeth, A., "History of Liturgies . . .," *Lutheran Church Review,* XVII, 93 ff.

Weaver, Glenn, "The Lutheran Church during the French and Indian War," *Lutheran Quarterly,* VI, 1954, 248-256.

Collections of biographical sketches are found in:

Dictionary of American Biography, New York, 1928 ff.

Jensson, J. C., *American Lutheran Biographies,* Milwaukee, 1890.

Sprague, William B., *Annals of the American Lutheran Pulpit,* New York, 1869.

Other biographical articles and books are:

Allbeck, W. D., "Jacob Leist, Pioneer Pastor and Synod President," *Wittenberg Bulletin,* LV, 4, May 1958.

————, "John Stough, Founder of Ohio Lutheranism," *Lutheran Quarterly,* XII, 1960, 25 ff.

Autobiography of Rev. James B. Finley, Cincinnati, 1853.

Autobiography of Rev. Joshua Crouse (unpublished).

Bell, P. G., *A Portraiture of the Life of Samuel Sprecher, D.D., LL.D.,* Philadelphia, 1907.

Buehring, Paul H., "William Frederick Lehmann," *Lutheran Quarterly,* VIII, 1956, 51-60.

————, "Wilhelm Schmidt, Founder of the Columbus Seminary," *Lutheran Quarterly,* VII, 1955, 348 ff.

Crouse, Joshua, *et al., The Life and Work of Rev. Francis Jacob Ruth,* published for the Wittenberg Synod, 1888.

Diehl, M., *Biography of Rev. Ezra Keller, D.D.,* Springfield, 1859.

Finck, W. J., "Paul Henkel, the Lutheran Pioneer," *Lutheran Quarterly,* LVI, 1926, 307 ff.

Haupt, C. E., *Emanuel Greenwald,* Lancaster, Pennsylvania, 1889.

Imhoff, Alex. J., *The Life of Rev. Morris Officer, A.M.,* Dayton. 1876.

Loy, M., *Story of My Life,* Columbus, 1905.

Meier, Everette W., "The Life and Work of Henry C. Schwan as Pastor and Missionary," *Concordia Historical Institute Quarterly,* October 1951 and January 1952.

Pershing, B. H., "Paul Henkel, Frontier Missionary, Organizer and Author," *Lutheran Church Quarterly,* VII, 1934, 125 ff.

Miscellaneous works which furnished data were:

Bernheim, G. D., *History of the German Settlements and of the Lutheran Church in North and South Carolina,* Philadelphia, 1872.

Churches in the Buckeye Country, Columbus, 1953.

Douglas, Paul F., *The Story of German Methodism,* Cincinnati, 1939.

Faust, Albert B., *The German Element in the United States,* Boston, 1909.

Ferm, Virgilius, *The Crisis in American Lutheran Theology,* New York, 1927.

Fortenbaugh, Robert, *The Development of the Synodical Polity of the Lutheran Church in America to 1829,* Philadelphia, 1926.

Harbaugh, Henry, *The Fathers of the German Reformed Church,* Lancaster, Pennsylvania, 1858–1859.

Heiser, Alta Harvey, *West to Ohio,* Yellow Springs, Ohio, 1955.

Kolehmainen, John I., "Founding of Finnish Settlements in Ohio," *Ohio State Archaeological and Historical Quarterly,* XLIX, 1940, 150 f.

————, "Finnish Lutherans in Ohio 1871–1937," *Lutheran Church Quarterly,* XI, 1938, 72-78.

Kraushaar, C. O., *Verfassungsformen der Lutherischen Kirche Amerikas,* Gütersloh, 1911.

Ledbetter, Eleanor E., *The Slovaks of Cleveland,* Cleveland, 1918.

Lengyel, Emil, *Americans from Hungary*, Philadelphia and New York, 1952.

Morris, John G., *Fifty Years in the Lutheran Ministry*, Baltimore, 1878.

Reed, Luther D., *The Lutheran Liturgy*, Philadelphia, 1947.

Schneider, Carl E., *The German Church on the American Frontier*, St. Louis, 1939.

Sweet, W. W., *The Rise of Methodism in the West*, Nashville, 1920.

Trepte, Helmut, *Deutschtum in Ohio bis zum Jahre 1820*, Dresden, 1931.

Tressel, E. L., *The Error of Modern Missouri*, Columbus, 1897.

Versteeg, John M., ed., *Methodism: Ohio Area (1812–1962)*, 1962.

Wargelin, John, *The Americanization of the Finns*, Hancock, 1924.

Wittke, Carl, *The German-Language Press in America*, Lexington, Kentucky, 1957.